FRANCE IN THE
SIXTEENTH CENTURY

FRANCE IN THE SIXTEENTH CENTURY

Frederic J. Baumgartner

St. Martin's Press
New York

FRANCE IN THE SIXTEENTH CENTURY
Copyright © 1995 by Frederic J. Baumgartner
All rights reserved. Printed in the United States of America. No part of this book
may be used or reproduced in any manner whatsoever without written permission
except in the case of brief quotations embodied in critical articles or reviews. For
information, address St. Martin's Press, Scholarly and Reference Division, 175 Fifth
Avenue, New York, N.Y. 10010

ISBN 0-312-09965-7 (cloth) ISBN 0-312-15856-4 (paper)

Lirary of Congress Cataloging-in-Publication Data

Baumgartner, Frederic J.
    France in the sixteenth century / Frederic J. Baumgartner. — 1st.
ed.
        p.   cm.
    Includes bibliographical references and index.
    ISBN 0-312-09965-7 (cloth : alk. paper). — ISBN 0-312-15856-4
(pb : alk. paper)
    1. France—Civilization—1328-1600. 2. Renaissance—France.
3. Reformation—France. 4. Monarchy—France.   I. Title.
DC33.3.B38   1995
944'.025—dc20   95-22423
                                                         CIP

Book design by Acme Art, Inc.

10 9 8 7 6 5 4 3 2

To Robert M. Kingdon
Mentor and Teacher

Contents

PART I: FRANCE, 1484–1530

PART II: FRANCE, 1530–1562

PART III: FRANCE, 1562–1614

A Note on the Monetary System

The monetary system in use in France around 1500 was highly complicated and confusing. What made it so was the existence of two types of money: a fictitious money of account, for which there were no actual coins; and a real currency, whose coins varied in value throughout the sixteenth century compared to the money of account. The gold coin in use—the *écu au soleil*—had become the sole gold coin minted in France by 1484. Its value was expressed in terms of units of *monnaie tournois*, a money of account originally from Tours, consisting of *livre tournois (l)*, *sol* (s), and *denier* (d). There were 20 s to the *livre* and 12 d to the *sol*, or 240 d to the *livre*, the system in use in England until 1971. By 1484, the *livre parisis*, whose value was 25 percent higher than the *livre tournois*, was obsolete. The official value of the *écu au solei*, as expressed in *livres*, was changed numerous times from 1484 to 1614, as a consequence of both inflation and the changing ratio of the amount of gold to silver in France:

1484 to 1498—1 *écu* = 1 *l*, 16 s 3 d
1498 to 1506—1 *écu* = 1 *l*, 15 s
1506 to 1519—1 *écu* = 1 *l*, 16 s, 3 d
1519 to 1533—1 *écu* = 2 *l*
1533 to 1550—1 *écu* = 2 *l*, 5 s
1550 to 1575—1 *écu* = 2 *l*, 10 s
1575 to 1614—1 *écu* = 3 *l*

In 1575 Henry III combined the two monetary systems, making the *écu* the monetary unit of account as well. In 1602 Henry IV reverted to the old system of the two units.

In respect to silver coins, the *franc*, a coin worth 1 *l*, was no longer being minted by 1484, but *franc* was often used for *livre*. The principal small coins, made of an amalgam of silver and copper called *billon*, were the *blanc*, 10 d, also called the *dixain*, and the *grand blanc*, 12 d, the *douzain*. These coins were useful for ordinary retail trade, but there were numerous transactions where a larger coin was needed. Thus Louis XII in 1514 ordered the minting of the silver *teston*, worth 10 s.

There were numerous foreign coins in circulation in France, and many accounts were expressed in them. Spanish coins of many values circulated throughout France but especially in the west. Other foreign coins included the *ducat* of Venice and Genoa, worth 1 *l,* 17 s, 6 d; the Flemish *florin,* 1 *l,* 4 s; the German *florin,* 1 *l,* 7 d; the papal *scudi,* 2 *l;* and the English gold noble, 3 *l,* 14 s. Another English coin, the rose noble, was valued at 4 *l.* The exchange rate for the pound sterling, also a money of account, was 8 *l,* 10 s, 2 d.

Preface

This book is organized around the Estates general, beginning with the meeting of 1484 and ending with the one in 1614. These two assemblies define well a distinctive period in French history—the "long sixteenth century," the era of the Renaissance and the Reformation. The constituent parts of the Estates general—the monarch, the clergy, the nobles, and the commoners—serve as themes for the chapters. The 130-year time span of the book is divided into three periods—1484 to 1530, 1530 to 1562, and 1562 to 1614—and a chapter is devoted to each topic for every period. The chapters on the monarchy describe the personalities of the kings, the organization of the court, the fiscal system and revenues, and an outline of the political events of each period. Under the topic of the church, the themes of the Calvinist challenge to Catholicism and the Catholic response are covered. Under the rubric of nobility, I examine the developments in the military across the three periods, and I discuss economic trends, both in the countryside and the cities, in the chapters on the commoners. Since the magistrates of the law courts were often regarded as a separate estates, separate chapters will be devoted to law and the courts, while a chapter will cover the cultural and intellectual developments in each period.

The scholarly apparatus for the work consists of two parts: the endnotes contain citations for sources for direct quotes and statistics and those articles that pertain to points being made in the text; books and articles that I consulted for larger sections of the book appear in the bibliography. Since this work is intended first of all for upper-level undergraduate students and graduate students or advanced scholars being introduced to a detailed history of sixteenth-century France, the citations favor works in English and those in French that are more easily accessible. When two works are nearly equal in their treatment of a topic, the more recent will be cited. Modern spelling of French words is used, as is the French spelling for French towns and French persons named in the text, except for French provinces and the names of kings, queens, princes, and princesses, which are given in the English spelling.

Many people contributed to the successful publication of this book. Some remain anonymous, such as the librarians and archivists at a large number of collections across the United States and France. In particular I need to thank the staff in the Interlibrary Loan office of Newman Library at Virginia Polytechnic Institute and State University. Linda Fountaine, Jan Francis, and Rhonda McDaniel, secretaries in the Department of History at Virginia Tech, put the work into the word processor and provided a wide array of other clerical skills. Cathy Gorman of the Virginia Tech Graphics Department produced the maps used here. My graduate assistants, Voula Saridakis, Kristin Vier, and especially Ginette Aley, helped in several valuable ways, but especially in proofreading Two friends and colleagues, A. Lynn Martin and Raymond Mentzer, gave me valuable advice and criticism. Special thanks are due to my first editor at St. Martin's Press, Simon Winder, who saw the possibilities in a short prospectus that I sent him, his successor, Michael Flamini, who saw the book through to print, and to the very capable staff at the press.

A vast number of people have aided my scholarship over the past quarter century, whose help was essential for my previous publications in the history of sixteenth-century France. Indirectly their aid is part of this book as well, since I have drawn extensively on my own works in writing it. I will mention only two here. My wife, Lois, has lived with French kings and queens for many years. Her help, encouragement, and, especially, her willingness to be left in charge of our children while I enjoyed the good life in the Parisian archives were essential to what success my academic career has had. This book, however, is dedicated to Professor Robert M. Kingdon, who first introduced me to sixteenth-century France and whose patient and kindly mentoring turned me into a professional historian, however limited in talent I may have been as a beginning graduate student and may be at present.

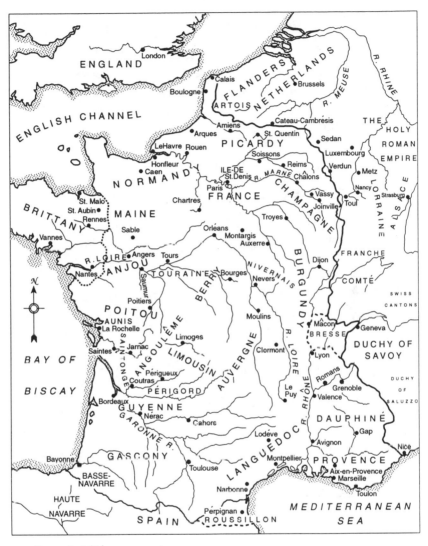

France in 1614

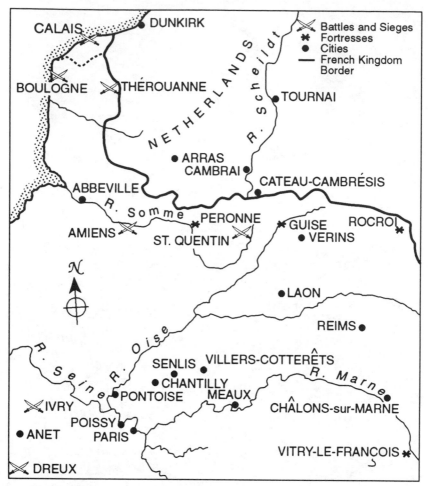

Northern France

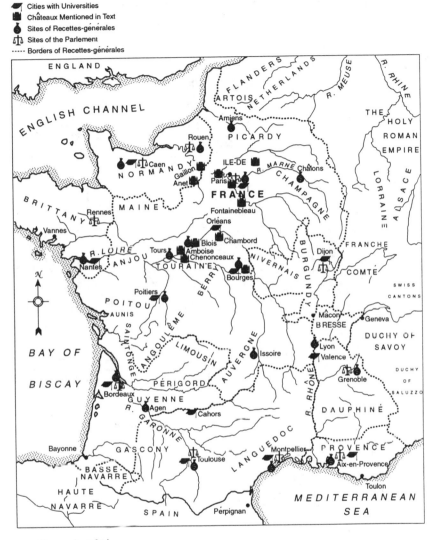

France in 1614

Northern Italy

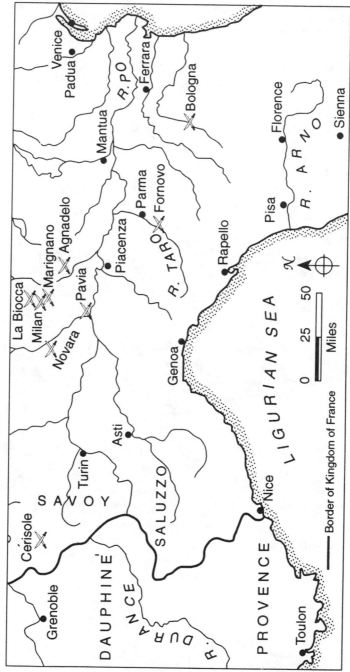

Part I

FRANCE, 1484–1530

1

Introduction

The young king, in his early teens, heavily weighted down with the ceremonial dress and symbols of his office, fidgeted with excitement as the heralds signaled the beginning of the ceremony. A woman at his side carefully observed the boy-king to ensure that he behaved as befitted the sovereign lord of France. On cue, more than 200 solemn men began to file into the hall, dressed in the finery of the nobility, the cardinal robes of the high clergy, the red robes of the magistrates of Parlement, and the more sober clothes of the bourgeoisie and occasional peasant.

This brief description of the opening of the French Estates general fits identically two meetings of the institution: that of 1484 in Tours, when the king was Charles VIII and the woman was his older sister, Anne of Beaujeu; and the one of 1614 in Paris, when the king was Louis XIII and the woman his mother Marie de Medici. These two assemblies, so similar in many ways, make up the bookends of the "long sixteenth century," the era of the Renaissance and Reformation in France. They constitute two of the three great meetings of the Estates general. (The third is the one of 1789 that precipitated the French Revolution.) These two Estates general mark off this era in French history far better than wars or the reigns of kings. In respect to both the issues debated by the Estates and the outcomes of the meetings, the meetings can be seen as defining the beginning and the end of a distinctive period of history called by some historians the Renaissance and by others the long sixteenth century. Even in areas of French life where the Estates had no impact, such as art, the dates mark changes in genre reasonably well, from the medieval to the Renaissance on one hand, and from the Renaissance to classicism on the other.

The Estates general, however, had a very limited autonomy in setting an agenda for France. Only the king could call meetings, and its convocation was sporadic at best. The Estates had no standing in the French code of law; it depended entirely on tradition and the goodwill or needs of the monarchy for its existence. At a time when tradition was being eroded as a basis for French government, it was not a sound footing for a stable or effective institution, and certainly not for the enhancement of the Estates's authority. The purposes behind its assembling were not consistent, although it usually was for approval of new taxes or a subsidy to the king. Nor was there consistency in the manner of choosing the deputies who attended, but there certainly was no sense that it was to be a popular or representative assembly. The Estates could not legislate or propose law; its sole function was to ask the king through documents called cahiers to correct grievances it identified in the functioning of royal government.

Despite the institutional weakness of the Estates general, the phrase "The King in his Estates" described a specific concept of royal authority that has been called the "Renaissance Monarchy." Certainly, the view that the king had absolute power, which so dominated the ancien régime, was already present early in the Middle Ages. The king's real authority back then, however, was sharply circumscribed not only by severe limitations imposed by the difficulties of transportation and communication, but also by the restrictions of feudalism. As feudalism's role as the defining principle of French society declined and the monarchy wrestled with the tremendous burden of waging the Hundred Years War, the kings had to draw on a wider range of the French population for support and validation. This was done largely through the Estates, both provincial and national. It is this consultative element that has held the center of attention over the king's absolute power in recent works on French government in the Renaissance era, but the kings never forgot their claim to absolute authority and frequently sought with varying success to use it. The extent to which the kings of the era 1484-1614 fit better into one or the other category depended a great deal on the character of each king. Kingship was largely what the individual king wanted to make of it and what effort he was willing to expend to be a strong ruler. Regardless of how a king regarded himself, a severely inadequate system of communications and the small size of the royal bureaucracy sorely limited his ability to be effective. The bureaucracy has been estimated for 1500 to have been between 8,000 and 12,000 officials, or about one for every 12,000 to 18,000 people.

What was most required for a strong king, however, was a willingness to brave the wrath of the corporate bodies that made up the French realm, should he violate their perceived rights and privileges. The most powerful such corporate body was the Catholic clergy. Controlling as much as 40 percent of the annual income of the realm, tied into every important family, and firmly buttressed by a tradition that was older than the monarchy's, the clergy was in a superb position to challenge the king over any issue that involved its interests. The nobility lacked the coherence and strong sense of common interest that marked the clergy, but the nobles had one clear advantage in any confrontation with the king: They could take arms against him. The cities, the king's *bonnes villes*, were still another corporate group that he had to take into account as he made decisions. The municipal governments, known as communes, were the urban bodies with which the king negotiated issues involving the cities, but the artisan and merchant guilds, which were largely coextensive with the communes, had a clear corporate identity that the king could not ignore. Even the peasants, usually seen as an amorphous mass who could not respond to injury except through violence, had their corporate bodies, the *communautés*, with some ability to resist royal edicts harmful to their interests. Of all the corporate groups in France, however, probably the most prickly in defending their perceived rights and privileges was the Parlement, the law court. For a royal institution, the Parlement had an amazingly strong sense of autonomy from the monarchy. Each of these corporate bodies had conflict and competition with every other one, but several of them, if not all, could act together to oppose the king, as they often did in meetings of the Estates. It was possible for the king to make decisions on minor matters without input from the corporate bodies on which they impinged, but major matters required consultation.

These corporate groups composed a clear majority of the French population, which in 1484 was about 13 million people and increasing rapidly. France then was about 20 percent smaller than the current republic, but it was the largest, wealthiest, and most populous state in western Europe. In the previous 150 years, it had expanded beyond its longtime borders set by the Treaty of Verdun (843), having annexed Dauphiné and Provence, but the king's authority in those provinces was still as "dauphin" and count, not as French king. Only in the central Pyrenees did the borders of 1498 coincide with today's. In the western Pyrenees, Navarre was a sovereign kingdom, although the French king regarded it as his fief. In the eastern Pyrenees, the provinces of Cerdagne and Roussillon, which had passed back and forth between France and Aragon, were again under Aragonese rule. On the frontier with Italy, the duchy of Savoy was an independent principality controlling the region from Geneva to Nice. West of Geneva lay the Franche-Comté and the county of Dombes, properties of the House of Burgundy that had passed to the Habsburgs. To the north, Alsace and Lorraine were units of the Holy Roman Empire governed by a myriad of nobles. Along the northern border, Flanders and much of Artois were also under

Habsburg control, although they were legally fiefs of the French crown. West of Flanders along the English Channel was English-held Calais, a remnant of the Hundred Years War. Beyond the borders, there were several small enclaves under French sovereignty; the most important was the city of Tournai in Hainault. Within the realm, there were two important independent enclaves, papal-ruled Avignon and the principality of Orange, both on the lower Rhône River.

Paris was, of course, the largest city. A well-founded estimate for 1547 is 220,000 people; there had been some increase in size since 1484. Foreign immigration, largely from Italy and Spain, was a factor in the growth of several of Paris's rivals. Lyon had a very substantial Italian community that helped make the city the French leader in banking and commerce and a serious rival to Paris as the cultural center. Lyon competed with Rouen, with some 40,000 people apiece, as the second city in the realm. Bordeaux, the home of several thousand Iberian Jews after the expulsions of the 1490s, was a city of some 20,000 people by 1500. Cities such as Bordeaux, Nantes, St-Malo, and Rouen prospered from foreign trade. Major French exports were grain, wine, woad for dye, coarse cloth, and salt; imports included fine cloth, spices, precious metals, and furs. After 1500 spices brought by the Portuguese from the Indies began to appear in France through its Atlantic ports. Despite that new competition, one winner in respect to trade was Marseille. Once Provence was annexed in 1481, Mediterranean trade was largely diverted there at the expense of Languedocian ports such as Narbonne and Montpellier, which were also hampered by the silting up of their harbors.[1] Despite constant complaints about the flow of bullion out of France, exports and imports were nearly equal; the greater quantity of exports largely balanced the more costly imports.

Internal transportation across France remained extremely difficult. Except in a few places where Roman roads were kept in good repair, roads were muddy or dusty ruts for travel on foot or horseback. Carriages were almost unknown. Only a small amount of trade traveled across land; for both commerce and people the preferred mode of transportation was by water. France was blessed with rivers, so that it was possible to go by boat, from Harfleur to Marseille, for example, with only one short portage. But the rivers, especially the Loire, were inconsistent, frequently too high or too low, and blocked by sandbars and fallen trees. Regardless of the mode of travel, highwaymen and pirates were a constant fear.

Nonetheless, the French traveled a great deal on business or pilgrimages. The royal court was highly peripatetic, despite the great number of persons and items that traveled with it. Rudimentary postal services run by the monarchy and the University of Paris existed in 1500. They were expensive but relatively quick. It took a letter sent in the summer from Brussels 44 hours to reach Paris, 60 hours to Blois, and 96 to Lyon. Winter added at least another day. The announcement of the election of a pope in 1503 reached Blois from Rome in less than four days, but it took nearly seven days for news of Charles VIII's death to reach Rome. The difficulty of communication meant that the spread of the king's French from the north was a slow process. In the provinces of the west and south, the average peasant probably knew only a few words of French; it was only in about 1500 that French became the language of the ordinary people of Bordeaux.[2] Breton was an entirely different language, being Celtic, not Latin, and its clear distinction from French surely was a major factor in Breton autonomy. The dialects of the Midi were closer to Catalan than to French, but they were also derived from Latin, and their similarity to French probably reduced the sense of particularism where they were spoken. Since Latin was still used in the law courts, there was less incentive for the speakers of the dialects to learn French. In 1484 most people in the realm regarded themselves as residents first of their towns or cities, then of their provinces. The idea of being *bon françois* (good French), which is found a century later, would have been highly unusual then. That different perception of who they were was one of the major changes that occurred in France during the "long sixteenth century."

2

The Monarchy:
Ascendant

The adage of "One Faith! One Law! One King!" sums up the essence of late medieval French kingship: the king was both head of the French Church and the embodiment of French law. In regard to religion, the king had borne the title of Très Chrétien since the twelfth century. He controlled the affairs of the Church to an extent that modern people, used to the authority of the papacy, would have a difficult time understanding. Monarchy was a divine office according to medieval and early modern theorists. The literal translation of the French word for coronation, *sacre,* is consecration, and the ceremony drew heavily on the liturgy for the consecration of a bishop. In the early Middle Ages, the *sacre* was regarded as a sacrament. A vestige of that belief survived in the privilege accorded to the new king of receiving the Eucharist in both bread and wine at the Mass of Consecration. It was the only time in early modern Catholicism a layman did that.

Royal authority in sixteenth-century France, as elsewhere in Europe, had powerful religious overtones. It came from God, to whom alone the king was responsible. On Judgment Day a king would account not only for his own sins but also for his stewardship of the realm and its people. Because only God could punish a bad king, rebellion was both treasonous and sacrilegious. Although the best-known statement on the divine right of kings came from Bishop Bossuet in the late seventeenth century, there was little in it that had not been expressed centuries before. A potent symbol of the king's special relationship with God was his ability to cure scrofula (a form of tuberculosis, disfiguring but rarely fatal) with his touch, especially just after his consecration. The king had a mystical relationship with his people, yet, unlike Christ, his blood certainly was not to be shed for them.

The French king, chosen by God the Eternal Lawgiver to rule, had the law of the realm "in his breast." French law had existed since time immemorial, and the king's principal responsibility was to discover what that law was and render justice according to it. True advocates of royal absolutism—contemporaries would have said royal despotism—were rare before 1614, but many political thinkers who were not absolutist approved of the maxim: "What pleases the prince has the force of law." The maxim was not interpreted in an absolutist way in the sixteenth century; if those thinkers agreed that the king indeed had the power to make law, that law had to be for the good of the realm to be legitimate. It could not please the king to ordain bad law. A good king allowed himself to be bridled by religion, justice, and polity—to use the terminology of Claude de Seyssel, the most important French political writer before Jean Bodin. By polity Seyssel meant the laws that the kings of the past had mandated for the good governance of the realm and the maintenance of royal authority. A king who allowed himself to be subject to law and tradition was more praiseworthy than one who tried to rule absolutely and, therefore, despotically.

The theory and the practice of kingship in sixteenth-century France thus combined absolutism and limitation. Some modern historians, looking largely at the evidence for arbitrary royal decision making, have deemed the sixteenth-century monarchy as absolutist. They use the term *New Monarchy* to emphasize the break with feudal kingship and the appearance of a new style of governance. Other scholars seize on the continuing consultation of the Estates general and, even more so, the provincial estates and the enduring power of the nobility, to argue that what change did take place was insufficient to designate the French monarchy as absolutist. These historians acknowledge that some change took place, but maintain that the French monarchy of 1614 was still closer in form to that of 1450 than 1715.

This sharp disagreement among historians and the great difficulties they have in identifying the nature of royal authority in sixteenth-century France is a product of the enormous variations in the modes of kingship throughout the era. The kings from Charles VIII to Louis XIII differed from one another in their styles of rule more than was true either of the kings of the Middle Ages or of the ancien régime. In a period of change, such as the era of the Renaissance, when the traditions of rule were being undercut without being definitively replaced, each king had a great deal of freedom to make of his authority what he willed. The "Renaissance monarchy" is a distinctive period in French history, and is difficult to define because each reign was essentially sui generis. To characterize the French monarchy in this way helps to explain why France was able to go, for example, from the consultative, limited monarchy of Louis XII to the more absolutist government of Francis I without pause or rebellion. Both forms had a basis in French law and tradition.

The hallmark of limited monarchy was the Estates general, although those who argue for the consultative nature of Renaissance kingship emphasize also the many meetings of provincial and local assemblies. Using the broadest possible interpretation of what constituted the Estates general, there were only ten meetings from 1484 to 1614. The meeting of 1484 was the first for which the term *Estates general* was used. Its convocation, however, was largely an accident and its achievements unexpected. When Louis XI—"King Spider" who weaved webs of deceit around his enemies—died in 1483, he left his thirteen-year-old son Charles VIII as his successor. An edict of 1374 had established the age of majority for a king as fourteen years, but there was a question as to whether that referred to having reached a fourteenth birthday or only of being in the fourteenth year by passing a thirteenth birthday. Consequently, there was disagreement in 1483 over whether Charles needed a regent, and if he did, who it would be. The queen mother, the traditional choice, was dying, and Louis XI had not named anyone in his will. He had, however, named as his son's guardians his older daughter, Anne, and her husband Pierre of Beaujeu, from the Bourbon family, a cadet branch of the royal family.

A number of great nobles, led by Louis of Orléans, third cousin to Charles and next in line for the throne, challenged Anne's claim to the regency. Louis XI had forced young Louis to marry his second daughter, Jeanne, who was so deformed it was believed from her infancy that she was unable to have children. Now in 1483 Louis of Orléans desperately wanted the regency in order to win a papal annulment, which he knew he would not get if Anne became regent. Thus, Louis and many other nobles, who had good reason to hate Louis XI and want his decisions reversed, pushed for a meeting of the Estates general. The Beaujeus agreed, expecting that it would ratify their right to power.

In October 1483 letters went out convoking the Estates at Tours. The letters contained a major innovation in the manner of choosing who would attend. Instead of the king naming the deputies for the clergy and nobility and the municipal governments electing their delegates, the local royal officials were told to assemble the members of each estate in their districts, of which there were about 100 in the realm, to elect a deputy to represent their respective estates. The new procedure produced a body of deputies who were more responsive to their constituents, and it probably explains why the Estates of

1484 became the benchmark meeting of the institution. For many historians, only those subsequent meetings for which the selection of deputies was the same as for 1484 warrant the name Estates general.

It surely was because of the new selection process that the Estates of 1484 produced an important list of cahiers, detailing the grievances of the deputies and suggesting corrections for them. Although the meeting of 1484 resulted in few immediate changes, failing even to name a regent, the monarchy responded positively to the request for a tax reduction. The system of revenues and expenditures of the French monarchy was highly complex and almost incoherent. There were two kinds of royal revenues—ordinary and extraordinary. The ordinary revenues were the products of the royal demesne, which referred to the king's position as feudal lord, both of the entire realm and smaller properties where he was the feudal seigneur. They included rents and profits from agricultural land, vineyards, forests, and fisheries; tolls from roads and bridges; and dues, fees, and fines that came to the king as the lord of his vassals. For example, royal rights in all forests of the realm brought in fees for collecting dead wood and cutting timber, pasturing animals (especially pigs), and an interesting fee on holders of forest land for the shelter they unintentionally gave to bandits and vagabonds.

The medieval king was expected "to live of his own," drawing enough from his ordinary revenues to carry on government. In fact, they were quite small; one estimate for 1500 put them at 231,000 *livres (l)*. Improved collection and the prosperity of the era increased that sum to 500,000 *l* by 1515, but that was as high as it ever reached. As the extraordinary revenues (the term used for taxes until the mid-1500s) rose throughout the sixteenth century, the ordinary revenues became a minor part of the royal budget. That is not to imply that the government ignored trying to increase them. They continued to be the subject of numerous edicts and judgments throughout the century.

Four royal treasurers supervised the collection of the ordinary revenues in the four great divisions of the kingdom—Languedoc, Languedoil (the Ile-de-France and the North), Normandy, and Oultre-Seine-et-Yvonne (the center). At the local level, the *baillis* and *sénéchaux* collected the taxes. Most of these revenues were farmed: wealthy merchants and bankers would bid at a public auction for the right to collect a specific revenue for a given region. The bidding began when a short candle was lit, and the high bid when it burned out was the winning bid. The high bidder paid the bid immediately to the royal officials; he then collected that amount and more for his profit; but he also had to cover any shortfall. The system provided the king with fairly stable revenues while it permitted the revenue farmers to make a profit. There were frequent complaints that the revenue farmers of an area were in collusion, allowing each member of their group to be high bidder for a specific revenue well below its real worth. Complaints about the collection of ordinary revenues were taken to the Cour des trésors, one of three royal courts that had jurisdiction over royal finances. The court for the extraordinary revenues was known as the Cour des aides, from the oldest tax, the *aides,* which arose out of the feudal lord's right to financial aid from his vassals for war and other obligations. They were apparently first collected for John II's ransom in 1357. By 1484 the *aides* had become a permanent sales tax placed on nearly every commodity sold in the realm. Some luxury items, such as spices, used by the nobility and clergy were exempt, as were small sales of the sort found in a little village. The *aides* were imposed at either wholesale or retail but not both, except for wine, which was taxed at one-twentieth of its price at wholesale and one-eighth at retail. The importance of wine in French life is already obvious from its place in the fiscal system. Although the *aides* rose from 400,000 *l* in 1461 to 480,000 *l* in 1523 to 700,000 *l* in 1547, it was common opinion that they were the fairest tax because nearly everyone paid them.

The *gabelles,* taxes on salt, increased from 150,000 *l* in 1489 to 720,000 *l* in 1547. Because the sources of salt were limited, it was rather easy for the government to impose a tax on it. The provinces of north and central France did not produce any salt and so were the most vulnerable to the tax. These *pays de grands gabelles* paid the highest salt tax. The salt was brought to royal salt warehouses and then sold to the populace with a hefty tax imposed, generally around 75 percent of its value. Families were required to buy a specific amount a year regardless of their needs. In the Midi and Burgundy, lands of the *petits gabelles,* the *gabelle* was levied at 20 to 25 percent of the retail value of the salt. The immediate areas of salt production, the coastal margins of the Atlantic from Normandy southward and the Mediterranean, were free of the tax. The vast difference in the price of salt within the realm encouraged large-scale smuggling, although the increased rate of taxation of later centuries would make smuggling worse than in 1484.

The newest tax, the *taille,* was also the largest. The *taille* had been irregularly levied as a war tax since the early years of the Hundred Years War. In 1439 the Estates general agreed to allow Charles VII to collect 100,000 *l* to pay the army. Both the clergy and the nobility were exempt. The Estates had no intention of making the tax permanent, but that was the consequence of its decision. Charles continued to collect it, increasing it to 1.2 million *l* by 1461. Louis XI raised the *taille* enormously, peaking at 4.7 million *l* at his death in 1483. The onerous taxation was the major reason why Louis was denounced as a tyrant. The Estates of 1484 demanded a return to the "standard" amount in place at the end of Charles VII's reign, and Charles VIII and Louis XII reduced the *taille* to 1.5 million *l* by 1506. Late in Louis's reign and under Francis I, it began to rise again. In 1515 and 1547, the tax totaled 2.4 million *l* and 4,889,000 *l.* Often after the *taille* had been set by the royal council for the year, financial problems, especially military expenditures, required increased funds. A surtax, the *crue* (fresh), then would be collected on top of the *taille.*

There were two types of *tailles.* In Languedoc, it was a tax on the non-noble land, or *terre roturière,* which was property that did not confer a title of nobility on its holder. When such a piece of land was purchased by a nobleman, it continued to be liable to the *taille.* In the rest of the realm, the *taille* was *personnelle,* a tax on the land and wealth of non-nobles. When a noble purchased a piece of property or a commoner property owner gained a patent of nobility, those properties escaped the tax. When that happened, the tax on the rest of the taxpayers of the parish was increased, since each parish was assessed a specific sum. Disputes over whether a piece of land had escaped the *taille* were frequently carried to the Cour des aides and sometimes to the royal council. Once the total *taille* for the year was set, it was divided among *généralités des finances,* which corresponded closely to the four treasuries of the royal demesne and were headed by the *généraux des finances.* These units were subdivided into some 100 *élections,* so-called because in the past the taxpayers had elected the *élu,* the officer who supervised the collection of the *taille* in each district. The *élus* informed the parishes of their assessments, and parish assessors informed the taxpayers of their tax based on the assessors' estimate of their wealth. By 1500, the *élus* were no longer elected but were royal officials who also supervised the collection of the *aides* and the *gabelles* in their *élections.*

In the *pays d'élection,* any local assemblies that existed had no significant role in approving the *taille* set for their provinces. The system of *élus,* however, predated 1453, and the provinces that had reverted to the crown after that—Guyenne, Gascony, Brittany, and Provence—along with Languedoc and Dauphiné had a somewhat different system of levying the *taille* from the rest of the realm. The Estates of those provinces met annually to agree to the sum requested by the king and also levy any *crue* needed. They were called the *pays d'état.* The distinction remained in effect for several centuries, and in the *pays d'état* the provincial estates continued to meet. The large cities were exempted from the *taille* on the grounds that it would have been too difficult to assess the wealth of the great number of persons who did not own property in a city. Instead, those cities would agree to an *octroi* (grant) of money to the king, which was taken largely out of tolls and tariffs that a city was already collecting for its own use.

The superior court for finances was the Chambre des comptes, the fiscal-policy setting offspring of the medieval royal council. Its purview over royal finances was very broad, although the royal council occasionally intervened, and it supervised the revenue-gathering officials. The Chambre des comptes collected the fiscal records in Paris, and the fire of 1737 that destroyed a large part of that collection was a serious blow to historians. Its judicial function was largely to settle disputes between tax collectors and the government. It was a sovereign court in that it had the power of registering royal edicts on finance and the right to refuse those it regarded as improper. However, the king could order it to register his decrees with a *lettre de jussion*. There were provincial Chambres des comptes at Aix, Dijon, and Grenoble.

In 1523, a major fiscal crisis caused by the rising expense of the court and war in Italy led Francis I to make extensive changes in the financial system, and he continued to tinker with it throughout the rest of his reign. Francis blamed the principal members of the fiscal system, the *gens des finances,* for the failure of a campaign in Italy because the army had not been paid. In order to get more control over the financial officers, Francis created a new office, the Epargne, with a new set of officials. The old *gens des finances* were not eliminated. They paid for their offices, and it would have cost too much to buy them out. Instead, their importance was drastically reduced. The Epargne now collected the royal revenues from the local districts, leaving in the districts those needed for the local royal bureaucracy. The royal treasure chests were now kept in the Louvre instead of being moved with the king, because under the new system far more gold was collected, and moving the chests as the king traveled about was becoming difficult. Revising the financial system hardly solved Francis I's financial problems. The government ran deficits nearly every year of his reign. He began to extract money from the clergy on a regular basis and to sell royal offices, including those of the judiciary, which previously had been regarded as inappropriate. The primary short-term solution was borrowing. The bankers were mostly Italians, but most other nationalities were represented as well. The French monarchy also drew on its own subjects for loans. Forced loans, often with no interest, were frequently imposed on wealthy subjects and the cities.

A large portion of the royal revenues went for expenses of the court and salaries of the large number of people associated with it. The size of the court increased slowly from 1484 to 1515, rising from some 320 persons who officially received a salary from the king to 380. The pace of increase picked up rapidly under Francis I, reaching 622 in 1535. There was double, perhaps triple, that number of people who made their living from the court but were not on the royal payroll. The head of the court was the Grand Maître de l'hôtel du roi, who always came from one of the highest ranking families of the realm. His duties included directing the security of the king. For that task he had 200 *gens d'armes,* who were recruited from the best families, two companies of French archers, a company of Scots archers, and one of Swiss pikemen. Supervision of the royal household fell to the grand chamberlain. The royal kitchen was known as the *bouche,* while the purchasing and care of furnishings, plate, and clothes was the responsibility of the *argenterie.* Also part of the royal household were physicians, surgeons, barbers, astrologers, historiographers, and jesters. There was also a "mistress of the daughters of joy" at the court, who supervised the large number of courtesans accompanying it. Her position dated back at least to the time of Charles VII. She had the pleasant task of offering a bouquet of flowers to the king on Valentine's Day.

There were other divisions of the court in addition to the *hôtel du roi.* The queen had a separate household, and there was one for the royal children. The king's oldest son, the dauphin, received his own household when he reached the age of ten. The royal chapel consisted of the grand almoner and his staff of almoners, who distributed the royal alms and supervised the hospital of the realm. The kings never were very generous in their almsgiving; under Louis XII the average annual sum for alms was 6,500 *l;* in 1548 it had risen to 8,400 *l.* Much of the money went to the clergy for masses and devotions, not to the poor. The chapel also included the king's confessor and the royal singers and musicians. The *écurie* provided horses, couriers, and transportation for the king. There were two divisions of royal huntsmen: one with dogs for hunting stags and boars, and another that provided falcons for birding. In addition there were merchants and artisans attached to the court, royal officials at the court on business, foreign diplomats and their entourages, and hangers-on, gamblers, prostitutes, and beggars. When the court moved, it was a major logistical nightmare, compounded not only by the muddy ruts that served as roads but also by the practice of stripping the current place of residence of nearly all of its furnishings to take to the next. One reason why the châteaux of the Loire were favored as royal residences was the ease of river transport compared to going overland. The French court moved about a great deal, especially under Francis I, who was rarely in the same place for more than three months. The royal love of hunting was one reason for the frequent moves; the huge royal hunting parties would quickly kill off the game in the large forests close to the royal châteaux. The frequent outbreaks of plague were another. Royal business and the need to show themselves to their subjects also kept the kings on the road. While the kings often needed to be in Paris for royal business, they preferred not to spend much time there.

The members of the royal councils and the major officers also had to be prepared to spend a great deal of time traveling. There were two royal councils. The smaller but more powerful was the Secret Council or Conseil des Affaires, made up of 8 to 12 of the king's closest advisers. It usually met in the early morning in the king's chambers. The most important matters of state were decided there. Decisions made in the Secret Council usually were taken to the larger Privy Council, the Conseil des Parties, which met in the afternoons. Its membership was much larger and far less consistent, and the king frequently did not attend. Besides some two dozen officials who were routinely at the court, the king invited provincial officers, nobles, and bishops when they made their infrequent appearances. By the late sixteenth century the Conseil des Parties was largely concerned with finances. When the king did not attend one of the councils, the chancellor presided. Every chancellor of the sixteenth century had been the first president of a Parlement, usually of Paris, since he was the head of the system of justice and presided over the Parlements when he attended them. The chancellor had the right to refuse to seal a decree that he felt was inappropriate, but the king, having heard his objections, could order him to seal it. As head of the royal chancellery, the chancellor had a hand, often the main one, in drawing up most royal decrees and edicts. His influence was paramount in the appointment of numerous royal officials. He officially spoke for the king at meetings of the Estates general, in the Parlement, and at ecclesiastical synods. The chancellor served for life, and his life tenure gave him a great deal of independence from the monarch and allowed him to object to royal decisions. If his criticism offended the king too much or he became incapacitated, the king could pass most of his duties to the Garde des sceaux. That official's regular task, besides having physical custody of the royal seals, was to oversee the royal chancellery and appoint its personnel.

The most powerful chancellor of the era was Antoine Duprat, Francis I's chancellor from 1515 to his death in 1535. He was the only sixteenth-century chancellor appointed at the beginning of a reign, since Louis XII had left the office vacant for the last two years of his reign. Perhaps because the other kings inherited chancellors from their predecessors, no other chancellor of the era matched Duprat's clout. Louis XII's powerful adviser, Cardinal Georges d'Amboise, had no position at the court; he had Louis's complete confidence and served in the Church as papal legate. He was the prototype for Cardinal Wolsey in England. D'Amboise's influence and energy were both so vast that the saying "Let George do it!" is supposed to have originated with him. Two queen mothers, Louise of Savoy and Catherine de Medici, and two royal mistresses, Anne d'Estampes and Diane de Poitiers, also wielded wide influence. The periods of their power ran nearly consecutively from 1515 to 1589.

The central government of France also included several royal secretaries, whose duties become better defined in the mid-1500s, the principal military officers, and the magistrates in the Grand Conseil and the Parlement. In the provinces the major royal officials were the governors, although only ten frontier provinces and the Ile-de-France had governors. It was originally a military office for the defense of the frontiers. By 1500, governors were being chosen from the princes of blood and the great nobles. They frequently had major responsibilities at court or with the army and could not reside in their provinces. Their lieutenants, also appointed by the king, generally made the routine decisions of the provincial *gouvernements*. Those decisions largely involved recruiting for the army, maintaining fortifications, and responding quickly to invasion.

Local civilian administration was in the hands of an officer called the *bailli* in the north and the *sénéshal* in the south. Drawn from the local nobility, they often served as military captains as well. Their responsibilities were broad, involving virtually every aspect of government from tax collection to justice, although the creation of other offices in the provinces had cost them much of their authority over both finances and justice. In 1515, there were some 100 *bailliages* and *sénéchaussées* in the realm; the number would increased considerably in the future. It was still common then to find a *bailli* or *sénéshal* holding high office in government or the army. By mid-century it was rare.

In the interior provinces, governorships had not been created in the late Middle Ages because those provinces had largely been under the regime of the appanage—the grant of a duchy or other substantial estate to a king's younger son. The system of appanage developed out of two facts: first, feudal law required that the king fill vacant fiefs; second, the late medieval monarchy was not capable of governing provinces outside of the Ile-de-France. Thus, major fiefs that fell vacant would go to royal sons in the expectation that they would keep them "in the family." The system rarely worked as intended. Even the first generation of appanage-holders often rebelled against the king, to say nothing of the succeeding ones. The worst case involved Burgundy, given to John II's younger son, Philip. His marriage to Margaret of Flanders in 1369 began the process of adding the Low Countries to his domains, which included the duchy of Burgundy itself, a French fief, and the Franche-Comté (Free County of Burgundy), a fief of the Holy Roman Empire. The threat that this powerful collection of lands posed to the French monarchy was reduced in 1477 with the death of Duke Charles the Bold at the Battle of Nancy, but it did not disappear entirely. Louis XI's efforts to coerce Charles's heiress Mary to marry his young son Charles were rebuffed; instead, she married her own choice for husband, Maximilian of Habsburg, the future Holy Roman Emperor, and passed to him her vast inheritance, less the duchy of Burgundy, which Louis succeeded in returning to royal control.

The successful reestablishment of royal authority in Burgundy was part of what is sometimes called "the gathering-in of the provinces." In a little more than a half-century, the monarchy recovered Normandy and Gascony-Guyenne from the English, eliminated all but one of the appanages, and brought Brittany and Provence into the realm for good. In 1480 Louis XI gained a major coup when he persuaded René of Anjou to will to him René's appanage of Anjou and Maine and the independent county of Provence, but along with them came his fateful claim to the kingdom of Naples. The long autonomous duchy of Brittany was securely tied to France through the successive marriages of Duchess Anne to Charles VIII and Louis XII. When Louis succeeded his cousin Charles as king, he brought his appanage of Orléans and Blois back under royal control. By 1500 the House of Bourbon had the only remaining appanage, consisting of the Bourbonnais and Auvergne in central France.

The nobility was not keen on enhancing royal control, which the gathering-in of the provinces entailed, especially as it took place largely in Louis XI's reign. In 1465 he faced a widespread revolt called the War of the Common Weal. His victory over the nobles did not reconcile them to the throne; those who survived bided their time until a new opportunity arose. That occurred in 1484 after Louis of Orléans and his allies among the nobles at the Estates general failed to strip Louis XI's daughter, Anne of Beaujeu, of her influence over her brother the king. The result was another revolt of the nobility called the Guerre folle (Fools' War). The Beaujeus badly outmatched the nobles, led by Francis of Brittany and Louis of Orléans, in political acumen and manpower. The rebels were soundly defeated in July 1488 at Saint-Aubin-du-Cormier in Brittany. Louis was captured and tossed into prison for three years, while Francis, heartbroken by his failure, died shortly after the battle.

Young Duchess Anne of Brittany was without hope of getting help from anyone, and the French were able to press her into marrying Charles VIII in 1491. In order to marry her, Charles had to break a marriage contract with Maximilian of Habsburg's daughter Margaret. She had already been living at the French court. With this humiliation added to the long list of grievances that Maximilian already had against the French, there is little wonder that he was always eager to sign on to any league against France. Now that Brittany, which had in the past been quick to aid France's enemies, was under French control and the French nobility cowed, Charles felt ready to turn his attention to a project that would become the identifying feature of his reign—the conquest of Naples. In 1265 Pope Clement IV, in the midst of the bitter struggle between the papacy and the Holy Roman Empire, had conferred Naples and Sicily on Charles of Anjou, the brother of Louis IX. French mistreatment of the Italians led them to revolt five years later. Aided by the king of Aragon, who claimed Naples and Sicily through his wife, they drove the French out. The Valois claim to Charles's realms passed down to René of Anjou, who left them to Louis XI in his will. Louis made no effort to make good these claims, but Charles VIII took the title of king of Naples.

Charles's focus was on Naples, but he also entertained the desire to lead a crusade against the Turks. Another factor was the influence of the ruler of Milan, Ludovico Sforza. The duchy of Milan in north-central Italy was one of the most prosperous and heavily populated regions of Europe. Like most of the states of Italy in the late fifteenth century, the legitimacy of its ruler was in question. The male line of the Visconti dynasty had died out in 1447, and Milan had reestablished a republic. Bitter factionalism disrupted it, and in 1450 Francesco Sforza, a condottiere (mercenary captain) in the pay of one of the factions, seized control of the city and proclaimed himself duke. Upon his death in 1466, his son ruled the duchy until his assassination ten years later. The title then passed to Francesco's seven-year-old grandson Gian Galeazzo. Gian's uncle Ludovico became his guardian and regent. Il Moro, the Moor, as Ludovico was called, soon arranged for the marriage of his nephew to the granddaughter of Ferrante I of Naples, which took place in 1489. The twenty-year-old duke, pushed by his father-in-law, tried to take control Milan from his uncle, but Ludovico refused to relinquish it. Restless to exercise power, Gian sought support across Italy. Milan's neighbors, Venice and Florence, signed on, as did Pope Alexander VI.

The Sforzas and the French kings had been on good terms since 1450, and il Moro even used the threat of French intervention against his enemies. While he may have been bluffing, Charles was quick to agree to lead an army into Italy. In order to gain the neutrality of neighboring princes and settle disputes that might prompt them to attack France while he was in Italy, Charles negotiated a series of treaties with them. The first was with Henry VII. In November 1492 Charles agreed to pay 1.24 million *l* that Anne of Brittany owned Henry for his aid in 1489 and 300,000 *l* in back payments of a pension Louis XI had agreed to give Edward IV. A treaty of January 1493 with Ferdinand and Isabella committed them to neutrality in return for the provinces of Cerdange and Roussillon, which Louis XI had annexed in 1463. The third, with Maximilian, arranged for the return of his daughter Margaret's dowry and several forts in Artois that Louis XI had occupied.

In late 1493 Charles began to collect the 3.5 million *l* needed for an expedition to Naples. He placed a crue of 800,000 *l* on the *taille,* imposed several new *aides,* and demanded a clerical tenth from the clergy on the grounds that he would lead a crusade against the Turks from Naples. Agents were sent into the Alps to recruit 6,000 Swiss pikemen. They joined 20,000 French infantrymen, whose quality was horrible, 1,500 French lancers, whose quality was superb, and 7,000 other cavalrymen to form Charles's army. It also included 70 large guns, the largest artillery train yet assembled. When all was ready in August 1494, Charles began the trek across the Alps. After conferring with

Ludovico Sforza, Charles proceeded southward. The amazingly quick reduction of several well-regarded fortresses by the French artillery convinced the Italians that resistance was futile. The massacre of the defenders also shocked the Italians, who were accustomed to the far less bloody style of warfare of the condottieri. Place after place capitulated to Charles without offering resistance. In Florence an anti-Medici faction took advantage of the passage of the French army to oust Piero de Medici and install a pro-French government. In January 1495 Charles crossed into the kingdom of Naples. Towns and fortresses fell with little resistance. The Neapolitan court fled to Sicily in mid-March, and on March 28, 1495, Charles entered Naples in triumph.

All the other states of Italy and Europe were upset at Charles's audacity and easy victory. Even il Moro repented of bringing the French into Italy. Ferdinand of Aragon, whose relatives had been ousted from Naples, created an anti-French alliance with the pope, the emperor, Milan, and Venice. Within days of his entry into Naples, Charles was informed of the creation of the League of Venice, whose announced purpose was to protect its members from the same fate as Naples. Charles, fearing that he would be trapped in Naples, left there in May with half of his army, leaving the rest to occupy the realm. Meanwhile, the allies collected an army about three times the size of the one returning to France with Charles and met him at Fornovo on the Taro River early in July 1495. In the battle that followed, both the bloody fighting style of the French and their superior artillery enabled the French to neutralize the great numerical advantage of the Italians. The Italians claimed victory, but Charles won what he needed—a safe retreat to France, where he arrived at the end of October. Once he reached Lyon, Charles largely ignored the army he had left behind in Naples and allowed it to atrophy. Naples soon fell to Spanish forces that had crossed from Sicily, but the French held on to several fortresses.

Charles's response to events in Naples was distracted by the devastating news of his only son's death. He resolved to reform his life and reduce taxes as requested by the Estates of 1484. Before he could proceed far, he died on April 7, 1498. On his way to watch courtiers play tennis in the moat of Amboise, he hit his head on a low archway and died ten hours later. It is not clear whether he died from the blow or whether the injury aggravated another condition.

At age thirty-five, Louis of Orléans was now king. Despite a prison term for treason and suspicions about his parentage, Louis became king without serious challenge. His easy succession was a clear victory for the Salic Law, which governed the succession to the throne and declared that no woman could wear the French crown. No notice was taken of any claim the dead king's sister Anne might have had to the throne, although she was over thirty years old and experienced in governing. Behind Louis was a four-year-old cousin, Francis of Angoulême, and no one was eager to reject Louis for a child. Louis also quickly overcame any lingering resentment toward him by confirming all of Charles's officers and continuing their pensions. When Louis saw Louis de La Trémoille, his vanquisher at St-Aubin, standing in a crowd around Charles's bier, he summoned him forward and asked him to be as loyal to him as he had been to his predecessor. However, it was not to La Trémoille but to a delegation from Orléans, which was apologizing for closing the city gates to him in 1487, that he made his most famous remark: "It is not honorable for a king of France to avenge the quarrels of a duke of Orléans."[1] The new king clinched the loyalty of the most important persons, the Beaujeus, by granting them something Charles VIII had refused—allowing their daughter Suzanne to marry Charles de Bourbon-Montpensier and combine the vast properties of both families.

As a young man Louis XII had a reputation as a frivolous womanizer and spendthrift, but much of his early irresponsibility arose from his marital situation. Coerced at age fifteen into marrying Louis XI's daughter Jeanne, he was repulsed by her deformed body. That Louis would seek an annulment was a foregone conclusion the moment he became king, for there was a great deal more at stake than even the question of a royal heir, his marriage being childless as expected. Anne of Brittany, the widow of the dead king, had again become the duchess of an autonomous Brittany. Her marriage contract with Charles had specified that should he die before her, the duchy would revert to its prior status. However, it also included a clause requiring her to marry his successor to the throne should he die without a son.

Shortly after Louis reached the throne, he sent La Trémoille to Jeanne to ask her to agree to an annulment, but she, convinced that she was his legal wife, refused. When Anne of Brittany agreed to marry Louis if he obtained an annulment in a year's time, he sent a formal request to the pope. Alexander VI, perhaps the most immoral pope in history, knew well how to take advantage of Louis's desperation. He demanded that Louis find a French bride for his son Cesare and give him a French title and pension. Louis granted him the duchy of the Valentinois near Avignon and persuaded the d'Albrets, the dominant family of southwestern France, to give him a wife. Alexander then commissioned three prelates to hear Louis' request. After three months of testimony, the matter came down to the question of whether the marriage had been consummated: Louis swore that it had not. Since the oath of a consecrated king was the strongest evidence, the tribunal had no choice but to return a verdict in favor of an annulment. Louis immediately gave Jeanne the duchy of Berry. She retired to Bourges, where she founded an order of nuns and died in 1505. Jeanne was canonized a saint in 1950. Louis and Anne were married in January

1499, but she remained the duchess of an autonomous Brittany, whose autonomy she defended to her death.

Louis XII intended from the moment he became king to dispatch an army to make good his rights to Milan and Naples. His claim to Milan came through his grandmother, Valentina Visconti, whose two brothers died without heirs, passing the claim to her descendants. After the second brother died in 1447, the Sforzas usurped the duchy. Louis expected that such a campaign would pay for itself, since the revenues of Naples were estimated to be 1.5 million *l* and those of Milan, more than 1.3 million *l*. Louis used diplomacy and bribery to gain the neutrality of his neighbors and secured the use of a small Venetian force for the attack on Sforza by promising Venice several towns in the eastern part of the duchy. Cesare Borgia committed his father to support the campaign. In July 1499, the French force began to cross the Alps into Italy. Its commander was Giangiacomo Trivulzio, a Milanese exile and a marshal in the French army. He was among the first of the many Italian exiles to play a prominent role in French government, military, and clergy in the sixteenth century.

In a month's time the superior French guns easily reduced a string of fortresses leading to Milan from the west, and Sforza fled from the city. A month later Louis entered the city in triumph and, as duke, established Trivulzio as his governor. The arrogant Trivulzio rankled his former compatriots, and the atrocious behavior of the French and Swiss troops soon made the Milanese long for Sforza's return. By February 1500, il Moro was back in the city. Louis wasted little time in gathering a new force to retake Milan. La Trémoille, now in command of the army, quickly cornered Sforza and most of his army at Novara to the west of Milan. Sforza was captured while trying to slip away dressed as a pikeman. He was taken to France, where Louis kept him imprisoned until his death in 1508.

Cardinal d'Amboise was named governor of Milan and received the city's submission. He held the office for the next three years; then his nephew Charles de Chaumont took it over. Louis was very generous to the city in victory. It helped to secure his reputation as a generous and merciful king, and it made French rule acceptable in Milan for the next decade, as there was little agitation against Louis. Once Milan was secure, Louis XII's attention turned to Naples, where he inherited Charles VIII's rights. French troops still had a toehold there, but it was clear that the powerful Spanish army protecting King Ferrante would make retaking the realm difficult. Louis decided to negotiate with Ferdinand of Aragon to divide it equally. In November 1500, the two agreed to such a plan. Both his contemporaries and modern historians have condemned Louis for this piece of "political robbery" in cahoots with "the worst rascal amongst many of them." If Ferdinand were willing to betray his kin, how much more eagerly would he turn on the French king? But for the moment, Ferdinand cooperated with Louis in ousting King Ferrante, who thought the Spanish army in Naples was there to protect him until it attacked him.

Louis had dispatched a galley fleet to Naples, which had already surrendered before it arrived. Louis agreed to send it on to the east to take part with Venice in a crusade against the Ottoman Turks. A poorly executed siege of a Turkish fortress on the coast of Greece failed, and the retreating Christian fleet was caught in a violent storm that sunk several French galleys with the loss of more than a thousand men. This ill-fated expedition was the last time the French battled the Muslims in what may be termed a crusade. Three decades of French inactivity in the Christian war with Islam followed, lasting until Francis I began to develop a tacit alliance with the Ottoman Empire directed against Charles V.

Meanwhile in Naples, disputes over the division of the realm's revenues caused tensions to rise, as each side accused the other of defrauding it. Adding to the combustible mix in southern Italy was the arrival of a new commander for the French troops, the young duke of Nemours, who was eager to prove himself in battle. The major battle for Naples took place a year later, in April 1503, near the town of Cerignola. The French suffered a crushing defeat, and Nemours was killed. But again, they held on to several forts, including the great fortress of Gaeta.

Louis XII quickly sent La Trémoille southward with a powerful force. As he approached Rome, word came of Alexander VI's death. Louis ordered him to halt near Rome in order to put pressure on the cardinals to elect d'Amboise pope. He did not win the election, and the delay of six weeks exposed the army to malaria, so prevalent around Rome. It was a decimated army that moved on toward Naples. In December 1503 the Spanish routed it on the Garigliano River. The fortress of Gaeta soon surrendered, and the kingdom of Naples, so easily won ten years earlier, was forever lost. Louis's rage at the loss of Naples was immense. Much of the blame was thrown on the fiscal officers for Naples, who were accused of defrauding the king of 1.2 million *l* intended for the army. Some 20 officials were found guilty of some degree of malfeasance, although the two condemned to death were pardoned before the sentence was imposed.

In 1505 Louis fell so seriously ill that he and everyone else thought he was dying. The prospect of death convinced him to undo a decision he had made four years earlier. In 1501, two years after the birth of his daughter Claude, he had signed a contract for her marriage to the son of Philip of Habsburg and Joanna of Spain. That son, the future Charles V, stood to inherit his father's Austrian and Burgundian lands and the Spanish realms from his mother, heiress to Ferdinand and Isabella. Claude would receive Brittany, and the first son from the marriage would become its duke when she died. In 1504 they worked out a new contract even more favorable to the Habsburgs, which stipulated that if the contract were broken by the French, Charles would receive Burgundy and Milan.

Facing death in early 1505, Louis suffered pangs of conscience at what these agreements threatened to do to his kingdom. He signed a new will that required Claude to marry Francis of Angoulême, and the Habsburgs demanded the compensation set out in the 1504 contract. Louis and his advisers, seeking to avoid the heavy cost, came up with the ploy of having the Estates general request that Claude marry the heir to the throne. In May 1506, a limited number of deputies assembled at Tours. Because the number was much smaller than in 1484, many modern historians do not label this assembly an Estates general, although all the sixteenth-century authors used the term. The speaker for the Third Estate, Thomas Bricot, addressed Louis with fulsome praise for how Louis had reduced the *taille* and established peace and justice in the realm. Therefore, Bricot proclaimed, Louis ought to be known as "The Father of His People." Having so honored Louis with a title unique in European history, Bricot turned to the real reason for the meeting: that the king agree to give his daughter to "Mister Francis here present, who is France's son!" The next day Louis announced the betrothal of Claude and Francis. The intriguing possibility of a union of the Habsburg and Valois dynasties disappeared.

The Habsburgs' anger over the broken contract did not last beyond Philip's death a year later, and the mercurial Maximilian soon was allied with Louis in a war on Venice. The Venetians were regarded as arrogant, deceitful, and too cunning for their own good, and a number of petty slights and injuries suffered by France, Spain, the papacy, and the Habsburgs led to the creation of the League of Cambrai in December 1508. Louis agreed to command a French army in person against Venice the next year. In May 1509, Louis led his army into battle at Agnadello, where the Venetian rearguard rashly took on the whole French army and was soundly defeated. Louis was content with having bloodied the Venetians and winning *gloire*. He returned to France in August with most of his army.

Louis's quick return home was a serious blunder, for it removed his influence from northern Italy at a time when a major revision of Italian politics was taking place. The catalyst behind the changes was Pope Julius II, who had joined the League of Cambrai in order to recover several towns in the northern Papal States from Venice. Having achieved that, he turned against France. Among the several causes for the violent confrontation between pope and king, the most important was Julius's zeal to free Italy of the barbarians, meaning all non-Italians, starting with the French because they controlled more of Italy than the others. Cardinal d'Amboise's death in 1510 removed the only person who might have been able to mediate between Julius and Louis. The pope was extremely busy in early 1510, persuading Venice to submit largely on his terms, fomenting rebellion in Milan, getting the Swiss Confederation to refuse a new recruiting treaty with France while signing one with him, and deeply offending Louis by investing Ferdinand of Aragon with the kingdom of Naples. Louis decided to use the spiritual sword against Julius, convoking a national assembly of the French clergy to threaten a schism. Julius responded by wielding the temporal sword. He attacked the duke of Ferrara, Louis's firmest ally in Italy. Louis ordered Chaumont d'Amboise, his governor of Milan, to go to the aid of Ferrara. When d'Amboise appeared before the walls of Bologna, where the pope was, Julius excommunicated him and his men. D'Amboise lost his nerve and withdrew.

When Chaumont d'Amboise died in early 1511, Louis replaced him with Gaston de Foix, the king's twenty-two-year-old nephew. Despite his youth, he was a better commander. Gaston quickly struck against the enemy forces—papal, Spanish, and Venetian. The crowning event of a brilliant campaign in early 1512 was the Battle of Ravenna on Easter Sunday, April 11. De Foix proved his military genius by winning this battle, the hardest fought and bloodiest of Louis's reign, but he was among its casualties. Without their commander, the battered French forces could not push on to Rome, as Louis had ordered them to do, but retreated in disorder toward France with a Swiss-Venetian army in pursuit. The Swiss moved into Milan, and the French presence in northern Italy was reduced to garrisons in a few citadels.

Louis XII was unable to prevent the incredibly rapid ruin of the French position in Italy because Spain, England, and the emperor had joined Julius's anti-French alliance. Ferdinand took advantage of the bind Louis was in to conquer the southern half of Navarre, where King Jean d'Albret's right to rule was being challenged by the de Foix, a cadet branch of his family. Gaston's death at Ravenna passed his claims to Navarre to his sister Germaine, who had become Ferdinand's second wife in 1506. In August 1512, Ferdinand sent his army into Navarre. A French campaign in late 1512 failed to drive the Spanish out, and southern Navarre was permanently annexed into Castile. Louis's fortunes took a turn for the better when Julius II died in February 1513; the new pope, Leo X, was far less hostile to France. Louis was able to make peace or truces with most of his foes. The one who refused any accommodation was Henry VIII of England, who was eager to win for himself martial glory and perhaps even make good his predecessors' claims to the French throne. In the spring of 1513, Henry crossed the channel with a vast army to Calais. The campaign of 1513 demonstrated the value of Calais to the English as a port of entry to invade France. From Calais Henry pushed on to Tournai, which capitulated in late September. More problems appeared at the same time for Louis in the form of a Swiss incursion into Burgundy and the death of his only ally, James IV of Scotland, in the battle of Fladden Field.

Ironically, it was another death, Queen Anne's in January 1514, that provided Louis XII with the opportunity to secure peace. She had given Louis two daughters, Claude and Renée, but no sons, and Louis was eager to remarry, although he was fifty-three years old and seriously afflicted with gout. In August 1514, Louis and Henry agreed to a peace treaty, which conceded Tournai to England, and a marriage between Henry's sister Mary and Louis. His new bride was eighteen years old and said to have been the most beautiful princess in Christendom. She arrived in France in October amidst great festivities. Louis was very much taken with his bride, and he disrupted what had become an very regular life-style, now going to bed at midnight instead of six. His health rapidly deteriorated, and the Parisian jesters cracked that the king of England had sent their king a filly to carry him off sweetly to hell or paradise. On January 1, 1515, Louis died, and his twenty-year-old cousin and son-in-law Francis I took the throne.

Francis I was a far different king from his predecessor. He had been raised by a doting but highly ambitious mother, Louise of Savoy, in the expectation that someday he would be king. The note of triumph in her journal for the day her Caesar, as she called him, became king is obvious. Until her death in 1530, Louise had a very powerful influence on her son.[2] The honors he gave her were unprecedented for a queen mother, although her service as regent for the times when he was out of the realm was not. Francis's sister, Marguerite, older by two years, was also very close to him, but her influence extended largely to cultural, intellectual, and religious affairs.

At Francis's succession, the two most powerful offices, those of chancellor and constable, were vacant. He named Antoine Duprat, the first president of the Parlement of Paris, as chancellor. An haute-bourgeois from Auvergne, he had risen in the judiciary until he reached the pinnacle of power. No other chancellor of the era was as committed to enhancing royal authority, nor as deeply hated. While there is no question that he reflected his master's views, he contributed substantially to the strengthening of royal power until his death in 1535. On the other hand, Francis's choice for constable, Charles de Bourbon, soon presented a severe challenge to royal authority. Charles stood second in the line of succession to the throne behind his cousin, Charles de Bourbon-Vendôme (grandfather to Henry IV), until Francis's first son was born in 1518. He was only twenty-five years old when appointed, but he already had a distinguished military career.

Francis I inherited the claims to Milan and Naples and was eager to make good on them. Louis XII had intended to lead an army against Milan in early

1515, so planning for an expedition was advanced. In August the king led his army across the Alps. His main foes were the Swiss, who had established a sort of protectorate over Milan, and its duke, Massimiliano Sforza, restored to power in 1513. Francis offered the Swiss a vast sum of gold to withdraw. Many accepted the bribe, but perhaps as many as 20,000 refused. They marched out of the city, "like bees swarming out of their hive," to take on the French, who were camped nearby. At the ensuing Battle of Marignano, the bloodiest of the Italian wars, the French *gens d'armes* and artillery played the major roles in the French victory. After a short siege Milan capitulated, and Francis had himself installed as duke. He was eager to negotiate with his recent foes—the Swiss and the pope. He needed access to Swiss mercenaries for his army, so he made a generous offer to the cantons. Eight of the 13 cantons accepted it, which gave the French monarchy the first right to recruit mercenaries within them and prohibited the Swiss from serving against France. Negotiations with Pope Leo X resulted in the Concordat of Bologna early in 1516, changing the governance of the French Church.

Francis returned home in early 1516 to the acclaim of his people, with the expectation that the pope would invest him with the kingdom of Naples when Ferdinand of Aragon died. His death occurred within days of Francis's return home, but it had far different consequences than what the French king expected. Ferdinand's heir to the realms of Aragon, Castile, and Naples was his grandson Charles of Habsburg. Already the prince of the Low Countries and the Franche-Comté, Charles's succession to the Spanish realms threatened France with a two-front war should he ever wage war on France, and he had plenty of grounds for war whenever he wished. However, he had difficulties establishing his rule in Spain, which precluded any war with France until after his grandfather, Holy Roman Emperor Maximilian I, died in January 1519. For the first time in two centuries, there was real competition for the election of the emperor. The Habsburgs had held the title since 1438, and they regarded it as hereditary. Both Francis I and Henry VIII decided to challenge Charles in the election. Henry did so largely for the prestige of the office, but Francis had a more compelling reason. Although by 1519 the emperor's authority in Germany was limited, he still had the power to direct the empire's foreign policy and call on the Germans for money and manpower to wage war. Should Charles become emperor, he would control land along virtually every mile of the French border.

Francis collected some 800,000 *l* to bribe the electors, but Charles outspent him and won the title. Francis then tried to detach England from its long-standing pro-Spanish policy. In March 1520, Henry returned Tournai to France for 1.2 million *l,* and it was agreed that the two kings would meet. The meeting took place in the Calais Pale in June and is known as the Field of the Cloth of Gold because of the gold cloth used for the tents. The most noted aspect was the exuberant wrestling between the two kings. Nonetheless, the camaraderie at Guines failed to produce any long-term benefits for France. Henry usually was either neutral or favored Charles in the contest for primacy in Europe.

Fighting between Francis I and Charles V erupted in 1520. Hoping to take advantage of the continuing revolt of the Spanish cities, Francis sent an army into southern Navarre to recover it for the d'Albrets. After initial success the French were driven out by mid-1521. That summer saw fighting along virtually the entire French frontier with Charles's lands. Again, Milan was the focal point. Charles claimed the duchy as a fief of the empire with the right to name its duke, while the administration that Francis had placed in the city had become very unpopular. When in late 1521 an Imperial force appeared before the walls, it received help from the residents. Odet de Lautrec, the French governor, abandoned the city in November, leaving a garrison in the citadel. Over the winter Francis recruited 16,000 Swiss mercenaries for Lautrec. Returning toward Milan with his augmented army, Lautrec ran into the Imperial army several miles from the city. The enemy had time to dig trenches, and Lautrec was reluctant to attack. The Swiss insisted, threatening to leave his army if he did not order an immediate attack. The resulting Battle of La Bicocca in April 1522 was a catastrophe for the Swiss and Lautrec; they had to abandon all of northern Italy except for garrisons in Milan and Cremona.

Serious financial problems hampered Francis I's ability to respond to this defeat. The heavy expenses of his court and wars had outrun the increase in taxation that had already taken place, and the creaky fiscal system in place made revenue enhancement difficult. Thus Francis made broad changes in fiscal administration, including the creation of the Epargne, which is one of the noteworthy achievements of his reign. The king, prompted by his mother, also became convinced that many of the *gens des finances* were defrauding the government in revenue collection. A special commission was established to audit their accounts, especially those of Jacques de Semblançay. One of a large number of royal officers from the region of Tours, he had become the chief royal financial officer and served the queen mother in the same capacity. He had gained so much wealth in royal service that he could lend the king huge sums. The audit commission found only a few minor errors in his books, but the report to Francis revealed how wealthy he was. Louise of Savoy also was very angry with him, because he had sent a large sum of her money to the French army in Italy without her permission. After three years in disgrace, Semblançay was suddenly arrested in early 1527 and put on trial for defrauding the crown before a *chambre de justice,* an ad hoc tribunal for hearing special cases of fiscal malfeasance.[3] He was quickly convicted and executed, although modern historians agree that at worst he was guilty of poor accounting.

A vindictive Louise of Savoy had a major role in the downfall of Charles de Bourbon. Francis had named him constable in 1515, but in 1521 relations between them deteriorated badly. The main reason was the death of Bourbon's childless wife, Suzanne de Bourbon, the heiress to vast properties in central France. He expected to take them over, but the king claimed them on the basis of feudal law, in which lands without an heir returned to the throne. Louise also laid a claim to her first cousin's properties. The case was taken to the Parlement of Paris, but prior to any decision, Francis appropriated Suzanne's lands and gave them to his mother. Contemporary rumor also claimed that Bourbon jilted Louise in a marriage proposal. A face-to-face confrontation between the constable and the king in early 1523 led Charles to renounce his allegiance to the French crown. He began to plot a rebellion, but word soon reached the king. The rebellion was not well organized enough to proceed, nor was Charles V ready to strike into France. Bourbon fled to the Franche-Comté in late 1523, and the next spring, he led an Imperial army into Provence. Pushing on to Marseille, he put it under siege, but had to withdraw to Italy when Francis arrived with a large force.

Francis was able to respond quickly to the attack on Provence because he had been gathering an army for a return to Milan. Having relieved Marseille, he crossed the Alps in October 1524, despite the late season. The Imperial army in Milan decided to withdraw to Pavia, which was more defensible, and Francis laid siege to it. A large relief force appeared in the area in January. Unable to draw the French forces out of their siege lines around Pavia, the Imperial commanders, who included Charles de Bourbon, decided to attack them. In the Battle of Pavia, February 24, 1525, the Imperial forces repulsed the assaults of the French *gens d'armes* and the Swiss pikemen. Both fled, leaving Francis to fight on alone with a handful of his bodyguards. His horse was shot out from under him, and he was obliged to surrender. He wrote to his mother, who was serving as regent for him, to assure her that he was still alive, adding the poignant phrase: "Nothing remains to me but my honor and my life, which are safe."[4]

Francis was taken to Spain, where he was locked up in a rude tower. Deprived of exercise, he soon fell seriously ill. He shortly agreed to the stiff ransom that Charles V was demanding. It required him to yield sovereignty over Flanders and Burgundy and concede his claims to Naples and Milan. Francis was also to reinstate Charles de Bourbon and marry Charles V's sister Eleanor, the widow of the king of Portugal; Queen Claude had died two years earlier. The French king proposed that he be released from captivity in order to effect the transfer of Burgundy, since the Parlement of Paris would refuse to alienate a part of the realm without his direct orders. Charles agreed to accept Francis's two older sons, Francis and Henry, as hostages for their father. The exchange took place in March 1526, on the Spanish-French border. The story goes that once Francis was released, he leapt on his horse, shouted "Now I am king once again!" and rode off without looking back at his sons. When he reached Paris, he denounced the agreement he had signed on the grounds that ill treatment had coerced it from him.

To ensure that the realm backed his position and would provide the financial aid needed for renewed war and the ransom of his sons, the king called an Assembly of Notables to meet in Paris during December 1527.[5] The distinction between the Estates general and the Assembly of Notables is not easy to make, since attendance at the former was not all that much greater than for the latter. The key difference was that the king chose the delegates from among the nobles, the clergy, and the Parlements, with Paris generally being the only city represented. Some 200 notables attended Francis's assembly. He explained why he did not feel bound to honor his ransom agreement and told the assembly that he would need 4 million *l* for war and the ransom of his sons. The delegates agreed unanimously that the king was justified in his decision and pledged the money he needed. The clergy agreed to give 2.6 million *l*.

Charles V responded to the broken agreement by resuming the war and making the treatment of the two French princes in Spain more and more harsh, gradually reducing the number of their French servants until none were left. Most of the rest of Europe was frightened by Charles's dominant position resulting from his victory at Pavia, and Francis was able to form an alliance with the remaining Italian states and England. With the threat of an English invasion gone and aided by the Italian states, Francis was able to raise a large army to send against Naples and a fleet to blockade it. The city seemed about to fall into French hands, when a dramatic change of alliance occurred. Genoa had a number of grievances against France, despite joining the anti-Habsburg league, and in July 1528, Andrea Doria, the Genoese admiral, signed a contract with Charles, committing his fleet to Imperial service. For the rest of the century, Genoa would be in the service of the Habsburgs and would provide vital seapower to their cause. The agreement resulted in the withdrawal of the Genoese fleet from Naples and the failure of the French siege.

By the end of 1528, both sides were ready to resume negotiations. The two most powerful women in Europe of the time served as negotiators—Louise of Savoy and Margaret of Austria, who was Charles's aunt and regent for the Low Countries. In August 1529, the Treaty of Cambrai, or the Peace of the Ladies as it was also called, was hammered out. The major change from the ransom of 1526 was the clause allowing Francis to pay four million *l* for his sons instead of giving up Burgundy. It took over a year to collect the necessary number of gold coins, and when they were weighed, they were found to be light because of debasement. Francis had to add 41,000 to make the proper weight. In July 1530, his two sons were handed over for the gold, and Eleanor of Castile, on her way to marry Francis, accompanied them to Bayonne. Henry, the younger son, strongly felt that he had been mistreated in Spain, and he nurtured a deep hatred for Charles V that would mark his reign when he became the royal successor after his brother died in 1536.

The catastrophe of Pavia proved to be costly to France both in monetary terms and in the concession of rights to Flanders and the Italian properties, but it inflicted no permanent damage on the French monarchy. The prosperity of the era allowed the crown to recoup its financial losses fairly quickly and alleviated the heavy tax burden the ransom created. Nor did the French kings concede the loss of the lands given to Charles in the treaty. They continued to seek to recover Naples and Milan until 1559, and they never conceded Flanders. It would remain a cause of war between Valois and Habsburg for nearly two more centuries.

3

The Church:
Unchallenged

The Catholic Church was a close second to the monarchy as the most powerful institution in France. It had wealth, a well-organized structure, its own educational system, and far greater autonomy from the monarchy than any other institution. Its domination over the religious, intellectual, and cultural life of the French people had gone unchallenged since the destruction of the religious movement known as Catharism in the thirteenth century. That power and dominance would come under fire in the sixteenth century, but it would emerge by 1614 largely unscathed.

All those who were tonsured and those in religious communities were designated as making up the ecclesiastical order. The term *clergy* referred more specifically to tonsured males, but it was usually used as a synonym for the ecclesiastical order, especially when it referred to a legal and political status within the realm, the First Estate. Calculating the proportion of the French population in religious life, both male and female, is a difficult task. Analyses done for three cities—Toulouse for 1400, Poitiers for a century later, and Dijon for 1556—place the figure at 4, 5, and 3.5 percent respectively. [1] Students of the universities, who were nominally all clerics, were present in large numbers in several cities, especially Paris, and members of the mendicant orders also made up a large portion of the urban religious. They were not present in the countryside, so one can assume that the clergy comprised a smaller percentage of the rural population. Until statistics are developed for the entire realm, the figure of 2 percent of the French population seems plausible for around 1500, although a lower figure is possible. The size of the clergy was increasing in the early sixteenth century and may have reached its highest ever by 1560, when it began to decline.[2]

Despite constituting such a small portion of the people, the French clergy had prodigious wealth. Since the Church was a permanent corporate body, land that it owned never left its hands, unlike a noble family, which may have had a daughter as its only heir, who then passed the family property to her husband's lineage, or whose line often died out entirely. The term *mortmain* (dead hand) was used to make the point that properties rarely changed hands once they passed into the Church's grasp. The resulting loss of income for the monarch, who as feudal lord collected fees when lands changed hands, led to a system of licenses in *mortmain,* which imposed a fee on lands transferred to the Church. Once that was done, the lands almost never passed out of the control of the clergy. Over the centuries the French Church had gained control of about one-third of the land of the realm.

Since the ecclesiastical order also held other sources of income besides land, it is possible that it collected 40 percent of the total income of the kingdom, as a Venetian ambassador reported in 1563. Those additional revenues included feudal dues and fees that most bishops and many monasteries still collected as the nominal lord of their towns and regions, although that income had declined substantially since the high Middle Ages. In addition to these "temporal" revenues, the clergy collected "spiritual" revenues. They included fines and fees from the bishops' courts, the *officialités,* which had jurisdiction over all cases involving clerics and anything touching on the sacraments. Thus, marriages and wills made up much of the case load, although for some time the kings had been chipping away at the broad range of jurisdiction of the church courts.

"Donations" for saying masses, performing the sacraments, burying the dead, and other clerical services provided a substantial part of the income of the average priest, although much of it passed up the hierarchy. These were theoretically free-will offerings, but the clergy had a hard-and-fast price list of fees. One of the most frequent complaints about the priests was that they extorted money from the faithful for performing religious services. For example, in Paris in 1509, the Parlement had to step in to force the local priests to reduce their fees for burying the dead, as many poor people were going unburied. Large bequests in wills were the usual way of seeking expiation for a sinful life, and they provided yet another source of clerical income.

Last but far from least as a source of income for the Church was the *dîme* or tithe. It was a universal tax on the fruits of the land and livestock, which all laity were obliged to pay. It rarely was as high as a tenth of production; a fifteenth was more common. It nearly always was paid in kind; the clerics kept some of the produce for their own use and sold the rest. The Church was especially vigilant in collecting the tithe, and excommunication was frequently used to force payment. Resentment toward the tithe was universal.

In canon (church) law, the vast revenues the ecclesiastical order collected were exempt from royal taxation. Its great wealth, however, was tempting to the monarchy, which was always in financial difficulty. At the time of Philip II's involvement in the Third Crusade, the papacy allowed him to collect a tenth of the clergy's income for the crusade. The proclamation of a pseudo-crusade became the means of levying a *décime*, as the clerical tenth became known. In the aftermath of the bitter dispute between Philip IV and Boniface VIII, it also became accepted that the king could ask for a *décime* from the clergy to wage a just war. The clergy always insisted that it was a gift to the king, and the pope had to approve its collection. In 1513, however, Louis XII, in the midst of his feud with Julius II and facing an English invasion, levied a *décime* of 300,000 *l* without papal approval. Three years later, Francis I, determined to make the clerical tenth a permanent part of his budget, gained from Leo X, who was cowed by the French victory at Marignano the previous year, the right to levy it without papal permission. Nonetheless, it remained in theory a gift from the French clergy, which always had to approve it in some sort of assembly, not that approval would ever be refused. Francis established a Département général des décimes, which determined and collected the proper levy for each French diocese. By 1532, the *décime*, set at 300,000 *l*, was being collected every year, although that sum was well below 10 percent of the clergy's income. Soon the king was levying more than one *décime* a year, and by 1547, four, or 1.2 million *l*, had became standard, which came much closer to 10 percent of the Church's revenues.[3]

In addition to their wealth and the privilege of having their own courts, the churchmen had a variety of other rights and privileges. They constituted the First Estate of the realm; in a society where rank was of vast importance that meant a great deal. The cardinals, for example, marched immediately behind the king in every royal procession (although a decision of 1560 put them behind the princes of blood). When the Estates general met, the speaker of the First Estate served as the spokesman for the entire assembly. All the bishops by virtue of their office had the right to sit in the First Estate, but in 1484 the Estates general decided that a bishop who had not been elected by his *bailliage* could not receive expenses or salary. That greatly reduced the number of bishops at the meetings; until 1614 they made up about a quarter of the First Estate's deputies.

Many bishops and some abbots had noble titles conferred on them by virtue of their offices. For example, the bishop of Tulle was also the viscount of Tulle. The most prestigious such title was bishop-peer. Six dioceses—Reims, Laon, Châlons-sur-Marne, Beauvais, Noyons, and Langres—conferred that title on their incumbents. They had major roles in the king's *sacre* and the right to sit in the Parlement of Paris. Ten additional bishops ex officio sat in the provincial Parlements. The people of the era regarded the title of bishop as enhancing the prestige of its holder, and the kings often gave bishoprics to their diplomats after they had demonstrated their talents and loyalty. In respect to the presence of a large number of prelates in royal service, their clerical status did not convey royal office; their frequent presence in the government reflected the attitude that the clergy provided a large pool of talented men who could be put to work for the monarchy. More cynically, the kings looked on high church office as a way to provide pay and rewards for loyal servants, which reduced the pressure on the royal treasury.

These last two points are part of the explanation for the rampant abuses in the clergy, especially one of the most common, absenteeism. At any time prior to 1600, most of the bishops were not residing in their dioceses. Many were at the royal court or abroad on royal business; others were in Rome; still others were absent for less valid reasons. It was said about Cardinal Duprat, Francis I's chancellor, that the first time he saw his cathedral at Lyon was when he was buried in it. With the overseer (the original meaning of bishop) absent, the lower clergymen were quick to absent themselves from their duties.

What was probably more scandalous about the lower clergy was the poverty-stricken condition in which so many found themselves, in contrast with the opulent life-style of the hierarchy. It was true that every parish was a benefice with a respectable income attached. The revenues were usually high enough that the pastor could hire a vicar, generally called the curé because he had the care of souls, to minister to the people. Often, however, the curé in turn hired unattached priests to perform the sacraments while he, like the rector, was absent. In the late fifteenth century there was a large number of unbeneficed priests who could be called a clerical proletariat, catching on to whatever positions they could find. They often lived with their families or in communities of other priests in the same condition. Differing little from their relatives in education and behavior, many of them turned to brigandage for their livelihood. Both the monarchy and the Church sought to reduce their number, with considerable success by the mid-1500s. Despite their circumstances and poor reputation, the lowest levels of the clergy were surprisingly conscientious, doing the work of saving souls that those higher in the hierarchy largely ignored.

A major reason for the wealth of the high churchmen was pluralism, the practice of allowing clerics to hold several church offices at once, which was also an important factor in absenteeism. Prior to the Council of Trent, it was all too common to find a prominent prelate holding two or more bishoprics at once. One cardinal had seven sees during the 1540s. A more common situation involved the practice of allowing prominent churchmen to hold monasteries *in commendam* (in trust). The commendatory abbot had no responsibilities in the monastery but drew the abbot's income and had the prestige of the title. It was not unusual for a cardinal to be the commendatory abbot of a dozen or more monasteries as well as bishop of two or three dioceses. When a great prelate was an absentee bishop of a large see, he often named as his vicar someone from the next level of the hierarchy, perhaps the bishop of a small diocese of the Midi. He in turn found a vicar from further down, creating a chain of absenteeism that reached to the local parish.

The French hierarchy was also notorious for its display of personal vices. Several prominent examples from the episcopate could be easily found for nearly every vice. Avarice certainly was common. The clerical revenues of Cardinal Charles de Lorraine from the see of Reims and eleven abbacies mounted to about 300,000 *l* in 1550. The Parlement of Provence once had to compel an archbishop of Arles to give alms to the victims of a great flood of the Rhône. Drunkenness was another problem, exemplified by the prelate called "the Cardinal of Bottles." But as usually has been the case, sexual incontinence was the most common vice. Concubines and illegitimate children were common for the prelates. Brantome, the eager gossipmonger who loved to tell tales on the hierarchy, told of one bishop who, "in order to build up his harem," gave pensions to ten-year-old girls so they would be available to him when they were older. Although the lower clergy did not share in the opulent life style of the prelates, the same vices were very evident.

The blatant corruption in the Church sparked a desire for reform, but it was far from an organized movement until after 1530. The Estates of 1484 made a strong appeal for reform in a number of areas, especially the elimination of pluralism, the appointment of worthy prelates, and a return to frequent diocesan synods. Charles VIII paid little attention to the need for reform until several months before his death. Undergoing a conversion experience of sorts, he announced his intentions of undertaking a broad range of reforms, beginning with the reformation of the monasteries and religious houses, whose disorder had become notorious.

Charles died before he accomplished anything, but Louis XII, his successor, followed up at least on the reform of the houses of religion. Louis was heavily influenced by Cardinal Georges d'Amboise, to whom the pope gave the office of permanent papal legate in France. His authority as legate extended to imposing reform on the houses of the Dominicans, Franciscans, and Benedictines in France without having to go through Rome.[4] It was reported about their houses in Paris that "they failed to observe all the rules of their orders and were dissolute in conversation and behavior." In all three cases the religious resisted the imposition of reform, and in two houses they took arms to thwart it. Louis had to force them to accept the reform commission into the houses. On the other hand, the reform of religious houses for women went much better; by the time of Louis's death, a large portion had been reformed.[5] When a body of clerics was determined to remain unreformed, as they usually were, it was most difficult to achieve reform. The clerics had the time to devote to defending their prerogatives, and they were quick to use the Parlement, which was usually sympathetic, to delay or avoid it.

Even a monarch truly committed to reform would have great difficulty in achieving it, but a king like Louis XII, despite hearing many sermons on the need for reform from his confessor Jean Clerée, was too comfortable in the conventional religion of his time to devote much time and effort to reforming the Church. The push for reform in France, what little there was before 1530, came from a small handful of individuals, who had little influence and less impact. The most visible reformers at the turn of the century were Jean Standonck and a small group of disciples in the University of Paris. A native of Flanders, Standonck was a prominent member of the faculty of theology. Familiar with the canons of Windesheim from his homeland, he invited the group, an offshoot of the Devotio Moderna, to establish a house in Paris. While the canons hardly succeeded in reforming the religious establishments of the city, they did raise the level of the Parisian clergy. Standonck also mounted a campaign to have himself elected archbishop of Reims. He hoped to use the office to push his reforms, but had no chance of getting it.

In 1491 Standonck founded a college in the University of Paris for poor students to create a better class of priests. It became the famous Collège de Montaigu. He had a strict sense of discipline in pedagogy, and the college became notorious for its severity yet famed for the quality of its education. Standonck had some interest in humanism, but after his death in 1504, the college became a stronghold of a rigid scholasticism. Leadership passed to conservative theologians, in particular Noël Béda, the scourge of humanist reformers during Francis I's reign. One of those Béda later went after was Jacques Lefèvre d'Etaples, the best known of the French humanist reformers. He returned to France from Italy in 1494 and became one of the founders of Christian humanism, by which is meant the application of the principles of criticism established by the Italian humanists to the history and earliest texts of Christianity. In 1509 he published a critical edition of the Psalms and three years later, the epistles of St. Paul. Both works emphasized the importance of reading and studying the Bible directly instead of approaching it through commentaries written by scholastic theologians.

Lefèvre had little direct contact with the monarchy, although he influenced Francis I's sister, Marguerite, whose idiosyncratic views on religion owed much to him. Her relationship with Lefèvre came through his principal patron, Guillaume Briçonnet, who became the bishop of Lodève at a young age and abbot of the great monastery of St-Germain-des-Près in Paris in 1507.[6] Briçonnet installed Lefèvre there as his librarian and spiritual director. When he became bishop of Meaux, he took Lefèvre with him to his new see. Free from the scrutiny of the reactionary theologians of the Sorbonne, they began to institute a broad reform program in Meaux. When Briçonnet first visited his diocese in 1518, he was shocked at how "starved his flock was of spiritual food." A group of activist reformers, including Guillaume Farel, the future reformer of Geneva, gathered in Meaux, creating what became known as the Circle of Meaux. Their program included an emphasis on preaching, and the bishop himself preached every Sunday in the cathedral, a truly rare event for a French prelate. Several of the Circle proclaimed their intention to preach "the pure Gospel," a phrase that later would become identified with Protestantism, and Lefèvre set to work to provide a French translation of the Bible, which he completed in 1530. In 1525 the queen mother, Louise of Savoy, acting as regent while her son was campaigning in Italy, received complaints that the diocese "smelled of heresy." Identifying heresy with lower-class sedition, as the monarchy continued to do until 1559, Louise feared that the terrifying disorders of the German Peasants' War, then in full riot, would spread to France. She moved to break up the Circle, and the more radical numbers, such as Farel, fled abroad and became openly Protestant. Briçonnet and Lefèvre at this point drew back from their former colleagues and never did break with the Catholic Church.[7]

Briçonnet's reform-mindedness certainly did not come from his family of wealthy merchants from Tours, who made large loans to the king and provided him with royal officials and prelates. His father had been a royal treasurer before becoming archbishop of Reims after his wife died. The careers of both father and son exemplified one of the major problems of the French Church of this era—the deep involvement of the king in appointing prelates and abbots. The bishoprics and abbacies of the major monasteries were the major benefices of the French Church. Benefices ranged from the curate of the local priest with an income as low as ten *l* a year to archbishoprics and abbacies with incomes as high as 30,000 *l*, the annual income of the see of Rouen. Other lucrative sees included Chartres, Toulouse, and Reims, all around 20,000 *l*. Several great monasteries matched that sum for their abbots. On the other hand, the revenues of small dioceses like Mirepoix and Tulle were in the range of 2,000 to 3,000 *l.* Pluralism allowed clerics to pull together incomes from many benefices of different types. By the mid-sixteenth century, French cardinals were drawing well over 100,000 *l* from their collection of benefices.

The ability to place one's relatives and clients in lucrative benefices, many of which were sinecures (from *sine cura,* "without care of souls") with few if any duties, was a powerful tool in the hands of those who had the right of collation (assignment) of benefices. Few aspects of the French Church were more complicated than collation. In theory the bishop had the power of collating every benefice of his diocese, but for a variety of reasons, his rights were severely reduced in most dioceses. For example, a noble whose family had founded a religious institution would collate its benefices, while the king had the right to fill a vacant benefice in every diocese at his succession. In most French dioceses the bishop's rights of collation extended to less than half of the benefices. In the diocese of Paris, the bishop collated only 215 out of 469 parishes, and it was as low as 4 percent in the see of Bayeux.

Far more valuable was the right to fill the 110 bishoprics and more than 600 major abbacies in France. They were called consistorial benefices because the pope would call a papal consistory—a meeting with the cardinals then present in Rome—to approve of the new appointees and draw up bulls of office in order for the new prelates to take office legitimately. The access to patronage, influence, and money that the collation of the consistorial benefices gave whoever held the right meant that it would be a matter of utmost importance for king and pope and a source of much conflict between them. The earliest way to choose bishops and abbots had been canonical election: the chapters of the cathedral clergy and the monks of a monastery had elected worthy men as bishops or abbots. But soon pope and king had become involved. The papacy gained the upper hand during the Investiture Controversy of the eleventh century. By the time of the Avignon papacy, the popes openly appointed bishops and abbots across Europe and collected a fee called the "common services" for drawing up their bulls of office.

After the papacy returned to Rome, the French kings, and perhaps even more their clergy, resented the interference of Italian popes in the process of filling the most valuable benefices of the French Church and in the affairs of the French Church in general. Their first response was to support the conciliar movement, which proclaimed that regularly convened general councils of the Church had the power to legislate for the Church and control the popes. When the pope ignored the Council of Basel of 1431-37 and its legislation limiting papal powers, the French clergy, which had been strongly represented at Basel, moved to formulate its own limitations on papal control. The result was the Pragmatic Sanction of Bourges, which a national council of French clergy recommended to Charles VII in 1438, who put it into effect. It returned the filling of consistorial benefices to the cathedral and monastery chapters by canonical election, but it allowed for the "sweet and honest prayers" of the king in recommending candidates to the chapters. The other major clause of the Pragmatic Sanction eliminated the payment of the common services and the annates, a papal tax of a year's income on a benefice when it was filled. The purpose was to stop the flow of money to Rome, although the French clergy was free to give a gift of money to the pope.

The Pragmatic Sanction failed to restore true canonical election to the French Church as intended. Bitter disputes erupted in the chapters over the elections.[8] Many of these struggles dragged on for years, and some became violent. For example, in 1507 at Poitiers, a cleric of the cathedral was killed over the episcopal election. The royal courts and the privy council were called on for decisions, while the king's "honest prayers" counted for a great deal when he made them, usually for the important dioceses and abbacies. By the time of Louis XII, the system had broken down.

The popes regarded the Pragmatic Sanction as a schismatic document and were constantly pressing the kings to eliminate it. With the anarchy in the French hierarchy increasing along with the number of court cases over disputed canonical elections, the monarchy was agreeable to a change. For some time, efforts to draw up a new system floundered on papal insistence on the right of appointment, but when Francis I won at Marignano in 1515, Pope Leo X became more accommodating. The next year, face-to-face negotiations between the two led to the Concordat of Bologna.[9] It gave the king the right to nominate a candidate for a vacant consistorial benefice. If the pope rejected the royal nomination, as was now his right, the king had to provide another nomination within six months. Should the pope find that candidate also unworthy, the right to fill the benefice passed to him. There was a fair number of cases before 1614 when the pope rejected the first royal nomination, but he never rejected the second. Other clauses required that the nominees for bishoprics be at least twenty-seven years old, be French by birth or naturalization, and have a degree in theology or law from a recognized university. These requirements, especially the last, were undermined by the clause that permitted the king to nominate members of the royal family or great noble families who did not meet them.[10] Over the next century, less than a fifth of the French bishops had the prerequisite degree. The Concordat also removed the royal ban on the pope's collecting the annates in France.

Although the Concordat of Bologna had been negotiated by the French king, there was strong opposition to it in France. The Pragmatic Sanction was the quintessential statement of a view known as Gallicanism, which postulated that the French Church, of which the king was the head, was free from papal control over the administration of its offices and finances, while accepting the pope's authority in matters of doctrine and discipline. While there had been vague expressions of the theory before 1400, the first clear statement of the concept dates to 1407 when Charles VI proclaimed two cornerstone edicts on the relationship between the French Church and the papacy. He declared that the Gallican Church had traditionally enjoyed certain liberties from papal authority, which the pope of his time was denounced for allegedly violating. In particular, they involved the freedom of France from papal appointive power. The principle of local control over appointments to the French hierarchy was made explicit in the Pragmatic Sanction, which reflected the idea that a French national council could legislate for the Gallican Church. It expounded the view that the king was able to call such assemblies and issue decrees in his authority as head of the French Church.

The Pragmatic Sanction espoused a point of view known as ecclesiastical Gallicanism, in that its crucial clause returned to the French clergy the power to fill the major benefices of the French Church. There was also a view known as royal Gallicanism, sometimes called parlementaire Gallicanism because the Parlement was its outspoken advocate, which endorsed the right of the king to fill those benefices. Regardless of which nuance of Gallicanism they advocated, most French until 1789 were passionate proponents of the general principle that the Gallican Church was autonomous from Rome. The opposition to the Concordat of Bologna remained strong for several years after 1516 and lingered through the sixteenth century. The University of Paris, the stronghold of ecclesiastical Gallicanism, objected, but the more serious opposition came from the Parlement of Paris, which believed that Francis had given up too much to the papacy. The Parlement refused to register the Concordat, as was required for it to take effect in France. The magistrates expected that the pope would use his right of refusal of nominees to pass to himself the right of appointment of French prelates. After two years of heated debate, Francis finally ordered the Parlement to register the edict establishing the Concordat.

The Concordat of Bologna remained in effect until the French Revolution, but it hardly ended disputes with the papacy. The major source of disputes in the several decades after 1516 was the clause that allowed the pope to fill the benefices of prelates who died at Rome. The French kings were determined to keep down the pope's opportunities to make such appointments by restricting the number of French prelates at the papal court, but that had the effect of reducing French influence in Rome.

However, the controversies engendered by the Concordat were minor compared to the row between Louis XII and Julius II.[11] As a territorial ruler in

Italy the pope was caught up in the conflicts sparked by the French invasions of Italy. Julius's election in 1503 put on the throne of St. Peter a firebrand determined to rid Italy of all foreigners, starting with the French. His Machiavellian mind was too subtle for the rather gullible Louis, who was rudely awakened one morning to find that the alliance he and Julius had forged with Spain and several other states against Venice had been turned against him. Louis chose to use the spiritual sword against Julius by calling a national council of the French Church to threaten removing France from obedience to the pope. When it met at Tours in September 1511, it authorized Louis to convoke a general council to reform the Church "in head and members," an obvious conciliatory tenet.

When nine cardinals and 24 bishops, nearly all French, assembled at Pisa in November 1512, Julius excommunicated them and the French king, and invited France's neighbors to invade the realm, dispose "the schismatic king," and divide his kingdom among themselves.[12] Only Henry VIII took Julius up on his offer, invading Picardy, since the pope had acknowledged his claim to be the rightful king of France. Louis stubbornly refused to concede anything to Julius until Papa Terribilis died in early 1513. The new pope, Leo X, soon extended an olive branch to Louis. The French king agreed to disavow his council, which had been transferred to Milan and then to Lyon, and Leo declared the excommunication had never applied to Louis. As part of the price for making peace with the pope, Louis also had to accept the decrees of the Fifth Lateran Council, which Julius had called to counter Pisa. Among them was an explicit denunciation of the Pragmatic Sanction of Bourges, which set the scene for its replacement in 1516.

The failure of the Council of Pisa dealt a final blow to conciliarism in France. When France became enmeshed in war in Italy, its kings had to relearn what Philip IV had fully appreciated: the election of the Roman pontiff was a matter of great importance. Charles VIII was too inexperienced to mount an effective campaign to influence the papal election of 1492. Nonetheless, some of the problems the French faced throughout the sixteenth century were obvious in the conclave that elected Alexander VI. There was no viable French candidate, and Charles had to support an Italian cardinal, Guiliano della Rovere, whom he expected to be a partisan of France. Charles spent 300,000 ducats to gain his election, but Rodrigo Borgia was able to outspend him by a wide margin. There were only three French cardinals in 1492, and just one took part in the conclave. Furthermore, France was just one of three major non-Italian powers (Spain and the Holy Roman Empire were the others) that were seeking to influence the mostly Italian cardinals. Last, there was a lingering suspicion of the French, a residue of the Avignon captivity and the Great

Schism, which would be compounded in 1494 when Charles led the First French Invasion of Italy. In short, French influence was of little matter in the election of Borgia as Alexander VI.

When Alexander died in 1503, circumstances seemingly had changed greatly. For the first time in a century there was a viable French candidate, Cardinal Georges d'Amboise. Alexander's son, Cesare Borgia, had pledged to help make him pope. A French army on its way to Naples happened to be passing by Rome when Alexander died, and Louis expected to use it to control the conclave. A Venetian ambassador in Rome reported: "The representative of the King of France has received a written instruction from his master to exhort all the Cardinals to consult his pleasure and make [d'Amboise] Pope. Every possible blandishment, promise, and inducement is employed."[13] Yet d'Amboise did not become pope. Only one other French cardinal was able to join him at Rome for the conclave, and Cesare's serious illness prevented him from influencing the election. Italian xenophobia was also a factor in the choice of the short-lived Pius II. His death was quickly followed by the election of della Rovere as Julius II in the shortest conclave in history. French approval of his election soon disappeared as his policy became clear. Louis's difficulties with Julius left only one French cardinal in Rome for the next election, in 1513, and with virtually no influence in the conclave. The selection of Leo X, who became increasingly concerned about Spanish power in Italy, reduced the damage of Louis's failure to influence the election.

French influence in the next consistory in 1521 was again small. A year earlier Francis had promised to spend a million in gold to secure a pope of his choice and threatened a schism if Charles V selected the next pope, a threat that was repeated at several elections. The Italian cardinals who dominated the College of Cardinals rushed the opening of the conclave so that none of the French cardinals arrived in time; only three of the 39 who elected Hadrian VI were not Italian. The choice of Charles V's tutor shocked Francis, but the new pope was a reformer, not a politician. His death less than two years later further reduced the impact of the French failure to prevent his election. Francis I's defeat at La Bicocca drastically affected his ability to play a leading role in the next conclave. The lack of a strong French partisan among the Italian cardinals also hampered the prospects of a favorable outcome of the election. But for the first time in decades a group of French cardinals took part. After a conclave of six weeks, Clement VII was elected. He was thought of as anti-French, but the growing domination of Italy by Charles V forced him to turn to France for support. In 1533 he and Francis sealed an alliance through the marriage of his ward Catherine de Medici to the king's son Henry, but the value of that alliance disappeared the next year when Clement died. There was little question that

Alessandro Farnese would now be elected, since he had been a strong candidate since 1513. Francis regarded him neutral in the bitter struggle with Charles V, and the fact that most of the French cardinals could not get to Rome quickly enough to participate in the very brief conclave that elected him Paul III was not seen as a defeat for France. Politically he proved to be pro-French, but the French monarchy found it could not support most of his reform program. The French kings consistently failed to gain the election of their papal candidates for the half-century after 1484, but it is hard to argue that the failure proved all that costly for France in the long term. Popes have usually been good examples of the adage "The office makes the man!" Had the French succeeded in electing their candidates, papal decision making may well have turned out little different.

This discussion of church wealth, benefices, and elections surely gives the impression that the French Church was about material things, and to a large extent that was true. The lack of any serious challenge to its domination over the spiritual life of the people made it difficult for the clergy to pay attention to their duties. Once Catharism had been eradicated by 1330, France was nearly free of organized dissident movements in religion, although communities of Waldensians continued to survive in the mountains of Dauphiné. They suffered sporadic persecution, but interestingly, in 1509 they won a judgment from the monarchy against the archbishop of Embrum and some local nobles who had waged a "crusade" against them some 20 years earlier, which ordered them to return confiscated properties to the Waldensians. Philip IV's expulsion of the Jews from the realm had not affected Provence, which was not then a part of France. Charles VIII and Louis XII issued several expulsion orders for those Jews who refused to convert. The final order, in 1501, largely succeeded in eradicating the once large Jewish communities of Provence. Nonetheless, large numbers of exiled Iberian Jews began to appear in Bordeaux, which had been under English rule in Philip IV's reign and also not subject to his expulsion edict. The monarchy made no effort to prevent them from settling in Bordeaux, where they became an important part of the region's economy.

Random calls for reform and rare attempts to implement it had virtually no effect before 1534 in lifting the spiritual level of either the French clergy or the laity.[14] Nor did the demands for reform alert Church leaders and kings to the growing resentment toward the Church, a trend appearing across Europe. Furthermore, there was no agitation by lower-class radical millenarian movements of the sort that convulsed much of the rest of the continent. Yet there were throughout the era the usual incidents of blasphemy and sacrilege, such as the case of the student from Abbeville who in 1503 stomped on a consecrated host of the Eucharist. Such cases kept the judicial machinery for dealing with heresy in tune, and the occasional execution for religious offenses, as happened to the Abbeville student, emphasized the seriousness of such offenses. The time was rapidly approaching when the courts and the executioners would be far busier than they had ever been.

4

The Nobility: Contented

The nobility was the principal rival of the Church in respect to power, influence, and wealth, although they were not exactly direct competitors because most of the Church's hierarchy were nobles. At meetings of the Estates general, the clergy and the nobility usually found that they had common cause against the Third Estate. More so than elsewhere in Europe, nobility in France constituted a legal status, which was transmitted in the male line from generation to generation. In 1468 the number of those expected to answer a royal summons to service as cavalrymen, the essence of noble status, was about 20,000, a number that was also true for 1547.[1] Using the most common multiplier of three other family members for every warrior, a total of around 80,000 noble persons, plus several thousand noble clerics and religious, seems plausible. There were, however, many thousands more who claimed noble status, who although their claims were tenuous or bogus "lived nobly," which meant they enjoyed the privileges of noblesse, even if they did not have a right to them.

According to the early sixteenth-century political thinker Claude de Seyssel, the legal privileges of the nobles were threefold: exemptions from the *taille* and most other taxes; the right to carry a weapon in all places and at all times, even in the presence of the king; and the honor of serving the king in the gendarmerie and royal offices, from which came salaries and pensions as a supplement to their incomes.[2] From these followed a number of other privileges, such as the exclusive rights to hunt, possess a rabbit warren and a dovecote, sit in a front pew in church, and begin legal suits at a higher level in the judicial system.

Only male nobles enjoyed many of these privileges directly; others affected the entire family. The status of noblesse allowed noble women to receive the deference of their inferiors, dress in a certain manner that indicated their noble status, such as using taffeta for their gowns, and occasionally wield considerable influence on the conduct of local and even national affairs. The daughters of nobles were tightly under their fathers' control until they married, and their marriages were always a matter of great scrutiny by their parents for the political and financial advantages they might bring. A marriage contract for a noble couple spelled out carefully and at great length what each party would bring to the marriage. If she had brothers, the woman received a substantial dowry from her parents; if not, the portion of her father's estate that she would eventually inherit was spelled out. The husband had the use of the dowry while the marriage lasted and it went to him if she died before him; if she outlived him, it was returned to her to enable her to live as appropriate for a noblewoman and provide for a new dowry should she remarry. The new husband usually provided her with income from designated lands, which was called a jointure, over which she had control and that often remained with her upon his death. The noble wife generally was expected to have a significant role in managing the noble household and perhaps even the family estates; but if she became a widow while the heir to the family estate was a minor, her authority would be vastly increased. That period when a widow's eldest son was a minor was the one time that a noblewoman truly exercised power and influence. If her relationship with her son remained close and he respected her judgment, she could continue to exercise broad influence until her death.[3]

Noblewomen from the better families frequently appeared at court as ladies-in-waiting to the queen or queen mother, where they could have a real if indirect impact on royal decisions. In those periods when the queen mother was regent, the noble ladies of her entourage had unusual power, which was certainly true for Catherine de Medici. Of course, only a small percentage of noblewomen found themselves in those favorable positions. The younger daughters in a large family often were dispatched to convents, because the sum needed to place a daughter in religious life was well below that for a dowry, although the convents provided their own opportunities for leadership. Those who did marry often found themselves in loveless marriages from which there was no escape. They also frequently found themselves raising their husbands' bastards with their own children, and illegitimate children often received estates and dowries from the family properties.

Noble privileges originally arose from the fact that the nobles' ancestors had put life and limb at risk defending the realm and the king, or so the theory went. In the early Middle Ages, the only way for a king to maintain fighting men as heavy cavalrymen (knights) was by granting them land so that they could outfit themselves with the horses, weapons, and armor needed for service as knights. Thus, the feudal system was first of all a military system in which military service was paid for with the right to the use of land and the peasant labor supply. The close identification between noble status and access to land remained intact from 1484 to 1614, although the monarchy recognized the possibility of a non-noble acquiring a piece of land, a *seigneurie*, which properly belonged to a nobleman, by requiring the payment of a fee called the *franc-fief*. The fee acknowledged that the king needed compensation for the loss of military service for a fief now in the hands of one who could not provide it, although many of the sons of these *anoblis* (new nobles) appeared in the military. In 1470, Louis XI issued an edict that allowed everyone who had been paying the *franc-fief* for at least 40 years to acquire noble status for a larger payment. Over the next century, the quiet practice of providing limited social mobility for wealthy commoners, largely to replenish the nobility, which constantly saw its families die out, became a legal right and a royal revenue device. It netted 47,250 *l* for Louis XI in Normandy alone. The *franc-fief* provided access to noble status for a significant group of families.[4]

Somewhat similar in its impact on both social mobility and the king's finances was the *lettre d'anoblissement*—the patent of nobility. It was usually granted for a hefty sum, although occasionally the king gave one for great service in war. There is no doubt that the established nobles, the *noblesse de race*, also called the *noblesse d'épée*, which reflected their military origins, resented these new nobles, who acquired noble status through the above two methods. However, the old nobles, reluctant as they were to acknowledge the newcomers, were willing to admit that the king had the power to ennoble men with certain credentials, in particular great wealth, through the *franc-fief* and patents of nobility, both in use for 200 years by 1500. The nobles of the sword were far more resentful of a new practice now beginning to appear: the ennobling of royal officeholders in the judicial and the fiscal systems. Before 1484 most officeholders came from the nobility, and the concept that serving the king in an office conferred noble status was not controversial. With the change in the social origins of the officers as the sale of royal offices accelerated, the old nobility perceived its interests were threatened. What in the past was a slow but complete acceptance of the *anoblis* was badly retarded in respect to these nobles of the long robe, the *noblesse de robe*.

Both the *franc-fief*, which required that the family being ennobled had paid it for at least 40 years or for two generations, and the royal patent of nobility raised the recipient's family to noble status and ensured that the *anobli's* descendants were also noble. But ennoblement through officeholding only ennobled the officeholder himself. Passing noble status to his descendants called into play another aspect of the French concept of nobility: A family that lived nobly for three generations had a permanent right to that status. Living nobly meant having an exemption from the tailles and a livelihood that did not depend on commerce and manual labor, and serving in the gendarmerie. The practice of law was not regarded as a noble enterprise, and perhaps it was the entrance of haute-bourgeois lawyers and their sons into the nobility through officehold-ing that so raised the ire of the old nobility toward the nobles of the robe during the sixteenth century.

The privileges of nobility were eagerly sought, and there were many who claimed them without legal standing. Their neighbors, both commoner and noble, were determined to prevent them from making good their pretenses, but enough were slipping into the nobility that the loss of tax revenue began to concern Louis XI. In 1461, he ordered an examination of the titles of nobility in Normandy, where the disorder of the last years of English rule and the French reconquest had given great opportunity to usurpers. Louis ordered that the claims to nobility of a large number of suspicious families be examined in a process called the *recherche*. Those deemed to be usurpers were returned to the tax rolls. Their loud complaints prompted Louis to halt the *recherches*, but the fact that his agents concluded that 301 out of 1325 claims checked in lower Normandy were fraudulent was surely a factor in his decision in 1470 to issue his edict on the *franc-fief*.[5] The *recherche*, however, proved to be a valuable tool for the monarchy, and it was used again in 1523 and eight more times until the most exhaustive one of 1666.

Another function of the *recherche* was finding out who among those of noble birth were no longer living nobly, usually because they were pursuing a trade that was unsuitable for the nobility. Nearly all who suffered the fate of derogation were petty nobles, whose income from appropriately noble sources was too small to support them as nobles. Nobility required a certain amount of income to maintain the proper life-style. While legally and, to some extent, socially, all nobles were the same, there were vast differences in wealth and political clout among them. The petty seigneur, the country squire, lived little different from his wealthier peasant tenants, except for those few occasions when he exercised his noble privileges. There was the late thirteenth-century example of a nobleman whose inventory of goods at death included only a chessboard as an indication of his status. Such a nobleman often could not afford the equipment to serve as a knight and was the sort likely to be subject to derogation. The exemption from the *taille* was truly valuable for a noble who was in such financial straits that he was threatened with derogation, and that helps to explain why cases often were pursued for decades in the courts.

Above the simple seigneur was a myriad of noble titles such as the baron, marquis, viscount, and, at the top, the dukes and counts. Already by the late fifteenth century there was a proliferation of high titles, which increased in the next. The most prestigious title was that of peer of the realm, conveyed to the holders of six of the principal fiefs in France—Burgundy, Flanders, Champagne, Guyenne, Normandy, and Toulouse—who, along with the bishop-peers, sat in the Parlement of Paris and assisted at the king's coronation. At the *sacre* of Louis XII in 1498, the only peerage that was occupied was Flanders, by Philip of Austria; the others were represented by prominent nobles and royal relatives. That situation was the result of an important development of the late fifteenth century—the extinction of an unusually large number of major noble houses. Certainly lineages died out before and after then, but the number was exceptional in that era. Deaths in battle, executions for treason, and barren marriages were unusually common for the great nobility in the fifteenth century. The decline in the branches of the royal family was most important. The direct male line of the Valois ended with the death of Charles VIII. The House of Valois-Orléans terminated with Louis XII. The succession of Francis I passed the throne to the cadet line of Valois-Angoulême, which lasted to 1589. The House of Valois-Burgundy ended at the death of Charles the Bold in 1477. The older royal lineages of Anjou and Artois became extinct in 1472 and 1481. The only cadet royal family that flourished was the Bourbon, descended from the sixth son of Louis IX. Besides the direct line of the dukes of Bourbon, which died out in 1503, there were two cadet branches, Montpensier and Vendôme, which were in little danger of extinction. Despite their status as princes of the blood, the Bourbons had little influence until 1560.

Several of the principal medieval noble houses also died out. The great family of Armagnac, based in the southwest, ended when Duke Louis de Nemours was killed in Italy in 1503. Another prominent noble house of the southwest, the de Foix, also was terminated in battle in Italy. The male line of the ducal house of Brittany ended with Duke Francis II's death in 1488. Except for properties of the de Foix, most of which passed to the Albrets, the lands of these extinct noble and princely houses escheated to the monarchy. (Eventually the de Foix lands did as well, via Henry IV.) Because of a series of untimely deaths in the royal family, few of the major properties thus "gathered-in" by the monarchy were given back out as appanages, and those that were did not stay out for long. Thus, by the mid-sixteenth century, the House of Bourbon-

Albret (merged by marriage in 1548) along with two noble families previously with little clout, the Montmorency and Guise families, emerged as leaders of the nobility.

The income of the noble magnates was impressive. The duke of La Trémoille, whose numerous estates were concentrated in west-central France, had an average annual income of 27,600 l from 1486 to 1509 from his properties.[6] The extensive records left by the La Trémoille enable historians to get an accurate picture of their income, but they were far from the wealthiest of the nobles. Louis of Orléans, admittedly a prince of the blood, had expenses for his household that mounted to 30,000 l in 1491, while the salaries of his retinue came to another 18,000 l. Noble expenses were as high as their incomes, or often higher. Every noble who could afford it had a retinue of lesser nobles, a court, and a bureaucracy of officers to collect their revenues from their estates. A man was not a *gentilhomme* unless he hunted; hunting dogs and hawks and their keepers were large and necessary expenses, along with horses, groomsmen, arms and armor. Louis XII was quoted as saying that a majority of the nobles of his realm was being bankrupted by their horses and dogs. Luxuries, large dowries for their daughters, and gifts to those above and below in the feudal hierarchy strained noble resources. Funerals had to be appropriately expensive for the family's rank, especially for the head of the house. The wills of nobles nearly always contained large sums for masses for their souls and alms for the poor as a way of atoning for a sinful life. Heavy debts were never anything unusual for the nobility. The key question about noble indebtedness was whether the French economy was prosperous enough to allow most encumbered noble families to recover solvency eventually. Even when it was, however, there were always some nobles who had to sell properties and rights, and others who fell into derogation because they could not carry on the activities associated with noblesse. In the period from 1484 to 1530, derogation was not a common event; the nobility fared well enough that chronic indebtedness was not a major problem for most noble houses.

An essential element of noblesse was a public display of largesse to the poor (never in large amounts), the Church, relatives, and especially the nobles of one's retinue. Miserliness was the characteristic of a commoner, which was the meaning of the insult thrown at Louis XII when the nobles called him *roi roturier* for his lack of generosity toward them. Not only the king, who obviously was the richest source of gifts and pensions, but every wealthy nobleman was expected to provide largesse to those below him in the feudal hierarchy. The king and greater nobles also had offices that provided the lesser nobles a salary and the opportunity for graft, although the number of haute-bourgeoisie in such offices was far higher in 1500 than a century earlier.

The most prized form of largesse was the royal pension, which often was substantial. For example, Louis XII provided a pension of 10,000 *l* to the duke of La Trémoille, although the members of the royal family drew more than that from the royal fisc. The pension rolls include nobles who received as little as 100 to 200 *l*. The annual total of royal pensions reached 500,000 *l* and more, except for several years under Louis XII, when it dropped to about half of that. A large pension almost always accompanied the hefty salary of a high office in the royal administration. La Trémoille received 4,000 *l* as the salary for being governor of Burgundy. The king also frequently dispensed large gifts in gold or revenues from a specific toll or tax. The nobles who received such sums from the king were expected to distribute much of the money to their retainers. For this system of patronage, historians of France often use the term *clientage*. As of 1500, traditional feudalism, with its lord-vassal relationship, remained in place in France, while clientage, by no means new to the realm, was rapidly becoming widespread. The result was a confusing network of relationships among nobles, which is most difficult to untangle. A nobleman might have been serving as the vassal of one aristocrat while acting as the client of another. By the mid-sixteenth century it was also possible to find the same man described as the "creature" of two prominent nobles.

The patron-client relationship was created when someone lower in the aristocratic hierarchy agreed, often in the form of an oath, to serve someone higher placed. The client gained from his patron gifts, pensions, and frequently offices, which may have come from the patron's resources or the king's; access to royal largesse for the benefit of clients was a key measure of the great nobles' influence. For example, when Charles VIII gave the captaincy of the château of Chinon to Pierre de Beaujeu in 1484, he immediately passed it, "with all the rights, privileges, and revenues" to his chamberlain. The client could also expect military and legal protection, even against the royal courts if the patron was well placed. In turn the patron expected loyalty and service. The client whom his patron placed in a royal office was expected to look after his patron's interests in the discharge of that office. For most clients the principal form of service was military. Every prominent nobleman had his retinue, dressed in his colors, which accompanied him wherever he went. When the patron went to war in royal service, he brought his clients with him. A large portion of the *gens d'armes* in the royal service were clients of the great aristocrats. The development of clientage boded ill for the monarchy, however, because it made the ability of the great nobles to raise forces a function of wealth as well as feudal position and kinship ties, which still played a role in recruiting a retinue. Before 1530, most of the high nobility used all three practices to raise retinues. After that, clientage became more important for such families as the Montmorency and the Guise, whose feudal lands were limited but who received vast sums from royal largesse. Thus it was the monarchy itself that created the potential for rebellion among its major subjects in the Wars of Religion.

The revenues, tax exemptions, and privileges of the nobles were based on the expectation that they would offer life and limb to defend the realm and its people. In the late fifteenth century, every fiefholder had an obligation to provide military service to the king. The problem that plagued the early feudal system—vassals answering only to their immediate lords and not to the ranks above, including the king—disappeared. When the king now invoked the *ban*, calling his immediate vassals to military service, and the *arrière-ban*, summoning their subvassals, most of those affected responded, although the percentage substantially declined in the course of the sixteenth century. In 1503 Marshal Pierre de Gié made an effort to get a count of all those liable to service under the feudal levy, but he was able to get a count for only two *bailliages* before he fell into disgrace. Under Francis I, further attempts were made to determine the number, but they were not very accurate.

A number of fiefholders were exempt from the *ban*, including royal officeholders, who paid 12 to 15 percent of the annual revenues of their fiefs for the exemption whenever the *ban* was mustered. Commoners who held noble lands paid up to 20 percent, but some did provide the required service in person, which was one means of achieving noble status. In the Middle Ages, service in the feudal levy went uncompensated except for recovering the loss of a horse, but by 1500, the king began to pay regular wages. For example, the captain of a cavalry company raised by the *ban* received 100 *l* a month, and an ordinary trooper, 20 *l.* The *ban* and *arrière-ban* were usually called to respond to an invasion. Under Louis XII there were four general summons, and five under Francis I. Local levies were called more frequently, but more often to crush rebellion than to drive out invaders.

The governor of the province, or frequently, his lieutenant, summoned the feudal levy once word came from the king. In turn the *baillis* and *sénéchaux*, who had more direct responsibility in those provinces lacking governors, ensured that those liable for service appeared. The response of those obliged to serve when summoned was still quite good before 1500, as high as 75 percent of some 16,000 nobles in 1492.[7] However, even when a large proportion of those with a feudal obligation did assemble, the forces created were of poor quality. Most of the wealthier fiefholders, who could afford the best horses and equipment, were exempt from the *ban* for a number of reasons. The natural warriors among them would almost certainly have joined the standing army, leaving mostly those who were reluctant to fight, physically weak, or slightly disabled to serve in the feudal levy. Those who by ill-health or age were unable to serve paid a fee. When the *ban* was summoned, the manpower assembled was a force of ill-disciplined and ineffective cavalrymen.

The poor quality of the feudal levy was obvious to the kings during the Hundred Years War. Charles VII acted to solve this problem in 1445 with a major edict on the French army. The Truce of Tours with England in 1444 had ended the employment of thousands of fighting men, many taking to a life of pillage. Charles issued an ordinance mandating the recruitment of the best among them for a royal army made up of 15 cavalry companies, hence the name *compagnies d'ordonnance.* Each company consisted of 100 *lances fournies,* the heart of which were the heavily armored lancers, whom the French called *gens d'armes* or *hommes d'armes.* Each lancer was accompanied by two mounted archers, a knife wielder, a page, and a valet, all of whom would be mounted although the last two were noncombatants. Thus, a lance company had 100 *gens d'armes* and 600 men in all. If the 15 companies had ever been at full strength, which is improbable, the royal army would have had 9,000 men, of whom 6,000 were fighting men. Louis XI increased the number of companies and their manpower, so that at the time of his death there were 2,092 lances, which totaled about 12,000 men. The ordonnance companies were commanded by captains from the high nobility and paid from the newly established *taille.*

Because of the use of both longbow and crossbow, the knight of the late Middle Ages had taken to the use of plate armor, which encased him from head to toe. Its ever-increasing weight required stronger horses, which were difficult to breed. Because French agriculture could raise the largest number of heavy chargers, the lancer remained the mainstay of the French army long after he had begun to be phased out of other armies. The French nobles regarded fighting on horseback as identifying their status far longer than nobles elsewhere did. In the theory of medieval warfare, the proper foes of the French *gens d'armes* were other lancers, but by 1450 the hardened mindset that had made it so difficult for the French knights to concentrate on the enemy's infantry, especially the English archers, had begun to crack. In order to take on other lancers in plate armor, a knight needed a heavier lance than had been the norm, and to be effective against infantry, a longer lance. The *gens d'armes* in the royal companies were paid an annual salary of 180 *l* in Louis XII's reign, but that respectable sum hardly covered the cost of outfitting a lancer. For example, a suit of armor cost about 45 *l,* and a good horse, 450 *l.*[8] It is obvious that serving as lancers required considerable wealth to begin with. Thus, they were recruited from the higher nobility. With the pride and arrogance of their class, the French *gens d'armes* remained convinced that they were the princes of the battlefield, even as new weaponry rapidly increased their vulnerability.

Few things are less clear about the French army of the late fifteenth century than the nature of the five support troops in the *lance fournie,* including questions of their social rank and weaponry. It is clear, however, that by 1484 the archers no longer carried the bow, despite continued use of the term archer, but had a light lance and limited armor. Paid 90 *l* a year, they came from the lesser nobility. The number of men in a lance declined from 1445 to 1534, when Francis I mandated that there be only three archers for every two *gens d'armes.* An company of 100 lances then had 250 men in all. By then, the size of the companies had also declined to the point that companies of fifty lances was the norm. Companies of 100 lances were reserved for the princes of blood and the highest ranking nobles. When Louis XII wanted to flatter Cesare Borgia, he gave him the command of a company of 100 lances. While the mounted archers of the lance companies originally were expected to carry a bow, they dismounted to fight. There was then no true light cavalry in the French army, by which is meant horsemen who used a bow or a throwing spear from horseback. The French saw Albanian light horsemen in the service of Venice in Italy and were impressed at their versatility. They began to recruit Albanians for their forces in Italy, although it appears they never served in France itself.

When Charles VII created the lance companies, it was expected that they would be disbanded after the English had been driven out. Nonetheless, Charles kept them intact after 1453 and continued to collect the *tailles* to pay for them, while increasing the size of the army. Many historians have seen the creation of this standing army as a major step toward royal absolutism. However, it is difficult to see that in respect to the first century after Charles VII's edict. It may have been the king's money that paid the troopers, but they were as likely to be loyal to their noble captains as to the king. In the revolt of the League of the Public Weal against Louis XI in 1465, perhaps half of the lance companies became part of the rebellion. When Louis of Orléans and Francis of Brittany rebelled in 1487, they also had several royal companies in their forces. Charles de Bourbon, however, received little support from the king's companies in his revolt of 1523.

Certainly, the monarchy could not use native infantry forces to dominate the realm. The feudal nobility had always been reluctant to put weapons in the hands of commoners, and after the Jacquerie (a peasants' revolt) of 1357 to 1358, it became a doctrine of the French aristocracy. The French government preferred to depend on mercenaries for the rest of the Hundred Years War, especially Italian crossbowmen. France of the fifteenth century, however, was not entirely devoid of infantrymen. The English had recruited infantrymen in Gascony, and a tradition of military service remained strong among Gascon commoners after its reconquest. A second source of French infantry was the urban militia. Every walled town had its guards and wardens, and the larger cities had its organized companies of militiamen, primarily pikemen and crossbowmen, until musketmen began to dominate after 1500. The large cities close to the frontier had especially large militias. While intended primarily to serve as garrison forces for their own cities, the militias sometimes were summoned to fight in the field. Last, there was a small group of fiefholders whose incomes were so low that they could meet their military obligation only as infantrymen armed with a pike or crossbow. There is limited evidence of this type of soldier answering the summons for the *ban* or appearing in battle after 1484.

Facing a lack of French infantrymen, Charles VII hoped to create a native infantry by forming a corps of *franc-archers*, made up of 8,000 men exempt from the tailles and funded by their villages. They were a hodgepodge of archers, crossbowmen, and pikemen, and this made the royal mandate that they drill together less than successful. In 1479, the *franc-archers* suffered heavy casualties in a battle in Picardy against Burgundian forces. Louis XI then abandoned the effort to organize them, although ill-disciplined masses of Gascons continued to be used. In 1510, Louis XII, then at odds with the Swiss, made a new attempt at organizing the French foot soldiers. He placed some of the most respected *gens d'armes* as captains of the new infantry companies in the hope that their prestige would enable them to impose discipline on their rowdy soldiers, but the effort had limited success. The French monarchy continued to depend on foreign mercenaries. The mercenaries of choice, at least until 1560, were the Swiss. Since 1315, when the Swiss first defeated the duke of Austria and asserted their independence, they had developed a style of war that had made them all but invincible on the battlefields of the fifteenth century. Wielding their eighteen-foot pikes, swinging their halberds—a heavy battle ax on an eight-foot pole—and wearing little armor so they could move rapidly, the Swiss advanced toward their foes in three columns already in battle order. Thus it often was only a matter of moments after "the forest of pikes" was first sighted before the lead center column smashed into the enemy's lines. In three battles in 1476 and 1477, the Swiss defeated the forces of Charles the Bold of Burgundy and in the third, the Battle of Nancy, killed him. Louis XI, vastly impressed by the Swiss victories, began to recruit large numbers for his army. For the next 50 years, except for the period from 1510 to 1515 when France battled the Swiss for northern Italy, Swiss pikemen were the main infantry force in the French Army.

Using Swiss mercenaries had its problems. They were expensive, second only to the *gens d'armes* of the lance companies in their rate of pay, and they often extorted more by threatening to leave French service just when they were needed the most. They often refused to take orders from French commanders, in particular insisting on rushing the enemy before some other part of the French army had executed its tactics. The French kings were quick to take advantage of a new source of mercenary foot soldiers, the German *landsknechtes*, when they began to appear by 1500. They were cheaper than the Swiss but fought in much the same style, at least initially. After 1525 there were more *landsknechtes* than Swiss in the French army, despite being of lower fighting ability.

The *landsknechtes* also were in demand after 1525 because they had a higher proportion of handgunners than either the Swiss or the French. Hand-guns dated to the mid-fourteenth century, but it was not until about 1470 that an effective matchlock musket, the harquebus, was developed. It began to occupy the niche held by the crossbow, since they were about equally easy to learn to use and cost about the same, but its shot provided greater penetration than crossbow bolts. It also belched fire and smoke and could be used as a club in hand-to-hand combat. Despite its advantages the French infantry was late in adopting the harquebus. One reason was the poor quality of the French-made harquebuses; the French bought Italian models whenever possible. Another was the attitude of the French nobility, which Marshal Blaise de Monluc expressed as late as 1570, as he ended a 50-year military career: "Would to God that this unhappy weapon had never been devised, and that so many brave and valiant men had never died by the hands of those who are often cowards and shirkers, who would never dare to look in the face those whom they lay low with their wretched bullets."[9] Despite Monluc's attitude, he tried to find musketmen for the company of foot he commanded in southern France in 1523, but he had to turn to Spanish deserters.

While French infantry forces were at best inadequate until the late sixteenth century, the contrary was true for the artillery. By 1460 France had a reputation for having high-quality guns. Under the impetus of the rivalry with Burgundy and the direction of the two Bureau brothers, the first French masters of artillery, French guns continued to improve rapidly. By 1494 the French had developed the high-wheeled gun carriage with its long tail, which could be easily attached to a horse team and moved. The main pieces in the French artillery train were culverins, muzzle-loaded bronze guns that shot iron balls, not the stone balls used in the wrought-iron bombards found elsewhere. Culverins took more gunpowder, but France had plentiful supplies of saltpeter, the key ingredient. When in 1494 Charles VIII took his army to Italy, his artillery train consisted of 70 large guns, whose quality was quickly demonstrated by the speed with which they reduced Italian castles and city walls. Those victories the French had between 1494 and 1559 depended in large part on their superior artillery.

With the development of the artillery came the creation of a new military office, the *grand maître de l'artillerie*. He took his place among numerous commissioned officers who had titles like *colonel-général d'infanterie* and *colo-*

nel-général des chevaliers. Usually from the upper nobility, they directed the various elements of the French military in peacetime. In war they fell under the command of one of the senior commanders of the French army—the constable, the marshals, or the king himself. French kings often commanded their forces in person. They were eager to prove themselves in war as worthy of the crown and to win glory, but it was also an axiom of the era that the men fought better when their king was present. If the king was with the army, then the constable, the highest ranking officer, commanded the vanguard; if he was absent, the constable was the commander-in-chief. He and the chancellor were the highest ranking officers of the crown, with salaries of 24,000 *l* and life tenure. But perhaps the kings felt that the tradition concentrated too much power in the constableship, since the office was left vacant from 1488 to 1515, until Francis I named Charles de Bourbon to the post. After his treason in 1523, it again remained vacant until Anne de Montmorency was named in 1538.

With the office of constable vacant for large blocks of time, the marshals became more important, and the office was further enhanced when two or more French armies began to operate in different theaters at the same time. After 1500 the marshals usually commanded forces some distance from the court, most obviously in Italy, since the constable, when there was one, had to stay close to the king in his role as a major adviser. In 1516 Francis I increased the marshals from two to four. The office of marshal was the highest ranking position, both civilian and military, in which foreigners—a Scot and several Italians—could serve.

While the exact duties of the marshals are difficult to define, even more unclear are those of the admiral. Even the origins of the word are unclear; it may have come from the French word for sea, *mer*, or it may have come from an Arab military title that had nothing to do with the sea. The admiral in the period from 1484 to 1614 never commanded a fleet at sea; his duties were concerned with coastal defense. The two most famous admirals of the sixteenth century, Bonnivet, who died in the Battle of Pavia, and Coligny, were army commanders. There were several provincial admirals, such as the admiral of Gascony, whose duties were more directly concerned with the sea.

The French navy of the early sixteenth century was in a curious situation. The many ports on France's long Atlantic coast provided a large merchant fleet of sailing ships, which had to be capable of defending themselves against the constant threat of piracy. In times of war, usually against England, the king would impress the merchant ships into royal service, perhaps adding to their crews with men in royal service and putting on more guns. This "Fleet of the Ponant" allowed France to project the threat of invading England, even if it never happened, and to go to the aid of the Scots. This Atlantic fleet was slow to adopt the enormous innovations taking place in the Portuguese fleet, but after 1500 the French began to use huge sailing ships built for war. These "parade ships" carried large numbers of guns in a vast range of calibers, and it has been argued that the French put the first gun ports on such ships shortly after 1500. Gun ports allowed heavier guns to be placed on lower decks, which provided more stability when they were fired. Parade ships were poor sailers, however, and they were incapable of projecting naval power any distance from home ports.

In the Mediterranean the situation was entirely different.[10] France did not have as strong a maritime tradition there as it did in the Atlantic, while the independent county of Provence had not been a major factor in the naval wars during the late Middle Ages. When in 1481 Provence passed to the French monarchy under the terms of the will of Count René, the fleet at Marseille consisted of about ten galleys. A few more were added under Charles VIII, but so small a fleet made France a third-rate naval power in the Mediterranean at best. Fleets there were based on the galley. The Mediterranean's light breezes from April to October and its many islands and peninsulas, which made it possible to traverse the sea without being out of sight of land for more than a day or two, made the galley its dominant naval vessel. An Atlantic sailing ship of 1500 would have too often found itself becalmed and swarmed over by galleys to be an effective vessel of war there, which remained true until late in the century, while the lightly built galley was not suited to the rough waters of the Atlantic. The two fleets were so different, both in the type of ship and the style of fighting, that they could not be used interchangeably.[11] In emergencies such as the English invasion of 1512, the "Fleet of the Levant" was sent to the Atlantic, but it was ineffective there. The necessity of operating two different fleets meant that the French government could not invest heavily in either one, and consequently France remained a second-rate naval power in both seas for the duration of the sixteenth century. It was only after 1600 when the galley had become obsolete for fleet action and been relegated to harbor defense that France could emerge as a major naval power.

On the other hand, the French army was vastly superior to the Italian forces it faced in 1494. It has sometimes been called the "first modern army," because it was the first to have in strength the three arms of the modern military—cavalry, infantry, and artillery. The quality of French cavalry and artillery, supported by Swiss pikemen most of the time, gave the French victory in a large portion of the battles fought between 1494 and 1525, the period of the three French Invasions of Italy, although the Italian wars continued to 1559. The period from 1494 to 1530 had an unusually large number of major battles. The extraordinary effectiveness of artillery against fortified places meant that sieges were brief, and armies moved about much more freely than was true in most other periods of European history. Commanders found themselves facing their foes in large-scale field battles rather than in extended sieges. Two important battles took place a week apart in July 1495 involving both parts of the French army that Charles VIII led to Naples the previous year. The Battle of Fornovo demonstrated clearly the differences between the French and the Italian styles of war. The Italians emphasized the need to outmaneuver an enemy and place him in a position where he had to surrender or fight a bloody battle, which the condottieri resisted because of the negative impact on recruiting. The French were far more willing to take heavy casualties, and they made effective use of their superior artillery.[12]

The part of the French army that Charles left in southern Italy easily crushed the Italian-Spanish force, thanks to the superiority of the French *gens d'armes* and the Swiss pikemen over their enemy counterparts. Gonsalvo de Cordoba, the Spanish commander at Seminara, and Ferdinand of Aragon were quick to take lessons from the defeat. There was little they could do about the Spanish cavalry, since Spanish agriculture could not raise enough heavy horses for an effective gendarmerie, but they could transform their infantry. Pikemen and harquebusiers replaced the ineffective Spaniard infantry. Cordoba began to use the two types of infantrymen in large squares that provided mutual support for each other. It was especially important for the harquebusiers to have support because of the slow rate of fire for the firearms of that era. This infantry formation become known as the Spanish Square. Although it became widely imitated across Europe, no one did it as well as the Spanish, and it was a major factor in their military superiority for the next 150 years. The French, on the other hand, were slow to adopt the formation.

The French received their introduction to the transformed Spanish army in 1503 at the Battle of Cerignola near Naples. Cordoba entrenched his infantry on the slope of a hill. When the duke of Nemours arrived with his French forces, he moved immediately to attack, as was typical of French commanders. He personally led his *gens d'armes* in a charge against the Spanish lines, but devastating harquebus fire quickly brought them to a halt. Nemours was killed by a ball. The Swiss pikemen advanced, but heavy harquebus fire halted their momentum, and they could not break through the lines of Spanish pikemen. The French army was thrown back with heavy losses, and Naples passed into Spanish hands for the next two centuries.

French military leaders were slow to recognize the significance of the defeat at Cerignola. The aristocratic prejudice against putting missile weapons in the hands of commoners made it difficult to introduce firearms to the French infantry. Few expressed it as bluntly as Blaise de Monluc, but there are numerous hints of the nobles' attitude throughout the sixteenth century. Nonetheless, France had its victories in the next quarter century. Genoa (1507), Agnadello (1509), and Ravenna (1512) resound to the glory of French arms. But there also were humiliating defeats. A powerful army was crushed at Novara near Milan in 1513 when their foes, the Swiss, charging through heavy artillery fire, reached the French lines and routed them. More embarrassing for the French was a small action that occurred later in 1513 in Artois. Henry VIII, on his way to Tournai, had stopped to lay siege to the fortified city of Thérouanne. Louis XII dispatched a small cavalry force with a supply train for the city but gave its captain strict orders not to engage the enemy. Thus when it unexpectedly encountered a much larger English force, the French quickly retreated, but what was to be a strategic retreat turned into a rout when the English pursued. The French flight became so precipitous that the incident became known as the "Battle of the Spurs," because it was said that spurs were the only part of their equipment the French had used.

The French *gens d'armes* had the opportunity to redeem their reputation two years later at Marignano. Fought between the French and the Swiss, who controlled Milan, it can be called the last battle of the late Middle Ages in that both armies emphasized the military arm and the tactics they had used for the previous two centuries. The Swiss, charging the French lines in their standard three columns, were brought to a halt by the countercharge of the French cavalry. That allowed the French artillery to tear great holes in the massed Swiss ranks, and they were forced to withdraw. Francis I, commanding his *gens d'armes* in person, proclaimed after the battle that no one ever again could call them "hares in armor."

Marignano dealt a devastating blow to the Swiss style of war, and they never again fought outside of their borders as a national army. It also resulted in the Treaty of Geneva by which the French monarchy had first call on the services of Swiss mercenaries. The battle, however, also convinced Francis and his advisers of the continued superiority of the French cavalry. No changes were made before the next great battle, which took place at Pavia, just outside of Milan, in February 1525. Francis had established siege lines around the fortified city of Pavia, when a large Imperial relief army arrived in the area. His army of about 25,000 men was encamped in a large walled park, where the walls provided an excellent defensive line, bolstered by 53 guns. Unable to draw the French out for a battle, the Imperial commanders moved under the cover of darkness to a corner of the park. There sappers broke out openings, and the Imperials slipped in and took up positions. Exactly when Francis became aware of the enemy inside the park is a matter of dispute, but he had sufficient warning to get a number of guns turned in the right direction. He decided to attack with the units he had in hand, mostly cavalry.

The French guns began the battle, scoring effectively on the large squares of enemy infantry; but then Francis charged his cavalry in front of the guns, silencing them. The French *gens d'armes* easily broke through the Imperial cavalry; but that exposed them to a solid line of Spanish harquebusiers, whose fire rapidly reduced them. By then Francis's Swiss had also advanced. Musket fire devastated them, and they barely came to a "push of pike" before pulling back. The king continued to fight at the head of a dwindling company of *gens d'armes* until his horse was killed, and he was captured. Pavia was a true disaster for France: the king was a captive and his army virtually destroyed—8,000 men dead and 10,000 captured.

Even the devastating defeat at Pavia did not end French reliance on the *gens d'armes*.[13] For three more decades they still held pride of place in the French army and made significant contributions to victory in several battles. More than for any other army in Europe, the French nobles continued to constitute the core of the army. They may not have regarded either Charles VIII or Louis XII as their ideal king, although Francis I probably was, but all three provided them with plenty of wars in which they exercised their God-given right to fight and win glory. The salaries for military service and booty from war also helped balance the budgets of noble households. There is little sign of noble discontent in the era, despite some annoyance over the rising number of new nobles and bourgeois purchases of noble estates. It is noteworthy that there was no protest in 1503 when Pierre de Gié, a prominent noble, was disgraced; and only a handful of nobles, nearly all his clients, followed Charles de Bourbon into rebellion in 1523. A fair-minded person would have regarded what the monarchy did to both men as unfair, but no one ever deemed the French nobles as having any concerns other than personal ones. The nobles revolted when they collectively had personal grievances. As of 1530, the nobles were contented, and the monarchy was on solid footing.

5

The People: "The very hens are safe from violence!"

France from 1484 to 1530 was unusually free of rebellions and unrest. While this internal peace and stability would not have occurred if the nobility had been discontented, it owed more to the sense of well-being and prosperity found among the French commoners. Thomas Bricot, the speaker for the Third Estate in 1506, related how "the very hens know they are safe from violence." That bit of hyperbole serves to underscore the fact that Louis XII's reign and the entire era were among the quietest in respect to popular uprisings in the history of the French monarchy. Those that did occur were neither widespread nor bloody in comparison with the ones before 1484 and after 1530.

One reason why this period was quiet was because of royal tax policy. Taxation dropped dramatically from 1481 to a low point in 1510. Then taxes began to rise again, but as of 1530 they were not at the levels of 1481, although increasing popular agitation by 1530 reflected rising taxes. Just as important for the internal peace in France was the demographic situation, which contributed to the prosperity of nearly every group. In 1340 the population of France may have been as high as 20 million. Because of a change in climate, the Black Death and recurring outbreaks of the plague, and the Hundred Years War, it declined to as low as 10 million a century later. Normandy and Picardy, areas badly affected in the last decades of the war, saw their populations drop by more than half. The population began to rebound after 1453, reaching 14 million in 1500 and continuing to increase at the accelerating pace that is typical of growing populations; by 1560 it may have returned to 20 million, the top capacity for preindustrial France. One factor in the population growth was the reduction in the age for marriage, especially among the peasants. In agricultural societies, when times are reasonably prosperous, couples tend to marry younger, because they have better prospects of being able to maintain a household. In regard to the late fifteenth century, the age of marriage was about two years younger than early in the century. This meant that the average woman was likely to have one more child than in the earlier period. Because of the presence of a stable food supply, more children also survived to adulthood, and the population increased rapidly.

In the half-century after 1453, as the population rebounded from its nadir while peace and a favorable climate stimulated an expanding economy, wages for both rural and urban laborers rose. Land that was abandoned in the previous era was returned to cultivation, which, along with warmer weather, provided a steadily increasing grain supply. It kept pace with the growing population, keeping the price of grain stable, except during the occasional poor harvest. From the nearly complete record of the price of wheat at Paris every Wednesday from 1439 to 1789 and shorter record runs for Rouen and Toulouse, it is clear that from 1484 to 1515 grain prices changed little over ten-year averages. Expressed in the number of days that a Parisian day-laborer had to work in order to buy a *setier* of wheat (156 liters in the Parisian system of measurements), which could feed an adult for about four months, the golden age for the French laborer in the three centuries after 1453 was probably 1460-70. Then it took slightly less than five days of work for a typical urban day-laborer to buy a *setier* of wheat. By 1484 that number rose to nearly ten days, where it remained until 1515, albeit with considerable year-to-year fluctuation. After that the rapidly increasing population and rising inflation forced prices up, and the larger labor supply halted the rise in wages. Consequently, after perhaps a decade of stagnation, the standard of living began to slip, at least in regard to the ratio of wages to the price of grain, its key indicator. By about 1530, it required some 15 days of work for an urban day-laborer to buy a *setier* of wheat. The price of other commodities and manufactured goods remained steady in relation to wages longer than did the price of wheat.[1]

The last decades of the fifteenth century were also the golden age for rural laborers. Their improved conditions were responsible for a decline in the number of vagabonds and brigands in the countryside, prompting Bricot's statement at the Estates of 1506 on how safe the countryside was. Rural laborers were the most marginalized people in society, because their villages lacked any system of charity except for small handouts from slightly better-off neighbors. Since a slight downturn in their circumstances sent large numbers of people onto the roads and byways, the near absence of complaints about vagabonds during the reign of Louis XII is a strong indication that the rural laborers were enjoying steady employment and good wages. That there even could be a problem of impoverished rural laborers taking to the roads was one result of the near disappearance of serfdom in France, although it retained some strength in the east-central region, especially Burgundy. The decline of serfdom provided a measure of personal freedom for most of the rural population, but it also eliminated the security and the paternalistic concern many of the manor lords gave their serfs. Most *manouvriers* (manual laborers) and *laboureurs* (plowmen) were paid at the end of every day's work, hence the term day-laborer, although the pay period was sometimes a week. The income of the day-laborers was reduced not only by the difficulty of finding work every day but also by the large number of days, about 100 per year, on which the Church prohibited work. While many of the rural laborers were established in their villages and unlikely to leave except in the worst times, others were restless and quick to migrate to towns, become vagabonds, or join the army, although the latter was not a real option for French peasants until after 1550.

A step above the rural laborers in income and security were the tenant farmers and sharecroppers, who constituted the majority of peasants. The term *métayage* was used for the system of sharecropping in which the landowner often took as much as half of the produce, largely in the form of an annual rent called the *cens*. The range in size of the holdings of both sharecroppers and tenants was broad. While some barely were able to make a living from the land and were forced to work for wages much of the time, others were able to afford plow teams and other equipment and rent it out and hire day-laborers themselves. Frequently their tenures were hereditary, and rents and shares usually were fixed for long terms, often for the lifetime of the tenant. In times of rising grain prices, the sharecroppers could do well if they were thrifty. In times of falling prices and crop failures, they were hard hit, first giving up their wage labor and, if times became bad enough, their holdings as well.

It was the next level of peasant, the *fermiers,* the small freeholders or yeomen, who frequently fell into the clutches of moneylenders in hard times, since foreclosing on them was highly attractive to land-hungry bourgeoisie. Freeholders, who owned land yet were not part of the feudal system, were more common in the Midi than elsewhere in France. In good times, their control of all the produce of their lands, except for paying the *dîmes* and the *tailles,* enabled them to profit greatly. They sometimes turned to moneylending or to farming royal taxes and the *dîmes* of a local religious institution. Those who were successful managers, whether of their own lands or other sources of income, were in position to buy the properties of the less successful, perhaps even before hard times hit. The trend after 1530 was toward a concentration of freeholdings and tenancies in the hands of a smaller number of large landowners, who often emerged in the seignorial class.

Ironically, the process of consolidating land in the control of "capitalist agriculturalists" was aided by a contrary process of land subdivision. As the rural population increased, family sizes did as well. It was more difficult for a peasant than a nobleman to insist on primogeniture, since the noble's younger sons had prospects of a career, generally in the Church or the army, apart from the family's landholdings. Frankish law insisted on the equal division of land among all the sons, and this remained tradition among the peasants in much of France while it largely disappeared among the nobles, especially in the north. Dowries for daughters and fragmentation of landholdings among the sons of the yeomen put severe pressure on those families, especially in the hard times after 1530. Their holdings often were broken into pieces that were too small to support a family. Moneylenders were quick to foreclose on such vulnerable people. Soon a large portion of what were prosperous landholding peasants was degraded to day-laborers, although many of the same class succeeded in adding the properties of the financially depressed to their own.

Regardless of the level of the peasantry in which a family found itself, it would probably have been involved in cultivating grain, which required the labor of women and older children at key times. The two basic crop rotations of the early Middle Ages continued to be used. In the Midi and a few small regions further north, the biannual or two-field rotation of the Mediterranean world, in conjunction with the wheel-less plow, controlled agriculture. The arable land was divided in two, with one half planted in a crop and the other left fallow to allow it to recover its fertility. This system was used for drier soils and rougher lands prevalent in the south. Farther north, where the soils were wetter and the land flatter, the use of the heavy wheeled plow was a factor in a triannual or three-field rotation. One field was planted with a winter grain; the second, with a spring crop; and the third was left fallow. The northern agricultural regime dictated the greater presence of draft animals needed for the heavy plow and long narrow fields, in contrast to the emphasis on human labor and square fields in the Midi.

Wheat was the most valuable crop, but it was finicky, quick to take umbrage at wet or cold weather and fail to produce, so rye, which was more reliable, may well have been the most common grain grown in France. Oats, used for both humans and horses, was widely grown, as were barley and millet.

Buckwheat, despite being regarded as a rough grain, was spreading rapidly across northern France because of its productivity in poor soil and bad weather. A family consumed most of the grain it produced, but some made its way to urban markets in exchange for a few *deniers*. Most of what was sold to the cities came from the granaries of the landlords and the clergy, who in most years accumulated far more grain from the peasants in the form of rents and fees and *dîmes* than they could consume. A portion, at least in good years, was exported, although virtually every king issued an edict banning export of grain.

There was a wide range of cash crops for the peasants with larger holdings: flax and hemp for linen and rope; woad, madder, and saffron for blue, red, and yellow dyes; and, of course, grapes for wine. The cultivation of woad probably contributed to improving agriculture, since growing it required more careful cultivation and manuring than growing grain. Growers of woad gave their neighbors lessons in better agriculture. The woad merchants were among the wealthiest persons in their regions; in particular they dominated Toulouse in the mid-sixteenth century.[2] Dyes not only were used in the French textile industry but were a major export, especially woad dye.

Wine was the most important French export and the major incentive to capitalist agriculture. Viticulture spread across France in the Middle Ages; in the warm thirteenth century it pushed well north of Paris. The return of colder temperatures returned the limits of wine production to the south. As of 1500 the vineyards around Paris were barely hanging on. Vineyards were attractive to the peasants because they rarely failed except at the northern edge of their range (although the quality of wine suffered in a bad year), and they could use marginal land where grain could not grow. There was always a strong market for wine even in the most productive years. Most wine was produced for local consumption, since it did not bring high enough prices to justify transporting it any distance, which was more difficult than hauling grain. High quality and easy access to sea transport were major reasons why Gascon wines, sold in England since the twelfth century, continued to appear on English tables after 1453 and across all of northern Europe.

Another source of income for the peasantry was rural industry. A village always had a number of artisans—millers, blacksmiths, masons—to provide skilled labor, but by the late fifteenth century, artisans who were turning out goods for market appeared in many villages. The major item produced was yarn, in what later became known as the "putting out" system: a merchant from a local town exchanged raw wool for yarn made in the peasant's cottage, usually by the women of the household. It was rare for a peasant family to depend on spinning for its livelihood, but it was often a major addition to agricultural income. Being midwives and wet nurses (breast-feeding someone else's child) also provided sources of income for lower-class women in villages and towns. In good times, peasant women mostly worked at home, taking care of animals and small plots of land as well as household chores and children. In hard times, female day-laborers, who were paid generally half as much as men, frequently joined their husbands in the fields or even replaced them, while the men were forced to migrate to areas where there was work.

An option for poor young women, perhaps the younger daughters in large families that could not afford dowries, was domestic service; not that every servant was female, but most were. Any household with a modicum of wealth, even those of tenant farmers, had a servant, although the portion of families with domestic help was far higher in the towns, where every artisan had at least one servant. Being a servant had its benefits. It attached a person to a household, which was absolutely necessary for respectability in sixteenth-century France. Generally, servants received their pay at the end of a year's service, while their employers took care of their basic needs. This allowed them to save money for doweries and marry. Of course, there were hazards associated with domestic service, such as having a demanding mistress with a difficult personality. The greatest danger, however, was being impregnated by the master. Pregnancy resulted in dismissal, and there were few options for a dishonored young woman except prostitution. It was a trade plied mostly in the towns; occasional acts of selling sex occured in the villages, but there was not a large enough market to make a living at it. A large portion of the prostitutes in any town did come from the countryside. In towns the children of unmarried lower-class women and destitute couples were usually abandoned at the door of a church or monastery, but infanticide was common as well. In economic good times abandoned boys were sent out as apprentices at a young age while girls became servants. In hard times, abandoned children had very poor prospects. Illegitimate children of rural people were more likely to be incorporated into the family, but at a lower status than the legitimate ones.

The broad forests of France, which by 1453 reclaimed much of the land cultivated prior to 1349, provided income for many people. Charcoal was rapidly becoming the principal fuel for ironmaking and other smelting industries. It was produced in the woods in kilns that were easily moved after the wood of one area was consumed. Large trees were logged for timber, and their branches were bundled for firewood. Both would probably be sold in the nearest town. In the Midi especially, chestnuts were an important source of food and income for rural people. Another potential use of the forests, hunting, was closed to the peasants: it was restricted to the nobility, and poaching was severely punished, even by execution. Someone like a bishop of Lodève, who in the mid-sixteenth century gained a reputation for his severity toward poachers, was deeply hated, since poached game was virtually the only source of meat for many peasants, especially after 1530.

This brief description of the economic activities in the French countryside indicates that the socially undifferentiated village of the early Middle Ages, which probably was rare even then, was not found in the late fifteenth century. Nonetheless, the *communautés d'habitants,* as most villages were called in royal documents, continued to be the focal point of virtually every aspect of peasant life, including collectively controlling their meadows and wastelands for grazing of animals, making them available to most villagers. The village usually coincided with the parish, but the earlier, nearly complete coincidence of the feudal *seigneurie* with the village disappeared, as the holdings of several nobles often divided a village. In much of western and southwestern France, the system of *bocage* made the parish the focus of peasant life. *Bocage* (from a word for hedge) referred to a rural population pattern in which the people lived in isolated homesteads and small hamlets, working land immediately adjacent to their homes, in contrast to the large villages found elsewhere, from which the cultivators went some distance to reach their fields. The village church and its square were the center of the social life of the villagers. Most games and recreation in peasant life took place after Sunday mass, and religious processions from the church around the village were high points of the year. The church was frequently the only stone or brick structure in a village otherwise entirely made of wood, and it was the place of refuge in case of fire, which frequently devoured an entire village in a matter of minutes. The church also served as protection against brigands or invaders, at least for a short time, until local forces were assembled. These unfortified places were known as the *plat pays,* often used as a general term for the peasant masses.

The *communauté*/parish was the basic unit of the tax system. The *élu* of the district informed the syndic, elected by the heads of the households in the village, including the widows, of the sum for which the village was liable for the *taille.* In turn several collectors, also chosen by the villagers, received it from the inhabitants, based on the syndic's assessment of their wealth. The villages had certain legal rights as a corporate body, including regular meetings, usually in the parish church, for electing the syndic and church wardens, agreeing to repair the church, and deciding to engage in litigation against almost anybody— neighboring village, local seigneur, curé or higher church authority, or royal official. Perhaps the most amazing thing about French peasants was the vast amount of litigation in which they were involved, despite being almost entirely illiterate and uneducated. One of the major innovations of the Estates general of 1484 was that the monarchy invited the *communautés* to send delegates to representative assemblies in each *bailliage* in order to participate in the election of deputies for the Third Estate. Some prosperous peasants actually attended the meeting as deputies.

When a *communauté* had a thousand or more residents, a wall around it, and a charter setting out its privileges, it was difficult to differentiate such a village from a town. As of 1500, there were some 1,200 *villes closes,* "walled places," but many could not be considered towns. However, the presence of agricultural workers in a *ville close* did not necessarily make it a village. Many townspeople had fields they cultivated outside of the walls, much like villagers across most of France. At Romans in Dauphiné, for example, a town of about 4,200 people in 1500, a third of the population consisted of plowmen and their families, working land owned by the wealthier residents of the town.[3] What then, distinguished a small town from a large village? Perhaps the key difference was that the monarchy exempted the towns from the tailles on the basis that it was too difficult to assess the wealth of townspeople. There were 226 such places in 1538, the king's *bonnes villes.* The king, however, frequently asked the towns for a subsidy, which was collected from the townspeople. Another difference between large village and small town was the far broader network of privileges that a town's residents, or at least its enfranchised citizens, had. A large number of French towns had charters from the monarchy or a powerful noble of the region, which set out their privileges. Many of the charters dated to before 1100, and some of the towns that received them early had either not grown since then or actually shrunk in size. Some such towns were hardly larger than nearby villages. Others never received charters but took on the privileges of the chartered towns, while some places received charters as late as the sixteenth century.

In the Middle Ages, the most important privilege found in an urban charter was personal freedom. A serf could not travel freely to buy goods nor sign a contract, both essential for commerce. By 1484, the broad reduction in serfdom reduced that aspect of the attraction of the towns to peasants, where living for a year and a day conveyed freedom to a serf immigrant; but the townspeople, even the lower classes, continued to have more personal freedom than did the peasantry. A more restricted privilege was the legal status of being bourgeois. The word meant, in its original sense, a member of the commune that governed the *bourg* or the *ville clos,* the walled municipal entity. Sixteenth-century French did not use the term except in that narrow sense; they used *honorable homme* to identify the wealthy merchants and members of the liberal professions of law and medicine, the people who later are identified as bourgeois. The requirements for membership in a town's bourgeoisie were usually spelled out in its charter. They included ownership of property in the town of a specified value, residence in the town with one's family for a year or more, regular attendance at church, service in the urban militia, and payment of town taxes. Immigrants requesting bourgeois status generally were held to higher standards, especially in regard to wealth, than noncitizens born in the town. Citizenship was hereditary but could be lost, particularly by long-term residence elsewhere. Each new bourgeois swore an oath to the commune.

Among the privileges enjoyed by the bourgeoisie of most towns was the exemption from the *taille*. The towns had their own taxes, usually a sales tax, but they did not match the *taille* as a burden on the bourgeois purse, even when the kings called on the towns for subsidies. The greatest privilege accorded to the bourgeoisie was the right to participate in the municipal government. There were three types of towns in France—those where the king or a powerful local seigneur exercised broad powers in the town, those where the commune of the bourgeoisie was in control, and those that combined features of both categories. Paris was the prime example of the first type. The king had his officials—the *prévôt* and his *lieutenant civil* and *lieutenant criminel*—in place at the Châtelet to administer Paris. Their policing duties included ensuring tranquility and security in the city and an adequate supply of food and other necessities. The Parlement supervised the work of the officials of the Châtelet and often stepped in to remedy a problem. The price a city with a Parlement paid for its presence was interference in municipal affairs by the parlementaires.

These royal officers shared the administration of Paris with the bourgeoisie organized in the Hôtel de ville, whose head was the provost of merchants, the mayor. There were sixteen *echevins*, aldermen, who were elected in the sixteen *quartiers* into which Paris was divided. The bourgeoisie elected these municipal officers, but the king approved them before they could take office, and he frequently made his choices known before the elections. Their duties included supervising bridges and roads. When the Pont Notre-Dame collapsed in 1499 during a flood of the Seine, the Hôtel de ville was responsible for rebuilding it. Its officers were responsible for organizing the first entries of the king and the queen, separate events that took place two years apart, which were second only to the coronation at Reims as major celebrations in a reign. When the king wanted financial aid from his *bonnes villes,* he first appealed to the Hôtel de ville of Paris, which also supervised the Parisian militia and the city walls. Besides the king, the local bishop frequently held some sort of seignorial power in a town. In the early Middle Ages, many towns were completely under the jurisdiction of bishops, but by 1484 the number had declined greatly. Nonetheless, the bishop of Gap in Provence was not the only bishop of the sixteenth century to claim: "Upon his bishopric depends total jurisdiction in this city of Gap and its territory, on all of its subjects and inhabitants as much in the temporal as the spiritual, and his judges and officers take jurisdiction in the first instance over all cases civil and criminal."[4]

The other type of town, administered by the bourgeoisie, was the more common by 1484, even if most towns were under the other type of regime centuries earlier. The commune of bourgeoisie administered not only the day-to-day matters of food, supply, roads, walls, and bridges, and militia, but also justice. In some places, such as Marseille, the communes claimed there was no appeal beyond their walls, but when the French monarchy took control of them, the right of appeal to a Parlement or the Grand Conseil was quickly imposed. Nonetheless, there were several cities, among them Marseille, Toulouse, Arles, and Bordeaux, that prior to 1530 can be called urban republics, for they carried on virtually all the business of an autonomous state except declaring war. Their response to royal requests for aid was more that of an ally than a subject. It has been proposed that the monarchy, especially under Louis XI, ruled France through the *bonnes villes*. After 1484 the monarchy worked to reduce the autonomy of such cities, but the anarchy of the wars of religion allowed them to reassert it for a decade or two.

In what was probably the largest group of towns, two or more authorities shared the administration and justice. Part of a town may have been under the authority of a bishop, another under the cathedral chapter, and a third part under the commune. Nobles and abbots might also have shared power in a town. Generally, the commune administered the newer part of such a town and encouraged commerce, while the other power brokers controlled older sections, such as around the cathedral, where business often stagnated. Beauvais and Tours were examples where authority was badly divided among the bishop, the cathedral chapter, several monasteries, and the commune.

Regardless of where political power lay in a town, the guilds always had a large share of it, and in those towns controlled by the commune, the dominant share. The guild, *communauté de métier,* appeared in France in the twelfth century. A key characteristic of the guild system was the specialization of labor, since there was a guild for virtually every economic activity in a town. Even the towncriers of Paris had their own guild. The number of guilds continued to increase through the late Middle Ages, not only because of the further subdivision of earlier guilds, so that, for example, a bakers guild and a pastrymakers guild could be found in many towns, but also because of the appearance of new trades like printing and silk-cloth making.

The guiding principle of the guild system was the mutual benefit of both producer and consumer. The guild existed to provide an adequate supply of a good quality product at a fair price to the town's consumers with an appropriate profit for its members. Each guild rigorously enforced a set of rules on the quality, quantity, and price of their product, and any guild master who was either above or below the standards was heavily fined. The guilds also controlled the training of new members through the system of apprentice and journeyman. An apprentice was committed to working with a master for as short as two years for some trades and as long as twelve for others. He learned a trade and earned his room and board under conditions that ranged from pleasant to dismal, although the latter was rare until economic conditions began to deteriorate for the guilds in the late sixteenth century. Once the required apprenticeship was completed, the aspiring tradesmen usually spent several years as journeymen. They would go from town to town hiring out to masters for periods ranging from a day or two to several years. This practice had two purposes: It provided the journeymen a broader training in the craft and enabled them to earn money to buy a shop. More than the apprentices, they were likely to be mistreated and exploited, since they often were from distant towns and provinces. In hard times journeymen had difficulties buying a shop, and their number began to mount. The presence in a town of a group of frustrated young men, deprived of what they felt was their due and unable to marry until they had a shop or were close to buying one, created serious problems. They were quick to take to the streets in violence or use the occasion of carnival to vent their frustration, which often took the form of sexual misbehavior and rape. The towns often sponsored brothels to reduce the incidents of sexual violence.

While a journeyman was saving up for a shop, he also had the major expense of producing on his "masterpiece," which demonstrated his skill in his craft. Other expenses for the would-be shopkeeper included fees to the royal government and to the town for citizenship, and gifts and a banquet for the guild masters. Unless a journeyman was lucky enough to inherit the shop from father or uncle, he had to work long years and be careful with his spending to accumulate the money needed.

A journeyman who lacked family ties also had competition from another group—the widows of the master guildsmen. A large proportion of the guilds allowed a widow to take over her husband's shop in which she almost certainly took a hand when he was alive. The master's wife usually was involved in supervising and disciplining apprentices and sometimes even journeymen, to the great resentment of the journeymen. It was common practice to allow the widow to run the shop as long as she did not remarry or, in some cases, if she married a master from the same guild. A widow who was close to 40 years old was not likely to remarry, and since there was likely to have been at least ten years of age between husband and wife in artisan families, the proportion of shops being run by the widows and the wealth they controlled would have been quite high.[5] In addition to the widows of masters, there were women who were masters in their own right but rarely in what were regarded as masculine trades. The cloth industry, beer- and ale-making, retail sales, and inns and taverns provided extensive trade opportunities for women. Some guilds, mostly those associated with clothing such as ribbonmakers and embroiderers, were exclusively female with their own system of training girls.[6] In general, the number of women masters was much larger in economic boom times. The large number of journeymen looking for their own shops in hard times put pressure on the town to reduce the contingent of women masters. Thus, in the course of the sixteenth century, the relatively broad opportunities for females in the guilds gradually declined, although they never disappeared entirely.[7] The monarchy kept a close eye on the guilds because of their economic impact, and there were numerous ordinances affecting them throughout the Middle Ages. By 1500 the kings began to interfere more directly in guild affairs, especially in their right to control their membership. In 1514 Louis XII, for example, granted his successor, Francis of Angoulême, the right to name a master in every guild across the realm. By then, it was accepted practice for the king to sell letters admitting someone to a guild. It was especially common for the more prestigious guilds of Paris. This blow to the autonomy of the guilds increased the number of permanent journeymen at a time when economic problems reduced the opportunities for them to obtain their own shops.

When a journeyman secured a place as a master in a guild, he also joined its confraternity. Most guilds had their own religious and charitable organizations, or several guilds in related trades joined together in one. A confraternity had its patron saint, whose feast day was celebrated with a procession and a banquet, and its special church, where guild members were expected to attend services. It had a chest for alms for the poor, especially its own needy, and dowries for the daughters of its poorer members. The members attended the weddings and funerals of their fellows and family members and provided money for masses for their dead. The confraternity provided an opportunity for bonding the guild members, who often were in sharp competition in their workday lives, and thus kept the guild viable. It also reinforced the oath, which most new masters took, that they were devout Catholics. When Protestantism began to appear in French towns, the confraternities frequently were the centers of opposition to religious change.

The term *guild* often is used as if it referred only to the associations of artisans and craftsmen, but in most towns there were also guilds for merchants. They brought products and goods into the town, selling at retail to the urban populace and at wholesale to artisans, who crafted the materials into finished products. Like artisans they were grouped according to their merchandise. Wine sellers, grocers, who sold spices and drugs *en gros* (in bulk), greengrocers, who dealt in vegetables, fruits, eggs, and cheese, and jewelers were all among the elite of French bourgeoisie, but it was the mercers who frequently were the wealthiest merchants. Originally dealers in textiles, their profits were large enough that they became involved in a broad range of products, squeezing the profits of other merchants and artisans. Mercers alone had a national organization to control price, quality, and quantity, whereas the guilds of all the other trades and crafts were strictly local in authority. The mercer guild of Paris was one of the Six Corps of the city, which included the drapers, grocers, hosiers, furriers, and jewelers; they had first rank among its bourgeoisie and wielded broad power. The power and wealth of the Six Corps increased in the sixteenth century at the expense of the artisan guilds.

Although the great merchants were not involved in creating the banking system of the late Middle Ages, many of them soon saw the vast profits to be made in banking. The cloth merchants of Florence were the first to become involved, and they dominated European banking until the late fifteenth century. By 1484, many French merchants also saw the profits in banking, although Italians continued to do much of the lending at interest in France from 1484 to 1530. The famed spice merchant of Bourges, Jacques Coeur, was in the mid-fifteenth century the prime example of a French merchant-banker, but in the long run he was far less successful than a group of merchants of Tours, the Tourangeaux, who began as merchants in Tours in the early 1400s. The founder of the de Beaune financial dynasty was a draper; the Briçonnet, a hosier; the Fumée, a mercer. They intermarried extensively and helped one another rise high in the government, especially the financial bureaucracy, and in the Church while making large loans to the monarchy.

Despite the power and wealth of the Tourangeaux, Tours never held first rank as the banking center of France; that title belonged to Lyon in the sixteenth century. Its access to Italy as well as to the whole of northern France and the Low Countries made it the center of a vastly growing trade between France and Italy. Huge quantities of spices and cloth passed through Lyon. Italians merchants and bankers settled there in large numbers in the late Middle Ages, and it received a great boost from Louis XI when he established banking fairs in the city in direct competition to the fairs of Geneva. These quarterly banking fairs were opportunities to settle accounts in international trade, but more important, at least from the king's point of view, they created great pools of capital from which he could borrow. Under Francis I and Henry II, the Lyon fairs were the principal source of loans for the monarchy. The interest for these loans was set from fair to fair, generally 4 percent for three months, or 16 percent a year.

These great banker-merchants were the dominant political influence in the towns where they lived. Every town had an oligarchy that controlled it, but in some the oligarchy was smaller and wealthier than in others. While the oligarchs had their own interests at heart, they also brought the mentality of the guild, to which nearly all of them belonged, to the governance of the towns. They believed that they were responsible for the well-being and security of all the urban residents and worked hard to secure them. With that mindset, the town administrators supervised carefully importing food, wine, and raw materials for manufacturing. They established regulations for sanitation, and butchers, tanners, and others who dealt with dead animals were frequently fined for leaving offensive wastes in the streets. Officials quarantined people stricken with the plague, organized the fire brigade, and worked to suppress violence.

Especially crucial was the supervision of the walls, the night watch, and the urban militia. Probably more than anything else, the walls defined urban life. They were responsible for the crowded conditions, since once they were built, centuries would pass before they were expanded, despite population growth. They defined the urban community that the commune supervised and controlled. Perhaps the most important aspect of the walls was psychological— the sense of security that they provided to the townspeople. At dusk the gates were closed and opened at dawn. No one was allowed in or out, and even approaching the walls at night was strictly forbidden. A resident who returned to the town after the gates were closed had to sleep under the stars. During the night the torches of the night watch atop the wall were a visible sign of security from the terrors of the night found on the outside. Accordingly, maintaining the walls was a major concern for town governments. On the frontiers, the king through the royal governors took responsibility for the walls of the border towns, since they were part of the defenses of the realm. Once Charles V gathered nearly all of the lands on France's frontiers under his rule, the monarchy took a greater interest in maintaining the walls of the border towns. One result of the intense rivalry between Habsburg and Valois was a dramatic increase in the authority of the royal military officer or governor in the frontier towns. These city governors did not have the broad authority of the provincial ones, but their power in their cities was considerable. By late in the sixteenth century, such governors began to appear even in the towns of the interior.

The night watch was also one of the major responsibilities of the town government. Its members were generally bourgeoisie from the artisan guilds, perhaps because they needed the extra income from serving, and they were regarded as more reliable than men of lower status.[8] In Paris, the bourgeois watch shared duties with royal guards. The former in theory comprised all the householders of the city but was restricted in practice to the lesser guilds, consisting of 40 men posted at fixed stations at the gates and the major intersections, while the royal guard was made up of 60 men, who alternated nights on patrol, 10 on horse and 20 on foot. Amiens, near the frontier with Flanders, had 10 companies of watchmen, while the gates were guarded by 20 squads of 10 men apiece; Toulouse, a larger city but away from the border, had only 40 men in its watch until late in the sixteenth century.

The urban militia was an old institution, dating to the founding of most towns. Usually every male householder in the town was liable to serve in it. Since they were busy in their trades and politics, they were reluctant to spend much time learning to handle weapons and drilling. The result was that the urban militias tended to make use of weapons, such as the pike and crossbow, and the harquebus by the late 1400s, which did not require a great deal of training to be reasonably effective. The crossbow and the harquebus were also effective when used on the walls against besiegers. As of 1500 Rouen had a regular militia of only 50 crossbowmen, but in the 1520s it added 104 harquebusmen. The militia was used mostly to defend the town against outside attack and internal disorder, but the kings sometimes ordered the militiamen to join the royal army to fight in the field. While they lacked the training and discipline to be rated as quality infantry forces, the men who served in them were more highly motivated and of better quality than peasant infantrymen. At the turn of the sixteenth century, the monarchy began to take a greater interest in the urban militias, especially those of the border towns. It began to regulate the militia companies in order to improve them for use in border defense. As the threat of Habsburg power loomed larger, royal troops were placed in those towns as garrisons, much to the annoyance of the townspeople. After 1500 the kings also provided artillery pieces for the walls of border towns.

For towns in the center of the realm, the threat against which the militia was poised was less likely to be foreign invaders than their own lower classes. As Robert Muchembled has said, "The style of urban life engendered an extraordinary aggressiveness."[9] Although respectable citizens were prone to violence themselves, they regarded most of it as coming from the lower classes. Consequently, the bourgeoisie policed the lives of the other residents of the towns as closely as they supervised their apprentices and journeymen. Day-laborers and piece-workers were a necessary part of the economy of a town, providing cheap, unskilled labor. The range of work they did was absolutely necessary for the well-being of the town, but they were hardly regarded as a legitimate part of the urban community. Quick to take offense and commit violence, which was often prompted by quarrels in taverns where they spent much of their time and meager incomes, the day-laborers deeply frightened the guildmasters, as did the beggars and vagabonds in the streets. Anyone who was not attached to a piece of property and a corporate body or a master fell under the suspicion of being involved in criminal activity.

That certainly was true of unattached single women who were not widows; they were usually assumed to be prostitutes. Prostitution was not illegal in late medieval France. Most towns had legal brothels and public bathhouses frequented by the best citizens. The medieval attitude was that it was better to provide an outlet for sexual tension, especially on the part of footloose journeymen, than risk having respectable women accosted or assaulted. A woman who was raped, even when it was clear that she was blameless, lost her honor. An unmarried woman who was raped was unlikely to marry at the same station as she otherwise could have. The young women who worked in the brothels often were domestic servants who were made pregnant by their masters. Their hopes of finding a respectable marriage were practically nil unless they could accumulate a dowry and go to another town to find a mate. Besides the legal brothels there was a large number of prostitutes working the streets and taverns, usually under the control of pimps. These women were more likely to be regarded as threats to society, as disorderly women to be controlled or punished. They tended to come from the same levels of society as the prostitutes in the legal brothels, but they more likely were women between jobs or recent migrants who had not found employment. Their hope was that they could quickly earn some money and quit without compromising their future prospects for respectable employment and marriage, as some did. It was true that the professional prostitutes of the brothels occasionally made respectable marriages, but those who stayed in the business long were likely to become madames. By the end of the fifteenth century, there was a growing movement to redeem prostitutes, based on the example of Mary Magdelene. In 1495 a Society of Repentant Women was found in Paris. Many women, however, were trapped in prostitution and died young from violence or disease.

Policing prostitutes and pimps was a major task of the towns, but the law-enforcement corps of a sixteenth-century town was small, often amazingly so. The term *police* in that era referred to the entire range of the administrative and supervisory functions of a government, and an *officier de police* could refer to a wide range of minor functionaries, such as measurers of grain, who checked the quality and quantity of grain brought into a city. The task of policing the countryside fell to the provosts of the marshals. Their jurisdiction originally included only the soldiers and the camp-followers of the army; thus they came under the authority of the marshals. They commanded units of *sergents* to enforce the king's peace on the troops and vagabonds; the latter, it was assumed, could only be deserters. Under Louis XI their authority was expanded to include anyone without occupation. By 1530 they had competence over criminals caught in the act or as a result of a public outcry, thefts committed on the highways, illegal assemblies, and counterfeiting. The provosts rendered justice in these cases, which included summary execution in cases of violators caught red-handed in capital crimes. Such authority gave rise to the worst abuses. The provost-marshals were, however, virtually the only sort of police force found outside of the towns.

The towns, on the other hand, did have police forces, in the modern sense of the word, even if they were tiny in proportion to the population. In Paris during the mid-sixteenth century with its 200,000 or so people, the Châtelet had 220 *sergents,* who provided the muscle to enforce the laws and arrest those accused of crime, and 32 commissioners, who investigated crimes and called on the sergents to make arrests. In 1526 Francis I established a "lieutenant of police" to patrol the streets and taverns of Paris and seize vagabonds and others without identification, who were regarded as the most likely to commit violence. The nightwatch was used to maintain order if a minor disturbance broke out; the militia was called out for a larger one. The Hôtel de ville also had a squad of armed men to enforce its rules. Tours had an even smaller number of peace officers—only 30 in the late 1400s, while Toulouse with a somewhat larger population had 40. In towns where a royal *bailli* or a local seigneur held a share of municipal governance, he would have agents to enforce his decisions. At Rouen, the *bailli* had 40 *sergents.* The respectable citizens of a town depended less on the presence of a large police force than on the collective pressure of the community to keep violence at a tolerable level. They took to the streets themselves to maintain order should a broader disturbance threaten.

The principal form of urban disturbance was the bread riot. There were numerous reasons why the price of grain suddenly skyrocketed: most obviously, a bad harvest in the region, but also the impact of war, a failure in the distribution system, or the efforts of monopolists. One town might have had a bread riot, while others in the region remained peaceful. Any hiccup in the price of grain had a serious negative effect on the urban poor, who were quick to take to the streets to demand relief. While their rioting frightened the town fathers, it became serious only when the lower levels of the artisans, who were only slightly less vulnerable to increased grain prices, joined in the rioting. Prudent town governments quickly opened the public granaries and forced wealthy residents and religious establishments to open theirs in order to reduce the threat of a serious disturbance.

Probably the largest bread riot of the sixteenth century (not that other motives were ever absent from any of these affairs) was the Grande rabeyne of 1529 in Lyons. A poor harvest the previous summer led to an enormous increase in grain prices. Rumors were circulating in the streets by early spring that Italian merchants had driven up the price by speculating and exporting wheat to Turin. In late April placards were posted around the city denouncing both the wealthy merchants for their crimes against the poor and the city government for letting the speculation in grain prices go unchecked. The placards called for the poor to assemble on a Sunday afternoon at a church to demand bread. When a thousand or more people, including a good number of artisans, gathered, it was easy for rabble-rousers to harangue them into taking action. With the city government momentarily frozen by fear that the mostly artisan militia was untrustworthy, the mob plundered the granaries of the wealthy and several religious establishments, and those of the city itself, which the city fathers were too slow to open to the poor. The rioters were also accused of looting other goods from the houses of the rich. With plenty of bread in their mouths, the poor were now satisfied; and the bourgeoisie, aided by royal troops, quickly restored order and exacted revenge. Rioters regarded as the ringleaders, mostly artisans, were hanged, and many more were jailed or fined. However, the city learned its lesson and had a more effective system of poor relief in place by 1531, another year of scarcity in the city.

For all of the threats to life and health in a sixteenth-century town—riot, fire, violence, contagious diseases, famine—the existence of the urban safety net in the form of a grain reserve was a significant factor in making migration to the towns attractive to the peasants. When a crop failure forced the local peasants to eat their seed grain, foreclosing on the possibility of a good harvest the next summer, the existence of alms in the form of free bread in a town lured many from the countryside to the town. The municipal governments usually tried desperately to prevent destitute people from coming into their cities, and sometimes ousted those already present, but they had only limited success. Because of the general prosperity from 1484 to 1530, these matters were of less concern than they would become later in the century.

6

Justice: "The Most Worthy of Virtues"

The social theory behind the three estates of the Estates general arose out of the medieval principle of the three divisions of society—those who prayed, those who fought, and those who labored. By the early 1500s, there was discussion about whether there was a fourth estate of those who judged. This view received its definitive statement in 1558, when Henry II summoned the presidents of all eight Parlements and the magistrates of the Parlement of Paris to a meeting of the Estates general as "the Fourth Estate of Justice." Such a step was too great a break with tradition to become permanent, and the parlementaires opposed it because they claimed the right to render judgment on the decisions of the Estates. Nonetheless, the fact there was such a discussion of the magistracy forming a fourth estate demonstrates the tremendous respect for law and its interpreters found in early modern France.

The French monarch was first of all the provider of justice in the realm. He was not a lawmaker; law already existed, although it needed codification and clarification, which were major functions of the monarchy. One of those attempts at codification, the Code Henri III from 1587, declared that of all the titles by which the French king was honored—among them August, Invincible, Victorious, Wise—only Just was unique to him.[1] The king was a debtor who owed Justice to his people, Louis XII's chancellor declared; and the preamble to Louis's 1499 code of French law stated: "Since Justice is the first and most worthy of virtues, also it is the first and most necessary part of all monarchies."[2]

It was from the king's obligation to give justice and provide order to his people that all of his other powers and responsibilities flowed.

The French of the sixteenth century were a people who respected law and loved litigation despite enormous complexity and confusion in the legal system. The only certainty about French law of that era is that any statement about it has many exceptions. French law was first of all protective of property rights, which included the right to enjoy the privileges and revenues of an office, whether royal or ecclesiastical. Second, it was designed to maintain proper order—the hierarchy of estates, ranks, and orders—against anyone who might threaten it, especially against those who ought to have had a master but were in fact masterless. The realm was divided into two zones of law. The *pays de droit écrit* (lands of written law) was found south of an undulating line from Bordeaux to Lyon and a few districts north of it, where Roman law had remained in effect throughout the Middle Ages. Early in the Middle Ages, Roman law functioned as customary law, but the return of the study of Roman law in the universities of the Midi reestablished it as statutory law. In the *pays de coutumes* (lands of customary law), in the center and north, local custom based on Frankish and feudal law was in effect. There were some 400 codes of law in place; their writ ranged from towns to small districts to whole provinces. For example, the midsized *bailliage* of Senlis, just north of Paris, was divided into three *coutumes*. The *coutumes* varied across France, some having only slight differences; others, vast ones. In a few places the *coutumes* had been written down, but in most they depended on the memory of the oldest influential men of the region. The result was a system of law that resulted in enormous confusion, protracted litigation, and frequent miscarriages of justice.

The lack of written law codes created difficulties for the Parlements when cases came to them on appeal. It also was clearly in the royal interest to have a single code of law across the realm, as part of the centralizing process that had been going on in fits and starts since 1200. No king of the late Middle Ages had the power or the audacity simply to issue a new code of law, although, as could be expected, Louis XI had hopes of creating a uniform code of *coutumes* for the realm. In 1454, Charles VII issued an edict mandating codification of the *coutumes,* but little was done in the next 30 years. The Estates general of 1484 admonished Charles VIII to speed up the process. He took the request to heart and established a procedure: royal commissions from the appropriate parlements were to visit the *pays de coutumes* and establish the text of the local law code through meetings with the local officials, nobles, churchmen, and others. The commissions were to get the approval from local estates where they existed, on the grounds that "there is no more clear and evident proof on the custom than that which is made by the common agreement and consent of the said estates."[3] Articles causing serious dispute were taken to the Parlement for final decision. The commissions would return to court with the written codes, which the king then officially promulgated. Charles also decreed that the commissions could make changes in the local *coutumes* to improve them, which provided some opportunity to make them more uniform. The process of writing down the law codes also allowed some opportunity for amending local custom that appeared unreasonable. In such cases Roman law often influenced the codifiers as they did their work, especially in regard to contracts and other aspects of commercial law, where the *coutumes* were sorely deficient because of the agrarian society that produced them.

Since it was only in 1498 that Charles established this procedure, it was left to Louis XII to pursue the task. In 1505 he accelerated the pace. Over the next ten years the *coutumes* of about 25 major districts were codified, including Paris. The work continued through the sixteenth century at a slower pace. While it benefited France to have its laws codified, there was a negative aspect as well: Unwritten customary law allowed for some change, albeit very slowly; a written code of customary law allowed for no change at all. The *coutumes* remained in effect as they had been redacted until the French Revolution. The continuing existence of a huge number of law codes led Voltaire to comment two centuries later that a French traveler changed law codes more often than his horse. Codification also had the effect of clearly differentiating French law from English law, with its national code of customary law, and German law, where Roman law was rapidly replacing the German equivalent of the *coutumes*.

Not only did late medieval France have numerous codes of law, there were also many different courts of law. The division of courts that most directly affected the French people involved the distinction between high, middle, and low justice, although the exact content of these divisions varied across France. This division of justice came from seignorial justice where the feudal lord had jurisdiction over the people of his *seigneurie*. Courts with high justice heard criminal cases in which the death penalty, corporal punishment, or banishment could be imposed, and adjudicated all cases where the fines were more than 75 *sous* (3.75 *l*), with the major exception of the *cas royaux*, which involved matters pertaining to the king's person, his family, officers, and enforcement of his edicts. The *haut justicier* had authority over a broad range of matters that made up the *police* of the district, and he had the right to the property of condemned persons and those who died without heirs and wills, and to half of the treasure troves found in his *seigneurie*. Middle justice pertained to criminal cases where the fine was below 75 *s*, and it was the court of first competence for all civil cases involving more than that. The *moyen justicier* could arrest persons charged with more serious crimes and hand them over to the court of high justice, receiving 75 *s* from any fines and fees imposed. Low justice referred to courts where criminal cases for which the fine was under 10 *s* and civil cases of less than 75 *s* were tried. A *bas justicier* also could arrest someone charged with worse crimes and receive 10 *s* for his service. Some areas had only courts with high and low justice. In those regions where feudalism had been strongest, there was yet another type of court, for *justice foncière*: the right of the feudal seigneur to collect his rents, fees, and dues and hold a court to coerce those who did not pay.

An enormous number of courts, well into the tens of thousands, exercised one, two, or all three levels of justice. The same person in one *seigneurie* might have had all three, while three different persons might have exercised them on the neighboring manor. Partition of seignorial justice was a common occurrence in the late Middle Ages in much of France, where custom proclaimed that "fief and justice have nothing in common." Thus, it was possible to sell, give, or will the power of justice to others while keeping control of the land of the fief to which it was originally attached, or, as often occurred, to divide seignorial justice among several persons while keeping the property of the fief intact. High, middle, and low justice was exercised in seignorial courts where cases involving feudal cases were heard, in manorial courts where the noble landlords dispensed justice to their peasants, and in municipal courts for the townspeople. Church institutions such as bishoprics, chapters, and abbeys held the three types of justice, and the principle of *mortmain* meant that they kept their jurisdiction intact while lay nobles were subdividing theirs.

The result of allowing seigneurs to alienate their judicial powers was the existence of an enormous number of courts of high justice, which continued to increase throughout the ancien régime. Since courts of middle and low justice were not as valuable, they actually were less likely to be divided into smaller units. For example, the *prévôté et vicomté* of Paris, which extended 20 to 30 miles outside of the walls of the city, had 364 courts of high justice. The city itself had 25, of which the bishop's court of high justice (not to be confused with the church's courts) was the largest, comprising 105 streets. Churchmen possessed all but two of the other courts of high justice; the smallest district comprised only eight streets. The much smaller city of Angers was said to have had 19 different courts with criminal jurisdiction. Regardless of how large (rarely more than ten parishes) or how small the districts of high justice were, the *haut justicier* had a number of obligations. He had to provide a courtroom and a jail (although both often were simply parts of his house or barn), a gallows, and a whipping post. He had to pay several court officers: a *greffier* to keep records and draw up legal documents, a *bailli* to administer the court, a *sergent* to keep order in the court and jail and serve warrants, and a *procureur fiscal* to collect fines and fees. Since fines and fees were an important part of the legal system, the latter generally served as the prosecutor as well. If the district of the *haut justicier* was large, these officers had their own assistants. The holders of low and middle justice also had to provide a courtroom and a jail, but their required personnel was fewer. While those who held the power of justice at any of the three levels could serve as the judges in their courts, they usually appointed professional men of law as judges. The salaries of all these officers and the fees for professional executioners, who did both hangings and whippings, came from the seigneur, but he collected all of the fees and fines imposed by his court. Injured parties received nothing, and to gain any compensation for injuries and loses, they had to begin a civil suit. The costs of providing justice in criminal cases fell upon the providers of justice, whether king or seigneur, and fines and fees often did not recoup their expense. There was, therefore, a strong tendency to ignore much of the petty crime that occurred, when the fines would not meet expenses. In cases that were not prosecuted by the proper authorities, the injured party had the right to initiate a civil suit, but that meant bearing the expenses without any certainty of winning a judgment. In many petty cases, it was easier and cheaper to ignore an injury, or seek private revenge, than to litigate. Whether seigneurs made any profit from administering justice varied from place to place and from year to year, but in the sixteenth century there was a downward drift. Profits from rights of justice became a smaller and smaller portion of seignorial income.[4]

In the early centuries of feudalism, there was no appeal from the courts of the *haut justiciers*, since the right of justice was inherent in the status of being a seigneur and had not come from the king. The frequent miscarriages of justice inevitable in such a system provided plenty of opportunity for the intrusion of royal justice into local seignorial justice. The lowest instrument of royal justice was the *prévôt*, also called the *châtelain*, whose district was a subdivision of a *bailliage* or *sénéchaussé*. Originally his court had first jurisdiction over minor matters involving royal rights and edicts, but it was expanded to include appeals from the seignorial courts. These appeals were sought out as a means of enhancing royal authority in the provinces. Most *cas royaux* were heard by the *baillis* and *sénéchaux*, who also heard appeals from the *prévôt's* court. It was an established principle of both Roman and canon law that there was a right of appeal to the highest authority; this principle, absent in the early feudal system, became entrenched in French law by 1484. This development strengthened the view that fief and justice were separate, and the latter came from the king. The rush of business for the king's *curia regis*, despite the high cost of such appeals, and the complexity of many cases made it difficult for the curia regis, made up of the king and his principal advisers, to hear all of the appeals as well as the cases involving the grands of the realm that came to it as the court of first instance.

The answer was the Parlement. By 1320 its basic organization, procedure, and permanent residence in Paris were well established. It had three chambers: Requêtes, where requests for justice were examined to see whether they should be carried forward; Enquêtes, where the testimony of plaintiff, defendant, and witnesses was heard and assembled, and the Grand' Chambre, which rendered and announced the final decisions, although in the course of the sixteenth century it lost those powers. By 1500 the Grand' Chambre consisted of 15 clerical and 15 lay judges presided over by five presidents, led by the first president, who often rose to the chancellorship of the realm. By then the *conseillers des enquêtes,* who often had to travel to the originating locale of a case, numbered 40 plus three presidents, while the chamber of Requêtes had five magistrates and a president. By 1500 the original equal number of lay and clerical magistrates began to edge in favor of the laymen, but the designation of half of the seats as *clerc* remained in effect. Although most of the cases the Parlement adjudicated were civil in nature, the criminal cases it handled were assigned to a separate chamber, the Tournelle, so-called because it originally met in the Tour St-Louis in the Palais royal. Magistrates from the Grand' Chambre were assigned to the Tournelle. In 1515 Francis I reorganized the Tournelle as a separate chamber, but continued the practice of staffing it from the Grand' Chambre.

In addition to regular members, the 12 peers of the realm had the right to sit in Parlement, but they rarely attended except for cases involving a fellow peer. Also considered part of the Parlement were eight *maîtres des requêtes de l'hôtel,* who also were part of the royal household. One of their far ranging duties was to bring before the Parlement those matters the king wanted it to consider. There was also a group called the *gens du roi,* who were attached to the Parlement but not regarded as magistrates. They included the *procureur général,* the king's representative and, as such, the prosecutor of *cas royaux.* He had several assistants, called the *avocats du roi,* who presented most cases before the magistrates. The Parlement also had its *greffier* and his assistants to keep its records, lawyers, ushers, and *sergents.* Equally numerous were the clerks, re-cruited from former law students who never finished their courses of study. They were called the Basoche, from *basilica,* which was an early term for the Palais de Justice. Their rowdy behavior and sharp wits earned them a place in French literature as authors of farces and satires.

All of these people shared at least partially in the privileges and prestige of the Parlement, of which the most important was gaining of noble status for serving the king as his judges. The more important support offices of the Parlement conferred noble status. This privilege, more so than the salaries of the offices, made them truly valuable. Salaries of the magistrates and other officials of the Parlement were quite low, although they were allowed to accept small gifts called *épices* from the litigators but only after the case was concluded. Both Charles VII and Louis XII made efforts to abolish the *épices,* but neither king would raise the magistrates' salaries, and the practice continued.

The privileges associated with them made the offices of Parlement an early object of venality—the practice of selling royal offices. In the late fifteenth century the practice began to appear in royal fiscal offices, because it was obvious that their incumbents usually became wealthy during their service and the king wanted his share. There was strong objection to venality in the judiciary, and Louis XII prohibited it in 1499. However, the concept developed in seignorial justice that rights of justice could be bought and sold was easily applied to royal justice as well. Like every other property right, the right to an office, whether given by the king or bought, could only be given up by the incumbent. The king could reclaim an office only upon the holder's death, something the king might have arranged through a charge of treason or malfeasance. Ordinarily, judicial officeholders were irremovable under normal circumstances. The contradiction between this practice and the king's authority as source of justice was largely ignored, but throughout the ancien régime it was a serious check on royal absolutism.

In desperate need of money for the war in Italy in 1512, Louis XII began to take large loans from several new officeholders, and it appears that repayment was not expected. Under Francis I, beginning in 1521, new appointees to the Parlement were obliged to make a permanent loan to the king. Their salaries served as interest, and the principal was never repaid.[5] In 1522 Francis created 20 new magistrates in a second Chambre des Enquêtes, in part to have more offices to sell. Francis also organized the Bureau des parties casuelles to direct the sale of all offices—financial, administrative, and judicial—for the profit of the royal treasury. Once the offices of the Parlement became venal, "legally available by purchase,"[6] any effort to eliminate the *épices* was doomed to failure, especially since salaries were not raised. Doomed too were attempts by the Parlement to keep the monarch from creating additional offices. By 1547 there were 150 magistrates in the Parlement of Paris.

In the late fifteenth century the Parlement, after examining candidates on their knowledge of law, lifestyles, and devotion to Catholicism, recommended three to the king, who chose the new magistrate. The king always named the presidents and, occasionally, the magistrates directly. The rise of venality in the Parlement did not end the traditional way to choose *conseillers,* for there had always been several candidates for each vacancy and nearly all of them could afford to pay for the office. The growth of another practice in the late fifteenth century had the effect of reducing the options available to the Parlement and the king. Following the church practice, a member of Parlement could resign his seat to his successor, usually a son or nephew. The Parlement undertook the usual investigation of a would-be magistrate, and if it found no cause to reject him, he would be seated. The use of venality in the Parlement actually increased the practice of "resignation in favor," already the method by which half of the new magistrates gained their seats in Charles VIII's reign, because it encouraged the sense that an office was a property right a man could pass on to his heir. The beneficiary of such a resignation did have to pay the king a tax of 10 percent of the price of the office. Lists of the prices of the venal royal offices were readily available. As it did in the Church, the practice of resignation in favor resulted in the appearance of parlementaire dynasties, as generation after generation of the same family took their seat in the Parlement.

These developments in the Parlement increased its sense of independence from the monarchy, since so many of the magistrates no longer depended on the king's favor for their seats. In fact, the Parlement had an amazingly strong sense of independence from royal control despite being a royal institution. It began to regard itself as the protector of the rights of corporate bodies against the king when he proposed to violate corporate rights and prerogatives. Soon parlementaires cultivated the view that they were obliged to defend the monarchy itself when a king, fallible human that he was and often surrounded by bad advisers, threatened to harm its best interests. The means by which the Parlement, namely, the Grand' Chambre, protected those interests was its right to examine royal edicts for errors and conflicts with established law and privileges. The Parlement sent a remonstrance to the king with its objections and, meanwhile, refused to enter the edict in its register of royal edicts. If the king was unwilling to make the desired changes, he ordered the Parlement to register the edict via a *lettre de jussion.* If it still balked at registering the edict, then the king, if the matter were important enough to him, would come in person to reclaim the authority that he had delegated to the Parlement and order its registration, a process known as a *lit de justice.*[7]

The monarchy called upon the Parlement not only for legal judgments but also for political advice. At times of trouble, such as Francis I's captivity in Spain in 1525, it took an active role in directing the government. Little wonder that its members and many contemporaries referred to it as the Senate, in the sense of the Roman Senate. Yet, it had its challengers even in matters of law. When the king removed himself from the routine decisions of the Parlement, which occurred by 1300, he did not shut the door on hearing appeals. The royal council continued to decide many cases involving important persons or issues. Since the council traveled with the king, it was difficult to get cases heard and decided. The cahiers of the Estates of 1484 contained a bitter complaint about the situation. In 1497, Charles VIII had taken a large step toward establishing a separate court of final appeal, the Grand Conseil, by defining the types of cases it would hear and placing it in Paris, despite the vigorous protests of the Parlement. At the beginning of his reign, Louis XII issued an edict establishing its membership as the chancellor and 18 magistrates. He mandated that cases involving persons of high dignity and disputed elections of bishops and abbots be brought to it. As had happened before with the Parlement, the absence of the king from the Grand Conseil meant that cases of great significance were still appealed to the royal council. However, the Grand Conseil reduced the judicial business of the royal council. Since the Grand Conseil did not have the tradition of independence that the Parlement developed over two centuries, the monarchy used it to enhance royal power, for it was far less likely to challenge the royal will. The Grand Conseil remained in existence until 1789, but it was never as powerful or as controversial as the Parlement.

One power of the Grand Conseil that the Parlement of Paris lacked was the right to take appeals from the provincial Parlements. The Parlement of Paris always regarded itself as the sovereign court of the entire realm with no appeal except to the king, and it looked down on the provincial Parlements that began to appear in the fifteenth century as mere branches of itself. Nonetheless, the monarchy was adamant from early on that they were sovereign courts in their own right over which the Parisian court had no jurisdiction. The first to appear, the Parlement of Toulouse, was erected for the *pays de droit écrit*. Prior to 1443, magistrates from the Parlement of Paris were sent to Languedoc to administer royal justice in what were called *grands jours*. They were special court sessions in which parlementaires would travel to areas where royal justice weighed lightly and enforce the king's law. In 1443 a permanent institution with jurisdiction over Languedoc was created. By 1500 its original small number of magistrates had grown to 50 plus three presidents. The court at Grenoble for the county of Dauphiné was raised to a Parlement in 1456. The *grand jours* for Gascony-Guyenne, begun once the region was recovered from the English, were replaced by a Parlement at Bordeaux in 1467. The dukes of Burgundy had an equivalent of the Parlement for their duchy. After 1477, the court existed in a legal limbo until Charles VIII gave it official status and residency at Dijon in early 1498.

In Normandy, the English administration left behind an institution called the Exchequer, which was more a judicial court than a financial body. Lacking supervision from London in the last decades of English rule, the Exchequer had fallen into some bad habits that were allowed to continue after 1453. There was inconsistency in its membership, since the grands who had the right to sit on it attended erratically. Bribe-taking and favoritism were rampant, and decisions were excruciatingly slow. When he became king, Louis XII summoned a group of prominent Normans to Paris to tell them he planned to create a parlement for the province. They asked that the provincial estates be convoked for consultation. When the Norman estates met at Rouen in early 1499, they agreed to the creation of a "Perpetual Exchequer" at Rouen. Francis I renamed it a Parlement in 1516 and set its personnel at four presidents and 28 magistrates. In Provence a similar state of affairs existed, although the faults of the old Conseil Eminent were not as notorious as the Norman Exchequer's. Louis XII established a Parlement at Aix in 1501 with one president and 12 magistrates.

As of 1530, there were seven Parlements. The disputes over jurisdiction between Paris and the provincial courts were often fierce. Despite them, provincial presidents frequently were appointed to the same office in the Parlement of Paris. The kings sometimes sent cases of special significance to the provincial Parlements rather than have them heard in Paris, as the provincial courts tended to be more amenable to the royal will. The provincial Parlements were organized along the same lines as the one at Paris, with *chambres des requêtes* and *enquêtes, grand' chambres,* and the same support personnel, but with fewer members. They had the same power to refuse to register royal edicts, which would not take effect in their regions until they did. In those few cases when a provincial parlement did refuse, it rarely took more than a *lettre de jussion* to gain registration.

Both the monarchy and the Estates general kept a close eye on the Parlements and frequently sought changes in their rules and procedures. Even such matters as the time when it began its work came under royal scrutiny. For example, an edict of 1493 from Charles VIII allowed the parlementaires to arrive at seven in the morning instead of six during the winter months. The most extensive examination of the whole judicial system came at the Estates of 1484. The cahiers of the Third Estate contained a great deal on the judiciary and its abuses. They denounced venality, which at the time took the form of paying an incumbent judge for a resignation in favor; pluralism in judicial officers; and the arbitrary removal of judges by the king, a practice especially used by Louis XI. The cahiers called for the return to the system of election by their fellows of judges, both the parlementaires and the lieutenants of the *baillis* and *sénéchaux,* in place of royal appointment, the payment of an adequate annual salary, and the elimination of the *épices*. The Third Estate also called for the publication of all royal edicts in every town of the realm. It complained that one of the major problems in the legal system was that only a handful of influential people knew what the edicts were.

Charles VIII issued an edict in 1493 that addressed some of these concerns such as forbidding any exchange of money for a judicial office and the paying of *épices*. His successor attempted to put more of the program of the Third

Estate into action with his Ordinance of Blois in March 1499, one of the major pieces of legislation in the history of the French monarchy. It consisted of a lengthy preamble and 162 articles. The preamble was careful to state that the 162 articles contained no new law but were only a return to the good law of the past. The majority of them dealt with the system of justice. Several were designed to protect persons accused of crime. Formal indictments were required before a trial could be held. Judges were told that they had to interrogate the accused and witnesses instead of having their clerks do it. The local language was to be used in the court procedures, not Latin, but this did not take hold until Francis I's edict of 1539. Interrogations were to take place as quickly as possible after an arrest and in absolute secrecy. The purpose of the judicial system was to find out the truth, and the theory of the medieval judicial system proclaimed that the judge and the *procureur du roi,* who served as the prosecutor in criminal cases, were equally committed to finding it, thereby protecting the rights of the defendant. Thus, the *procureur du roi* had a major role in interrogating the defendant and in finding and questioning witnesses. The never-ending complaints about the *procureurs du roi* indicate that this ideal was rarely achieved.

Judicial torture, or extraordinary procedure as it was called, was an integral part of the system of justice of that era. The edict of 1498 dictated that torture was to be used only once on an accused person who refused to confess unless there was new evidence or new testimony. In cases where it was impossible to determine the truth from the testimony (usually in the form of written depositions) of the defendant and the witnesses, torturing the defendant was prescribed as the means of reaching it. Safeguards existed to avoid overly zealous use of torture, but they were too often disregarded. Louis's edict was intended to reinforce the safeguards; he had no intention of eliminating judicial torture. Nonetheless, it was used rather little, and in some cases the "torture" involved only a mock performance, such as throwing water into the face of the accused in place of forcing them to drink huge amounts. Since the defendant remained in prison until the process was completely over, including appeals, other articles were designed to speed up justice, such as requiring judges to pass sentence within six months of the interrogation. In criminal cases, an even split among the judges rendered a verdict of acquittal. Louis also sought to deal with the expense of justice, mandating a reduction in the fees paid to the courts and lawyers.

In regard to the judges, the Ordinances of Blois made sorely needed reforms. Article 40 prohibited the sale of judicial offices, and it mandated that if the chancellor by mistake approved appointees who later were proven to have purchased their offices, the appointments were null and void. However, Louis had to repeat his decree in 1508, and under Francis I, the sale of judicial offices became as common as the sale of financial offices, which Louis did allow. Another article forbade father and son or two brothers from serving together in the same Parlement. Absenteeism from the courts except for other royal service was interdicted. Louis even set out the number of days and hours per day that parlementaires had to attend court and required them to possess a book of all royal edicts. Yet another article obliged the members of the Parlement to assemble one Wednesday a month for self-examination of their procedures and behavior. The *mercuriale,* from *mercredi,* became a standard part of the procedures of the Parlement, but it never met as often as intended. In 1500, Louis attended a *mercuriale,* the only king to do so until the infamous one of 1559 attended by Henry II. Article 48 established the prerequisite of a degree in law for appointment as the lieutenant of a *bailli* or *sénéchal.* Since the lieutenants performed the judicial work of those offices, the article resulted in significant improvement in the local courts and took justice largely out of the hands of the local nobles who were at best amateurs in law, and gave it to professionals. The reforms of 1499 did not eliminate the nobility from the administration of justice completely. They continued to sit in the Grand Conseil and the Parlements and some seignorial courts, but most of the judges were now professional men of law.

There was a number of other courts whose responsibilities were restricted to a specific group of people or economic activity. The sovereign fiscal courts were called sovereign because appeals from them went directly to the royal council. Another financial court, the Chambre des monnaies, which heard cases of counterfeiting and other matters pertaining to the coinage, was not sovereign as of 1484 because appeals from its decisions went to the Parlement. It did have the right to register royal edicts on the money system. Under Louis XII the number of *généraux des monnaies* increased from four to eight. No other court saw its membership increase as dramatically in the course of the sixteenth century, reaching four presidents and 20 magistrates by 1570.

There was another group of courts that met around the same marble table in the Palais at Paris, hence the name Table de marbre for them. The principal one was the constable's court, in which he exercised his jurisdiction over the soldiers of the realm. Since it was assumed, not very accurately, that every footloose brigand or highwayman was a deserter from the army, this court also had competence over crimes they committed. By 1484 separate but similar courts for the marshals had merged with the constable's. These high officers rarely attended the Table de marbre, leaving the task of hearing the cases to the *prévôt général de la connétablie* and a group of professional judges. By then officers called the *prévôts des maréchaux* maintained law and order on the highways with a squad of *sergents;* they had the power to call on royal troops if needed. The provost marshals were notorious for their arbitrary decisions and rough justice, but they provided something of a national police force when nothing similar existed. Another officer with a court at the Table de marbre was the admiral, whose jurisdiction was over sailors and pirates. Francis I added the *grand maître de l'artillerie* to those military officers who had their own tribunals. His position was especially concerned with acquiring saltpeter for making gunpowder. This court sat at the Arsenal in Paris, not the Table de marbre.

The busiest of the courts at the Table was that of the Grand maître des eaux et forêts. Because of their love of hunting, the French kings took a special interest in the forests of the realm. Early on, the office had authority only over forests in the royal demesne, but by 1484 it had been extended to the entire realm. The king had special rights over forests and rivers, which the master of waters and forests and his officers in the provinces enforced, and they collected the fees for their use. They also had jurisdiction over crimes committed there. Unlike the other tribunals of the Table de marbre, the court for waters and forests had provincial tribunals in the major provinces. None of the courts of the Table were sovereign, since there was a right of appeal to the Parlement. In numerous cases, the right of appeal was meaningless, since summary execution was the common penalty for many of the crimes that came under the jurisdiction of the courts of the Table.

The courts of the Table de marbre demonstrate two major points about French law. First, the early medieval tradition of collective justice, in which a community rendered justice, had not entirely disappeared. All the members of a court would sit in judgment regarding important matters, while single judges decided less significant cases. This was in sharp contrast with ecclesiastical courts such as the Inquisition, in which sole judges had the authority to render decisions. Second, those with the power of rendering justice also established the rules and regulations, albeit not the law, that formed the basis of their judgments. This arrangement was the result of the medieval mindset, which held that the same people who had the authority to make rules ought to judge those accused of violating them. This was true for the seignorial courts, although custom prevented the seigneurs from establishing new regulations. It was clearly true of the courts of the Table de marbre and the fiscal courts, but it also applied to the Parlements in a limited way. True, they were courts of appeal from the lower courts in areas where they had no other authority, but they had broad administrative authority in the cities where they sat. The one exception to this principle was the Grand Conseil, which had no administrative responsibilities, perhaps because it was created after the Middle Ages.

It should come as no surprise that this view prevailed in the sixteenth century, since ultimately it was based on the theory that the king was the source of both justice and authority. He joined in himself the legislative, executive, and judicial functions of government. When he gave a portion of that authority to others to see to the proper administration of the realm, he did not parcel out his authority among different institutions for each separate function but handed down a small portion of his complete power to those who needed it. As the "fountainhead of justice," he could recall his authority, define the law, and render final justice.

7

Culture and Thought: A Bursting Forth

France in 1484 was still a medieval world; in no aspect of French society was that more true than in culture. Currents of change rippling through the economy, the government, and the military were slow to affect the realm of the mind. In particular, the ideas of the Italian Renaissance, which were taking root elsewhere in northern Europe, had yet to have much impact in France. The University of Paris remained the dominant center of French thought, yet not to the extent it was two centuries earlier. It lost respect among the French people for supporting the English monarchy after 1420 and playing a major role in the trial of Joan of Arc. For the same reasons the French monarchy no longer gave "the eldest and dearest daughter of the king," a phrase first used in the reign of Charles V, its virtually unconditional support. Nor was the papacy as fond of "the masters and scholars of Paris" as it had been, due to their staunch conciliarism and Gallicanism. After the mid-fourteenth century the student body declined in size as a result of the Hundred Years War and the competition of numerous new universities both abroad and in France. Since Paris could not teach civil law because of the papal mandate of 1219, which was intended to keep students from being lured away from the study of theology, the great surge in civil law studies of the late fifteenth century passed Paris by.

The papal ban on civil law at Paris led the other universities in France to emphasize law. Several of them were nearly as ancient as Paris, and the University of Montpellier may have existed even earlier as a medical school. It was the medical center of France throughout the Middle Ages, but for several centuries it also served as the school for the study of Roman law in the *pays du droit écrit*. The old cathedral schools in Orléans and Angers owed their development into universities largely to the ban on the study of civil law at Paris; both enrolled large numbers of arts graduates from Paris to take a degree in both canon and civil law, a desirable combination.

These four universities grew out of early medieval foundations, even before they received papal bulls recognizing their right to grant degrees. All other French universities were consciously founded by a pope, king, or prince for a specific purpose. The papacy created the University of Toulouse in 1229 as a weapon to combat Catharism. It was the second French university to get papal authority to grant theology degrees, but in the late fifteenth century its strength was teaching civil law, replacing Montpellier as the law center in the Midi. With perhaps 4,000 students, it was second in size to Paris. The third school in the Midi was the work of Pope John XXII, who gave his native city of Cahors a university in 1332, but it never had more than 200 students.

The fifteenth century saw a dramatic upsurge in the founding of universities, as the cosmopolitanism of earlier times declined drastically, and students stayed closer to home. The count of Provence persuaded the papacy to license a university at Aix in 1413. He stipulated that all Provençal students had to study there. The Hundred Years War led directly to the founding of three universities. Charles VII erected one at Poitiers in 1431 to counter the University of Paris, then in English control. Once the French recaptured Paris, the English government created universities at Caen (1437) and Bordeaux (1441). Despite their suspect origins, both survived after 1453, albeit as minor institutions. The proliferation of universities continued under Louis XI, who procured papal statutes for one at Valence while he served as the governor of Dauphiné. By 1500 it emerged as a major center for the study of Roman law. If a French prince could found a university, would the duke of Brittany be far behind? In 1460, the duke received papal bulls for a school at Nantes, which survived the end of Breton autonomy. Lastly, Louis XI, who was fond of his native city of Bourges, persuaded the pope to erect a university there in 1464, which also became noted for the study of Roman law. The University of Paris and other established universities objected loudly to the creation of the last several schools, especially Bourges. The Parlement supported the old schools, and Louis XI had to write a *lettre de jussion* to get it to register the papal bulls for Bourges.

In the late fifteenth century, most of these universities had small student bodies. Two or three of them may have been under 100 students, while only Toulouse and Paris were clearly above 1,000. The number of students at Paris is difficult to determine. A source from the 1490s indicates that 25,000 to

30,000 men claimed the privileges of a student, but only a fifth of that number were truly students.[1] Many of those claiming student privileges were employed by the university or licensed to it, as booksellers were; but a large number were former students who hung on indefinitely in Paris. The great number of former students and pseudo-students was a consequence of the vast range of privileges accorded to the students and the masters of the universities. Riots, violence, and defiance of authority were routine in the universities, but nowhere was the problem more serious than at Paris. The sheer size of the student body and the mobs of hangers-on was a factor, as was the great number of arts masters in Paris who were only a few years older than their students and nearly as likely to get into trouble. Students and masters were all nominally clerics, so they held the special rights of the churchmen. They won more by means of the "cessation": stopping all lectures and sermons in the city. Since most of the curés of the city parishes were university graduates still bound by the oath they took as students to obey the university, they also were obliged to obey a cessation. It was through the cessation that the university won its special privileges in the early 1200s, and it used the tactic to defend them down through the years. From the papacy the university members gained the right to be absent from their benefices, have their cases tried in Paris regardless of the place of origin, and, when found guilty of an offense in a church court, be warned twice before being excommunicated if they ignored the court's verdict. This was in sharp contrast to the speed with which a layperson was excommunicated for ignoring a church court's decision. The church courts were in fact extraordinarily lenient toward students, and the last privilege was rarely needed. A Conservator Apostolic of University Privileges, usually a bishop from a neighboring diocese, was responsible for seeing that the papal privileges given to the university were followed. He had his own court to hear appeals.

The French kings also granted special privileges to the university. Among them were exemptions from the *aides* on wine and food, which ordinary clergymen paid. They had the right to bring any civil case in which they were involved to Paris for trial. More pertinent to the masters was their freedom from civic responsibility to the city. The royal *prévôt* of Paris served as the Conservator of Royal Privileges of the University. These privileges and the ardent defense of them by the university via legal appeals, violence, and cessation meant that students went virtually unpunished for all but the most serious crimes, and even then it was not certain that student perpetrators would be punished.

By the mid-fifteenth century, however, neither pope nor king was as eager to defend the university's privileges. Louis XI began to cut into its independence, but it was Louis XII who put an end to the practice of cessation. The university's claim to exemption from the *aides* had been extended to include all former students and anyone with a license to sell to it. That seemed unreasonable to Louis XII. In 1499, he ordered that the exemption apply only to full-time students and masters, and he specified the length of time that students in the various faculties could claim it. The university was already in his bad graces because a number of faculty members criticized the annulment of his marriage to Jeanne of France. When word came to Blois that placards and sermons denouncing him and Cardinal d'Amboise were rife in Paris, he gathered an armed force and marched on Paris. Cries for a cessation thundered across the university, but as the king approached the city, university leaders met him and conceded defeat. The university never again attempted a cessation. Francis I quickly nipped in the bud an attempted cessation by the University of Toulouse in 1533, ending the practice there. Although student violence and turbulence did not disappear with cessation's demise, the royal government had corrected the worst abuse of university privilege and succeeded in reducing the autonomy of the most independent of medieval corporations.

It is difficult to avoid the conclusion that Louis XII won an easy victory over the University of Paris in 1499 in large part because its reputation then was at one of the lowest levels in its history. This was especially true in respect to its Faculty of Theology, commonly called the Sorbonne, after the Collège de Sorbonne, a residence for poor theology students, although in this era the colleges of Montaigu and Navarre had greater prestige. The university remained the stronghold of scholastic theology, but after Jean Gerson's death in 1429, no Parisian master of theology came close to matching the importance of the dozens of great theologians of the previous 300 years. It is true that three of the most important names in the history of Christianity—Erasmus, Calvin, and Loyola—were students there, but only Loyola stayed for any length of time. The first two found the Nominalism of William of Ockham (who died in 1349), which was the dominant theological system of the Faculty of Theology, highly uncongenial. Nominalism, which had a brief, brilliant period in the mid-fourteenth century, had by 1484 degenerated into the pursuit of increasingly trivial and esoteric questions. That, along with theologians' distaste for the learning of the Italian Renaissance, led the humanists to insult them by calling "Théologastres," from *theologian* and the Greek word for belly, as well as other epithets.[2]

We must not take at full value the bitter criticisms of the humanists and the early Protestants, and conclude that the University of Paris declined into insignificance or mindless obstructionism in the face of the superior ideas of humanists and reformers. It continued to be called upon to render judgments on major issues of the day. In 1514 the celebrated Reuchlin case was brought to the Faculty of Theology. Reuchlin was a German humanist whose study of

Judaic works led to charges of error against him. Reuchlin studied arts at Paris and law at Poitiers. The Paris Faculty decided against him, much to the anger of most humanists, who had taken up Reuchlin's cause. In 1519 the theologians were asked to assess the works of Martin Luther, a development that Luther himself supported at first. After a long debate the Faculty condemned them as heretical. The most famous case for which the Faculty served as a consultant was Henry VIII's annulment. Eventually, a small majority of the theologians sided with the English king, but by the time the opinion was published, it had little impact on events in England.

Mutual antagonism between the University of Paris and the humanists, which the Reuchlin affair exacerbated but did not create, has obscured the fact that prior to 1515, the university had a tolerant attitude toward humanism. Humanism can be defined as an intellectual movement that emphasized an education in the ancient classics and believed that anything worth saying had to be said in classical Latin or Greek. Several of the first humanists in France taught at the university. Guillaume Fichet was a member of the Collège de Sorbonne who became immersed in the works of Italian humanists, especially Petrarch. In 1470 he and another member founded the first printing press in France on the grounds of the college, bringing three German printers to Paris to operate it. The next year they printed a work by the Roman author Sallust, the first classical book published in France. In 1472 Fichet went to Rome and never returned to Paris, but his press continued to publish a mix of scholastic and classical works for the university market. Lyon had a press by 1478, and by 1500 some 20 French cities had them in operation. The presses at Lyon were more productive of classical scholarship than those of Paris, even without a university. Lyon's proximity to Italy and the presence of numerous Italians who took up residence there made it a near equal of Paris as a center of early humanism in France.

Fichet's place as a teacher of classical rhetoric at Paris was taken by Robert Gaguin, a teacher of canon law who also taught classical Latin to select students, including Erasmus. Erasmus's first published work was a dedicatory poem to Gaguin's *History of France* of 1495, which became the model for humanist histories of France. Gaguin's translation into French of Caesar's *Commentaries on the Gallic Wars* was his chief contribution to humanism. His work embodied Christian humanism in his promotion of classical Latin as training for the Christian mind.[3]

Several Italian humanists also came to teach in the University of Paris to promote their humanist agenda. The most important was Girolamo Aleandro, already a noted scholar of Greek when he arrived in Paris in 1508 at the urging of Erasmus. Soon he was lecturing in Greek to vast crowds at the university and taking part in its governance. He served as proctor of the Collège de Sorbonne and rector of the university. In a letter of 1512 to Erasmus, he complained that the faculty was harming him, not honoring him, by all the offices it was thrusting on him. Aleandro's later career as a Catholic controversialist against Luther revealed a conservatism in theology that may explain the university's ready acceptance of him. By the time he left it in 1514 to become a secretary to the bishop of Paris, the battlelines between the theologians and the humanists were drawn up. Theologians began to conclude that humanism was not simply an inappropriate emphasis on the study of ancient languages, but constituted a real threat to their authority and prestige, in part because a mere undergraduate in arts who knew a little Greek could challenge the most senior theologian's understanding of scripture.

Desiderius Erasmus, partially a product of the Paris Faculty of Theology, had much to do with that development. A native of Holland, he studied theology in the Collège de Montaigu for two years, from 1495 to 1496, but he concluded that the study of scholastic theology was a dreadful waste of time. Erasmus later quipped about Montaigu: "where the eggs were stale, and the theology staler." He returned to his first love, classical learning, and published his first humanist work, the *Adages*, in Paris in 1500, the year before he left the city. Having developed a bitter dislike for scholasticism, Erasmus could not simply ignore it; instead he devoted his sharp wit to satirizing it and its devotees. More important, in 1515 he published his edition of the Greek New Testament, applying to the Scriptures the principles of text editing that the Italian humanists had developed. He believed that the Bible ought to be accessible to all, and that establishing the correct text of the original Greek was the first step toward producing accurate vernacular translations for use by the common people. That idea was a direct challenge to theologians, who proclaimed that they were the sole interpreters of Christian doctrine.[4]

Francis I had barely become king when the earlier relationship of cordial competition between humanists and scholastic theologians in Paris degenerated into mutual suspicion and open antagonism. The conservative Noël Béda, who followed Jan Standonck as director of the Collège de Montaigu in 1504, was emerging as the dominant voice in the Faculty of Theology. He was convinced that the humanist approach to the Scriptures threatened to undermine Christian doctrine as well as the Faculty of Theology. Béda was prepared to denounce many of the humanists as heretics. Francis I, on the other hand, was deeply sympathetic to the humanists. His expedition to Italy in 1515 increased manyfold his strong interest in Italian civilization. Upon his return in mid-1516, several French humanists including his secretary Guillaume Budé and his former tutor François de Rochefort convinced him that France needed a place for teaching ancient languages. In February 1517, the king announced his intention to create royal chairs of Greek, Hebrew, and classical Latin at the university.[5]

Francis wanted Erasmus as the principal chair, but the great humanist was not ready to disrupt projects he had going on elsewhere. The king then chose Jan Lascaris, a native of Greece, who spent the years from 1496 to 1504 in France teaching Greek. He then served as Louis XII's ambassador to Venice. In 1517 he was the director of Leo X's college of ancient languages in Rome. Lascaris returned to France but spent less than three years there before Francis sent him to Milan to direct a college of languages and collect Greek manuscripts for him.

The plan for a college of ancient languages in Paris languished for a decade while Francis was caught up in the Italian wars. By the late 1520s, however, his entourage included many more humanists, and his sister Marguerite of Angoulême, who always had a great deal of influence on him, openly supported the humanist agenda. In 1530 Francis returned to the idea of teaching ancient languages and appointed four *lecteurs royaux,* two for Hebrew and two for Greek. Since the king paid them, their lectures were free to the public. Francis intended to leave the teaching of classical Latin to the traditional faculty, but they soon made it clear that they had no intention of pursuing this, and a chair of classical Latin was added. Almost immediately the royal professorships expanded beyond their original purpose with the addition of Oronce Finé to lecture in mathematics.

Besides the king, the person most responsible for what soon became known as the Collège des Trois Langues was Guillaume Budé. He probably had mastered Greek better than anyone else in France, but he was also the greatest legal scholar of the Renaissance. Budé came from a well-placed family of royal officials in Paris. As a student in law at the University of Orléans, he was noted for the little time he devoted to his studies. Nonetheless, he became interested in ancient learning and taught himself classical Latin and Greek. As a *sécretaire du roi,* he undertook several diplomatic missions for Louis XII but truly came into his own with the succession of Francis I. In 1522 he became the first Master of the King's Library. He had numerous agents and fellow humanists searching for manuscripts of classical works for it. The library was at Blois until it was moved to the new château at Fontainebleau in 1544. An inventory done in 1518 tallied 1,626 books, mostly manuscripts, in the royal library.

Budé's reputation as a scholar began with his translations of several of Plutarch's works from Greek done in 1503-05. In 1508 he published a commentary on the first 24 books of Justinian's *Digest* of civil law. It was a powerful attack on the study of law as it was done in the universities, which, like scholastic theology, was the study of medieval commentaries, not the original text. Budé largely created legal humanism. While he spent most of his time at Paris or the court, legal humanism was centered in the universities where civil law was taught. The second major contributor to its creation was an Italian law scholar, Andrea Alciati, who joined the University of Avignon in 1518 and went on to Bourges in 1528. Toulouse, Orléans, and Valence were other early centers of the genre, but literary humanism also was strong in them. However, with the exception of a few prominent humanists such as Jean de Pins, who arrived at Toulouse in 1523 and whose Latin style was highly praised, these provincial centers of ancient learning began to flourish only after 1530. Budé's modern standing as one of the great French humanists rests heavily on his work in Roman law, but in his own time his prestige depended more on his *De asse et partibus eius* (*On Coins and Measurements* [1515]). It was a study of the Roman monetary system and included a vast array of information on prices, weights, and measurements. The work placed Budé on a level with Erasmus among humanists and helps to explain why Erasmus was eager to carry on an extensive correspondence with him. Later, Budé's interest in these decidedly nonreligious topics declined, and he argued that some aspects of the study of ancient culture might actually lead to religious error. Nonetheless, he regarded its study as a worthy handmaiden to the science of God.[6]

One group of French humanists, of whom Budé was the foremost, had interests that were secular; religion rarely intruded in their scholarship. Another group, like Erasmus, placed religion at the center of their interests. They can properly be called Christian humanists, for they applied to the study of the Christian classics the philological principles of humanism so profitably used by Budé. Of these humanists, the most renowned of the French among them was Jacques Lefèvre d'Etaples from Picardy. He took a master's degree in arts at the University of Paris and by 1490 was lecturing there. Two years later he traveled to Italy. Although he spent little more than a year there, he was inspired to work on a critical Greek edition of several of Aristotle's works and translate them into Latin. After a second trip to Rome in 1500, he turned his attention more to the Christian classics and religious interests. Lefèvre published critical editions of several of the Latin Church fathers and Latin translations of Greek fathers in order to bypass the texts of scholastic theology and go to the earliest sources of Christianity. Soon he realized he needed to go directly to the Bible itself. In 1509 he published a critical edition of the Psalms in which five important translations from the early Church were printed side by side. Much more important was his Latin edition of the Epistles of Paul: He printed the Church's official translation of St. Jerome side by side with his own commentary, which owed virtually nothing to scholasticism; it was, in comparison with scholastic ones, a simple exposition of the literal meaning of the words of St. Paul. Lefèvre's commentary included several points on the sacrament of the Eucharist and human salvation that anticipated Martin Luther.

Lefèvre, unlike most humanists in France, never received patronage from the king, although Marguerite of Angoulême gave him support. His principal patron and pupil was Guillaume Briçonnet, who rose rapidly in the church, becoming bishop of Lodève at age fifteen and abbot of the great monastery of St-Germain-des-Près at Paris in 1507. That appointment allowed Lefèvre, who was Briçonnet's secretary for three years, to become the librarian of the large library in the monastery. The careers of both men took a drastically different direction in 1516 when Briçonnet became bishop of Meaux. Astounded by the lack of religious zeal and understanding of both the clergy and laity of his diocese when he visited it for the first time in 1518, Briçonnet invited Lefèvre to join him and help reform the church at Meaux. When Lefèvre arrived there in 1521, French humanism crossed the line separating the Renaissance from the Reformation in France.

Although the humanists in France became, through the work of Erasmus, Lefèvre, and others, a major element in the push for church reform, humanism was first of all a literary movement. The first evidence of the influence of humanism on literature was found in the group of poets called the *rhétoriqueurs,* who included Robert Gaguin, Jean Bouchet, Jean d'Auton, Jean Marot (father of Clément), and Jean Lemaire de Belges. More than most other literary schools, the *rhétoriqueurs* had a number of common characteristics: a love of classical Latin, even if their knowledge of it was mediocre; close association with the French court; and an interest in history. None of these authors today are highly regarded for their literary work, except perhaps for Lemaire; but they did help popularize classical Latin in France. Most *rhétoriqueurs* wrote chronicles, which are of varying value for writing the history of that era, and several inserted poetry into their prose chronicles. All of the *rhétoriqueurs* drew on ancient models both for style and content in their French writings. Lemaire's *Les Illustrations de Gaule et Singularitez de Troye (The Illustrations of Gaul and the Peculiarities of Troy,* two volumes published in 1510 and 1513) was responsible for popularizing the myth that Gauls founded Troy (based on the presence of Celts in Galatia), and that after the fall of Troy the surviving Trojans fled back to Gaul to create Gallic society and culture. Thus the king of France was the descendant of Hector and Aeneas.[7]

In the first years of the reign of Francis I, native French writers were overshadowed by the Italian humanists whom the king invited to France; and the French language deferred to Latin. The superiority of Latin was something on which the professors of the universities and the humanists could agree, even if they disagreed strongly on what was proper Latin. French was changing rapidly, and the stability of Latin appealed to those who believed that what they had to say was worth keeping for the ages. Today, the French poetry of the *rhétoriqueurs* is more highly regarded than their Latin; but they and their contemporaries were convinced that their best work was in Latin.

The major exception to this point was the theater. French drama during the last years of the fifteenth century was heavily medieval and religious in character. The mystery plays from a century earlier were still being staged by guild confraternities, corporate groups, or entire villages. Charles VIII's reign has been called "the great epoch" for mystery plays of Christ's passion.[8] A successful mystery play had its serious elements, depicting the events from the Bible or the lives of the saints and emphasizing a moral point, and its comic side, injecting farce into the midst of the play. It was the production of farce that was the most noteworthy aspect of French theater in Louis XII's reign, and the best writers of farce were members of the Basoche, the society of the law clerks of the Parlements. Several other government institutions had similar organizations of clerks involved in producing farces. These comedies and farces put on for the public, which often included Louis XII, were called *sotties* (farces performed by *sots*—jesters or fools). Since the writers and performers were minor government functionaries, their topics were usually political, and they often satirized members of the court and even the king and queen. Perhaps the most notorious was the *sottie* "Le Monde et Abuz," produced by the Basoche of Toulouse, which satirized Louis by praising his vices, especially his miserliness. The king tolerated the *sotties* because, he was reported as saying, they informed him of the faults and corruption of his ministers, although he made it clear that he would not tolerate attacks on his wife.

Louis XII employed the best of the writers of *sotties*, Pierre Gringore, as part of his effort to convince the French people of the righteousness of his struggle against Julius II. Gringore wrote a number of popular poems and plays for the royal campaign. The most important of Gringore's attacks against Julius was the *sottie* "Le jeu du Prince des sotz." It was performed at Les Halles, the main marketplace in Paris, on Mardi Gras in 1512. Highly praised as one of the best medieval plays for its drama and eloquence, it combined a cutting attack on Julius with satirical asides on nearly every aspect of society, except the king. The *sotties* were written in colloquial French and reveal no influence from classical or Italian plays. Francis I did not have Louis's liberal attitude, and the genre quickly disappeared in the first years of his reign. Although farces and satires continued to be performed, the objects of their ridicule were clerics and monks rather than royalty, and their authors no longer were exclusively from the Basoche and related societies. The plays also began to show the influence of classical satirists such as Juvenal.

The world of science (natural philosophy as it was called in that era) and mathematics remained equally conservative. The flash of innovative thought at Paris in the fourteenth century from several Ockhamist theologians, such as Jean Buridan, had burned out. Teaching natural philosophy in the universities involved the use of commentaries on Aristotle and other ancient works. Humanists, especially Lefèvre, made a small contribution, despite concentrating on literature and religious works, by providing critical editions of Aristotle's scientific works and those of some other ancient scholars. Mathematics, for instance, received a great boost when some of the major ancient works on the subject were translated into Latin in good critical editions. The best French mathematician of the era, Nicolas Chaquet, should be seen as the culmination of the medieval tradition. He finished his *Triparty* in 1484, but it remained in manuscript for four hundred years and had little impact on the sixteenth century. Had his ideas about algebra, such as the use of *p* and *m* for plus and minus, been in wide circulation, they surely would have hastened the development of modern notation.

The one scientific area in which some work of note was being done was astronomy, because of its association with astrology. Astrology was the dominant "scientific" discipline of the late Middle Ages, because like any modern science, it was believed to predict the future. The arrival of Arab astrological works in the West in the previous century provided a boost to a field that was ignored in the early Middle Ages. As of 1500, every one, or so it seems, availed themselves of the services of astrologers, and the kings of France had one as a permanent member of their courts at 200 *l* annual pension. Because astrology depended on interpreting the movements of the heavenly bodies, astronomy was essentially its handmaiden. Work in astronomy had the purpose of making astrology more accurate. In 1524 a major astrological event took place—the conjunction of all the planets in the constellation Pisces, which mandated careful astronomical observation. Astrologers proclaimed that the conjunction of the planets in a "water" sign meant a second Great Flood. Much later, opponents of astrology used the fact that 1524 was hot and dry to discredit astrology.

In the field of medicine, the era was a period of tentative steps toward the use of ancient learning. In 1514, Henri Estienne published a small collection of texts of Galen translated into Latin by an Italian. About the same time, the faculty of medicine at Paris began to teach Galen in a limited fashion. The publication in Paris in the same year of an Italian work on anatomy also indicated new currents in medicine. Dissections became commonplace by 1515, and their occurrences and locations no longer received special note in the records of the medicine faculty. The prominent physician Symphoren Champier of

I. The Hôtel du Sens, Paris. Built for the archbishop of Sens between 1475 and 1507, it is regarded as the prototype of Parisian hôtels.

Lyon wrote extensively on medical topics and fostered humanism, especially the study of Plato, in his enormous corpus of printed works.

In art and architecture, the influence of the Italian Renaissance was more powerful than in natural philosophy. The date when that influence clearly began to be felt is easily pinpointed for architecture—Charles VIII's return from Italy in 1495. He decided before 1494 to rebuild the château of Amboise on the Loire River, his favorite residence, and brought back from Italy artisans and artists, including Fra Giocondo, the noted engineer, to work on it. The plan and exterior appearance of the château remained that of a medieval castle, but much of the decoration and the new gardens were Italianate. That combination of characteristics was found in most of the building projects of the early Renaissance until 1530,[9] such as the Hôtel du Sens in Paris, built between 1475 and 1507. (See illustration I.)

The next king, Louis XII, did much the same for his favorite château, Blois, but the changes were more extensive. The most significant impact of Italian architecture was in the idea that a château need not be a defensive stronghold. By 1500, Italian châteaux were not being designed to protect the occupants but to provide pleasant space for receptions, balls, and gracious living. Louis felt secure enough in his control of the realm and the affection of the nobility to live in a "defortified" place. The great tower of Blois disappeared (it may have been torn down before 1498), and ditches were replaced by gardens. Blois can be seen as the prototype of the royal châteaux of the ancien régime, which were the centers of life for an absolute monarch secure among his subjects, and not the castles of a medieval king.[10] Several of Louis's advisers also incorporated Italian elements in their new or reconstructed châteaux. In rebuilding his château of Gaillon near Rouen, Cardinal d'Amboise introduced Italian influence to Normandy.[11] The best known of these châteaux is Chenonceaux, begun in 1513 by Thomas Bohier, a finance minister. (See illustration II.) His wife, Catherine de Briçonnet, one of the most learned women of the era, is given much of the credit for the design of this beautiful building.

Francis I was much more of a builder than his two predecessors and more influenced by Italian ideas. The massive château at Chambord, with its square keeps, round towers at the corners, and moat, is essentially medieval, but much of its decoration is Italian. (See illustration III.) Da Vinci probably had a hand in its initial planning, but he died the same year that the final design was drawn up in 1519.[12] Several French master masons were more responsible for building it. Francesco Primaticcio did most of the decoration after he arrived from Italy in 1531. Despite the Renaissance decor, Chambord apparently was not a comfortable place to live, as the French kings spent little time there, although Francis did entertain Charles V in the château in 1539. Another of Francis's early projects was adding a wing to Blois, for which the inspiration was probably Bramante's design for the Vatican Palace. In 1524 Francis's building program was interrupted by the Italian war and his subsequent captivity.

In painting, French artists of the last years of the fifteenth century were influenced by Flemish painters, whose style revealed the detailed realism made possible by the use of oil paint. The Flemish school was noted for its portraiture. Its best representative, Jean Clouet, moved to Burgundy shortly before 1515

II. The Château of Chenonceau. It was begun in 1514 for Thomas Bohier, a royal secretary; Philibert de L'Orme designed the bridge (1556-59) over the river, and Jean Bullant did the gallery over the bridge (c. 1580). Giraudon/Art Resource, New York.

III. The Château of Chambord. Leonardo da Vinci may have had a part in planning this massive structure when it was begun in 1519 for Francis I. It was completed by 1540. Giraudon/Art Resource, New York.

IV.   Francis I. By Jean Clouet, c. 1535, in the Louvre. Giraudon/Art Resource, New York.

and then became court painter to Francis I. His portrait of the king is the best known representation of Francis. (See illustration IV.) A French painter, Jean Perréal, noted for his portraits of Louis XII and Queen Mary, introduced Leonardo da Vinci to painting with tempera while he was with the king in Milan. Louis met da Vinci there in 1499 and admired his work. He asked him to come to France with him, but da Vinci refused because he had too many projects in Milan. It is probable that Louis commissioned Leonardo to paint his *Virgin and Child with St. Anne* for Queen Anne.[13] Louis had more success in luring several lesser-known artists to France, such as the painter Andrea Solario, whose *Madonna With a Green Cushion* was done at Blois.

The Italian influence was more pronounced in sculpture, perhaps because there was no competing Flemish influence. Charles VIII brought Guido Mazzoni to France in 1495, where he remained until 1516. Louis XII commissioned him to do two important projects—the tomb of Charles at St-Denis and the equestrian statue of himself at Blois. The three Giusti brothers worked in France after 1507. Their most important commission was the tomb of Louis and Anne at St-Denis, which Francis I commissioned in 1517. It was finished in 1531.[14]

Francis succeeded in persuading da Vinci to move to France in 1516 and become court painter with a pension of 500 *l.* He brought with him several of his best known paintings, including the *Mona Lisa,* which explains why it is in the Louvre Museum today. The king wanted da Vinci to serve primarily as an architect for his building projects, but he died in 1519 before he did much in France. Andrea del Sarto also arrived in France in 1516 and painted *Charity* there before returning to Florence in 1523 to serve as an art agent for Francis. The impact of Italian artists increased dramatically when a large number of them were brought to Fontainebleau after 1530 to work on the new château.

In music the currents of influence went in the opposite direction from the other arts—from Flanders through France to Italy. Charles VIII and Louis XII patronized a large group of Flemish composers who settled in France as singers in the royal chapel. They contributed to the development of polyphony and counterpoint. The best known among them was Jasquin des Prez, who is regarded as an important precursor to Palestrina. He became the music director of the royal chapel in 1500 after 13 years in the papal chapel. He left France upon Louis XII's death. Louis's trips to Italy with his chapel singers in tow was one means of bringing Flemish polyphony to Italy. Francis I was somewhat less interested in music, and his reign saw the continued development of trends already in place in 1515.[15]

As of 1530, 40 years of broadening Italian influence in art and literature and increasing royal patronage of Italian humanists and artists prepared the ground for a bursting forth of a brilliant Franco-Italian culture in France in the next 30 years.

Part II

FRANCE, 1530–1562

8

The Monarchy: Dark Clouds on the Horizon

With the Peace of Cambrai (1529) in hand and his sons back home, Francis I had several years to attend to other matters besides war. The enormous cost of the war with Charles V, the ransom of his sons, and the bad harvests of 1530-31 led to popular unrest across France. While his financiers examined changes in the fiscal system, Francis decided to make a "progress" through the realm to show himself to his people. Personal contact between king and subjects was regarded as the best way to reaffirm loyalty to the throne.

In early 1532 the king spent six months traveling through Picardy, Normandy, and Brittany. At Rennes he watched as his eldest son, Francis, was invested as duke. The final act of the duchy's incorporation into France would come when his second son and heir to Brittany, Henry II, became king in 1547, irrevocably attaching it to the crown. In the late fall of 1532 the king returned to Paris via the Loire Valley. The next spring he began a longer trek, traveling through Champagne and on to Lyon, Clermont, Le Puy, and Toulouse. When he reached Marseille, he remained for more than a month. The extended stay had an important purpose—the marriage of his second son, Henry, to Catherine de Medici, the cousin of Pope Clement VII (she was usually called his niece). Francis was eager to wean Clement away from his pro-Habsburg policy before making another try at recovering his Italian lands. The marriage contract between Henry and Catherine included the pope's pledge of support for the French recovery of Milan, which the young couple would then receive. King and pope remained in the wedding suite to ensure that the marriage was consummated, since both bride and groom were only fourteen.

Thus Catherine de Medici arrived in France, where she remained until her death in 1589. Popular opinion felt that she was too lowborn to marry a French prince, since she was only "an Italian shopkeeper's daughter." The insult failed to acknowledge that her mother had come from high French nobility. There was more grumbling a year later when Pope Clement died, and the new pope, Paul III, refused to recognize any obligation under the marriage contract. The feeling that the marriage had been a mistake increased over the next years as the couple remained childless, until they had a son in 1542. By then, Henry's older brother had died, and Henry had become dauphin.

Marrying his son to the pope's relative to create a French-papal alliance against the Habsburgs proved disappointing to Francis. Another diplomatic initiative with the Ottoman Turks proved to be more fruitful, although it was a public relations disaster for the king. After the failure of a Franco-Venetian expedition against the Turks in 1502, the French had withdrawn from crusading activity. By the late 1520s Francis had begun to regard the Ottoman sultan as a powerful counterweight to Charles V and began secret contacts with him. In 1530 a French agent appeared in Constantinople to persuade Sultan Suleiman the Magnificent to attack Charles. Francis preferred that the Turks strike Italy, to draw Imperial troops away from Milan, rather than Austria, which would rally the Lutherans to the emperor. It was Austria that Suleiman attacked in 1532, but the failure of that campaign and the rallying of the Lutherans to Charles did not dampen French enthusiasm for conspiring with the Infidel.

Having taken the plunge, Francis began to broaden his contacts with Constantinople. In 1540 an Ottoman diplomat appeared at the French court, and discussions over the next year led to a tacit alliance. In early 1543, an Ottoman fleet left Constantinople with a French agent aboard. It cruised along the west coast of Italy, raiding the coastal towns. Francis agreed to allow the Turks to winter in Toulon instead of returning home. The residents were forced to evacuate, and for eight months Toulon was a Turkish town. When they left, six French galleys accompanied them to Constantinople, where Suleiman himself welcomed their crews. The outrage at this was intense across Europe; even many of his subjects criticized Francis for his pact with the devil. Although the loss of goodwill probably was a factor in the decision to push the Turks to leave Toulon, Francis did not denounce the alliance with them. "When the wolves attack my flock," he allegedly said, "I do not hesitate to call on the dogs."

Less scandalous and more productive was Francis I's relationship with the German Lutherans. In 1531 the Lutheran cities and princes founded the Schmalkaldic League to protect their interests against Charles V and called on the French king for help. Francis was torn between his hatred of Charles and his distaste for the Lutherans. His policy toward the Lutherans was ambivalent—eager to use them against the emperor yet careful not to endorse openly their cause. For nearly ten years, as Francis vacillated between war and accommodation with Charles, his policy toward the Lutherans in Germany was also inconsistent, keeping them at arm's length or embracing them. In the late 1530s, as Valois and Habsburg edged toward war, Francis sought to strengthen his ties to the Schmalkaldic League. Among the factors preventing a formal alliance were the Ottoman threat to Germany and Francis's policy of sporadic persecution of Protestants in France. Despite these difficulties, the Lutherans and the French reached the point of discussing the possibility of replacing Charles V with Francis or his son.

The most important relationship for France in the bitter competition with the Habsburgs was the one with England, whose king still called himself king of France. Aware that he held the balance of power between Francis and Charles, Henry VIII played off one against the other, thereby gaining, for example, French approval of the annulment of his marriage to Catherine of Aragon. The rivalry between the two egocentric kings of nearly the same age and the old hostility between the two kingdoms made the relationship shaky at best. In 1532 Francis annoyed Henry by marrying his daughter Madeleine to James V of Scotland. When she died within months of arriving in Scotland, he provided another French bride for James. She was Marie de Guise, the eldest daughter of Claude de Guise, who came from a cadet branch of the House of Lorraine. Marie's marriage to James Stuart was short and tragic. Her two sons died within a week of each other in 1541, and her husband a year later, only a week after the birth of their daughter Mary, who became queen of Scots at the youngest age of any European monarch.

The relationship between Francis and Charles remained tense throughout the 1530s, although there was only limited military action. As eager as ever to recover Milan, Francis became enraged when the duke of Savoy refused in 1536 to allow his army to cross his duchy to strike at Milan. The French army occupied Savoy and drove the duke into the service of the Habsburgs, whom he served as a captain until 1559. Charles became so angry at this act of aggression that he challenged Francis to settle their differences in a duel. Probably to the relief of both, the pope refused to allow them to fight. Charles instead responded to the French provocation by invading Provence in July 1532, although there had been no declaration of war by either side.

Francis sent Anne de Montmorency, regarded as his best captain, to defend the region. Montmorency belonged to a family that claimed the title of "First Baron of the realm," on the grounds that it was descended from the first

Frank baptized after Clovis. He was close to Francis in age and had been raised with him. The king gave him high office at a young age. He had commanded the French army that defended Provence against Charles of Bourbon in 1524, for which he gained fame as a master of defensive war. In 1537 Montmorency imposed a rigorous scorched-earth policy on the towns and villages of eastern Provence while he posted his army on the Rhône to prevent Charles from crossing it. Brought to a halt short of the Rhône, the Imperial army soon ran out of supplies and had to retreat after a month.

After driving out a second Habsburg force that had invaded Artois, Montmorency marched back to the southeast, crossed the Alps, and took several forts in the duchy of Milan in late 1537. By then Charles was ready for a truce. Montmorency's credit rose to its highest level, and in February 1538 he was rewarded with the office of constable. It had been vacant since Charles of Bourbon's defection, and Francis conferred the title on him at Moulins, site of the old Bourbon court.

Despite Montmorency's new office as the head of the army, he advocated a policy of peace and persuaded Francis to meet with Charles V at Nice in May 1538. It was not face to face; the pope served as a go-between. A month later as Charles went by sea to Spain, he stopped at Argue-Mortes for a personal meeting with Francis. Although no specific agreements came out of the meetings, the spirit of reconciliation continued into the next year when Charles visited Francis on his way from Spain to the Netherlands. Francis thought he had an agreement that his third son, Charles, would marry the emperor's daughter and receive the duchy of Milan. When Charles dashed that hope by investing his son Philip as duke of Milan, Francis's rage knew no bounds. It was directed as much at Montmorency as Charles, since he had been advocating the policy pursued in the past two years. It cost him his place at court despite the support of the dauphin, and gave the advantage to the opposing faction, led by Prince Charles, Admiral Chabot, a personal enemy of Montmorency's and the Duchesse d'Etampes, the king's mistress. Francis was an enthusiastic womanizer and loved being surrounded by beautiful women. It was largely he who turned the French court into a center of fashion and beauty.

The Duchesse d'Etampes was the first royal mistress to have a strong influence on royal decision making. She was strongly anti-Habsburg, and she probably influenced the change in foreign policy of 1540. French agents again made contact with the Lutheran princes, but the immediate cause of the war that broke out in 1542 was the murder of two French diplomats near Milan. France took the offensive by striking at Luxembourg in the north and Perpignan in the south. Henry VIII's declaration of war on France early the next year compounded the consequences of the failure of both attacks. Francis had not been paying the annual pension to keep England neutral, and French pressure had persuaded the Scots to repudiate a marriage agreement for Queen Mary Stuart and Henry's young son Edward.

The theaters of the war were the usual ones of Milan and the frontier between Picardy and Flanders. In 1543 the French army won a major victory near Turin, the battle of Ceresole, when the Imperial commander, a Spanish veteran of Pavia, overestimated the ability of his harquebusiers to take on the French *gens d'armes* and Swiss pikemen. But the French could not follow up the victory, because an English attack in northern France forced a quick recall of troops from Italy. In May 1544, Charles and Henry coordinated a two-prong invasion of France—Charles from the east and Henry out of Calais. Both were stalled for some time before two powerful frontier forts, Boulogne and St-Dizier. The forts fell after sieges, but Henry refused to advance any farther. Charles advanced into Champagne within a hundred miles from Paris, but by then it was too late in the campaigning season to push on to the city. Charles was also eager to settle accounts with the Lutheran princes who had rebelled. He quickly agreed to peace when French representatives approached him. The resulting Peace of Crépy obliged the French to aid Charles against the Turks and, in a secret clause, against the Lutherans. The war with England continued beyond the Peace of Crépy, as Francis was determined to recover Boulogne. For one of the very few times since 1340, the French fleet took the offensive against England, but it returned home after burning a few coastal villages. In June 1546 the war sputtered to an end with a peace treaty that required the French to pay 4.5 million *l* for Henry's unpaid pension and the return of Boulogne in eight years.

By then it was clear that Francis I's health was deteriorating badly. The factionalism at court grew worse, as the party of the dauphin became bolder with the sense of the upcoming transfer of power, while Duchesse d'Etampes's faction sought to entrench itself in power before the king's death. Francis himself engaged in a furious round of hunting and travels before his weakened condition forced a halt at the château of Rambouillet. He died there on March 31, 1547.[1]

Henry II was twenty-eight years old at his succession to the throne. He already had a coterie of close friends and advisers who immediately moved into positions of power or, in the case of Constable Montmorency, returned to it. He remained Henry's most influential adviser throughout the reign. He had married late, and his sons were still young in 1547, so it was his nephews, the three Châtillon brothers, who profited from Montmorency's clout early in the reign. The eldest became a cardinal, while the second, Gaspard de Coligny, soon was named admiral. It was also clear that the two eldest sons of Duc Claude de

Guise, François and Charles, would be highly influential. François, the same age as Henry, proved to be a successful military commander, while Charles, whom the pope named a cardinal in 1547 as a favor to the new king, was a talented politician and churchman.

The new royal mistress, Diane de Poitiers, quickly took over Anne d'Etampes's place at the court. In 1548 Henry gave Diane, who was 20 years older than him, the title of duchess of Valentinois. The king remained deeply in love with her to the end of his life, despite the age difference. It meant that in his personal life Henry paid little attention to Catherine de Medici, although they continued to have children up to 1557, seven of whom survived infancy. She, nonetheless, received an apprenticeship in state affairs, since she served as regent during the several occasions that Henry was outside the realm.

In the three-way competition for influence over Henry II, Montmorency generally held the upper hand. He used his clout to rein in Henry's enthusiasm for war against Charles V; as he once said, he no longer was eager to go to war. The king, on the other hand, was eager to avenge himself on the emperor for what he regarded as the mistreatment he had received while a prisoner in Spain. At the beginning of his reign, however, he was convinced that his father had left the French army in too poor a condition to go to war immediately. There were also the unresolved problems with England, where Edward VI had succeeded his father a few months before Henry's own succession. One was the English effort to force the young queen of Scotland to marry Edward. In 1548 Henry, determined to prevent that from happening, sent a fleet to whisk Mary Stuart from Scotland to be raised at the French court among her Guise relatives. In due course, Mary's betrothal to Henry's first son Francis was announced. The other major problem involving England was the continued occupation of Boulogne. Henry had commanded the French army that had been defeated there in 1544, and he was eager to redeem himself. He also cringed at paying out 4.5 million *l* for it, which would bring no return in glory. The king sent his forces against Boulogne in late 1549, but winter set in before it fell. Early the next year he accepted a treaty returning it to France for 900,000 *l*.

Henry continued the tacit alliance with the Turks. While he never did anything as blatant as giving them a harbor for their fleet, he quietly tried to coordinate his attacks against Habsburg lands with theirs. More public was the French alliance with the Lutheran princes. They had been badly defeated in 1547, and Germany had been quiet for several years until Lutheran resistance reappeared again in 1551. That same year Henry and the Schmalkaldic League signed an alliance. He agreed to provide the League with a large subsidy in exchange for recognizing French rights to those places in the Holy Roman Empire where French, not German, was spoken, although the French king was to rule them as vicar of the Empire, not as sovereign prince. The most important places were the Three Bishoprics of Lorraine—Metz, Toul, and Verdun. In April 1552 Henry set out to secure his new lands in an expedition known as the "Promenade to the Rhine." The French-speaking cities of Lorraine quickly opened their gates to him. When he entered the German-speaking region of Alsace, the open hostility he encountered persuaded Henry to retreat. Having "watered his horses in the Rhine," he returned to France, bringing in tow the young duke of Lorraine, who was shortly betrothed to Henry's second daughter Claude. The French presence in Lorraine was irrevocable.

Habsburg fortunes turned for the better the next year with the death of Edward VI, who had followed a largely pro-French policy, at least in his last years. Charles's cousin, Mary Tudor, was in line for the throne, but the French tried to keep her off it by supporting the candidacy of Lady Jane Grey. French machinations failed to keep Mary off the throne while costing Lady Jane her head. French anxiety increased apace when Mary announced that she would marry Prince Philip, Charles's heir. England would be securely in the Habsburg camp. Henry aided several rebellions against her and did his best to make her life miserable.

Success in the south balanced Henry's problems in England. In 1553 a combined Franco-Ottoman fleet landed an army on Corsica and seized it from Genoa, Charles V's ally. Despite the success on Corsica, however, the tacit alliance between the French king and the Ottoman sultan was, for the most part, a record of missed opportunities caused by poor communications and mutual suspicion and resentment. Far more beneficial to Henry was the election of Pope Paul IV in 1554. A native of southern Italy, he hated the Spanish for their harsh rule in his homeland. Soon after his election Paul signed a secret treaty of alliance with Henry against the Habsburgs. Rumors of the alliance caused Charles and Philip, who was taking on more and more of his aging father's authority, to accept a five-year truce in February 1556.

Paul IV was determined to use the French to oust the Spanish from Naples; Queen Catherine eagerly embraced the cause of Italian exiles seeking to return home by overthrowing the current governments in Naples and Florence; and the Guise saw continued war as the way to increase their power at the French court. The pressure on Henry to resume war on the Habsburgs was intense, and it became stronger when the pope promised to give Naples to one of Henry's younger sons and Milan to another if the French occupied those places. In September 1556 Henry agreed to dispatch a French force to Italy under the duke of Guise, while proclaiming that the truce held only on the frontiers of France itself. It was broken in January 1557, when forces under Admiral Coligny unsuccessfully attacked Douai. Why the attack occurred has remained a mystery, but it seems unlikely that Henry ordered it. Philip, who had taken over rule of the Netherlands from his father, ordered his forces to retaliate, which led Henry to declare war in February. French aid to English rebels led Queen Mary to go to war on France in June.

A sharp disagreement with Paul IV over how best to proceed and the usual heavy losses to disease and desertion that hit every French army in Italy, hindered Guise's move against Naples, while Philip moved to reduce French pressure in Italy by attacking northern France from Flanders. In early August 1557, a Spanish army (by then Philip had become king of Spain and the term Spanish will be used for his forces in the Netherlands, although few were Spaniards until 1566) crossed the frontier and halted before the fortified town of St-Quentin, which blocked the route to Paris. Henry ordered Montmorency to rush forces there to relieve it. The resulting Battle of St-Quentin was a disaster for the French. In the rout of his army, Montmorency and numerous other great nobles were captured. Philip decided to take St-Quentin before pushing on to Paris. It fell a month later, but by then Philip felt it was too late in the season to conduct a siege of Paris. By mid-October most of his army was in winter quarters.

Meanwhile Henry had been collecting his reserves and numerous mercenaries, and Guise and most of his men had returned from Italy.[2] When it became clear that the Spanish would not advance on Paris, Henry decided to plan a winter campaign, still a rare event in that era, against Calais. The recovery of Calais was the fervent hope of all the French, not only because of the ease with which English forces attacked France from it, but also the boast the English had posted over its main gate: "Then the Frenchmen Calais shall win; when iron and lead like cork shall swim." A winter attack on Calais was good strategy, because it would surprise the English with a reduced garrison and the shallower marshes around it would be frozen. It worked to perfection; only eight days after the French army entered the Pale, Calais surrendered.[3] The Hundred Years War had truly come to an end.

The Calais campaign was one more heavy expense for a royal treasury already badly depleted. One response Henry made to the crisis was an assembly he called for Paris in January 1558. About a third of the episcopate, the *baillis* and *sénéchaux*, the court nobility, representatives of the *bonnes villes*, the magistrates of the Parlement of Paris, and the presidents of the provincial Parlements were invited to attend. An interesting innovation was the use of the term *fourth estate of royal justice* for the parlementaires present, and the king referred to the assembly as a meeting of the Four Estates. Should it be considered as a meeting of the Estates general? Its membership, especially for the Third Estate, was well below those meetings accepted as full-fledged Estates general, but most contemporaries referred to it as an Estates, not an Assembly of Notables. Regardless of what name one wants to give to the meeting, it dealt exclusively with royal fiscal affairs. The cities and the clergy agreed to provide the king with loans totaling 7.5 million *l.* In their elation after the victory at Calais, they turned the money into an outright gift to the monarch.

The war between Henry II and Philip II had resulted in a great victory and a major defeat for both sides: God intended them to make peace. Negotiations began in early 1558 but made slow progress, and fighting continued through the summer. Henry balked at the heavy demands, including the stiff ransom for Montmorency. In October 1558, he was given a parole to participate in the negotiations. The Spanish expected that his desire to be ransomed would make him push Henry to accept their terms. It probably worked, as the Treaty of Cateau-Cambrésis of April 1559 was largely favorable to Philip. Henry conceded everything in Italy, agreeing to withdraw his forces entirely and recognizing Philip's rights to Milan and Naples. Genoa received Corsica back. The border between Flanders and France was returned to the status quo of January 1557. Philip had a protest included in the treaty against French occupation of the Three Bishoprics of Lorraine, but he made no effort to have them returned to his uncle, Ferdinand I, the new Holy Roman Emperor. The peace called for the return of Calais to England after eight years for 1.25 million *l,* but if there were any English violations of the truce, Calais would remain French. France invoked that clause in 1563 when England provided aid to the Huguenots.

The Treaty of Cateau-Cambrésis also arranged for two marriages. Henry's daughter Elisabeth, who had just turned fourteen, would marry Philip II, now a widower after Mary Tudor's death in late 1558; and Henry's sister Marguerite, still unwed at age thirty-six, would marry the duke of Savoy, who would return to his duchy 20 years after Francis I had forced him out. Many contemporaries, especially the captains who had fought in Italy, sharply criticized the treaty for conceding too much to Philip. Others praised it for extracting France from the Italian sinkhole of French manpower and money, while keeping French control of Calais and Lorraine, which strengthened the French position on the northern frontier.

The defects of the treaty from the French point of view were made clear in the decades after 1559, but they were largely a product of the weak French monarchy following Henry's death. His death was a result of the peace, albeit an unexpected one. Henry planned a great festival to celebrate the peace and the two marriages. In mid-June 1559 the duke of Alba arrived in Paris as Philip's proxy both for swearing the peace and wedding Princess Elisabeth. Still very much a part of any such festival was a grand tournament. On June 30 the king himself took to the lists to joust. He ran the usual three courses, winning the first two but losing the third against Gabriel de Montgommery, captain of the Scots Guards. Henry, determined to make a better showing, ordered Montgommery to run again, despite the rule that no one was to run more than three courses in a day. When Montgommery shattered his lance on the king's breastplate, the inexperienced knight brought the broken lance up instead of dropping it immediately. The shattered end struck Henry in the face and drove several splinters into his head above his eye. The blow was not in itself fatal, and Henry was expected to recover until blood poisoning set in four days after the accident. He died on July 10, 1557.[4]

Henry left to his fifteen-year-old son Francis II a government that had undergone considerable change in the previous 30 years and was deeply in debt. Both Francis I and Henry tinkered regularly with the systems of administration and finances. One office that was substantially changed was that of royal secretary. At the beginning of Francis's reign, they were designated *secrétaires des finances* because a large portion of their workload involved writing financial documents. He broadened their responsibilities, and the title *secrétaire d'état* became used for the most important. Henry II reduced the number of those who used the title to four, defined their duties more exactly, and raised their salaries. Each of the four had responsibility for expediting the affairs of state and preparing dispatches for a specific group of provinces and the foreign countries next to them. For example, the secretary responsible for the Midi also had responsibility for Spain and Portugal. Prominent members of the *noblesse de robe* were normally the *secrétaires d'état,* and their families often held the office for generations.

Provincial affairs were the concern of another important development in administration. Francis I had begun to use the eight *maîtres des requêtes de l'hôtel du roi,* who originally took appeals and requests to the king, to supervise provincial officials of justice. By 1547, now 18 in number, they traveled fairly regularly to the provinces. An edict of 1553 further enlarged their number to 20 and defined more clearly their duties. Six *maîtres* were routinely sent on tours of the provinces to supervise both financial and judicial systems. An officer with the title *intendant de la justice* was placed in the provincial governor's council with the authority to supervise the royal officials. The terms used to define the power of the one appointed to serve with the French governor of Corsica were virtually identical to those for the intendants of a century later.[5]

The heavy expenses of the nearly continuous war with the Habsburgs, the increasingly lavish court, and the largesse to the royal favorites meant that the changes in the fiscal system would be more extensive. The first major change was a decision in 1542 to divide the four *généralités des finances,* which had encompassed most of the realm for the previous century, into 12. The four smaller financial divisions were kept the same size but were put under the same regimen, creating 16 *recettes générales*. Each was given a *receiveur général* to supervise the collection of the king's ordinary revenues from his demesne and the extraordinary ones from taxation. To increase efficiency, a *receiveur-générale* was given the power to pay local expenses of royal government out of the revenues of his *recette-générale*. This meant that far less money was in transit to and from the royal treasury, but it also meant less bullion would be in the royal treasure chests in wartime. Supervision of the entire royal revenue system was given to two *intendents des finances*, whose number soon rose to 12. In 1562 Charles IX gave the title of *surintendant des finances* to their president, who emerged as the minister of finance. In 1557 Henry II, facing a serious shortfall in the midst of war, ordered all the revenues again brought to Paris, since war needs were immediate while payments for local expenses could be put off indefinitely. The system of the *recettes-générales* was maintained, because it gave the king greater control over the fiscal system and provided better knowledge of the current state of revenues and expenses.

The old distinction between the two types of revenue disappeared. Combining the two types of royal revenues made sense, because the ordinary revenues constituted a smaller and smaller proportion of the total royal income, as taxes rose dramatically: 22 percent from 1523 to 1547 and another 23 percent to 1559. Those large increases came nowhere close to meeting the demand for money, so in 1549 Henry created a new tax, the *taillon*, which was sold to the people as a way to support French troops so they would not pillage towns and villages. It was intended to produce 720,000 *l*. Three years later he persuaded an assembly of clergy to levy a tax of 20 *l* on each church steeple, to total 1.4 million *l*, indicating that there were 70,000 steeples in the realm. The churchmen had already been giving the *décime*, the clerical tenth, on a regular basis. By 1542 Francis I was asking for four *décimes* a year, which represented 4 million *l*, or about a true 10 percent of the clergy's income. Four *décimes* became the clergy's routine "gift" to the monarch, except in 1550, a year of peace, when Henry II asked for only two, and 1558, the worst year of Henry's reign for war expenses, when he demanded eight.[6]

The money derived from taxes and the clergy's contribution could not keep pace with royal expenses. Another source that was ever more exploited was the selling of royal offices. Venality was already being practiced in 1515, but Francis I greatly accelerated its spread, especially by extending it to the judicial offices. By 1547 the royal treasury was collecting as much as 900,000 *l* from venality. Henry II greatly accelerated the creation of new offices for venality. It seems to have a factor in every administrative change Henry made in the government, even those justifiable in their own right. In 1560 it was estimated that the royal treasury collected 3.6 million *l* a year from the sale of offices, but the wages paid out for all the new officers Henry had created consumed a third of that sum.

All the changes in the fiscal system failed to solve the king's financial problems. Both Francis and Henry had to resort to large-scale borrowing. They drew on their own subjects for loans, which were often forced loans at little or no interest. The most common loans from French subjects were a type called *rentes*. Someone, such as the king, would rent out a source of income, like a toll or a tax, for a lump sum that served as the principal. The income then served as interest for the loan until the principal was repaid in a lump sum at the end of the contract. This system was seen as avoiding the Church's ban on interest-taking. The most important source of *rentes* was the city of Paris, where the Hôtel de ville collected money for the loans from its wealthy bourgeoisie and paid them interest from tolls collected in the city. Because they were backed by the city whose credit was better than the king's, the interest on the *rentes* was $8^{1}/3$ percent, or about half of the interest on loans from bankers. These *rentes sur l'Hôtel de ville de Paris* did not become a major source of money for the monarchy until late in Francis I's reign. At his death about 720,000 *l* in *rentes* on the Hôtel de ville were outstanding. Henry II vastly expanded the practice, drawing an average of 500,000 *l* a year for the 12 years of his reign. Since some were repaid, the total of the Parisian *rentes* outstanding in 1559 was 3 million *l.*

The major source of loans was Lyon with its quarterly banking fairs, where bankers and borrowers assembled to do business. They dated to before 1500, and the monarchy often borrowed funds there, but it was after 1542 that the French king became the major consumer of the capital collected at Lyon. The interest unusually was 4 percent from fair to fair, or 16 percent per annum, although it dropped as low as 5 percent in 1550, when peace reduced the demand for money.

Henry II's principal contribution to the system of royal borrowing was the creation of the Grand Parti of Lyon.[7] Any group of bankers lending to the king was called a *parti*. Because of the size of the sums involved and the number of bankers, this one was the Grand Parti. Henry pledged to use the most secure revenues of three *généralités* of the southeast for repaying the loans. What was innovative about the Grand Parti was its system of payment of interest and principal. At the time of each fair of Lyon (four a year) the king would repay a sum equal to 5 percent of the original loan. The first payment consisted of 4 percent for the interest (16 percent per year) and 1 percent to repay the principal. But since the interest was on only the unpaid principal, a larger part of the 5 percent payment at every fair went to amortizing the principal. The loan was to be repaid in full after 41 fairs, or ten years and four months. It was the first time that any monarch in Europe had set up a definite schedule of amortizing a loan. To avoid being charged with breaking the Church's laws against usury, the interest was described in the contract as a gift.

In 1557, Henry was forced to suspend payment to the Grand Parti for a quarter, but he did not default on his loans, as often has been said. The interruption in payment did not shake the lenders' faith in Henry's ability to repay his loans; they continued to lend to him at the same interest rate. At his death Henry owed the Lyon bankers 16 million *l.* His total indebtedness may have reached 43 million *l,* more than two and a half times the king's annual revenues. In the next decades the impact of that debt, which was not paid off until 1600, was enormous. The debt required exorbitant taxes, resulting in the defection of much of the Third Estate from the monarchy. It prevented the kings from being as generous to the nobles as Francis and Henry had been, causing the defection of many. It largely eliminated the prospect of a foreign war, which would have drawn most of the fighting men out of the realm and pitted them against a foreign enemy instead of each other. In short, the huge royal debt in place in 1559 ensured that the religious division already renting France would become civil war.

The political situation at the court after Henry II's death also was a major element in the outbreak of the civil war. Francis II, who had turned fifteen in June 1559, was legally old enough to rule in his own name, but it was expected that a youth of his age would have to have a great deal of help in ruling France. Furthermore, Francis was sickly and not very bright. There was little doubt that those who emerged as his chief advisers would dominate France for some time to come. Nor was there much doubt about who they would be. The young king never liked Constable Montmorency and sent him and his nephews back to their estates, depriving them of all their royal office that did not confer life tenure. It was his wife's uncles, the Guise, who immediately stepped to the fore as the power brokers in the kingdom, although the queen mother's influence over Francis was not as slight as is often portrayed.

When the membership of the new royal councils was announced, notably absent were the entire Montmorency clan and the Bourbons, who as princes of blood ought to have been included. The head of the House of Bourbon, Antoine, who was married to Jeanne d'Albret, queen of Navarre, was at his wife's court in Pau when he heard of Henry's death. He leisurely made his way to Paris, fully expecting to take the reins of power. When he finally arrived six weeks later, he found the Guise already entrenched. The angry protests of Bourbon, his brother Louis of Condé, and their supporters failed to effect any change. They began to cooperate with Montmorency's nephews, with whom they had long been at odds.

By mid-1559 the Guise had become symbols of Catholic repression of the Protestants. To what extent the adherence to Protestantism by most of the Bourbons, Admiral Coligny and his brothers, and other prominent nobles excluded from power was a protest against the Guise is difficult to evaluate, but there can be little question that it was a factor for many of them, and the principal one for some. Because of the financial crisis, the Cardinal of Lorraine, who had taken charge of administration and finances, was forced to decrease the pensions for the nobility drastically, while his brother the duke, as lieutenant-general of the realm, had to reduce the size of the army. Such blows to the financial well-being of the nobility could only result in opposition to the Guise, who easily could be cast as the "evil advisers to the king," from whom Francis had to be freed. Once that was done, all would be right with the world.

At first the Huguenots pinned their hopes on Antoine of Bourbon, but his commitment to Calvinism was not very firm, especially when he was away from his wife. He was eager to gain support for the recovery of southern Navarre from the Spanish, and accepted a promise of help from the Guise in exchange for attending the royal council without demanding its presidency. The Huguenots turned to his brother, Condé, who was both far more committed a Calvinist and more ready to oppose the Guise. He also was far more amenable to one tactic endorsed even by Jean Calvin for undermining the Guise—calling for the convocation of the Estates general, which, it was expected, would strip them of their power. When a petition was presented to the king, he flatly refused to accept it.

Bitterly disappointed by the king's reply, or perhaps anticipating it, several Protestant nobles, led by the sieur of La Renaudie, once a client of the Guise, began to plot to take control of the government.[8] By March 1560 as many as 500 nobles, mostly Huguenots but also some discontented Catholics, had agreed to participate. However, the Protestant owner of a house in Paris where La Renaudie was directing the plot revealed it to the government. Francis II moved from Blois to Amboise, which was better fortified. In mid-March bands of armed men began to appear near Amboise, many of whom were arrested and brought to the château. A larger body of men, some 500, was discovered on March 16, and the king gave the duke of Guise authority to punish them as rebels. La Renaudie was killed in a fight away from the château, but at least 300 of his followers were executed, the commoners by drowning or hanging, the nobles by beheading. The climax of the affair was the public execution of 56 nobles on March 30.

The conspirators had solicited the advice and aid of Calvin, Queen Elizabeth, Antoine of Bourbon, and Louis of Condé. Calvin brusquely forbade rebellion against established authority; Elizabeth may have provided a small sum of money; Bourbon turned down the offer to head the affair; only Condé responded positively. He agreed to take his brother's place as head of the government once the Guise had been eliminated. Arriving at court just as the conspiracy was being broken up and confessions extracted, he was accused of complicity in the rebellion. By a show of bravado, challenging anyone who accused him to a duel, he avoided penalty, but had to withdraw from the court and was open to future charges.

As the "Tumult of Amboise" was unfolding, Chancellor François Olivier was dying. His successor was Michel de L'Hôpital, a protégé of Marguerite d'Angoulême and now of Catherine de Medici. A humanist and a moderate in religious matters, he expounded a point of view that later became known as *politique*: religious differences should not be allowed to damage the state and the interests of the monarchy. Toleration of religious dissent was to be preferred over civil strife. L'Hôpital was also a strong advocate of regular meetings of the Estates general but only as a way to keep the king in touch with his people, not to control him. His hand seems apparent in the Edict of Romorantin of May 1560, which restored the distinction between religious heresy and political sedition. The former was returned to the church courts, which had not become any more effective. While it was certainly not an edict of toleration, it did reduce the likelihood that a Protestant not involved in activities defined as seditious, such as preaching heresy to a group, would be dragged into court.

The Tumult of Amboise and the presence of the new chancellor were responsible for the decision to hold an assembly of notables in August 1560 at Fontainebleau. Among the 54 grandees present was Constable Montmorency, making his return to politics after Henry II's death. Reporting on the royal finances, the Cardinal of Lorraine revealed that there was a 2.5 million *l* deficit for the previous year. The assembly soon turned to matters of religion. Coligny, who had accompanied his uncle, presented a petition to Francis, asking for religious toleration and the right to have at least one place in every town for Protestant services. Two liberal bishops, Jean de Monluc and Charles de Marillac, seconded his call for a general council of the church to settle the religious issues or, failing that, a national Gallican one. They, and others, also called for a meeting of the Estates, a constant refrain of Huguenot literature of this era. Even Lorraine seconded it. At the close of the assembly, the king announced that he was calling the Estates for December and the national council of the clergy would also meet, unless the pope convoked a general council first.

Bourbon and Condé were summoned to Orléans to prepare for the Estates general. When they arrived at the court in October 30, Condé was arrested for *lèse majesté* (treason). He demanded to be tried by his peers in the Parlement of

Paris. This Francis refused, but a resolution to the case was delayed when the king fell ill. He lingered for two weeks and died on December 5, 1560. His mother moved immediately to claim the regency, since the successor to the throne was ten-year-old Charles IX. Catherine skillfully maneuvered Antoine of Bourbon into accepting her right to the regency before his own, while the other powerful courtiers had no right to object.

The Estates general had been called to meet on December 13. It was decided to go ahead with the meeting despite the king's death. For the first time since 1484, the selection of delegates was made in the same fashion as then. The return to a more representative system was noteworthy, but also remarkable was the large number of Huguenots among the deputies. For several years, Calvin had been calling for the Estates to meet, and once their convocation was announced, he actively pushed his followers to see that Protestant deputies were chosen. It appears that a majority, or close to one, of the Second Estate were Huguenots, and a significant percentage of the Third was also. Even in the First Estate there were a number of deputies sympathetic to reform and several who were or would become openly Protestant.

The first matter of business was the huge royal debt, which was threatening to ruin the monarchy. The chancellor put the debt at 43 million *l*; 19 million *l* in loans had come due. If every *denier* the monarchy collected in a year was paid on the loans, they would not have been paid off. All three estates objected to the solutions proposed to raise more money for the monarchy. The nobility, which had been asked to accept taxes on itself, responded by voting to deny Catherine the regency, as one of the functions of the Estates general was to approve of the government of a minor king. Learning that many of those who had so voted were Protestant or clients of the Bourbons, she ordered the release of Condé. This appeased much of the opposition, and the effort to deny her the regency was aborted. The Estates, however, refused to accept new taxes. The Second and Third, with their large Huguenot contingent, made a strong attack on the Catholic clergy for its vices and wealth. They proposed that the monarchy solve its fiscal problems by seizing much of the Church's wealth. That was too radical, and Catherine moved quickly to close the meeting, which ended on January 31, 1561.

The Estates had accomplished nothing to solve the financial crisis, and only two weeks later Catherine was forced to convoke a new meeting. Its opening was eventually put off until August. The instructions sent to the election districts included a change in the voting procedure and the charge that the deputies attend only to the royal debt and not politics or religion. Catherine felt that Orléans had failed because of the large number of deputies present. She ordered each of the 13 *governements* in France to elect one deputy, a total of 39 delegates in all. However, Catherine also convoked a meeting of the French clergy at Poissy. It had not been intended to overlap in time with the Estates general, but a delay in assembling the Estates had that result. Most of the clergy's deputies assembled at Poissy, and, except for a few sessions, the Second and Third Estates met alone at Pontoise. Without the influence of the clergy, the deputies at Pontoise easily agreed that the Church should bear the weight of the monarchy's fiscal demands while making no offer to increase taxes on themselves. Frightened by the schemes being proposed at Pontoise, the assembly of clergy made a generous offer of money to the king, but it was not enough to solve the financial crisis. When the Estates of Pontoise closed on August 27, 1561, having tried Catherine's patience with a call for religious toleration, they had not provided any solutions for the problems plaguing the realm—massive royal debt and religious division. The next response would be civil war.

9

The Church: The Protestant Challenge

Casting his eyes about Europe in 1517 just as the Reformation erupted in Germany, Desiderius Erasmus remarked that France was the purest place in Christendom, free of heretics and Jews.[1] While the kingdom had its share of cases of blasphemy and sacrilege typical of the late Middle Ages, there was no organized dissenting movement, nor would there be one until after 1540. For the French kings, the appearance of Lutheranism in the Holy Roman Empire was almost a godsend, preventing Charles V from drawing on the whole range of German resources for his anti-French policy. As late as 1551, Henry II objected to recalling the Council of Trent: Since France was largely free of heresy, he did not need a council to keep it so, while a council might help Charles in solving the religious problems in his domains.

Despite Henry's bravado, his assessment was not accurate for 1551, and it would not have been 20 years earlier, but France's religious situation for the four decades after 1517 was quite different from most other European countries. While there was no organized Protestant movement until late in the period, there were many Evangéliques, those early reformers, not necessarily Protestants, who insisted that the Scriptures were the only source for religious truth. L'évangélisme was the view that the Church could be reformed and the pure Gospel preached in French without necessarily breaking with the Catholic Church.

In Lucien Febvre's words, this was a period of "magnificent religious anarchy,"[2] in which there was a full range of religious opinions expressed, without any one dominating. France was unlike Spain and Italy, places where vigorous state repression and cultural revulsion kept the number of reformers very small, but it also differed from the many places across Europe where state fiat imposed the Reformation. Thus explanations for the state of religious affairs in France are difficult to formulate, because they have to account for individual decisions by thousands of persons to accept a faith different from traditional Catholicism. Even after Calvinism became the standard for French Protestantism, there remains the difficulty of finding an explanation of why portions of every social class and corporate body accepted it, while the rest remained loyal to the old Church.

The first appearances of Luther's books in France date to 1519. They were sold openly for two years before the Faculty of Theology ordered a crackdown. After 1521 the number of heresy cases in the courts rose noticeably, but with a few exceptions, there was little that was specifically Lutheran about the beliefs of the accused. They usually revealed dissatisfaction with the Catholic Church and its clergy, which Luther's writings stimulated and validated but did not create. In 1523 an artisan from Meaux was the first Lutheran (the general term for Protestants in France until 1559) executed for his heretical beliefs. Later Protestant authors hailed him and other early victims as Protestant martyrs, but it is not clear how true to Protestantism they really were.

The social background of most accused of heresy in the first 15 years after 1517 had changed very little from the previous century. They were largely artisans and day-laborers, whose response to their dismal living conditions usually took the form of a poorly articulated but angry anticlericalism.[3] Whether they espoused age-old popular heresy or Lutheran ideas is generally impossible to determine. A good example of the doctrinal confusion of this time is found in the Sorbonne's condemnation in 1525 of Jacques Pauvan, a student at Paris who had gone to Meaux. It declared that he derived his ideas from Waldo, Wyclif, Hus (three medieval heresiarchs), and Luther. Pauvan briefly recanted his beliefs but soon changed his mind, and he was burnt as a relapsed heretic in August 1526.

Nonetheless, there were some French dissidents whose beliefs came from the major Reformers. Among them were the more radical members of the Circle of Meaux—Guillaume Farel, Michel d'Arande, and Gérard Roussel—who drew on the Swiss Reformers, especially Huldrich Zwingli, more than Luther. When Louise of Savoy, as regent for her son, moved to break up the Circle in 1525, they fled abroad.[4] Farel emerged as an important leader of the Reformation, most notably having a major role in reforming Geneva even before Jean

Calvin arrived there. Soon d'Arande and Roussel returned to France and received appointments as bishops in the Midi through the influence of Marguerite of Angoulême. Despite the Sorbonne's protests about their suspect doctrine, both kept their offices until their deaths some 20 years later.

The most notorious case of heresy in the 1520s involved Louis de Berquin, a Picard nobleman and friend of Jacques Lefèvre. He was the first to fall under the royal edict of 1523 prohibiting possession of Luther's works. Francis I intervened in Berquin's trial before he was convicted, but his library was burned. In 1529 Berquin was arrested again and quickly found guilty as a relapsed heretic. He was sentenced to life in prison, but his appeal to the king angered his judges, who included Guillaume Budé, and they sentenced him to death. Two days later he was strangled and then burnt. Berquin had the most prominent rank of anyone executed for heresy in sixteenth-century France.

Francis I's attitude toward the reformers was ambivalent. He regarded heresy as a vice of the lowborn, who were as likely to commit treason against the king as against God, *lèse-majesté divine,* as heresy was often called. He was truly attracted, however, to the Evangéliques and liberal humanists, several of whom were very close to him, and was sympathetic to their calls for moderate church reform. As long as they stuck to satirizing the clergy and espousing Evangélisme, the king supported them. He saw nothing dangerous in the ideas of scholars such as Erasmus and Lefèvre, while he had mostly contempt for their opponents in the Sorbonne. When the Sorbonnists and their allies in the Parlement of Paris sought to try several humanists for heresy, Francis intervened to protect them and exiled the most outspoken of the Sorbonnists, Noël Béda, to Mont-St-Michel in 1534.

The king's forbearance toward moderate reformers was tested in late 1533, when the rector of the University of Paris, Nicolas Cop, delivered a controversial address to the university community. He drew heavily from Luther and Erasmus and denounced the execution of religious dissenters. Informed of Cop's views, the Parlement moved to arrest him, but he fled from Paris with a number of his friends. Francis, who had not been in Paris, gave the Parlement power to crack down on "that damned heretical Lutheran sect." When the king returned to the city in early 1534, however, he found the situation less serious than he had been told and called off the heresy hunters.

Late in 1534 a far more notorious episode, the Day of the Placards, occurred. In the morning of October 18, placards (broadsheets nailed to a board) were posted in a number of public places in Paris, several other cities, and the château of Amboise where the king then was. Whether a placard was nailed to the door of the king's chamber remains uncertain. The author of the text was Antoine Marcourt, a Frenchman who had fled to Switzerland several years earlier. A group of radical dissidents had smuggled the placards into France. The placards contained a very strong attack on the Catholic doctrine of the Eucharist, which the author defined as being only a symbol of Christ's sacrifice. He vehemently denied the real presence of Christ. That point of view, largely advocated by the Swiss Protestants, was called "Sacramentarian." The outrage of the Catholic populace was intense. Within six weeks a wealthy cloth merchant and five artisans were executed, as were several more persons in the next few months.

The Day of the Placards was the first manifestation that at least some French reformers had gone beyond Lutheran ideas and anticlericalism to adopt the more radical doctrine of the Swiss Protestants. The episode coincided with the worst excesses of the Anabaptists in the German city of Münster, which fell to Catholic forces in early 1535 after a long siege. The king was badly shaken by what he saw as the blatant call to rebellion obvious in both events, and he began to back away from the Evangéliques he had always protected. Some fled to Strasbourg and Switzerland; others, to Marguerite of Angoulême's court at Nérac near Agen and to Navarre, where she was queen as the wife of Henri d'Albret.

By mid-1535 the king's fury had eased. Foreign policy considerations, especially his relationship with the Germans, required that he slacken the prosecution of Lutherans. For much of 1535, Francis was in contact with Philip Melanchthon, the German humanist who was Luther's principal assistant. They hoped to arrange a debate with the Paris Faculty of Theology in order to reach a compromise that could be adopted in France and Germany. Hard-liners in the Sorbonne and the Lutheran camp prevented any meeting, but Francis was ready to make far-ranging concessions to reach an agreement.

By then, however, the Reformation in France was rapidly going beyond the relatively conservative position of Melanchthon. Its social makeup also was very different from his party of liberal humanists. Artisans and journeymen were among the most affected. The journeymen traveled extensively and were exposed to new ideas; they resented the rigid controls society placed on them; and they did not have the social and religious bonds that membership in the guild confraternities placed on the masters. The relatively new printing industry seems to have had the largest number of proto-Protestants, perhaps because its members were less bound by tradition.[5] The artisans and journeymen had a strong streak of anticlericalism, probably because they saw the large number of well-fed clerics about their towns while they struggled for survival despite their skills. It is hard to find evidence that Lutheran theology directly influenced many of them; more important was the image of Luther as one who had challenged the power of the pope and the clergy. The ideas of the proto-Protestants were disorganized and incoherent, and they had only a loose network of individuals and clandestine cells. Often they were centered around defrocked priests and religious, frequently former Franciscans, who provided much of what leadership they had.

That was less true for the small but important group of haute-bourgeoisie attracted to Protestantism. They were far more likely to have read the major Reformers and express their discontent with the established Church in theological terms. They also were far more eager to replace the Catholic Church by a different style of church organization. They tended to be similar in their beliefs because many were educated in the humanist colleges that had been founded earlier in the sixteenth century. Colleges appeared in well over a hundred towns where there was no university, although the universities themselves, even Paris, did have their share of liberal humanists. The town councils had usually erected the colleges to provide a humanist education for the sons of the bourgeoisie. By 1530 numerous headmasters and teachers were being arrested or dismissed for suspicion of heresy. Antoine Saunier, who was arrested in 1530 while at the college of Reims, later became principal of the college of Geneva, while Mathurin Cordier, ousted from the college at Bordeaux, became its best-known teacher.[6]

The combination of artisan attraction to Reform and bourgeoisie education in the colleges ensured that the early evangelical movement was primarily an urban phenomenon. Few rural dwellers appear in the court records as charged with heresy, although that may have indicated simple indifference on the part of authorities in what the peasants believed, until they began to refuse to pay the tithes to the Church. The only rural region with any evidence of evangelical strength early on was the Cévennes.[7] Paris, with its large number of liberal humanists and artisans and the site of the principal heresy-hunting institutions, the Sorbonne and the Parlement, was the focus of attention until 1535, but from then to 1562, cities such as Lyon, Caen, Nîmes, Montpellier, and Rouen became the centers of French Protestantism.

It was a bourgeois from Noyon in Picardy who provided leadership, coherence, and structure to French Protestantism. Jean Calvin, who used the Latinized version of Cauvin, his family name, was born in 1509. His father, Gérard, was a notary for the cathedral chapter, a position of respectable income and prestige. Eager to secure his son's future, Gérard Cauvin procured a benefice in the cathedral for him and dispatched him to the University of Paris to prepare for a career in the Church. When he arrived in Paris, the arts faculty had a number of scholars of classical Latin, despite the university's later reputation for extreme conservatism. Calvin acquired an excellent training in classical Latin, albeit largely on his own, while earning the bachelor and master of arts degrees.

Before Calvin began his study of theology, his father had a quarrel with the cathedral chapter of Noyon and was excommunicated. Angry at the church, he sent Jean to Bourges for legal studies. Calvin spent the years from 1528 to 1533 at Bourges and Orléans, both centers of legal humanism. At Bourges he studied Greek with Melchior Wolmar, a German with Lutheran sympathies. When his father died, Calvin abandoned a legal career, although he did receive his license to teach law, and returned to Paris, where he studied Hebrew with one of the royal lectors. He clearly demonstrated his humanistic bent of mind and training in his commentary on Seneca's *On Clemency,* which was published in Paris. There is no hint of Protestant beliefs in it, unless one wants to see it as an appeal to Francis I for leniency toward accused heretics. His circle of friends at Paris was, however, made up of Erasmians and evangelicals.

When Nicolas Cop, one of those friends, created the uproar with his rector's address in late 1533, Calvin fled from Paris with him.[8] He went first to the court of Marguerite of Angoulême at Nérac, where he met Lefèvre and several others from the Circle of Meaux. In the spring of 1534 Calvin returned to Paris a fully committed Reformer. Much later in life he made a reference to a sudden conversion but gave no date. It had to have occurred before May 1534, when he made a quick trip to Noyon to resign his benefice. Soon after that, he wrote the preface to Pierre Olivétan's French translation of the Bible. Olivétan, Calvin's cousin from Noyon, was already in Geneva.

Soon Calvin himself was in exile, fleeing France in the aftermath of the Day of the Placards. He went to Basel, where he spent a year writing his theological masterpiece, *Institutio Christianae Religionis (The Institutes of the Christian Religion),* which was published in 1536. After Basel Calvin went to Ferrara in Italy, where Louis XII's daughter, Renée of France, was duchess. Highly sympathetic to evangelicals, she welcomed numerous French exiles. Calvin did not stay long in Ferrara, as he heard that French refugees in Strasbourg needed a pastor for the Reformed church they had organized. He dashed back to France to settle his inheritance and set out for Strasbourg. Detoured southward by war in July 1536, Calvin stopped in Geneva, a French-speaking Swiss city already home to a good number of French exiles. It had become Protestant largely through the influence of Farel. When he heard Calvin was staying overnight in his city, Farel rushed to him and begged him to remain there, overcoming his reluctance finally by telling him it was God's will. Calvin's leadership skills quickly pushed him to the forefront of the church of Geneva. He suffered a setback when he and Farel were expelled in 1538 by a faction opposed to his system, but three years later he was invited back, and remained there until his death in 1564.

Calvin was an extremely productive writer and had an enormous range of correspondence, scriptural commentaries, and sermons, but his key work was the *Institutes.* Written in a fine Latin style that revealed his humanistic interests and organized in the precise logic of his legal training, the first edition of the *Institutes* is an amazingly mature theological work for someone who barely two years earlier was unsure of his beliefs. Dedicated to Francis I, Calvin wrote it to show him that the Protestant beliefs Calvin had accepted were not the dangerous doctrines of the Anabaptists, whose often violent denunciations of political authority terrified the rulers of Europe. Although Calvin revised the *Institutes* several times up to his death in 1564, the essence of his theology was clear in the 1536 edition. Any summation of his doctrine will risk overemphasizing certain elements; nonetheless, it is necessary to take note of the key doctrines, not so much as Calvin regarded them, but as his followers did, since it is their understanding of his teaching that explains Calvinism's remarkable success.

The starting point of Calvin's theology is the overwhelming sense that God's will determines everything that happens in the universe. If not even a sparrow falls to the ground without God willing it, how much more does the fate of human souls depend on divine will! Souls are predestined from all eternity to salvation or damnation. Nearly all other Christian theologians have accepted some form of predestination but have shrunk back from what Calvin called the doctrine's "awful consequences": that God has predestined both the saved and the damned from all eternity. Calvin fully embraced the belief that God has chosen to give grace to some, who fully deserve damnation for their sins, and not to others, who thus are damned for perhaps no more serious sins. God thus is responsible for damnation as well as salvation. Christ's death earned the salvation of some, not all.

Calvin proclaimed that those who lived a good Christian life according to the precepts of the Scriptures as taught by the Reformed Church should have reasonable confidence that they were among the elect. This confidence, taken more as a guarantee by his followers, gave the Calvinists the courage to confront the evildoers and correct them, especially the princes who were harming the true religion, and go to their deaths with Psalms on their lips. Calvin's doctrine of predestination was a serious stumbling block for many who otherwise were attracted to his vision of Christianity, but it gave to those who did accept it a powerful courage of their convictions to change the world. It made them a revolutionary force in western Christendom in the century to come.

Even more important in explaining Calvinism's success in places like France, where the rulers persecuted its adherents, was Calvin's form of church government. The Reformed Church in Geneva had as its major governing body an institution called the consistory. When created in 1542, it had 12 lay members chosen by the city council and the 9 pastors then in the city (the number of pastors had increased to 19 by 1564). The consistory had the power to enforce strict discipline on the church members through excommunication. Unlike Zwingli, Calvin insisted that the authority to excommunicate belonged to the consistory, not the city council.

Calvin's ecclesiastical organization had two major consequences: the laity had a major voice in the Church through their role in the consistory, and the Church was regarded as independent from secular control, at least in those lands ruled by hostile princes. The two in combination allowed a small group, recently converted to Calvinism in a hostile land, to organize a church despite the lack of a pastor. Once it was organized, a request could be made to Geneva for a Reformed pastor. Calvinism was far more flexible than was Lutheranism in dealing with both different lands and persecution.

Jean Calvin was regarded from very early on as the most brilliant mind among French Protestants. He had met a vast number of French dissidents before he went to Geneva, and he carried on an extensive correspondence with sympathizers in France. It was the publication of the French translation of the *Institutes* in 1541 that was the turning point for the French Reformation. Printed in thousands of copies in Geneva and smuggled into France, it replaced the anarchy of the early French Reformation with uniformity and agreement, although it took ten years before French Protestantism became predominantly Calvinist. Not all who had been part of the early evangelical movement agreed with Calvin's clear rejection of Catholicism. A large portion of the Evangéliques drew back, and few of the lower-class evangelicals were attracted to Calvin's relatively conservative social and political positions. These aspects, however, and Calvinism's coherent theology made it attractive to wealthy merchants, educated lawyers and notaries, and even some nobles. As the royal government increased its pressure after 1541, the artisans and lower-class dissidents eager for a more radical Christianity found that they had to associate themselves with the better-placed Calvinists for what protection they could provide. By 1559, there were few French Protestants who were not Calvinists.

Calvin was very eager to win his homeland for Reformed Christianity. He wrote to Francis I in hope of winning him over or at least convincing him to tolerate it. He welcomed thousands of French refugees to Geneva, which had the result of strengthening his position in the city. Many of the exiles were trained in Geneva and sent back to France as Reformed pastors. Beginning in 1555, Geneva-trained ministers were dispatched into France, often at the fervent request of local churches organized without a pastor.

It took very little time for the French government to realize Calvin's importance to the Protestant cause. A royal edict of 1542 condemned his *Institutes,* among a number of Protestant works, and made possession of them a civil crime, with hanging the mandated punishment for possession. Any bookseller caught selling them was liable to burning. The edict labeled as seditious the condemned religious beliefs and required the king's faithful subjects to inform on their adherents.

Francis I's campaign against heresy accelerated in 1545. His first target was the Waldensian communities in the high valleys of Provence. The increase in the number of accused heretics in the realm had called attention to the Waldensians again, and Francis I promised the pope that he would purge his realm of heresy. The appointment of a new president for the Parlement of Aix, Jean d'Oppède, who coveted their lands, was largely responsible for the ferocious enforcement of the king's edict of early 1545 against them. At least 2,700 were killed by royal troops or executed. A suit by a major landholder of the region led to a trial of Oppède and his accomplices under Henry II, but he and most others accused were acquitted; only two individuals were punished. The surviving Waldensians were badly scattered by the massacre, and most joined with the Protestants in the next few years.

Francis also turned his attention to Meaux, which continued to be a stronghold of dissent despite the breakup of the Circle 20 years earlier. The spark it had given to reform had not been extinguished among a group largely made up of artisans. By 1546 the Protestants of Meaux had organized a church of 300 to 400 members, based on the model of Strasbourg. The house of a wealthy merchant served as its meeting place, while an artisan was its minister. In September 1546, 64 men and women were arrested. Except for the owner of the house they were all artisans or laborers. Fourteen were eventually executed, making them the largest group of victims in a widespread campaign against heresy in 1546. The next year had fewer executions because of the ill health and death of Francis I and the succession of Henry II.

For the new king the "conventicle" at Meaux with its lowborn members confirmed that heresy was a seditious affliction of the lower classes. Henry II was a conservative Catholic deeply loyal to the traditional faith. In October 1547, he created a new criminal chamber, the Second Tournelle, in the Parlement of Paris to hear heresy cases exclusively both as a court of first instance and appeals. The new chamber's zealous pursuit of heresy led to the name of the *chambre ardente*. It was not true, however, that this "zealous chamber" burned "all who fell into its clutches." In the 23 months it functioned, it handled 323 cases of accusations of heresy, blasphemy, and sacrilege: 37 persons were condemned to death; 39 were acquitted; 142 were given penalties ranging from a public reprimand to exile; and 105 were remanded to the Church courts when the Second Tournelle was shut down in 1550. Only 29 persons were identified as "Lutheran" or Sacramentarian; more vague charges of heresy and blasphemy overwhelmingly predominated.

Henry II abandoned his experiment in less than two years because the other parlementaires objected strongly to the innovations involved and, even more so, the Catholic hierarchy protested the loss of its competence over heresy. Henry issued the Edict of Châteaubriand in June 1551, which clearly equated heresy with sedition and public disorder. One important clause banned importing books from Geneva and any contact at all with the city. The new edict was unsuccessful in eradicating religious dissent from France, despite Henry's ardent desire. War against the Habsburgs was a major distraction, which also required him to hire Protestant mercenaries and placate Protestant princes by reducing highly visible heresy trials and executions. Another factor in that failure was the king's attitude that heresy was a vice of the lowborn. It blinded him to the fact that a number of prominent nobles, especially the nephews of Constable Montmorency, were openly sympathetic to the Reformation. Although the Protestants were increasing rapidly, there were fewer heresy trials in the years from 1555 to 1559 than in the previous four years. An attempt to create the Inquisition in France failed when the Parlement of Paris refused to register the edict establishing it, and Henry did not require them to do so.

By 1557 reports reaching the court told of whole towns and districts becoming Protestant. In July Henry issued the Edict of Compiègne, which mandated the death penalty for the "Sacramentarians" only (the Calvinists), thereby avoiding trouble with his mostly Lutheran allies and mercenaries. The king declared that since the heretics had become openly seditious, he would use force to crush them; the Battle of St-Quentin, barely a month later, prevented him from making good his threat. By the time Henry was able to return his attention to the religious situation after the Peace of Cateau-Cambrésis of April 1559, several events in Paris had raised the stakes considerably. The "Affair of the rue St-Jacques" of September 1557 involved some 400 people attending Protestant services. About 120 persons were arrested, and eight were executed.[9] In May of the following year, a larger Protestant assembly took place over a three-day period on the playing fields of the university students, the Pré-aux-clercs. The assembly reached 10,000 by the third day, including Antoine of Bourbon and his wife Jeanne d'Albret. Bourbon insisted to Henry that he and his wife were only curious onlookers, and the king accepted his explanation. A third episode, which occurred either in 1557 or 1558, was an assassination attempt on the king near Sainte-Chapelle in Paris. A young man, who may have been a brother to two men executed at Meaux for heresy, rushed at him with a sword. Henry avoided the thrust, and his guards seized his attacker, who was quickly executed but not before allegedly confessing to being a Protestant. Henry clearly needed peace with Philip II, if he was to be free to deal with the Protestants.

On the heels of the courier bringing the king news of the peace with Spain came word that the bishop of Nevers, Jacques Spifame, had defected to Geneva.[10] He was not the first French bishop to turn Protestant, but his flight gained far more attention because of the importance of his family of wealthy Parisian merchants. His apostasy emphasized that the Catholic episcopate was far from being made up of ardent heresy hunters. Briçonnet of Meaux was not the only bishop who actively patronized liberal humanists and moderate reformers. Prelates, including some such as Charles de Guise, the cardinal of Lorraine, who would later have a reputation as bitterly anti-Protestant, patronized the humanists. Francis I had placed many humanists in the episcopacy. A number of them came under suspicion of heresy, and several clearly became Protestant.[11]

In the early decades of the Reformation, most of these humanist bishops refused to make use of the legal machinery they controlled to prosecute accused heretics. A greater number of bishops, out of indifference, failed to pursue heresy as their offices required them to do. As one Protestant historian has written, "The reformers . . . might well be justified in regarding the negligence of the bishops as a wise providential arrangement. Many a feeble germ of truth was spared the violence of persecution until they had gained greater powers of endurance."[12] There were few French bishops before 1562 who actively tried heresy cases in their courts.

The Protestant threat to the Catholic Church and its bishops did little to persuade the prelates to reform themselves. The problems of pluralism and absenteeism in the hierarchy were at their worst in the late 1550s, 40 years after the Reformation had begun. In 1559, more than 60 percent of the French bishops had not set foot in their dioceses in the previous 12 months. The French reaction to the effort to reform the Church through the Council of Trent was decidedly negative. When Pope Paul III convoked the council in 1544, Francis I refused to allow French bishops to attend. He objected to its location in Trent, an Imperial city; he had no interest in helping the emperor solve the religious problems in Germany; and neither he nor the French hierarchy were interested in promoting reforms that would reduce the king's control over the Church and the prelates' privileges and income. Although Francis sent a few bishops to Trent eventually, they added little to its discussions; and the monarchy refused to begin to implement its decisions. Henry II's attitude toward the council when Julius III reconvened it in 1552 was even more hostile. He spoke of allying with the Swiss and the English to prevent it from meeting and prohibited French prelates from attending.

The French attitude toward Trent was very much a reflection of Gallicanism. The French Church felt it was free to make decisions on most ecclesiastical matters by itself, in national synods presided over by the king. That attitude was made all the stronger because the monarchy's relationship with the papacy was generally poor in this era. The French regarded Paul III as too sympathetic to Charles V, so when he died in late 1549, Henry II was determined to get a Frenchman or a French client elected. The conclave that followed was the second longest of the century, and it served as a clear example of blatant political interference in a papal election. Both Henry and Charles V spent great sums in bribing the cardinals and put heavy pressure on them to elect their candidates. Their activities deadlocked the conclave until Julius III, a compromise choice, was elected after 72 days.[13]

Henry accepted Julius because he expected him to be a compliant French client. When it became clear that he was recalling the Council of Trent against French wishes, Henry reacted angrily. He withdrew all the French cardinals and diplomats from Rome except for a secretary and ordered his prelates to prepare for a national synod.[14] The pope in turn threatened to excommunicate the king and give the French throne to Charles V or his son. In August 1551, the royal council discussed the possibility of establishing a French cardinal as patriarch of a national church. Henry also commissioned an ardent Gallican lawyer, Charles Du Moulin, to write a book attacking papal pretensions of authority over the Gallican Church.[15] These developments led the Swiss and the English to think that France was turning Protestant.

When both king and pope realized how close they were to schism or worse, they backed down, and the "Gallican Crisis" of 1551 ended without schism. Julius conceded more than did Henry, especially on several disputed points concerning the Concordat of Bologna, but one point on which he refused to accommodate Henry was the right of the pope to fill the benefices of French prelates who died at Rome. The king in turn refused to allow his cardinals and bishops to attend the papal court. When Julius III died in March 1555, no French cardinals reached Rome in time for the conclave, which elected Marcellus II, regarded as an implacable foe of France. Fortunately for Henry, Marcellus died within two months, and the French cardinals, who had not left Rome, secured the election of Paul IV, a bitter foe of Spain.

The political calculus of Italy changed dramatically with Paul as pope. He actively sought French aid in driving the Spanish out of Naples, setting in motion the events that led to the Battle of St-Quentin and the Peace of Cateau-Cambrésis. Paul also pressed Henry hard on eradicating heresy in his realm. With peace with Philip II in hand, Henry was able to attend to that issue after April 1559. He reportedly began to plan a military expedition to the southwest, the region said to have the most Protestants. Before he could take that step, he felt he had to deal with the Parlement of Paris, where a group of liberal magistrates were seen as thwarting heresy prosecution. In March 1559 the highest chamber reduced three death sentences to exile. Henry and the conservative Catholics were enraged, and the king ordered the Parlement to purge itself by a procedure called the *mercuriale,* a process for reviewing the handling of cases and the behavior of the magistrates.

When it became clear that a number of magistrates were liberal in their religious beliefs and that the Parlement seemed unwilling to do anything about them, the king attended the *mercuriale* in person. When Henry appeared in the court on June 10, 1559, it was the turn of the most liberal magistrates to speak. His presence did not stop several of them from openly chiding the king for preventing the reform of the Church. Henry became enraged when Anne Du Bourg, the most outspoken of the magistrates, condemned the burning of those who only called on the name of Christ while adulterers and murderers went unpunished. Henry apparently took the reference to adulterers as directed at his relationship with Diane de Poitiers. He ordered the arrest of Du Bourg and seven other magistrates. Du Bourg, who at his trial openly admitted taking Communion in the Reformed Church in Paris the previous Easter, was executed in December 1559.[16]

Despite Henry II's reputation as a relentless persecutor of Protestants, at his death in July 1559, the Huguenots, as French Protestants were being called by that time, had achieved remarkable success in increasing their numbers and organizing themselves. If one does not count the ill-fated church at Meaux in 1546, the first Protestant church was organized at Poitiers in 1554, followed by one in Paris the next year. In two years Reformed churches were organized in at least ten cities across France, and the number rose rapidly. In 1559 the Calvinists held their first national synod in Paris. It was a small group of ministers and elders under the leadership of François de Morel, the pastor at Paris, who had come from Geneva the year before. Meeting in secret, they were able to agree on a confession of faith and a statement of church discipline. The Reformed Churches (French Protestants preferred the plural) were organized along lines of semiannual provincial synods and an annual national synod.[17] By intriguing coincidence, therefore, the Protestants had created a national organization just as the political situation in France took a dramatic turn with the death of Henry II.[18]

The dynamism of the French Reformed Church was obvious in the first years after its initial national synod. Reports from across the realm revealed its incredible growth; only Brittany remained largely unaffected, perhaps because the Calvinists emphasized the use of proper French and avoided Breton. Determining its strength at the time of its zenith has proven to be impossible. An accurate count cannot be made, because there are far too many regions for which there are no numbers known, and the percentages of Protestants in those places where a count has been made fluctuated too widely to propose a norm. In early 1562 Catherine de Medici asked Admiral Coligny to assess the numbers of his coreligionists in case she needed to call on them for help. He reported that there were 2,150 churches that had pledged their help. No modern historian has compiled a list of churches larger than 1,400, or two-thirds of Coligny's figure.

Since most of the Reformed churches were newly formed in 1562 and situated in small towns or villages, it is improbable that they averaged 1,400 members, which is the number needed to reach three million people or 15 percent of the population, which is the traditional assessment of Huguenot strength. It is true, however, that several churches were huge, in particular, the one in Rouen, which may have reached 16,000 members by 1565.[19] A secret Catholic census of Paris and Lyon in this era, however, placed the number of Protestants at three or four for every hundred Catholics. Across France the total number of Protestants was probably somewhat under 10 percent, but in some regions, especially the Midi, it was well above that. There certainly is no need to argue for great numbers to explain the impact of the Huguenots. They came largely from the nobility and bourgeoisie, the two groups most active in so many aspects of French life, and they were filled with the ardor and zeal of the newly converted, while much of the Catholic population was sunk in apathy and indifference.

From early on the Protestants, following Calvin's lead and seconded by a small but vocal group of liberal Catholics, had been calling for a meeting of the Estates general and a national council, expecting that they could carry the day for their beliefs in both. Calvin had very high expectations of the Estates general of Orléans, which may have had a Protestant majority in the second and third estates. The government's success in keeping religion from being debated extensively at Orléans did little to dampen his enthusiasm, since almost immediately afterward Catherine de Medici agreed to reconvene the Estates and hold a national council.

The Estates met in 1561 at Pontoise northwest of Paris. The Second and Third Estates met alone for all but a few sessions, since the clergy was meeting largely concurrently at Poissy, eight miles away. Huguenots and Catholics opposed to the privileges of the clergy were strongly represented at Pontoise, and they presented several plans to use the church's wealth to solve the monarchy's financial problems. One, for example, would have set the annual income for the higher clergy at 6,000 *l* for bishops, 8,000 *l* for archbishops, and 12,000 *l* for cardinals. The most radical proposal called for the seizure of all the church's property, except for the buildings used for worship, and one house for each benefice-holder. It was estimated that the monarchy would have realized 120 million *l* under that proposal.

These schemes terrified the churchmen as they met at Poissy. They quickly agreed to provide the king with 1.6 million *l* a year for six years and 1.3 million *l* a year for the next ten years, for a total of 22.6 million *l*. The clergy would supervise the collection of the money, thereby avoiding the detailed scrutiny of its properties and revenues that the other two estates were demanding. Church courts had initial jurisdiction over any disputes involving money. The agreement strongly emphasized that the money was a gift to the king, not a tax, and left in place the principle that the clergy could not be taxed.

Far better known than the Contract of Poissy was the theological debate at Poissy. Catherine de Medici was determined to secure a compromise between Catholics and Calvinists for the French church, and she arranged for Theodore Beza and several other Reformed theologians to come to Poissy under royal protection. She flatly vetoed Calvin's participation. The Cardinal of Lorraine was her active partner in the colloquy, which made it more acceptable for the 50 bishops who attended; meeting face to face with a prominent heretic like Beza otherwise would have been too much for their sensibilities. Beza spent two weeks at the château of St-Germain-en-Laye where the court was, while the clergy hammered out the Contract of Poissy. He gave daily sermons in the apartment of Condé or Coligny, which half of the court attended. He sent glowing reports to Calvin that he expected the monarchy would accept the Reformed faith.

On September 9 Beza, together with eleven other Reformed ministers and a number of lay representatives appeared in the assembly at Poissy. The king and the royal family were present as Beza was called to present his case. He first enumerated the points on which both sides agreed. When he turned to those in dispute, he quickly reached the heart of the matter—the Eucharist. When he denied the real presence of Christ in the sacrament, the Catholics present shouted "He blasphemes!" Several demanded the king halt the meeting, but Beza was allowed to finish his address and present to Charles a Reformed Confession of Faith. Despite the uproar among the prelates, Catherine was determined to continue on. A week later the Cardinal of Lorraine presented the Catholic response. He surprised everyone by proposing that the Lutheran Confession of Augsburg be accepted as a compromise, but it was unacceptable to both sides. Catherine, recognizing the futility of continuing in so highly charged an atmosphere, took Beza, four of his colleagues, and five liberal Catholics to St-Germain in the hope that a small, more private discussion would be more conducive to agreement. The Catholics were more willing to compromise than were the prelates at Poissy, but when the agreement hammered out at St-Germain was presented to the latter in late September 1561, it was quickly rejected. The queen mother asked Beza to stay for three more months, essentially as an ambassador for the Huguenot party. In early 1562 he took the road back to Geneva, his mission a failure and the realm he was leaving rushing toward civil war.

10

The Nobility:
Stirrings of Trouble

The situation of the French nobility in the years between 1530 and 1562 was less unsettled than was the clergy's, at least until the last years of the era. Until then, most nobles remained reasonably prosperous. The wars that provided them with income and glory continued, and the upsurge in religious dissent little troubled them until 1559.

Economic trends, in particular the steady inflation of 2 to 3 percent per annum, were not that unfavorable to the nobles, despite the fact that they exacerbated their cashflow problems. Many nobles made the adjustments needed to keep their incomes in pace with rising prices or even ahead of them. Modern studies, however, concentrate on the great families—Albret, La Trémoille, Montmorency—who had access to talented officers to manage their estates.[1] To what extent the petty nobility took advantage of the same strategies for increasing revenues has yet to be examined, but there was nothing in what the magnates did that could not be employed by the lesser nobility as well. The diary of the sieur of Gouberville, a petty nobleman of Normandy, revealed a keen sense of how to maximize the revenues from his properties. It is impossible to say how typical he was. The most notable change the nobles made was reducing the length of leases and revenues farms, to avoid being tied into long-term leases and contracts and unable to raise rents and fees. The greatest inflation occurred in the price of grain, which had less affect on the nobility than most other groups because the grain their households used came from their own lands. It is clear that some nobles raised their income substantially, beyond the rate of inflation.[2] Both Francis I and Henry II were generous in their pension-giving, increasing both the number of nobles given pensions and the sums dispensed.

Yet many nobles failed to make the necessary adjustments, and they had to sell a considerable amount of property to cover their debts. The selling of noble estates accelerated in the 1550s and reached serious proportions by 1562. What also changed was the status of the purchasers, who were more likely to be from the haute-bourgeoisie, since they were eager to establish themselves as noblesse. This trend, along with the rising sale of royal offices to wealthy lawyers and merchants, led to bitter complaints from the nobles of the sword against venality and the nobility of the robe. These complaints reveal the perception, which had little basis in fact, that commoners were overwhelming the true nobles. By 1562 there was considerable agitation on the part of the old nobility to reverse the situation. It is clear that the nobles of the sword were not as badly off as their rhetoric suggested, but that hardly alleviated their sense of grievance. In the cahiers that the nobles prepared for the Estates of 1561, there were powerful attacks on venality and the concept that nobility was something that could be acquired by means other than birth and military service for the king.

One significant change in the privileges of the nobles was the disappearance of the right to judicial combat with a personal enemy. The old Germanic ordeal by arms in which the tribal king served as the judge evolved through the Middle Ages among the French aristocrats into judicial combat. This was a highly ritualistic affair involving a point of honor between two nobles who fought in single combat in a closed field before the king. One of the participants had to petition the king for the combat to occur, and he frequently refused permission. It was part of the tradition that a prince could not participate because of his royal blood. The winner of the combat was deemed to be in the right over the point of honor, but the fight did not have to be to the death. The victor could humiliate the vanquished even more by giving up his right to inflict the penalty of death, or the king could stop it, as Francis I did in one case in 1538 after both warriors had been injured.

There were in fact few instances of judicial combat after 1484, but the most famous was the last one. In 1544 the Dauphin Henry reportedly accused the sieur of Jarnac of being incestuously involved with his young stepmother. Jarnac denounced it as a lie, but he could not demand judicial combat because of Henry's status. One of the dauphin's friends, the sieur of La Châtaigneraie, then said he was the source of the story. Jarnac "gave him the lie," and demanded the right of judicial combat. Francis I refused it supposedly because the slight and inexperienced Jarnac was a friend of his mistress, who expected he would be killed. Henry II agreed only days after he became king. In the combat Jarnac quickly disabled La Châtaigneraie with an unexpected thrust to the back of the knee. As the injured man lay slowly bleeding to death, Henry, stunned by the quick defeat of his champion, took an excruciatingly long time before he acknowledged that Jarnac was the victor. The death of his friend and the fact that he had come close to disgracing himself by his delay led Henry to oppose judicial combat. There is disagreement over whether the edict of 1550 Henry issued applied to the entire realm or only to the army, but Henry never again approved of a request for judicial combat, nor did any future king.

Single combat was a rare event in France before 1562, but war was not. Had the nobles at the Estates of 1561 had any knowledge of how long it would be before the monarch would again direct French troops against a foreign enemy, some might have wanted a request for war included in their cahiers. War provided the nobles with wages, booty, and glory. It was, however, costly for them, not only for those whose lands near the frontier might be ravaged, but also for the many who went into debt by the cost of being fighting men. Thus, the nobles found war a two-edged sword, but it was the source of their claim to elite status and the center of life for many.

The mounted lancer was still the prince of the battlefield, at least from the French point of view, despite the changes taking place, which produced a vague sense of concern about maintaining that status. In 1534 Francis I acknowledged that the original composition of the lance companies was obsolete and reorganized them to put them in line with practice. He ordered that a lance company have three archers for every two lancers. A typical company now had 50 lancers and 75 archers, who were lightly armored lancers, despite their name. In 1549 Henry II raised their pay for the first time since before 1484, from 180 *l* a year to 400 *l* for a lancer and from 90 *l* to 200 *l* for an archer. The same edict set the age for joining a lance company at twenty years for a lancer and eighteen for an archer. The number of mounted troops in the companies remained in the range of 7,500 to 8,750 troopers until the Peace of Cateau-Cambrésis, when it dropped to 5,000. The mustering out of a large portion of the *gens d'armes* was a considerable factor in the unrest that precipitated the religious wars.

The cavalrymen whom the monarchy could raise through the *ban* and *arrière-ban* were now of even lower quality than they had been in 1484. Henry II, hoping to put some order into a highly disorganized system, established some standards for the nobles subject to the *ban* in 1549. Those whose fiefs were worth more than 500 *l* a year were to appear armed as heavy lancers accompanied by a pikeman and an harquebusier. Those with incomes below that were to assemble equipped as a mounted archer with an infantryman of either type.

Royal efforts to improve the *ban's* quality and turnout had few results. Generally, at mid-century, only one out of four fiefholders answered the summons to serve. Specifically, only 12 percent of those liable to the *ban* in the *élection* of Bayeux in 1562 turned out, although another 8 percent were serving in the royal lance companies.[3] Those who did answer the *ban* were mediocre fighting men, with poor equipment and horses. Frequently, those whom the *ban* brought out were *anoblis,* who usually had neither the training nor the spirit of the nobles of the sword. The latter frequently complained that the *anoblis* who the *ban* called to service were not worthy of the title and privileges of nobility.

Both Francis and Henry remained convinced that the armored lancer was the heart of the French army, but they also began to develop a lighter cavalry using a pike or scimitar from horseback. The latter was in imitation of the Albanians who served the French in Italy. By 1557 there were about 3,000 such troops in the army. By then there was also a corps of mounted harquebusiers who had to dismount to use their weapons. They were attached to the lance companies to provide some firepower. Not even the most arrogant lancer of 1557 was willing to charge an entrenched Spanish square of pike and harquebus until it had been softened up by firepower.

By the mid-sixteenth century, the French nobles could not ignore the fact that the infantry constituted a major threat to the lancer's domination on the battlefield. The centuries-old prejudice against arming French commoners meant that the monarchy had a great deal of difficulty in raising a native infantry force and continued to rely on foreign mercenaries. Foreigners, however, were expensive and difficult to handle, and their availability depended on political events usually beyond the control of the king. In 1534 Francis I issued an edict intended to create a powerful native infantry. It established seven legions of 6,000 men with noble commanders; they received the title of colonel, the first time the term was used in the French army. The edict set the composition of the legions at 60 percent pikemen, 30 percent harquebusiers, and 10 percent halberdmen. The legions found it difficult to fill their quota of harquebus, since firearms were still rare in France. Each legion also included fifes and tambourines for marching in step, which had become a practice for infantry. The officers were exempt from the feudal levy and paid all the time; the soldiers were freed from the *tailles* but paid only in wartime—6 *l* a month for harquebusiers and 5 *l* for the others, which compared to 7 *l* for Swiss mercenaries. The edict creating the legions also imposed strict discipline on the troops and required them to muster twice a year in peacetime to drill. The legion system, however, failed to work as intended. The infantrymen lacked discipline and usually ravaged the districts, even the French ones, through which they passed, largely because their pay was usually late. The *gens d'armes* often refused to cooperate with the legions. By 1544 the legions had fallen badly below strength, and the monarchy continued to use the older infantry companies, usually made up of Gascons, called the "bands of adventurers," alongside the legions. Foreign mercenaries remained a crucial part of the French army.

It was, therefore, a thoroughly heterogeneous army that fought the only major battle of the last decades of Francis's reign, at Ceresole in northern Italy in 1544. The army under François de Bourbon, who was only twenty-three years of age, had all of the elements noted earlier, but was especially strong in cavalry and weak in firepower. He laid siege to a town near Turin, and an Imperial army about the same size but strong in firepower and weak in cavalry approached to drive him off. Leaving some of his infantry in the siege line, Bourbon took his army to meet the enemy. The Imperial commander was a Spanish veteran of Pavia, who was convinced that firepower was the key to victory over the French. Thus, he did not entrench his army as the Spanish had done in nearly every battle since 1503 against the French, but moved directly to the attack. Harquebus fire inflicted heavy casualties on Bourbon's infantry, but it held its lines until the French cavalry, having driven off the enemy's horse, returned to smash into the flank of the Imperial infantry. This action disordered the Imperial lines and brought victory to the French. Although the *gens d'armes* had served as little more than auxiliaries, they were credited with the victory, and the battle reaffirmed French faith in the heavy lancer.

The French victory at Ceresole had no major long-term consequences in the ongoing struggle with Charles V. By 1550 it had become clear that the new style of fortification design, called the Italian trace since Italians were responsible for it, was changing warfare. Confronted by the ease with which French artillery using iron balls had battered down the high but relatively thin walls and towers of medieval fortresses in 1494, Italian military architects designed low, thick walls with triangular bastions at regular intervals. When it became obvious that the Italian trace was a significant improvement over old designs, it spread out of Italy to the north. Francis I ordered the building of a new-style fort at Vitry-le-François in Champagne to replace the one Charles V had destroyed during his invasion of 1544, which the French victory at Ceresole had not prevented. Residents were lured to the new town by a 20-year exemption from the *tailles* and other privileges. The town was laid out in a purely geometrical pattern with broad, straight streets so that troops and cannon could easily be moved from one section of the wall to another. Under Henry II the frontier with the Low Countries became a major theater of war, and he strengthened it with extensive new fortifications and reconstructed forts. The place of pride belonged to the fortress of Rocroi, which Henry ordered built in 1554, to counter a powerful Habsburg fort across the border. It blocked a major invasion route into northern France, a role that made it a major element in one of the great battles of the Thirty Years War.

Besides the negative effect the extensive fortification projects had on the royal treasury, they had a direct impact on the way war was fought. Major battles had dominated the era from 1494 to 1525 in a way that has been true for few other periods of history, since fortified places had not been able to impede the easy movement of armies. Because of the new superiority of artillery over fortification, a siege usually lasted only a few days, and an army was then free to move on to face the enemy in the field. By 1550, the use of the Italian trace was rapidly reducing the easy movement of armies in the field. The Battle of St-Quentin in 1557 was an important illustration of this point. After his forces had been victorious in the field, Philip II felt he dare not leave the major fortress of St-Quentin in the rear of his army if it pushed on to Paris. He ordered a siege of the place, which fell after six weeks but not before delaying the move on Paris until it was too late in the campaigning season. Ironically, Paris's defenses had not yet been modernized, and it would have been highly vulnerable to an attack.

The Battle of St-Quentin had another aspect that was even more indicative of trends in warfare. The Spanish army included 8,000 German pistol-carrying horsemen, whom the French called *reitres*. The pistol had been developed about 1530, but the cost of its wheellock mechanism (an early version of the later flintlock) and its unreliability limited its use to the nobility for hunting. As the quality of the pistol improved, German petty nobles began to use it off horseback for war. While they continued to wear armor, it was lighter and less expensive than that used by the lancers, and the horses they needed were smaller and more mobile. Carrying three or four loaded pistols in their hands and boots, the *reitres* rode toward the enemy line, fired their pistols at close range, and retreated to the rear of their line to reload. The pistols frequently misfired, and as a short-barrel, smooth-bore weapon they were highly inaccurate. Nonetheless, the *reitres'* mobility enabled them to use their pistols with some effectiveness and, perhaps more importantly, get out harm's way quickly.

Reitres had appeared in several battles before 1550, but they caught the attention of the French in a cavalry skirmish in 1552, during the Imperial attack on Metz. The French *gens d'armes* could not stand up to the numerous blows from the pistols. Henry II was astounded to hear that a force of pistolers not much larger than his own had so easily defeated it. He ordered Constable Montmorency to arrange for every company of *gens d'armes* to include an accompanying unit of *reitres*. This mandate was slow to be carried out until Henry received forceful proof of the *reitres'* effectiveness at St-Quentin. According to the accounts of the battle, the *reitres* played a major role in the Spanish victory. The French *gens d'armes,* on the other hand, fought very poorly. They fled the battlefield soon after the fighting began, leaving the enemy lancers and pistolers free to devastate the French infantry. Since the battle proved to be a pursuit of the panicked French army, the *reitres'* speed was a real advantage to the enemy. Henry was informed of the conduct of the battle, for he was reported as determined to rebuild his shattered forces with a large contingent of *reitres. Reitres,* he said, "are all found loaded with pistols and seemed to have been invented for the stunning and breaking up of the French men-at-arms."[4] When Henry reviewed his army a year later, he had recruited several thousand *reitres.*

Henry II's death while jousting dealt another major blow to the traditional heavy lancer. His widow, Catherine de Medici, ordered an end to jousting at the court. While tournaments did not disappear entirely from France, they received another jolt when a twelve-year-old from the House of Bourbon was killed in 1561 while he was practicing with a lance. Certainly, other factors contributed greatly to the dwindling numbers of the traditional lancers on the battlefield: their vulnerability to gunfire, their expense at a time of increasing economic trouble, and the difficulty of breeding horses strong enough to carry the lancer; but the tournaments served to emphasize the traditional values and skills of the knight. Without the opportunity to practice their skills in tournaments and impress noble ladies, the nobles let the old style of combat die in France, where it had endured longer than elsewhere in Europe.[5]

If the decline of the knightly style of fighting was upsetting to the nobility, so too was the end of war in 1559. The monarchy, faced with its enormous debt, rapidly reduced the size of the army. In a year's time, 2,000 members of the lance companies were mustered out, and the infantry saw a comparable reduction. The economic hard times of the era compounded the impact of the decline in opportunities in war. A wave of discontent spread across the French nobility, much of it directed against the monarchy after an inexperienced Francis II succeeded the old veteran Henry II. The nobles, while acknowledging that the king had a responsibility for the entire realm, believed that he had a special obligation to look after their interests. Collective bad times for the nobles had always translated into rebellion against the monarchy, and the period after 1559 was no exception.

The nobles had a high regard for Henry II, even if some of his captains objected strongly to the concessions made in the Peace of Cateau-Cambrésis. He was very much one of them—jousting, hunting, and playing sports—and he provided them with plenty of opportunity to win fortune and glory in war. It is unlikely that there would have been many defections from Henry among the nobles had he lived. His son and successor, Francis II, a sickly fifteen-year-old, could not garner the same respect from the nobles, and he openly antagonized many of them by accepting the tutelage of the House of Guise, the uncles of his queen, Mary Stuart.

The Guise were a cadet branch of the House of Lorraine, which claimed to be descended from Charlemagne. In 1503 the duke of Lorraine sent his second son Claude to France to take over the family's French fiefs, the largest of which was the county of Guise north of Paris. The same age as Francis I, Claude rendered him valuable service, especially during his captivity in Spain, and the king raised his title to duke and expanded his holdings in France. Of the ten children of Claude de Guise and Antoinette de Bourbon, the eldest three have major places in history. The first daughter, Marie, married James V of Scotland. After his death she served as regent for her daughter Mary Stuart, who was being raised at the French court. The eldest two sons, François, duke of Guise after his father's death in 1550, and Charles, the cardinal of Lorraine, had broad influence during Henry II's reign. They emerged without rivals as the dominant power at the court of Francis II within days of his succession. Their obvious ambition and their status as quasi-foreigners created deep resentment, especially in those who felt they deserved the first place at the court. The Guise's ardent Catholicism compounded the resentment among those with sympathy for the Reformation. Many nobles easily slipped into rebellion, arguing that they were only seeking to protect the king from his evil advisers. Rebellion was a habit of which the French nobility had not purged itself, despite limited practice in the previous 75 years.

Most unsettling of all to the French nobles was the presence of a new religion in the kingdom, even if the eruption of the civil wars known as the French Wars of Religion provided them with the opportunity to ply their trade again. Perhaps the most difficult aspect of sixteenth-century France to explain is the appeal of Calvinism to a significant portion of the nobility. Noble status and privileges depended upon much the same age-old traditions as did those of the Catholic clergy. James I's dictum of the next century "No bishops, no king!" applied nearly as well to the nobles. The strong bourgeois element in Calvinism could not have been appealing to them. Much of the nobility had profited from having access to high church offices for their younger sons, and being able to place their younger daughters in prestigious convents, often as abbesses, saved them from laying out large sums for dowries. There was a myriad of ways in which the nobles could siphon off some of the Church's wealth. Why then did perhaps close to half of the French nobles, including some from the highest-ranking families, become Protestant?

Certainly, the vast properties of the Church must have been tempting to the nobility, even those who had close relatives in the hierarchy. Many of the nobles had fallen afoul of church courts; they must have resented the severe disadvantages under which laypersons found themselves when involved in suits with clerics. Some were excommunicated for trivial offenses against the Church and the clergy. An important factor in the conversion of many families of the high noblesse was the influence of women.[6] Although French women did not become Protestant at a rate any higher than the men, a number of noblewomen were highly visible in their support of church reform and their adherence to the new faith. They often converted their families to their cause. Two princesses, Marguerite of Angoulême and Renée of France, had a similar range of activities in support of the reformers. Renée, who survived her cousin's death in 1549 by 25 years, made a commitment to the new religion that Marguerite, dying before the lines had hardened, had not felt obliged to make. Both princesses welcomed liberal humanists and reformers to their courts in southwestern France and Ferrara. Jean Calvin, for example, spent brief periods with both before reaching Geneva. When Renée returned to France after her husband, the duke of Ferrara, died, her château of Montargis became a place of refuge for Calvinists, until her son-in-law, François de Guise, captured it in the first war of religion. She, however, did not convert her children despite her zeal for religious reform. Marguerite's legacy was far different in that regard: her only child, Jeanne d'Albret, queen of Navarre, became a leading supporter of Calvin, with whom she carried on an extensive correspondence. In 1548 Jeanne married Antoine of Bourbon-Vendôme, the head of that cadet line of the royal family. Two years later she became queen of Navarre upon her father's death and began to implement the Reformation there. After her husband's death in 1562, she formally established Calvinism in her realm.

Jeanne d'Albret persuaded her husband Antoine to support the Reformation, although he never was as committed to it as she was. He vacillated a great deal on the matter of religion, responding to the political pressures of the moment. Nonetheless, his presence at a number of Calvinist assemblies, such as the Affaire du Pré-aux-clercs in 1558, provided encouragement to the Protestants and seemed to suggest that they had a powerful protector. Antoine's brother, Louis of Condé, also was married to a committed Calvinist, Eleonore de Roye, and converted through her influence. Louis was far more constant in his faith than was Antoine and emerged as the principal Huguenot leader in the first years of the religious wars.

The next level of the nobility had many examples of women converting their husbands and children. In the case of Louise de Montmorency, the sister of the constable, it was her children, not her husband, whom she brought to the Reformed faith, but her sons—Admiral Gaspard de Coligny, François Dandelot, colonel-general of the French infantry, and Cardinal Odet de Châtillon—were of crucial importance to the Reformed cause in France. They married noble women who converted before they did. When Odet openly became Protestant and married in 1563, he refused to give up his title of cardinal; his wife was called Madame la cardinale. The political and military leadership of the Huguenots in the religious wars included several dozen nobles whose wives or mothers brought them to the Reformed faith. Among them, to name four of the most famous, were Philippe Duplessis-Mornay, Antoine de Croy, René de Rohan, and François de Rochefoucauld.

Sincere religious conviction was the reason behind the conversions of many French nobles, as the significant number who became Reformed ministers demonstrated. Out of the 88 ministers whom Calvin sent back into France from Geneva between 1555 and 1562, 14 of the 42 for whom social status could be determined came from the nobility.[7] Nonetheless, it is hard to avoid the conclusion that for many others, politics, both national and local, played a major role in their decisions to join the Huguenots. When a well-organized and powerful Huguenot party appeared in 1560, it seemed to provide the clout needed by those whose well-being was being threatened by the economic and political changes taking place. Objections to the enormous power wielded by the Guise under Francis II were a factor in the presence of many prominent noblemen in the Huguenot ranks; in particular, that was true of the Bourbons.

The sieur of Gouberville, however, was probably more representative of the nobility in his response to the appearance of the new faith. In his diary he reported attending Reformed sermons in 1561 and 1562, using the Calvinist term *temple* for the place where he heard a sermon in August 1562. Yet, later in 1562 he took an oath of obedience to the king and the Catholic Church and reported hearing the sermon of a Franciscan. He also described arranging to be buried in the local Catholic church. Unlike many of his fellow nobles, Gouberville was not a warrior and avoided getting involved in the fighting that was breaking out in his region of western Normandy. Had he been more eager to fight, he might well have taken arms for the Huguenot cause in 1562, thereby making a commitment to both the new religion and rebellion that later would have been difficult to undo. It is probable that many petty nobles found themselves committed to the Protestant camp before they fully realized what was involved.

On the local level it is intriguing to note how often a noble family, which was involved in a long-term feud with another local noble house, joined the Huguenot party, while the rival family became active in the Catholic opposition. Many nobles also followed their patrons into one or the other of the religious factions, but there were frequent defections from patrons as well. Other factors often were more compelling than the client-patron relationship. One was simply the opportunity to fight; there is little doubt that a large portion of the fighting men on both sides of the religious wars fought with little or no religious conviction.

The Tumult of Amboise of 1560 demonstrated several of these points. The Huguenot high nobility had little to do with the conspiracy; only Condé knew of it in advance, and he did not take an active role. The leader of the conspiracy was involved in a bitter feud with a prominent Catholic noble of the robe over lands and church benefices. Two noble Calvinist ministers were actively involved, as were several nobles who were the clients of prominent Catholic magnates, including the duke of Guise. It is clear that for many of those who were implicated in the conspiracy, the political mandate of saving the king from the usurpers was their overriding concern.

That so many of the nobles of the sword took part in what the crown saw as treason was the major reason why the Estates general was convoked later that year and again the next. The cahiers of the Second Estate at Pontoise with its large Huguenot contingent included bitter recriminations against venality, the inclusion of non-nobles in the judicial and royal offices, the practice of admitting commoners into the nobility for reasons other than for service in war, and indirect taxes such as the *aides* and *gabelles* that the nobles had to pay. The noblesse called for meetings of the Estates every two years. As of 1561 there was a strong sense that the monarchy was slipping away from its traditional support of noble rights and privileges, and the nobility had the right to use force to bring it back to its proper policy. For many nobles, that, not religious doctrine or the right to defend the true religion, was the principal reason for what violence had already occurred, and for the far greater violence that was about to erupt.

11

The People:
Hard Times Looming

The most powerful force affecting the lives of the common people of France in the years from 1530 to 1562 was the accelerating population growth. It was so obvious, at least in Languedoc, that someone remarked the people there were breeding like mice in a barn.[1] As is usual for populations, the rate of growth accelerated as France approached the "full world," the peak carrying capacity of the land, which for preindustrial France was about 20 million people. In some areas that full world was reached by 1560; in others it took another decade or two.

By 1530, however, French grain production was close to its maximum output. The enormous rise in production since 1450 was achieved by putting all arable land under cultivation rather than by introducing new agricultural techniques or new crops. There was little additional land available that was suitable for grain. Therefore, as the population continued to surge upward for several more decades, tremendous pressure was placed on the grain supply, which was reflected in rising bread prices. The price of wheat more than doubled between 1510 and 1540, while prices for products such as wine, eggs, and mutton lagged well behind. The production of these products could be expanded more than wheat, since they did not require good land.

It was not only the pressure of population growth that created rising prices; the inflow of American gold and silver through Spain also had an inflationary impact. The Spanish suffered from greater inflation, and since French prices lagged behind theirs, they found that many French products were cheaper. Most French kings issued edicts forbidding the export of wheat, but it was impossible to control. Furthermore, the export of wheat was a major source of bullion for a realm with few native sources. The export of grain and other commodities had a twofold inflationary impact: It reduced the supplies available in the French markets and increased the amount of money in circulation. The overall rate of inflation was low, not more than 2 percent annually until 1562, but the steady price rise over several decades, in a society that had no understanding inflation could occur, had a profound impact on the economy.

It was the poor, both rural and urban, who first felt the pinch of the deteriorating economy. Wages were stagnant, as population growth increased the supply of labor and prices climbed. Extraordinary inflation in the price of bread hurt the poor the most because it always was their largest expense. Population growth hurt the poor day-laborers in another way. Most jobs required a set amount of labor; if more laborers were available, the overseers would hire more to finish the job quickly, thereby reducing the number of days of work for each laborer. As economic problems began to press the landlords, they often used female laborers, who were paid considerably less than men.

Changes in land tenancy patterns also reflected economic developments, especially the trend toward consolidation of holdings. Families in trouble borrowed heavily and then found they could not pay off the loans. They were often forced to concede their properties or rights of tenancy to their creditors. Larger families also had an impact: the sons divided the family holdings and the daughters required dowries. Last, the heavy royal taxes had the worst impact on the rural poor. All of these factors created a dramatic surge in the number of vagabonds, beggars, and highwaymen. Becoming soldiers was not yet an option for more than a few of the dispossessed laborers. As a result the roads and byways were more dangerous than they were around 1500. The monarchy enacted harsh edicts against vagabonds, which required royal officers to prevent the formation of large groups and force the able-bodied to work. In 1537 all vagabonds were declared rebels against royal authority, and anyone was free to kill them.

The price rise did not make everyone in the countryside destitute, even if it benefited the urban merchant class the most. Tenants and sharecroppers whose leases provided them with a large portion of the crop profited from the rise in grain prices, although many landholders soon recognized the trend and put much effort into revising leases in their favor. Vineyards expanded greatly. Planting a vineyard was labor-intensive, and a large supply of cheap labor and good wine prices encouraged landholders to put marginal land into vines. The vast expansion of wine production kept prices from rising as rapidly as those for grain and most other commodities. Even the expansion in wine exports to England, made possible in large part by improvements in sailing ships, did not noticeably affect the prices. The rapid expansion of brandy production after 1550 provided wine producers with a product that had a high profit margin and was easily shipped abroad. The production of woad near Toulouse benefited its rural producers even as it created vast fortunes for the woad magnates in the city. Silk was another luxury item whose demand increased more rapidly than did the economy overall, as tends to be the case for luxury items. Silk production benefited a broader number of urban participants, such as weavers and merchants, than did woad, but in the countryside around centers of the silk industry such as Lyon and Nîmes, landholders and tenants planted mulberry trees and supplemented their incomes.

While vagabonds and highwaymen were a more serious problem overall, the monarchy was more concerned about the larger, more organized episodes of popular violence, which increasingly involved opposition to heavy taxes. The largest popular revolt before the religious wars erupted in 1547 over the *gabelles*.[2] In 1541 Francis I mandated a large increase in the tax for the provinces of the southwest, which been nearly exempt. The edict put the tax there at the same high level as in the rest of the realm. The drastic increase in the cost of salt, coming on top of other royal infringements on local autonomy in a region that less than a century earlier enjoyed vast autonomy under the English, led to riots and violence in La Rochelle and the countryside around it. The king temporarily backed down, ending the riots, but in 1546 he issued a new edict reestablishing the new *gabelle*. It went into effect after Henry II succeeded his father. As soon as it did, tax farmers swarmed into Guyenne "like locusts" to take huge profits. In April 1548, violence erupted near the town of Saintes and quickly spread across Guyenne. One of the several ragtag armies of the Pétaults, "disorderly ones," near Périgueux was said to have numbered 40,000 men. Peasants and urban laborers and artisans cooperated in seizing control of numerous towns and Bordeaux itself. Nobles, wealthy townspeople, and especially royal officials were murdered. Most ominous for the monarchy, Tristan de Moneins, the lieutenant to the governor of Guyenne, was struck down as he negotiated with the rebels.

Henry II dispatched Anne de Montmorency with an army to crush the revolt. Although most of the violence ended by the time the constable arrived in the southwest, he imposed harsh retribution on the rebels. Hundreds were executed, often after gruesome tortures, and the townspeople of Bordeaux were forced to exhume Moneins's body and rebury it in the cathedral with proper ceremony. The harshest penalties, beyond the executions meted out to rural and urban dwellers alike, were reserved for the towns that revolted. The towns had charters and royal privileges that were revoked, and even the Parlement of Bordeaux was dissolved for a time for failing to maintain law and order. The rustics, however, had little to lose besides their lives for rebellion.

The Gabelle revolt demonstrated a characteristic that was fairly common among the popular revolts of the later sixteenth century—cooperation between the rural and the urban *menu peuple* (little people). Their worlds were different in many ways, but their responses to onerous oppression, heavy taxes, and food shortages were similar in the nature of the violence they used. Many of the urban day-laborers had close ties to the villages in the region, having migrated to the town only recently. It was easy for them to find common cause with their rural relatives and friends. A portion of the urban day-laborers were seasonal or longer-term residents who intended to return to their villages or, often, were forced to return.

With wages stagnant and consumer prices rising, the urban day- laborers found themselves increasingly on edge. The municipal governments in turn became concerned about the presence of poverty-stricken persons in the cities and sought remedies. One was a significant increase in organized municipal poor relief, which supplemented or even replaced the traditional handouts to beggars by individuals and religious establishments. Although conservative Catholics protested the change, those advocating it included Catholics as well as Protestants, at least in Lyon where the new system was put in place in 1539. Some 5 to 7 percent of the population received aid.[3] Francis I in 1544 granted Paris the authority to supervise and conduct poor relief , and seven years later, Henry II allowed the city to collect a poor tax. The changes in poor relief, however, were haphazard at best; there was no effort to systematize it across the realm. As conditions worsened after 1560, even improved poor relief could not accommodate all the destitute. The towns then worked to improve their ability to prevent the poor from entering and ousting those already in residence. With religious tensions drastically increasing, those towns in the control of one or the other religion sought to prevent the poor from entering because it was assumed they were adherents of the opposite faith and would cause religious riots.

Artisan guilds were instinctively conservative when it came to business, and found it difficult to adjust to rising prices. Accordingly, many of the guild masters and the journeymen who worked for them fell behind, while others, especially but not exclusively from the newer trades, rode the crest of rising prices to prosperity. One new trade, the printing industry, had a great deal of difficulty with its journeymen. In 1539 they engaged in a strike against the masters in the two major centers of printing, Paris and Lyon.[4] The removal to the countryside of much of the cloth industry hurt the weavers in many towns, and reduced significantly the number of women who participated in the guild system. Growing economic difficulties also negatively affected the ability of widows to take over their dead husbands' shops. That trend hardly placated the large number of journeymen, whose acquisition of their own shops was adversely affected by the economic problems and the practice of passing shops to the masters' male relatives. Last, artisans felt the impact of efforts to reduce their influence in the communes or eliminate it entirely. In many French towns, the bourgeois elite took steps to create an oligarchy made up of themselves, often with the cooperation of the monarchy or local royal officials. Artisans frequently responded with violence, and tensions in French towns were considerably higher after 1530.

As a group the merchants prospered. They were more capable of keeping up with inflation, or even ahead of it, than the other urban classes, which resulted in a substantial redistribution of wealth into their hands. The gap between merchants and artisan guild masters increased considerably, but the most obvious development was the enormous growth in the number of mercantile magnates. Many of them made their fortunes in new commodities or through changes in the trading patterns of old ones. The woad merchants of Toulouse were prime examples of how in the space of a generation a handful of merchant families gained incredible wealth and dominated their city. The diversion of much of the spice trade from the Mediterranean to the Atlantic benefited the spice merchants of Rouen and Bordeaux. The growth of the silk industry in Lyon and Nîmes led to the appearance of silk magnates in those cities. The shifting of at least some trade to the Atlantic coastal cities had no impact on Lyon, which remained the commercial center of France. A great deal of Lyon's commerce was in the hands of Italians, who controlled much of the business in the entire realm.[5]

Italians had an even larger share of Lyon's banking business, which was the major reason for the city's importance in the French economy. The vast expansion of royal loan-taking was centered in the Lyon banking fair. Henry II's suspension of payments for one quarter in 1558 hardly affected the eagerness of bankers to lend to the king. It was not only the Lyonnais bankers who profited from filling the monarchy's need for credit; wealthier merchants across France also did. Lending vast sums to the king at high interest rates was the major way that wealth was redistributed to the urban elite in the sixteenth century.

Far more productive of change in the social and political structures of French cities was the dramatic growth in the sale of royal offices to wealthy bourgeoisie. The sale of a royal office was quite similar to a loan in that the king received a lump sum, the principal, from the would-be officer and paid out a salary, which served as interest; but in the case of venality the arrangement lasted for the officeholder's lifetime. Venality became a significant factor in wealth redistribution and the urban political and social structures when Francis I began the large scale sale of offices. Once all the offices in place in 1515 were sold, Francis, and more so his successors, created new offices within old courts and entirely new courts. Provincial branches of courts long established in Paris proliferated, with the result that the growth in royal offices was probably more obvious in provincial towns than in Paris.

The Parlement and several other royal courts long exercised the dominant role in Parisian government; the proliferation of royal offices had little obvious impact on either Paris's political or social structures. In many of the provincial towns, the impact was much greater. At Montpellier, for example, not only did the number of royal offices in its *généralité* rise from 111 in 1500 to 252 in 1575, but the portion who lived in the city increased also. Even more dramatic was the change at Dijon, where the number of high officials went from seven in 1464 to 70 in 1556.[6] Following closely in the train of the royal offices were lawyers, whose numbers grew with the royal offices. The royal officers accumulated properties both in and outside the towns. Given that most officers came from bourgeois families already well off, the additional income, often considerable, moved them to the top of the pyramid of wealth for their towns. With wealth, of course, came political power. More and more, royal officers replaced the merchants as the dominant oligarchy in many cities.

This trend was acceptable to the monarchy, notwithstanding Henry II's edict of 1547 prohibiting royal officers from holding high positions in municipal governments. Since many of the high royal officials were exempt from taxes, it was presumed that they, as municipal leaders, would be more likely to acquiesce in the king's demands if new taxes had little impact on them. Many of the *bonnes villes,* at least 37, maintained their exemption from the *tailles,* but in 1538 Francis I requested all 246 towns to contribute to a special tax to pay 20,000 foot soldiers. Henry II increased the personnel thus supported to 50,000 men and made the *soldes pour les 50,000 hommes de pied* a regular part of the royal revenues. In time of war it totaled 1.2 million *l* but was reduced during peace. The kings also asked for gifts of money from the cities, which the municipal governments had to raise by taxing their inhabitants, including those otherwise exempt from taxes. Requests for these gifts were nothing new, but the sums involved now were far larger. In 1557, for example, after the defeat at St-Quentin, Catherine de Medici went to the Hôtel de ville of Paris to request 300,000 *l* from the city. Whatever Paris agreed to provide constituted 20 percent of the total sum the cities of the realm would provide the king, but it is not known how many cities contributed to the 1.5 million *l.* The crushing tax burden of the last years of Henry II's reign weighed heavily on the commoners in general, but the urban artisans probably felt the new load the most. They paid a disproportionate share of the drastically increased taxes on the *bonnes villes,* and over several decades they went from being undertaxed to overtaxed. By the time of Henry's death, unrest in the cities, led by the artisans, was becoming serious.

From the monarchy's point of view, a great deal of the sedition and agitation among the common people was created by the presence of heretics. There is little question that there was a close correlation between unrest among the French commoners and attraction to the Reformation in the several years after Henry II's demise. A factor in many towns was opposition to the churchmen, usually a bishop but often a monastery or cathedral chapter, with feudal rights over them. The Protestant party provided coherence and added motivation to the task of stripping churchmen of their power. The groups active in the urban communes—merchants and artisans—were those primarily interested in overthrowing the authority of the ecclesiastical seigneurs. In many towns, where political power was restricted to an oligarchy of merchants, the tension was between merchants and artisans. In such places the incidence of Protestantism among the artisans was unusually high.[7]

Among the urban classes the artisan journeymen early on were most attracted to Reform. By 1559, the economic downturn left a large portion of the journeymen with little hope of owning their own shops. Frustrated and bitter at the comfortable existence of much of the Catholic clergy they saw about the town, the journeymen found the revolutionary elements implicit in Calvinism appealing. There was something of a generation gap involved, as the journeymen from those trades where the masters mostly remained Catholic had the largest percentages of converts to the new church. In the next generation the most ardent Catholics were often journeymen working for Protestant master artisans.

The attraction of Protestantism was strong among master artisans as well. Although much research has gone into identifying specific trades that had a large Protestant cohort, such as printers, there was little consistency across the entire realm. Local circumstances appear to have had much to do with such patterns. A large portion of the artisans was literate, and the Protestant emphasis on direct access to the Word in their own language had to be highly satisfying to those who felt most keenly the injustice of the special status of the Catholic churchmen.

Merchants were less well represented among the Calvinists across France, although in many towns they made up a significant part of the leadership. In the Midi merchants and town officials constituted a larger part of the Calvinist movement than in northern France. In many small towns in the Midi, and several of the larger ones such as Nîmes, Calvinists took control and established

"Protestant republics," dominated by a Calvinist magistracy. They established the Reform in the towns in much the same fashion it been done in the cities of the Empire and Switzerland. It was the strength of Calvinism in the southern towns that was responsible for the term "Protestant Crescent": the band of land where Calvinism was the strongest, stretching from La Rochelle in the west through Guyenne, Languedoc, and up the Rhône valley to Lyon. Protestants may have constituted a majority of the townspeople within the crescent. Even there, however, the attraction of the Reformation to the peasants was weak, albeit stronger than in the rest of the realm.

Is there in this social and geographical distribution of French Protestantism any validation of Max Weber's thesis, which proposed a causal relationship between Protestantism, especially the Reformed churches, and the development of capitalism? The appeal of Calvinism to many French artisans and merchants may well have come from Calvin's call for the sanctification of work. A religion proposing that rewards ought to come to those who worked hard instead of to an indolent clergy, who seemed to prosper regardless of whether it worked or prayed, to say nothing of being holy, surely had to appeal to the urban middle classes.

Should not the same elements have appealed to the French peasantry? The ritual and practices of Catholicism were the products of the agrarian society of the early Middle Ages: highly visual for an illiterate society, in contrast to Calvinism's whitewashing of the churches; and filled with devices to gain control over nature, whose dangers pervaded the life of peasants. Calvin not only abandoned those elements but also loudly denounced them. Catholicism also provided a vast number of feast days as obligatory days of rest. For peasants, whose labor was largely expended for others, feast days came at little or no cost, unless they fell during the harvest, which, it is worth noting, few did. For the middle classes, a holy day was a missed opportunity to make a profit. Perhaps one should ask why any peasants became Calvinists at all.

One should not assume, however, that French peasants and bourgeoisie who remained Catholic accepted the privileges of the clergy and their abuses without criticism. In the countryside many peasants, Catholic as often as Protestant, refused to pay the tithe. Catholic deputies for the Third Estate at the Estates of 1560 and 1561 collaborated with the Calvinists and demanded dramatic reductions in the church's wealth and even its confiscation. The cahiers of the Third Estate and the address of its orator also denounced the heavy taxes imposed by the monarchy. The Third Estate at the meeting in Orléans had a large number of Calvinist deputies, and they had a major role in drawing up the 13 cahiers, one for each of the *governements*. The orator of the Third summarized them in his address, which attacked the corruption and wealth of the clergy, the abuses in the system of justice, and the excesses of the court. Although the Third Estate included a few remarks about the nobility's abuse of privilege, the meetings of both 1560 and 1561 were unusual in the close cooperation between the Second and Third Estates. It made the denunciation of the clergy's wealth more ominous for the churchmen.

Schemes for using the clerical revenues to relieve the royal financial crisis and the tax burdens on the people have received the most attention, but there was more to the program of the Third Estate. One proposal called for meetings of the Estates every two years, although the nobility was ready to accept ten-year intervals between assemblies. Another demanded that the Estates general be convoked to approve of any new tax and any declarations of war and peace. Concerning the church the Third called for the election of bishops by the curés of the diocese and the archbishops by the bishops of the archdiocese. A more radical proposal would have added a number of lay notables to the electors. The deputies of the Third Estate wanted to enhance the ability of bishops to visit and reform monasteries and convents and prevent persons from taking religious vows before the age of thirty for men and twenty-five for women. They also called for a drastic limitation of the scope of ecclesiastical jurisdiction beyond what been done in the Edict of Villers-Cotterêts of 1539, and a sharp reduction in the use of excommunication and other spiritual penalties.

The monarchy conceded a few points, especially concerning the clergy, in the Ordinances of Orléans, but they remained a dead letter. While the meetings of the Estates in 1560 and 1561 produced little in the way of permanent reform, the cahiers of the Third Estate provide insight into the views of some of the more articulate commoners. They were opposed to royal absolutism and promoted the idea that the people in the Estates general shared sovereignty with the king. While the Third was eager to give the wealth of the clergy over to the monarchy, it did not offer anything of its own. Feeling that they were already taxed far too heavily, the commoners refused to take on any more of the realm's tax burden. Given the radical nature of the cahiers that the Third Estate produced and its failure to accommodate the king's desperate financial needs, there was no chance that the cornerstone of its program, frequent meetings of the Estates, would be met.

12

Justice:
Missed Opportunities

The complaints of the deputies at the Estates general of 1560 and 1561 focused first on the wealth and corruption of the clergy, but close behind were concerns about the legal system. The previous 30 years had seen an explosion in the number of judicial offices in the realm and a drastic expansion of venality to the entire range of royal offices, except, significantly, those in the military, where a combination of rank and, less so, merit remained the criteria for appointments. Once Francis I became comfortable with the concept that judicial offices could be sold, he quickly saw how it could be a relatively painless way to raise money for the royal fisc. Early in his reign all of the fiscal offices were venal, but it was in justice that the expansion of venality was most obvious. In the Parlement of Paris, for example, the number of magistrates increased from near 80 to 150 in Francis's reign, while the Parlement at Bordeaux went from 29 to 66. Another device was creating new chambers in the Parlements, such as a Chambre des enquêtes in Paris and a Chambre de tournelle at Dijon. All of the new offices were venal. In addition to increasing the number of conseillers in every Parlement, Francis also added to their staffs—*avocats du roi,* ushers, notaries, bailiffs—while putting these offices up for sale. Both the price of royal offices and the salaries paid to their incumbents increased sharply in the course of Francis's reign.

Francis I made other changes in the Parlements in order to increase the royal take. Resignation in favor was a device by which an incumbent could pass his office on to his heir without paying a fee. Francis required the person receiving an office in this way to pay a fee of 10 percent of its value to the king. If the resigning magistrate died within 40 days after he agreed to resign, the office reverted to the king, who could then charge the full price for it, usually from the recipient designated in the resignation. The king also used the threat of creating new offices in a court to extract money from the incumbents, who feared that new offices would reduce the value of theirs. When, for example, he proposed the creation of 20 new seats in the Parlement of Paris, he responded to the complaints of the parlementaires by telling them they could pay him the 120,000 *l* he expected to get from the new offices. In this case, they refused. When, however, in 1543 he threatened to erect a Chambre des comptes for Normandy, he extracted 246,875 *l* from the Norman Estates to abandon the idea. The purchasers of the offices expected to recoup the cost with the salary for the office and, more so, the opportunities for graft and bribe-taking. For many it was the prestige attached to a royal office that made them worth purchasing, not the possible financial gain; the haute-bourgeoisie in particular were purchasing the noble status that many offices conferred. By 1547 the monarchy collected about 900,000 *l* annually from venal offices.

If Francis I established the practice of venality in France, Henry II carried it to unimagined heights. In addition to his father's technique of creating new offices and courts, Henry struck on an innovative approach—the semester system for the Parlement of Paris and the *alternatif* system in the fiscal offices. In the semester system established in 1554, each office had two incumbents who exercised its authority for six-month periods. Having paid 10,000 *l* apiece, up from 6,750 *l* before 1547, they received the same salary and shared equally in the fees and gifts. The king made a major concession to the magistrates: He reduced the number of offices to 87, what it was in 1515, so that the semester system resulted in a relatively modest increase in the total number of parlementaires. The system of *alternatif* was identical, except that the term of office was for a full year. About 310 offices were doubled by the edict of 1553 establishing the *alternatif* in the fiscal system.[1]

In the short term Henry's changes brought in vast sums of money to the royal treasury, but in the long run, the additional salaries for the new officers began to put an enormous new burden on the royal fisc. The innovations, however, did not last long. Several of the new financial offices were dropped as early as 1555, and most of the rest by 1560, because of expense and inefficiency. Many cases brought to the Parlement had to be heard twice. The semester system caused a great deal of tension between king and magistrates. In 1558 the king agreed to end the semester system, but he did not remove the additional magistrates, who were utilized in a new Chambre du conseil.

While the semester system was a blatant financial expedient, Henry II was responsible for two more changes in the legal system that were better justified, even as they created new offices to be sold. One was the erection of a Parlement for Brittany in 1554. Courts with that title had existed off and on since 1491, but Henry made it permanent, having it meet alternately at Rennes and Nantes. After 1569 it always met at Rennes. The court was organized with four presidents and 32 conseillers; half of the latter had to be native Bretons. More significant a change was the erection of the presidial courts. The legal system provided for an almost unlimited right of appeal to the Parlements for the most petty cases, and even to the king. Cases often took a decade or more to resolve, and minor litigation choked the higher courts. Henry II, probably responding to complaints from the parlementaires, issued an edict in 1551 that created the *siège présidial* as an intermediate court to serve as the court of final appeal for all cases involving a value of less than 250 *l.* The new courts were erected above the local *baillis* and *sénéchaux* and their districts consisted of several of the older units. Eight venal offices were created for each new court, and the personnel came from the lower courts.[2] In 1557 Henry created a chancery and an office of president for the presidial courts and raised the upper limit of cases it heard to 1,000 *l.* The new limit was set too high and failed to take hold, but overall, the new presidial courts worked well, effectively reducing the caseload of the Parlements and rendering justice more quickly and cheaply in minor cases. Henry and his successors, however, tinkered with these courts to increase the number of venal offices, and thereby reduced their effectiveness.

Unlike the numerous changes in the judicial system, there was only one substantial edict on the law itself from 1530 to 1562, but it was the most important one of the century. The Ordinance of Villers-Cotterêts of 1539 "on the subject of the legal system" consisted of 192 articles. The first eight dealt with changing the relationship between the royal courts and the church courts in favor of the former. The Catholic Church had its own set of courts. Every bishop possessed a court called the *officialité*, whose presiding judge was the bishop's *official.* Like every medieval court it had assistants, lawyers, notaries, and prosecutors. It had two vast spheres of jurisdiction: cases involving churchmen and those touching on the sacraments. Every tonsured cleric came under the official's competence, according to canon law, but church courts also claimed cases involving those who fell under the special protection of the Church—pilgrims, crusaders, and widows and orphans. Whether a matter was criminal or civil, it was heard in the *officialité* if it involved one of those groups, regardless of whether the other party in civil cases was from the laity. In the church courts' second area of jurisdiction, anything involving marriages, wills, and burials was included, as were violations of church law on such matters as usury, working on Sundays and holy days, and eating meat during Lent and on Fridays. More obviously, the *officialité* handled accusations of heresy, sorcery, witchcraft, and blasphemy.

In order to enforce its decisions, a church court had to "call on the secular arm," since it had no *sergents* of its own. It was actually the state that executed recalcitrant heretics, sorcerers, and blasphemers. Generally such executions were done by burning at the stake. Other penalties for "religious" crimes included public whippings, exile, fines, and confiscation of goods. Most of those found guilty were obliged to make an *amende honorable,* in which they stood at the main door of the local church on Sunday or a feast day, holding a candle of specified size, and dressed in a white shift. They had to proclaim their sins in a loud voice and beg the forgiveness of God and the king.

The royal government nearly always was cooperative in regard to religious crimes, but the church courts frequently had difficulty in enforcing their decisions in civil matters between the clergy and the laity. The churchmen, therefore, were quick to use excommunication as an enforcement tool. Laypersons who refused to pay disputed debts of a few *livres* to clerics often found themselves denounced from the pulpit as excommunicates, outside the community of the faithful and damned to hell unless they conceded. In canon law, appeals from an *officialité* went directly to the papal court, which was a truly expensive proposition. However, the monarchy usually sought to prevent appeals to Rome, creating never-ending disputes with the papacy.

Since the French kings were subjected to the church's "spiritual arm," excommunication, they were attentive to suggestions from their advisers, many of whom were trained in Roman law with its strong streak of caesaro-papism, to curb the power of the church courts. It was also a major tenet of Gallicanism to limit papal jurisdiction in France to a minimum. The principal means of achieving these goals was a legal device called *appel comme d'abus.* It appeared in the mid-fifteenth century and involved an appeal to a royal court on the grounds that the church court did not have jurisdiction in the matter in question or its sentence was excessive. Even if the appeal was not taken to the Parlement immediately, the case nearly always wound up there, since the lower secular courts invariably decided against the church court, while the clergy was determined to defend its prerogatives. The Parlement and the royal council, which heard its share of appeals from the Parlement, rarely decided in favor of the church courts. By 1539 the use of *appel comme d'abus* began to narrow the range of cases heard in church courts. In particular secular courts had jurisdiction over serious criminal cases involving clerics. The Ordinance of Villers-Cotterêts forbade the citing of laypersons before church courts, except for matters that were clearly spiritual or pertained directly to the sacraments. The civil courts gained jurisdiction over every cleric accused of a crime involving "public scandal," not only the most serious crimes. What was meant by public scandal was left undefined, allowing the royal courts a great deal of latitude in deciding what cases to take from the church courts. The *procureur du roi* in the local royal courts had the authority to invoke *appel comme d'abus* without a request from a party in a case. In the long term the church courts lost perhaps five-sixths of their case load as a result.

The most famous article in the Ordinance of Villers-Cotterêts mandated the use of French in place of Latin or any other language in the royal courts, both for the oral procedures and the written documents. The purpose was to ensure that there would be no misunderstandings before the court and eliminate the need for translation. There is no reason to suppose that it was intended to further the use of Parisian French in place of the various dialects, but that was the result. The spread of the king's French into the regions of the Occitan and Provençal dialects was swift after 1539, and its use in Brittany also increased significantly, although Breton held out far more successfully than did the other dialects.

The main concern of the edict, however, was speeding up legal procedures in both criminal and civil cases. The French of the sixteenth century were a highly litigious people, and petty civil suits were crowding criminal cases off the court dockets. Francis I's solution mandated that criminal proceedings take priority. It may seem surprising that such a matter of common sense needed an edict, but the civil suits of the elite were being heard before all but serious criminal cases. The edict also contained a number of articles designed to speed up the handling of civil suits, some of which applied to criminal cases. It was in the context of reducing litigation over property rights that the ordinance required parishes to keep a register of births and deaths, but the church was slow in implementing the new law.

French criminal justice depended on written depositions from accusers, accused, and witnesses, which were taken mostly at royal expense, and little on evidence in the modern sense. Francis's solution to the problem of cost denied the defendant legal counsel to interrogate witnesses and draw up appeals to a higher court. Denying bail to the defendants, which the edict also mandated, hampered their ability to produce new witnesses after the process began, which was a major cause of delay. "Justice delayed is Justice denied!" became a major principle of the French legal system after 1539. This, not reducing the rights of defendants, was the motive behind yet another change requiring that the decision to use judicial torture be communicated to the defendant immediately and carried out promptly. Any appeal of the decision to submit a defendant to torture had to be taken directly to the local Parlement instead of going through the several layers of the judicial system under the Parlement, which was delaying the process. Nonetheless, torture was not common in France until the late sixteenth century when it was used routinely in cases of witchcraft. In 1539-42, the Parlement of Paris ordered torture in only 8.5 percent of the criminal cases it heard.[3] It was used little more in heresy cases; the special heresy chamber of the Parlement of Paris, the Chambre ardente, notorious for its severity, applied torture in only 11 percent of its cases. The major exception was witchcraft, because most of those accused were innocent and often would not admit guilt except under torture. The number of executions per year for crimes other than witchcraft in cases heard by the Parlement of Paris edged slowly upward from about 60 in 1540 to 70 in 1610, but its case load also increased substantially. All sentences of capital punishment were automatically appealed to the Parlement.

Henry II published no major ordinance on law, but he did have an impact on the legal status of marriage through an edict of 1556 that outlawed marriages made without parental consent. Priests performing weddings were obliged to publish the banns of marriage before they took place, ensure that there were four witnesses, not two, and know the age of the couple. Henry's motive for drawing up the edict may have been to accommodate Constable Montmorency, who was furious with his oldest son for pledging marriage to a woman of lower status than the father thought appropriate. But it may have come out of complaints that young Protestants were marrying without the consent of their Catholic parents, or it may have reflected a growing sense that marriage vitally concerned the state as well as the church. Clandestine marriages were henceforth deemed invalid, and the penalty for undertaking such a marriage was disinheritance. Prior to the edict, the courts were involved in marital matters through disputes over wills and inheritances; now they were to sit in judgment on the nature of the marriage itself. The law also dramatically increased parental authority over even adult children and ensured that marital alliances were made with the interests of the family in mind, not the emotional fulfillment of the couple.[4] The same edict contained a draconian clause on infanticide. Every pregnant woman was obliged to register her pregnancy and have a witness at the birth. Should the child turn up dead and one of these two mandates not been followed, the presumption was that the mother was guilty of infanticide, with the penalty of execution.

The growing tendency to involve the royal government in overseeing the morals and behavior of its subjects was also revealed in the edict of 1561 that banned brothels from the realm. The Third Estate asked for such a law at Orléans. A reforming spirit in regard to prostitution was already in evidence, which led several cities to close their brothels even before 1561, as Toulouse did in 1557. Another factor may have been the connection between brothels and the spread of syphilis, although the length of time between the appearance of the disease and the law argues against a close connection. Syphilis was called the Italian pox or the Neapolitan disease because soldiers returning from the campaign of 1494 brought it to France. The edict also was directed against the disorder associated with brothels and taverns at a time when the urban elite were becoming concerned about the large number of masterless people and the increasing incidence of lower-class violence in the towns. The law, of course, failed miserably in ending prostitution but resulted in more prosecution of prostitutes and pimps. It had the effect of increasing the burden on poverty-stricken women who were forced to sell sex at a time when honorable employment was becoming harder to find. It was applied erratically across the realm, and as of 1614 some towns, such as Montpellier, had reputations as places with lax enforcement of the legislation on morality.

In the mid-sixteenth century, the royal courts also became more involved in the prosecution of witchcraft. It was another area where Roman law had a strong impact, although its influence was filtered through the procedures of the Inquisition and not applied directly. To be precise, it was the Roman law on treason with its emphasis on the necessity of the testimony of two witnesses and the use of torture to secure confessions, which the Inquisition adopted in the thirteenth century. After all, were not heresy and devil worship treason against God? Inquisitional procedure gave the inquisitor a great deal of freedom to seek out evildoers instead of waiting for accusations, on the grounds that these crimes would be committed in secret. Consequently, witch-hunters were far more aggressive than those with authority over other types of crime.

The great witch-hunt of the early modern period owed much to the *Malleus Maleficarum (Hammer of Witches)*, published in 1486 by two Dominicans who were inquisitors in Germany. Written and published under papal commission, it was quickly translated into most European languages and became a handbook for witch-hunters. It spread several key changes in the understanding of witchcraft. In the Middle Ages, witchcraft was seen as the use of black magic to bring harm to other persons or their possessions; since *maleficia* was done through the agency of demons, it was a crime against God and under the jurisdiction of church courts. The *Malleus* popularized the idea that witches made a pact with the devil to worship him in exchange for the power to do evil. This was far more terrifying than simple black magic, and punishing those guilty of devil worship became the central focus of witch-hunting. Unlike black magic where eyewitnesses were easier to come by, only those who attended the witches' sabbath, where unnatural sexual acts with the devil took place, could serve as witnesses, and they were not likely to testify freely against themselves. Torture of suspected witches, therefore, was in order if authorities were to learn the truth and the names of other participants, since where there was one witch, there certainly would be more. Judicial torture thus had a snowballing effect, as those named by one tortured person would be tortured in turn and add more names, often creating a frenzy of accusations, trials, and burnings. The *Malleus* also urged secular authorities to become involved in witch-hunting, since witchcraft was a secular crime as well as a religious one. By 1560, secular prosecution of witches was an idea whose time had come, as part of the general trend toward the royal courts taking jurisdiction away from the church courts.[5]

The *Malleus* was responsible for yet another major aspect of the witch craze—the idea that women were far more likely to be witches. During the Middle Ages, those who were accused of practicing black magic were about equally women and men. When perverted sex acts with the devil became an important part of the popular perception of witchcraft, it was argued that Satan was far more likely to seduce women and make them witches. By 1560 a clear majority of accused witches were female. In that year the first hint of the impending witch craze was made at the Estates of Orléans, when both the First and the Third Estates complained that witches were rapidly multiplying in the land. The clergy asked that they be expelled, but the commoners demanded that they be put to death without appeal. There was, however, no royal edict on witchcraft until 1682, which was intended to rein in witch-hunters. The witch craze in France was largely the work of local officials with almost no direction from higher authorities.

It was, however, heresy that dominated the French legal system for the two decades after 1539. How to deal with the upsurge in cases seen as involving sedition against the king as well as religious error deeply vexed the French government. A long tradition that heresy was a matter for the civil government dated back to Emperor Constantine, who first used the power of the state to enforce the decisions of the church against the persons and property of heretics. In 382 Emperor Theodosius declared heresy a capital crime and ordered the burning of heretical books. Justinian included those statutes in his code of Roman law. In the thirteenth century, Pope Innocent IV accepted Holy Roman Emperor Frederick II's edicts on the use of torture and burning for obstinate heretics and thereby established these practices in medieval Europe. Accordingly, medieval French law defined heresy as a matter of importance to the civil authorities, who accepted responsibility for punishing convicted heretics.

When the law clearly defined heresy as sedition, major disputes quickly erupted over which courts had first instance in heresy cases. Traditionally church courts had original jurisdiction; persons they judged guilty were handed over to the "secular arm" for punishment. This system began to malfunction when the number of cases proliferated after 1534. Church officials often found that secular authorities were reluctant to cooperate in arresting heresy suspects or in punishing those found guilty. More serious a problem from the monarchy's point of view was the lack of zeal for prosecuting heresy suspects exhibited by a large part of the French hierarchy. Some refused to be involved because they were humanists and sympathetic to reform; others simply were indifferent. Francis I's first edict on heresy procedure of 1541 expanded to the entire kingdom an innovation used in Languedoc two years earlier—giving the royal courts original jurisdiction over laypersons accused of heresy. The church kept authority over clerics so accused. Immediately the clergy vehemently protested the loss of jurisdiction. Three years later the king gave equal authority to both civil and church courts, but that only created vast confusion and gave those in both the civil judiciary and the hierarchy who were sympathetic to reform an excuse to do nothing. The issue of who had original jurisdiction over heresy continued to be a problem under Henry II, and it stymied his desire to enforce the laws against heresy. In particular, the clerics' complaints about the Chambre ardente were a major factor in Henry's decision to close it down, despite the record it was building in heresy prosecution. The solution in effect when he died involved giving the civil courts jurisdiction over those accused heretics who were regarded as seditious, while the clergy maintained competence over simple heresy. Since heresy almost by definition was seditious, few cases were left to the church courts, but the clergy's complaints effected no further change before the edicts of toleration began to remove Protestants from the purview of the courts.

The confusion in heresy prosecution was not an issue at the meetings of the Estates general in 1560 and 1561, although the matter of religious toleration was broadly discussed. Attention was focused on the Ordinance of Villers-Cotterêts. Loud complaints of the Estates in 1560 and 1561 about the edict reflected the fact that this was the first time they had an opportunity to register their objections. The deputies objected not only to specific clauses but also to the theory of royal power that lay behind it: The king had the power to mandate new law without consultation. When the Parlement of Paris refused to register the ordinance until it had the opportunity to examine it closely, Francis I ordered its immediate registration. The theory behind this dramatic enhancement of royal authority came from the Roman Empire. Royal absolutists found in the works of Ulpian, the noted Roman legalist, two famous sayings that could be used for an absolutist view of royal government: "The emperor is free from the law!" and "What pleases the prince has the force of law!" They were well known to medieval commentators, but it was only with the rise of legal humanism that they were studied in their imperial context, which gave them considerably more force than they had in the Middle Ages.

By 1530 the efforts of Guillaume Budé and Andrea Alciato, the creators of legal humanism, to emphasize the study of Roman law in its original context began to have an impact on the French universities where civil law was taught. The law was another area in which the humanist principles of proper understanding of classical language and history were regarded as applicable. This approach became known as the Mos Gallicus iuris docendi (the Gallican Method of teaching law) because of its strength in French universities. The established method of studying law, similar to scholastic theology in that it involved reading medieval glosses on the text of Roman law, was called the Mos Italicus. As was true of most areas where the humanists took on the established practice of a discipline, they directed satire and ridicule at their opponents, as Rabelais demonstrated in his *Pantagruel,* where he devoted a great deal of attention to the cause of legal humanism.

The earliest and long dominant center of legal humanism was the University of Bourges, where Alciato taught from 1528 to 1533. John Calvin studied with him there, making clear the close correlation between legal and religious reform. The antagonism between the two groups of legal scholars was often fierce at Bourges, but the situation at Toulouse was much worse. Jean de Catuce, a law professor, was executed in 1532 for heresy, and another, Jean de Boysson, recanted his errors in public. Etienne Dolet was a law student at Toulouse. He created such an uproar by his wide-ranging verbal attacks, especially on his old-style professors and the Gascon (southern) law students, that he was forced to flee Toulouse.

At mid-century the two most famous law professors at the university were Jacques Cujas and Jean de Coras. By 1550 Cujas became the leading advocate of the Mos Gallicus in the realm. He was so committed to the study of Roman law that he refused to consider French law. He left Toulouse in 1554, teaching at a number of other French universities before he died in 1590. Coras, who spent most of his career in Toulouse, where he investigated the famous case of the false Martin Guerre, was willing to touch on French law. He exemplifies the close ties between legal and religious reform, as he died in the St. Bartholomew's Massacre. Coras and other legal humanists such as Etienne Pasquier, François Connan, and Charles Du Moulin were practicing jurists as well as scholars. They were, as Pasquier said, eager to naturalize "in our France the civil law of the Romans." Du Moulin was the most important of these legal scholars who used Roman law to deal with contemporary French problems. A strong advocate of a powerful French monarchy, he used the concept of imperial authority found in Roman law to argue for the greatly enhanced authority of the French king. He regarded the monarchy as the protector of the common interest against the special interests of the nobility and corporations. It is no surprise, therefore, to find Du Moulin writing in 1551 a sharp attack on papal pretensions in the Gallican Church. His hostility to Rome led him to identify with Calvinism for a time, but he found it uncongenial. His ideal almost certainly was a French version of Anglicanism.

Being Gallican did not necessarily make one an advocate of religious toleration or freedom of religion, but Gallicans were generally less concerned about specific points of doctrine over which Calvinist and papist raged. Recent scholarship has found a distinction between toleration and freedom of religion in sixteenth-century French thought: The first indicated "a temporary acceptance of something undesirable;" while the latter meant the freedom of individuals to choose their own religious beliefs.[7] Few French, not even the Calvinists, advocated religious freedom. For most, truth in religion was certain, and the state had an obligation to enforce the truth by force if necessary. There was a group, later called Politiques, who argued that while the state did have the right to enforce religious conformity, it also could tolerate religious dissenters temporarily, if it were expedient.

The question of whether the French monarchy could for a time tolerate another religious faith, at least a variant form of Christianity, was a matter that lawyers debated; the theologians were nearly unanimous in asserting the negative. Those who answered in the affirmative were mostly legal humanists. The king's chief lawyer, Chancellor L'Hôpital, emerged as the principal advocate for toleration of the Calvinists.[8] The Edict of St-Germain of January 1562 was largely his work, although Catherine de Medici's role in getting it promulgated must not be underestimated. It was intended to separate the purely religious elements of Protestantism from those regarded as seditious. Thus it was harsh on those who created disturbances by seizing church property or holding services without permission from a local royal official. The death penalty for such acts remained in effect. Religious meetings, however, were permitted with prior permission, if the men attending were unarmed. Calvinist ministers were allowed in the realm, provided they swore to observe the edict. The Parlement of Paris refused to register it, despite two *lettres de jussion* from the king, and it remained a dead letter because events quickly overtook it.

L'Hôpital studied law in Italy, where his father fled after being implicated in Constable Bourbon's treason. Although there is little of the academic interests of the legal humanists in his writings, he was highly sympathetic to their agenda beyond religious toleration, including the need to reform French law in accordance with the principles of Roman law. L'Hôpital and other legal humanists found much to object to in the Ordinance of Villers-Cotterêts. Du Moulin, an eminent jurist, and another legal humanist, Pierre Ayrault from Angers, wrote commentaries on it. Both denounced the secrecy in which the edict veiled criminal proceedings, especially the interrogation of witnesses. They attacked the requirement that defendants produce the names of their witnesses immediately, without even the time to understand the charges. Ayrault was especially eloquent in expressing the need for public proceedings as the means by which bad judges would be exposed and good judges encouraged to do their best. It was Du Moulin, however, who penned the best known comment on Villers-Cotterêts: "See the tyranny of this impius [Chancellor] Poyet!"[9]

Since prominent legal scholars criticized the ordinance of 1539, it is no surprise that the Estates general of 1560 made a sharp attack on it, in much the same terms. The focus of complaints was criminal procedure. All three estates raised objections to the pervasive secrecy in criminal cases. Deputies argued that public procedures were far more likely to reach the truth in a case and serve to deter crime. The First Estate demanded that the king rescind those clauses giving the civil courts jurisdiction over so many matters formerly heard in church courts. The nobility, which had less reason to be concerned about the new legal procedure than the commoners, registered a complaint about the practice of not giving the defendants the names of their accusers. The noblesse also wanted an end to the practice of preventative detention of nobles except in cases of capital crime. The Third Estate was far more expansive in criticizing Villers-Cotterêts. It strongly protested against the practice requiring defendants to register immediately their objections to witnesses as soon as they were told the witnesses' names. It was often difficult for defendants to know if a witness would be testifying for or against them, and a hasty mistake on their part could result in a witness favorable to them being impeached or allow a hostile one to testify against them. The deputies alleged that many innocent persons were being convicted because of the inability of the accused to learn the names of those informing against them, and they asked that judges be allowed to grant a delay when the defendants asked for it.

Members of the Estates also complained about the greatly enhanced power of the provost-marshals. The expansion of their authority in the previous half-century gave them a vast scope within which to commit abuses. The delegates wanted to limit their judicial authority, but not their authority to make arrests, to cases clearly involving only soldiers. Virtually the only concession made to the Estates was the elimination of a special type of *sergent* that had appeared in previous decades; their sole responsibility was conducting prisoners from local jails to the Parlements. They abused their authority by extorting bribes from their charges and frequently mistreating them. The local judges were again made responsible for the transportation of prisoners.

Complaints from the estates had little impact on the monarchy; the royal council declared that the edict of 1539 would continue to be enforced.

Nonetheless, Chancellor L'Hôpital reflected the cahiers of the Estates in the Ordinance of Orléans, which was published in early 1561. He ignored the request of the Protestants for a separate set of courts, which they sought because of their fear of facing Catholic judges in the established judiciary. The area where L'Hôpital was most responsive to the estates was in their denunciation of venality. He could not have gone much further without denouncing the very concept of selling offices. He ordered the suppression of all offices created since 1515, eliminated the semester and alternatif systems, and prohibited close relatives from serving together on the same court. However, the monarchy's desperate need for money made it impossible to abandon venality, which L'Hôpital recognized,[10] and the anarchy of the coming religious wars rendered futile attempts to implement the other changes the edict endorsed. And, to be fair to L'Hôpital, the Parlement of Paris vigorously opposed much of what the edict proposed in regard to the judicial system, in large part because it adversely affected the parlementaires. The chancellor conceded a number of points to the magistrates, but when they refused the necessary registration, Charles IX issued a *lettre de jussion* to gain it. Nonetheless, most of the Ordinance of Orléans remained a dead letter because of the opposition of the judiciary, the nobility, and the clergy to key elements of it, especially those regarding justice. By ignoring the complaints that the French populace had against the system of justice as it was amended in 1539, the monarchy missed an opportunity to demonstrate its concern for the people. It was not a good time for the king to be unresponsive to popular opinion.

13

Culture and Thought: The Glory of the French Renaissance

The period from 1530 to 1562 was the high point of the French Renaissance. The lion's share of literary works and artistic projects most associated with the Renaissance in France were produced in those years, largely through the patronage of Francis I, "the Father of the French Renaissance." It was the era of three of the major glories of French culture: the Renaissance châteaux, Rabelais's novels, and Ronsard's poetry.

To be sure, the design and decoration of Francis's châteaux involved a large dose of Italian influence. He brought numerous Italian architects and artists back with him after his Italian expeditions and lured many more to France with promises of lavish patronage. Despite the financial burden of his wars and the ransom of his sons after his return from captivity in 1526, he immediately set into motion plans to build two châteaux, including the most expensive and finest of all the royal châteaux, Fontainebleau. The first, begun in 1528, was set in the Bois de Boulogne just to the southwest of Paris. As was true of most of Francis's building projects, it was intended to provide the king a comfortable residence and a place for short hunts close to Paris, where the press of royal business was taking him often. In 1528 he stated he intended to make the city his usual habitat. Paris did not have a comfortable royal residence; the Louvre and the Bastille were still medieval fortresses, while the Tournelles was decrepit. The new château became known by the implausible name of the Madrid.[1] The name was used because Francis based its design on a building he had seen in Madrid. Nothing of the château remains today; it was demolished in the eighteenth century. Although it was apparently similar to Chambord in its plan, it less resembled a fortress. It had no moat, and while the presence of towers was detectable, they had no defensive function. The floor plan, the high-pitched roof, and the tall chimneys suggest a French master mason rather than an Italian as its designer, but the decoration, especially the use of colored terra-cotta, was said to be completely Italian, done largely by Girolamo della Robbia.

Later the same year, work began on the reconstruction of an old castle deep in the forest of Fontainebleau. The excellent hunting there frequently attracted Francis, and he decided he needed a larger and more comfortable residence to enjoy the experience fully. The French master mason, Gilles Le Breton, was commissioned to rebuild the castle. Le Breton's contract reveals that the alterations and additions Francis originally wanted were limited, but they included a new entrance, the Porte Dorée, which was one of the most noteworthy features of the château. The lines of Le Breton's work were simpler and more regular than those of Chambord and Madrid and therefore more classical in appearance. Once the building began, Francis began to think of his new château in increasingly grandiose terms. It required nearly a century to finish all the wings and other elements, but the château as a whole has a great deal of uniformity, mainly because the simple design of Le Breton's original work at Fontainebleau became a model for a classical movement that spread across the realm. The tendency of past historians to see the château as designed by Italians has been supplanted by the view that it was French with some Italian input. The interior decoration, however, which is one of the glories of the Renaissance in France, was done mostly by Italians. Its influence on French art was so extensive that the term "The School of Fontainebleau" is used for the group of artists that imitated it. Two Italians, Gian Battista Rosso and Francesco Primaticcio, who arrived in France in 1530 and 1532 respectively, were responsible. Both artists are considered to be mannerists. Mannerism, an artistic movement of the late Italian Renaissance, was moving away from the classical simplicity of the High Renaissance toward a greater enthusiasm for movement, a crowding of human figures that are elongated rather than perfectly proportioned, and the elegant. It caught the lingering taste for the late Gothic still present in France. Mannerism also looked forward to the rococo of the next century.

Both Rosso and Primaticcio were primarily experts in decorating interiors, and they brought to France a style unlike anything previously used in the realm.[2]

Unfortunately, most of Primaticcio's work in the château, especially the decor in the Gallery of Ulysses, was destroyed during the building's many renovations. His principal remaining piece is the fresco over the fireplace in the Chambre de la Reine. Fresco was Rosso's medium of choice, and his pieces dominate the showpiece room of the château, the Galerie François I. (See illustration V.) This long, narrow room, originally planned as a corridor joining the Porte Dorée to the older part of the château, was trimmed with elaborately carved wainscot (wood paneling) on the bottom half of its walls. The top half was adorned with Rosso's frescoes with the spaces between them framed by stucco molded into fantastic shapes. The themes of the frescoes were taken largely from classical mythology and history. They are noteworthy for their crowded masses of human figures, often nude, with the elongated features that mark mannerism.[3] Francis was enchanted by the decoration in the new château, which became his favorite residence. He had an elaborate set of tapestries made from Rosso's frescoes, and he took them with him on his journeys across France. French artists also did numerous engravings of the works. These copies, and the many artists who actually executed the designs he planned, helped to spread the style of Rosso, who died in 1540, across France. Primaticcio remained active at Fontainebleau for another two decades. After 1550 he collaborated closely with Niccolo Dell'Abbate and created large murals to decorate the wings and pavilions finished under Henry II.

Francis's building projects continued to the end of his life. In 1532 he commissioned two Le Bretons, probably Gilles's brothers, to build the château of Villers-Cotterêts north of Paris, also in the midst of a broad forest. A high-pitched roof and tall, narrow windows mark its design as French, while the interior decoration was thoroughly Italian. The château of St-Germain-en-Laye was begun in the same year. Just to the west of Paris it became the principal residence of the court when the king had extended business in Paris. Under Henry II it served as the royal nursery as well. A French architect later described Francis I as almost being his own architect at St-Germain. Whether or not this was true, the work was directed by a French master mason, Pierre Chambiges, who also built several smaller châteaux for the king.

In Paris, Francis set about to transform the Louvre from a medieval fortress into a palace. In 1528 he ordered the great tower demolished, and renovations were made in order to entertain Charles V there during his stay in Paris in 1539. Unsatisfactory attempts at renovating the Louvre convinced the king of the need to rebuild it extensively.[4] The work began in 1546, when Pierre Lescot received a commission for the work. It continued under Henry, with the original design vastly expanded, and Lescot's principal contribution is known as the Henry II wing. (See illustration VI.) Although Lescot's Louvre had the

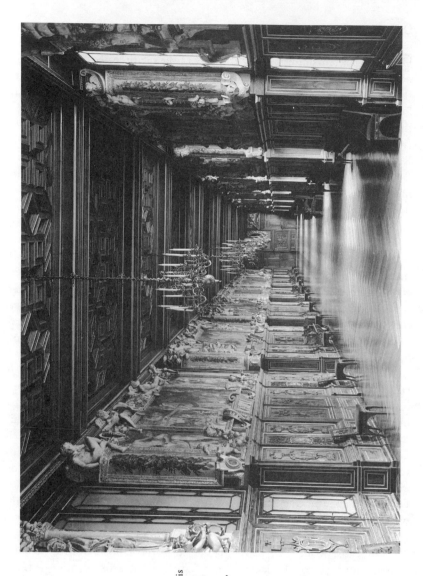

V. The Galerie François Ier, the Château of Fontainbleau. By Rosso Fiorentino, 1535-40. Giraudon/Art Resource, New York.

VI. The Henri II
Wing, the Louvre.
Designed by Pierre
Lescot, begun in
1546. Giraudon/Art
Resource, New York.

typical high-pitched French roof, its basic lines were classical. Unlike Italian Renaissance designs, Lescot's exterior is highly decorated with bas-relief and Corinthian capitals. Most of it was done by Jean Goujon, who was Lescot's partner in creating the new Louvre. Relief sculpture was Goujon's forte, but his masterpiece was the caryatid portico, where four three-dimensional statues of Greek goddesses supported the ceiling. His inspiration came from Vitruvius, the Roman architect whose works on architecture described the concept. Goujon had used the caryatids on a smaller scale for the tomb of Diane de Poitiers's husband, but not even Italians used them on the scale he employed in the Louvre. Goujon and Lescot also collaborated on the famed Hôtel Carnavalet in Paris, begun in 1545, which is similar to their work on the Louvre. Henry II did not favor Lescot, but he allowed him to continue working on the Louvre. Lescot's other projects were for private individuals, including the château of Villery for Marshal Saint-André.

The most influential architect in sixteenth-century France never did any work for the monarchy. Sebastiano Serlio was an Italian who published a treatise on architecture that described the work being done in Italy in the first decades of the sixteenth century. The first published portion (actually Book 4) appeared in 1537. He sent a copy to Francis I and asked to join his service, but it was not until after he dedicated Book 3 to the king in 1540 that Francis called him to France as royal architect. Serlio served as an adviser on numerous projects such as Fontainebleau and the Louvre, but he never had a direct role in designing a royal building. Serlio continued to publish his work on architecture until 1551, although the last three books were still in manuscript at his death in 1554. His treatise was intended to be a practical guide for architects, with an extensive number of plans to provide them with solutions to various problems. The work had a great impact on French architecture after 1550, especially since he incorporated French concepts such as the high-pitched roof into the plans he made after his arrival in the realm.

Henry II had his own favorite architect, Philibert de L'Orme, who began working for him even before his succession. L'Orme spent three years in Italy, the first French architect to study there and the first to combine the building skills of the French master mason with a thorough knowledge of ancient and Italian architecture. In 1547 Henry appointed him superintendent of buildings, which gave him broad purview over all royal buildings except the Louvre. His masterpiece was the château of Anet, which he did for Diane de Poitiers between 1547 and 1552. (See illustration VII.) He also designed the famous bridge at Chenonceaux, when the château was in Diane's hands, and the tomb of Francis I. His works and treatise on architecture demonstrate extensive classical and Italian influences put into a French context. He is regarded as having great

VII. The Château of Anet. Designed by Philibert de L'Orme for Diane de Poitiers, 1549-52.

influence in creating a French classical style, which dominated French architecture for well over a century.

In sculpture, the trends were nearly the same, because most of the statuary of this era was used to decorate buildings. Primaticcio, Rosso, Dell'Abbate, and Benvenuto Cellini were the principal Italians who contributed to bringing ancient and Italian models to France. The first three were primarily makers of engravings and bas-relief, but Primaticcio was sent to Rome in 1540 to collect statuary from the ancient world for Francis I. He returned a year later with casts

VIII.   Salt Cellar. By Benvenuto Celleni, commissioned by Francis I, 1540. Kunsthistorisches Museum, Vienna. Erich Lessing/Art Resource, New York.

from about a dozen famous ancient statues, including the *Laocoon,* which were turned into bronze statues in France and placed in the new château at Fontaine-bleau. Cellini's work was free-standing statuary. One of the most colorful characters of the sixteenth century, he arrived in France in 1540 after Francis asked Paul III for his release from prison, where he had been sent for insulting the pope's artistic taste. The king gave him an old tower near the Louvre for his workshop, which Cellini filled with prostitutes who served as his models. He did a great deal of work for Francis, who often came to watch him work, but chafed at being under his control, and he was rude to everyone but the king. In 1545 he received Francis's permission to return to Italy. Cellini did a vast amount of work while in France, but only two pieces survive. Fortunately, one is his masterpiece, the gold salt-cellar, which is one of the glories of European art. (See illustration VIII.) The nude figures of a woman and a man on it represent the earth and the sea. It is an exquisite example of mannerist art.

Henry II appreciated the mannerist style but preferred to patronize French artists instead of Italians. The sculpture from his reign was heavily influenced by classical and Italian models but given a French flavor. Goujon was the best sculptor working in France in Henry's reign. While much of what he did was bas-relief for building decoration, he also produced a number of free-standing statues. (See illustration IX.) His pieces followed Greek prototypes so closely that "they might be mistaken at first sight for Greek statues . . . but these graceful reinterpretations of the Greek ideal are treated in a personal manner."[5] His principal rival among French sculptors was Pierre Bontemps, who was influenced by the Italians of the Fontainebleau school. Not much of his work has survived, but a splendid example of it is the sculpture on the tomb of Francis I, which L'Orme designed. Bontemps also did the monument for Francis's heart, which by French tradition was entombed separately from the rest of the body. Germain Pilon, a younger sculptor, also did some work on Francis's tomb, but he is better known for the statuary on Henry II's tomb. (See illustration X.) The tomb itself was done under the direction of Primaticcio from 1561 to 1570. Pilon was responsible for the monument in which the heart of the king was encased. The urn holding the heart was supported by statues of the three Graces, who with their flowing drapery, long necks, and small heads are exemplary models of mannerism.

In respect to painting, Francis was also an avid collector of Italian works. Paintings by Michelangelo and Titian highlight the pieces sent to the king from Italy, most of which were placed in Fontainebleau. One was Angelo Bronzino's *Venus, Cupid, Time and Folly,* which is often regarded as the archetypal mannerist painting. In France, Rosso, Primaticcio, and Dell'Abbate did considerable painting as part of their building decor, especially at Fontainebleau. Primaticcio did several independent works, in particular the well-known portrait of Henry II from early in his reign. Mannerism was the dominant style of their paintings, but the best-known French painters of the era worked in a different style. Jean Clouet and his son François were primarily portrait painters who continued the Flemish style of the previous period. Clouet père, a native of Flanders, arrived at the French court about the time Francis became king. When he died about 1540, his son assumed his position. There are several paintings that can be attributed to either Clouet, in particular the famous portrait of Francis I. It depicts the king at a younger age than François could have painted him, but it is more in the son's style than the father's. François is credited with a wider range of paintings than is Jean, although portraiture was still his forte. (See Illustration XI.) They included full-length portraits with backgrounds, absent in Jean's work. François seems to have had a broad range of influences—Italian, Flemish, German—that are obvious in different paintings. A third famous portrait painter of the time was Corneille de Lyon, a native of the Low Countries, who settled at Lyon. In his lifetime he was highly regarded

IX. Diana with a Stag.
Attributed to Jean
Goujon, c. 1550, in the
Louvre. Giraudon/Art
Resource, New York.

X.   Effigies of Henry II and Catherine de Medici. By Germain Pilon, c. 1583, in the Abbey Church of St. Denis. Giraudon/Art Resource, New York.

for his small portraits of various notables, but only one surviving work can be attributed to him with certainty.

In some of the French art and architecture of the mid-sixteenth century, there is a tension between classicism and mannerism, to say nothing of the lingering influence of the late Gothic. In Italy the classicists were the dominant influence long before the mannerists began to move away from it. Both arrived in France at virtually the same time, but the two genres were not entirely

XI. Charles IX. By François Clouet, c. 1570, in the Louvre.
Giraudon/Art Resource, New York.

compatible, even if Frenchmen such as Goujon attempted to make use of both forms at once in some of their works. The château of Fontainebleau showcased classicism, mannerism, and the French versions of both. During few other times and places has one building been so influential in defining artistic and architectural trends. Fontainebleau truly was a school for the new culture in France.

Fontainebleau also had an impact on the literary side of French culture, after Francis I transferred the royal library there from Blois in 1544. He was an avid collector of books and manuscripts, especially in Greek. A large portion of the materials his agents in Italy sent to him went to Fontainebleau directly, so it already had a noteworthy library when the 1,894 volumes from Blois arrived. Francis also had a small library, strong in romances and Roman history, which he took with him on his travels. He had an official reader to read to him at mealtimes. The king devised a way to increase his library at little cost: In 1539 he mandated that every book printed in France be deposited in the royal library, while booksellers were to make available a copy of every foreign book brought into the realm for examination and possible purchase. The edict's stated purpose was to demonstrate France's cultural glory and encourage the royal progeny to study literature and history. As of 1544, the edict had not had much effect, judging by the small number of printed books listed in the inventory of the library when it was transferred to Fontainebleau.

The second focus of Francis's patronage of literature was the Collège de Trois Langues, which began functioning in 1530. He intended it to be a part of the university, and its members at first were called the royal lectors of the university. The regular faculty did not make them welcome, and they had difficulty finding a permanent place to lecture, even resorting to the streets on occasion. The Faculty of Theology censured them in 1530 for teaching theology, as they were accused of doing in their lectures on the languages of the Bible. There is no question that several gave a humanistic gloss to their study of biblical language. In 1532 Francis paid 2,310 *l* in salaries to five lectors in Greek and Hebrew and one mathematician who made up the college, although getting their pay on time was a persistent problem. Because the king paid them, they were expected to give free lectures, in contrast to the university, where the students paid their teachers.

The practice of students paying the faculty directly was creating problems in the university. The idea that a faculty position was a property right similar to a royal office led faculty members to sell or rent their positions to unqualified persons. Attendance certificates, which were necessary to enjoy the privileges of being a student, and degrees were openly sold. Probably because of the great value of a law degree, corruption was the worst in the law faculties in the universities with law schools. The attacks of the humanists on the University of Paris surely helped to undermine its prestige and create the image of bitter reaction against new ideas. Its own hidebound conservatism, however, and the onslaught of corruption did even more to destroy its reputation. The university did nothing to restore its prestige prior to 1614.

The negative image of the University of Paris in place by 1530 helps to explain the widespread support for the royal lectors and the efforts to free them from university auspices. The name of Collège des Trois Langues came into use by 1539, which remained its title until about 1610 when the term *Collège Royal* appeared. Today's name, Collège de France, did not appear until the French Revolution. The members, called the "professors of the king," increased to 11 by 1547, and in 1551, Henry II added a 12th chair for Peter Ramus. Ramus (the latinized version of de La Ramée) was from a noble family of Picardy that fell on such hard times that his father had to take on manual labor and was derogated. Although Ramus was educated at the University of Paris, he received an excellent humanist training in classical Latin and rhetoric. In 1536, he supposedly chose as his thesis for his master of arts degree the proposition: "Everything said by Aristotle is false." Seven years later Ramus published two works that openly challenged the way Aristotle was being taught in the university and attacked the Aristotelians who dominated it. His attack was centered on the proposal that Aristotelian logic, the heart of the arts curriculum, should be replaced by rhetoric. The Arts Faculty responded by persuading the king to form a commission to settle the matter and arranged for a debate between Ramus and his fiercest opponents. The commission decided against him, and he was prohibited from teaching logic and philosophy. Since he remained a member of the Arts Faculty, he turned to mathematics, in which he was self-taught. A major concern of Renaissance mathematics was squaring the circle, and Ramus gave considerable attention to that problem. His knowledge of mathematics was actually mediocre compared to that of his close friend, the mathematician Omer Talon; royal favor and a reputation for encyclopedic knowledge won him the royal lectorship. Ramus's curiosity extended to being one of the few Frenchmen of the sixteenth century who was acquainted with Copernicus's heliocentric theory. Ramus, however, criticized the Pole for using hypotheses in astronomy and called for a reformed astronomy without hypotheses, even proposing to give up his royal professorship to an astronomer who would develop it. All of this was part of his program to create mathematics as a discipline in its own right, separate from natural philosophy.

Ramus's fortune changed for the better when Henry II became king, since Ramus dedicated a book to him before his succession. In 1557 Henry granted him a royal "privilege to print" that covered not only all of his completed works but everything he might want to publish in the future. As a royal professor he was permitted to lecture on virtually anything he wished, except for theology, and he dabbled even in that discipline. His theological writings reveal nothing of any Protestant inclinations before 1562. Until that year he was a practicing Catholic, at least in public. Even after his conversion to Calvinism, he remained in the good graces of Charles IX, Catherine de Medici, and even the cardinal of Lorraine until 1570.

Another royal lectorship went to Guillaume Postel, a savant who was even more wide ranging and eccentric than Ramus. A Norman by birth and mostly self-educated, his brilliance allowed him to advance rapidly in the world of letters. Fluent in classical Latin and Greek at an early age, he learned Hebrew from a French Jew and Spanish and Portuguese from a Spanish merchant. In 1532 he published his first works, on the alphabets of 12 different languages and Hebrew grammar. Francis I sent him to the Ottoman Empire to collect manuscripts in Oriental (Middle Eastern) languages for his library. While there he learned Chaldean and Arabic. Upon his return to France in 1537, Francis gave him a royal chair in Oriental languages. Five years later he antagonized the king by defending Chancellor Guillaume Poyet, his major patron, who was disgraced, thus losing his lectorship. He conceived of a plan to convert the Muslims of Palestine by demonstrating to them in their own language the errors of the Koran. Thus, he was attracted to the new Society of Jesus, whose first members he probably met in Paris; its original purpose was also the conversion of the Muslims. Postel, however, could not accept the strict discipline of the Jesuits, and he soon left the order. He spent most of the next 20 years traveling in Italy, Austria, and the eastern Mediterranean. While in Venice in 1547, he fell seriously ill and was nursed back to health by a woman named Joanna. She became for him the new Eve through whom the human race would be redeemed. For this and other heterodox ideas, Postel found himself in trouble with Church authorities, one of whom deemed him "more mad than bad," and spent several terms in prison, although he always denounced Protestantism.

François Rabelais was less eccentric than Postel but far more famous. A native of Touraine, Rabelais joined the Franciscans at an early age but became restless because of the order's lack of enthusiasm for humanism. Hoping for a more congenial atmosphere among the Benedictines, he entered one of their monasteries but abandoned religious life entirely by 1530. Despite the religious orders' reputation for being hostile to the new learning, Rabelais was one of several major humanists who received excellent educations while in religious life, but it is also true that they all abandoned monastic life eventually. By then he had received a thorough training in the classics, law, and medicine. He earned a medical degree at the University of Montpellier and supported himself as a physician to a prominent churchman, Cardinal Jean Du Bellay, a supporter of humanism and Evangélisme, until his literary reputation gained him a minor royal office from Francis I in 1538. Exceptionally learned in virtually every aspect of human knowledge, widely traveled if his many precise descriptions of places can be taken as firsthand accounts, and equipped with an unusually keen sense of the comic, Rabelais made use of laughter, vulgarity, and absurdity to make deeply perceptive comments on the human condition. In 1532 he published two text editions on medicine and one on law, which demonstrated his talent as a classical scholar. In the same year *Pantagruel* was published at Lyon. Rabelais turned Pantagruel from the dwarf of French folklore associated with drunkenness into a giant, whose gigantic tastes, lusts, and instincts provide much of the humor in his novel. Pantagruel, however, also received a university education, which provided the opportunity for satirizing the theology and law faculties. Rabelais's sympathy for Evangélisme and church reform came through clearly in the book, as did his antipathy toward those he regarded as obstructionists.

Two years later, Rabelais published the "prequel" to *Pantagruel.* It is the story of Pantagruel's father, the king of a race of giants, married to the daughter of the king in More's Utopia. It is one of many references to contemporary humanist works found in Rabelais's works. By making Gargantua essentially a comic version of Plato's philosopher-king, Rabelais gave himself the opportunity to pronounce on a very wide range of topics, including pacifism. In what is really a lengthy tangent to the plot, such as there is, the description of the abbey of Thélème allows the author to present his concept of the proper monastic institution. It is, of course, a complete antithesis to virtually every aspect of traditional monasticism, and it enables Rabelais to discuss such matters as free will, celibacy, and the teaching of the pure Gospel. Rabelais, however, pulled his punches in his attacks on the Sorbonne and other opponents, which was true of the second edition of *Pantagruel,* which also came out in late 1534, after the Day of Placards. Two books published in 1546 and 1552 continued the stories of Gargantua and Pantagruel, while a third of questioned authenticity appeared in 1562.

Rabelais's frequently coarse and vulgar humor has often offended scholars who have studied his works, and many of them have deemed him not a true humanist for it and for using popular French. In regard to the latter, he contributed significantly to strengthening French as a mature language and made the dialect of Touraine a significant factor in modern literary French. In respect to the first point, few of his contemporaries in France signed on to the humanist agenda as completely as Rabelais did. That agenda included puns and witticisms, a keen interest in languages and the use of language, and Evangélisme. His profession may explain his frequent references to urine and defecation, since studying both was a major aspect of the physician's duties.

Even if few reading his works today can fully appreciate his humor and vast range of references, many modern critics still regard *Pantagruel* and *Gargantua* as the greatest French novels.

Rabelais's trademark, broad and bawdy humor, is also present in the most famous work from a unlikely source—Marguerite of Angoulême. Francis's sister was not only a major patron of Renaissance culture, a close second to him in that regard, but also was a noteworthy author in her own right. She received an excellent humanistic education and became well versed in classical Latin, Italian, and Spanish; later in life she learned a little Greek and Hebrew in order to read the Scriptures in the original languages. Her combination of humanistic interests and religious views serve as an excellent example of Evangélisme, with her keen interest in reading the Bible, personal and mystical sense of religion, and deep distaste for the emphasis on formal doctrine and ritual in contemporary Catholicism. Marguerite protected a large number of Evangelicals and early Protestants. Much of her literary work, some of which remained in manuscript until the nineteenth century, was highly religious in content. The opinions expressed in her poem "Mirrour de l'âme pércheresse"("Mirror of the Sinful Soul," 1531) were deemed sufficiently heterodox for the Faculty of Theology to censure it after its anonymous publication. When it became known that the king's sister was the author, the faculty backed down. In sharp contrast with the mystical tones of her poetry stands her famous prose work, the *Heptameron*. Written late in her life and published ten years after her death in 1549, the work was left unpolished and probably incomplete. Marguerite was heavily influenced by Boccaccio's *Decameron*, which she commissioned to be published in French. The *Heptameron* is a collection of 70 tales told by ten Frenchmen and women while isolated in the Pyrenees for a week. Like Boccaccio's, her tales were often bawdy and risqué, but they had a serious purpose: examining the many aspects of love, both human and divine. Her discussion of the latter clearly reveals her Evangélisme, which subjected this work also to the Sorbonne's censorship.

One of Marguerite's principal clients, and also an advocate of Evangélisme, was Clément Marot. He was the son of Jean Marot, a *rhétoriqueur*, and like him a minor functionary of the royal court. Marot's poetry served as a transition from his father's generation to the Pléiade of the next. He wrote poems on a wide range of subjects, including events of the court, the pleasures of wine, women, and song, and religion. One of his poems was entitled "The Lovely Breast." Another was written to the king, asking to be released from jail, where he had been tossed for helping a friend escape from it. When he was in a playful mood, his language could be nearly as bawdy as Rabelais's. As a poet Marot is credited with introducing the sonnet to France, for he was an avid reader of Petrarch, although there are several other poets to whom that honor might be given, including Marot's friend Mellin de St-Gelais. Marot also made extensive use of classical allusions and forms in his works, such as the elegy, which Marot was the first French author to use. His sharp wit was often employed in satirizing the clergy, for he strongly believed in the need for church reform. His most important contribution in regard to religion was his translation of the Psalms into French, which he began in 1533 with the king's support. He was one of those who fled France after the Day of the Placards. He returned in 1537 but left again in 1543 for Geneva, where 50 of his French Psalms were published. Finding Calvin's city too puritanical for his tastes, he went to Italy. Despite the importance of his French Psalms to French Protestants, for whom they served as a trademark, he seems to have remained a Catholic to his death in 1544.

Marguerite, Rabelais, and Marot reveal a key characteristic of the literature of the early French Renaissance: a blend of the humorous and the serious, the profane and the sacred, the crude and the refined. In general they provide a wide-ranging analysis of the human condition. By the time Henry II reached the throne, these characteristics were less likely to be found, and the taste for refined sensibilities was more obvious, especially in the poetry of a group of French poets known as the Pléiade, referring to the constellation in which none of the seven stars outshines the others. They originally were known as the Brigade, when seven young poets came together in Paris to study with Jean Dorat, an accomplished poet in his own right and a fine Greek scholar. In 1560 he received a chair in Greek in the Collège de Trois Langues. The Pléiade received patronage from the king but not as much as they thought they deserved. Although they were heavily influenced by Latin and Italian models, in particular Petrarch, they wrote mostly in French. More than one literary historian has said that modern French poetry begins with the Pléiade. In 1549 one of their number, Joachim Du Bellay, wrote what could be regarded as their manifesto, the *Défense et illustration de la langue française,* which proclaimed the legitimacy of the French language for use in literature. The author, however, admitted that French writers needed to study the classics and imitate them in order to achieve the highest level of excellence.

The best known of the Pléiade was Pierre Ronsard, whose poems, especially the *Odes,* are the sixteenth-century poetry most likely to be read today. He was a nobleman from the Orléanais. His career in diplomacy was cut short by deafness, and he turned to writing poetry, which gained him a royal pension of 1,200 *l* from Henry II. He published the first four books of the *Odes* in 1550, which served as a concrete expression of the principles Du Bellay set forth in the previous year. Like the other members of the Pléiade, he was heavily influenced by the Romans Pindar, and Horace, and Petrarch. He wrote a small number of poems in Latin but most were in French. Ronsard used a large number of Frenchified Latin words in his work and at times seemed consciously imitating his ancient models, which in that era was common. But his standing as one of the great poets would not be as high as it is, if he were not more often original in his expression.

Etienne Jodelle, a native Parisian, was the one member of the Pléiade who was known for something other than poetry, namely the theater. He produced what is regarded as the first French tragedy, staging his *Cléopatre captive* in 1552 for Henry II. In his prologue Jodelle emphasized that his play, which drew heavily from Plutarch, was written in French and owed little to classical models. He played the title role himself, which was not unusual as women rarely appeared on the stage in that era. Several others of the Pléiade had roles in the play. Jodelle also wrote a comedy, *Eugènie*. In its prologue he expressed his intention to write a comedy that was neither a *sottie* nor a mere imitation of classical comedy. Since the plot involved an abbé and his mistress, the play included considerable anticlerical satire.

Nearly all of the literary figures discussed thus far were associated with the court or Paris, but Lyon lived up to its place as the realm's second city with its own long list of authors. Perhaps its proximity to Italy helps explain the large group of poets who wrote in Latin. Etienne Dolet is the best known among them but more for being a printer and a victim of the heresy hunters than for his poetry. He was the most famous of the large group of printers in Lyon. His support of the printers' apprentices in their strike of 1539 created enemies for him among his fellows, but his arrest in 1544 was caused by the publication of banned books. His interrogation revealed an enthusiasm for several ancient thinkers regarded as atheists, and that charge was leveled against him as well. He was executed at Paris in August 1544.

Among the Lyonnais poets, the best regarded in his own era was Maurice Scève. As much as Marot, he was a transitional figure between the *rhétoriqueurs* and the Pléiade. His poetry was marked by an enthusiasm for Petrarch, and he claimed to have discovered the tomb of Petrarch's Laura in Avignon. His love poems imitating the Italian are his best work, although he never adopted the sonnet. What makes the literary scene at Lyon particularly interesting was the presence of two women. Little is known of a close associate of Scève's, Pernette Du Guillet, except that she died at age twenty-five. She learned classical Latin and at least a little Greek. Several of her poems mention Scève in very laudatory terms. In their imitation of Petrarch's love poems to Laura, they suggest that she had an unrequited love for Scève, but there is evidence in Scève's poetry that they were lovers. She wrote several pieces in Italian and was heavily influenced by Italian works.

Louise Labé, the daughter of a wealthy Lyonnais ropemaker and wife of a wealthy merchant, had the opportunity not available to most women of her era to acquire learning and write poetry. She was notorious for her refusal to conform to the expected behavior for women of her class. She often wore male attire and was trained in arms, having a reputation for her skillful use of the sword, and horsemanship. While the legend that she took part in a battle against Spain is certainly untrue, she probably did participate in a tournament before the future Henry II in 1542. Labé was friends with a large number of literary figures, and it is probable that she hosted a salon in Lyon. The preface to her first collection of poems, published in 1555, is an exhortation to women to take up learning and put aside their spinning and demonstrate to men that they are capable of great achievements. For that reason, she said, she was publishing her poetry. Petrarch heavily influenced her poetry, both in the sonnet form and the nature of his love poems, but she was no mere imitator.[6] Labé's love poetry, which makes up the larger part of her work, is much more passionate and physical than any other sixteenth-century French poet. The object of her love has never been determined, but it probably was not Henry II, as some accounts have it. In her life and her writings, Labé was the strongest example of feminism in sixteenth-century France.

In literature, art, and architecture, France of the mid-sixteenth century produced some of its greatest achievements of its history; in science and mathematics, however, the realm continued to lag behind much of the rest of Europe. In 1543, Nicolaus Copernicus touched off the Scientific Revolution with the publication of his *De Revolutionibus,* but its impact in France was limited. While Henry II acquired a copy for the royal library, there is no evidence that he ever read it. Like most other books he placed there, it was rebound with the royal coat of arms, and the copy remains an exquisite example of bookmaking. There is little evidence that many French scholars of the time read Copernicus. For the few who seem to have, it was a curiosity. Most lacked the necessary training in astronomy to make an informed judgment on heliocentrism. At a time when astronomers in central Europe were making important contributions to the development of technical astronomy (making use of observation), the French continued to regard the discipline as purely speculative. For all of his complaints about hypothesizing in astronomy, Ramus remained a theoretical astronomer.

The closest France came to a competent technical astronomer was Bishop Pontus de Tyard of Chalon-sur-Saône, who was also a poet of sufficient talent to be included in the Pléiade. The marginal notes found in his copy of *De Revolutionibus* indicate a good understanding of the use of star tables. He adjusted the tables found in Copernicus to his own time, which has been shown to have been 1557. Tyard's attitude toward Copernicanism was typical of a number of Frenchmen of that era: Astronomy was one of many areas concerning nature in which the human mind was incapable of reaching certainty. Hypotheses about the physical world neither could be proved nor disproved.[7] This was the attitude of Jean de la Pène, who is better known for his Latin editions of several of Euclid's works, especially the study of optics. La Pène's work in optics led him to the conclusion, as was befitting for a friend of Ramus, that the Aristotelian crystalline spheres, in which the heavenly bodies moved about the earth, did not exist. He based his argument on the lack of refraction of light from the stars, which should occur as starlight moves from one medium, crystal, into the next, air.

For the vast majority of the French, astrology was still the true science. One scholar, for example, argued that heliocentrism could not be true because the earth had to be in the center of the universe in order to receive the influence of the heavenly bodies. This was the era of the most famous astrologer of all times, Nostradamus (Michel de Nostradame), who even today is the focus of intense interest. A quatrain in his *Centuries* was said to have predicted the accident that killed Henry II, although it is not clear that it was taken to refer to the king before the event, and Nostradamus quickly reached the heights of fame from which he has yet to descend. One reason, however, why he could not have intended his predictions to apply to the twentieth century is the fact that he, like most of his contemporaries, expected that the world would soon come to an end. An important part of astrology was predicting the moment of the Second Coming or the appearance of the Antichrist and the dreadful days before the Second Coming. There was general agreement in the French populace, Jean Calvin being the major exception, that astrology could predict the last days. For Catholics the presence of the heretical Protestants was one sign of the approach of the Antichrist, who severely would test the faithful before Christ would vanquish him. The outbreak of the violence of the religious wars in 1562 confirmed their fears. More importantly, the civil wars had a severe impact on the achievements in art and literature from the generation of French artists and writers who had come to maturity after 1530. Their substantial record might stand considerably higher had not the religious wars intervened.

Part III

FRANCE, 1562–1614

14

The Monarchy:
Order out of Anarchy

On March 1, 1562, François de Guise was traveling through Champagne on his way to court with his retinue of armed men. Complaints from the bishop of Châlons about the presence of a large congregation of Huguenots in the village of Vassy prompted him to go there. While attending Sunday mass in Vassy, Guise was angered to hear the sounds of a Calvinist service coming from a nearby barn and sent some men to silence it. Violence quickly erupted, each side accusing the other of starting it, and Guise rushed over with the rest of his men. When quiet returned, as many as 30 Huguenots lay dead.

Although sporadic sectarian violence had already erupted elsewhere in France, especially in the Midi, the Massacre of Vassy is regarded as touching off a series of civil wars known as the French Wars of Religion. The Huguenot leaders were prepared for war, since exactly a month later Louis of Condé seized Orléans. In rapid order other towns of the Loire Valley fell to local Calvinist forces, while the urban Huguenots staged coups in numerous cities, most notably Lyon, Rouen, and Le Harve. Meanwhile, local Catholic forces prevented the Calvinist takeover of Bordeaux, Amiens, and Toulouse, among other places. Within three months France was clearly divided into two armed camps.

Catherine de Medici responded to this dangerous threat to Charles IX's authority by ordering the leaders of both sides to come to the court, but they refused and continued to arm. Believing that the Guise were more a threat than Condé was, she sent the prince a confidential letter that indicated she understood why he had to take arms. He published sections of it out of context, which suggested that she urged him to arm. Her anger at this betrayal led her back to the side of the Catholic champions—Guise, Constable Anne de Montmorency, and Marshal Jacques de St-André, who became known as the Triumvirate. She reluctantly provided them with legal sanction for assembling forces. They had been rivals for influence under Henry II, but they now were prepared to cooperate in defending the traditional faith. The constable's participation was a surprise because his nephews were on the other side, but he was loyal both to Catholicism and the crown. With the blessing of the crown, they drew on most of the royal forces and recruited Swiss mercenaries. The triumvirate was able to use the royal tax system to pay their troops, although much of the realm had stopped paying taxes.

Early on the Huguenots had the advantage of enthusiasm and discipline in their forces. Observers in the first several years of the wars often commented on their good behavior. The support of a large portion of the nobility, perhaps close to a majority, provided the Huguenot side with plenty of cavalry troops. Since they were volunteers, however, they were quick to leave for home when word came of fighting in their localities. The Huguenot leaders had to look to Germany and England for help. In September 1562 Queen Elizabeth agreed to provide 6,000 men and money for the defense of Rouen, which the triumvirate had under siege, in exchange for use of Le Harve as a harbor for the English troops. The English intended to exchange it for Calais when the eight years of French control of Calais set in the Treaty of Cateau-Cambrésis was up. In 1567 the French monarchy declared the arrival of the English at Le Harve was a violation of the treaty and refused to give up Calais.

By mid-1562 the Catholics had recovered from the surprise of the Huguenot uprisings and regained some of the places initially lost. The triumvirate made Rouen their special concern, since the expected arrival of the English threatened all of Normandy. The English did not move fast enough after they landed to relieve Rouen, which fell to the Catholic/royal forces in late October. Before it fell, Antoine of Bourbon was fatally wounded. He had committed to the Catholic side when he received a pledge from the triumvirate to help him recover Haute-Navarre. His death meant that the authority of his brother Condé and widow Jeanne d'Albret vastly increased. She was an ardent Calvinist who quickly established the Reformed Church in her lands.

Condé, believing his forces were too small, did not try to relieve Rouen until a band of German mercenaries joined him. Moving into Normandy in December, Condé ran into his foes commanded by Montmorency near Dreux. In the hard-fought battle the triumvirate won an indecisive victory at a heavy cost: St-André was killed and Montmorency was captured. However, Condé was also captured. The Battle of Dreux has the unique distinction of having both commanders captured by the other side. Instead of pursuing the Huguenot army, Guise returned to the siege of Orléans, which had begun in June. In February 1563 a Huguenot named Poltrot shot him to death. He had feigned desertion from the Huguenot army in order to get close to Guise. Poltrot was captured, and under torture he implicated Admiral Coligny and Theodore Beza. On the scaffold he retracted his accusation. The Guise, convinced of the efficacy of torture, as was normal then, remained convinced of Coligny's guilt and thirsted for revenge.

The death of the duke freed Catherine de Medici from the triumvirate, and she returned to her policy of reconciliation. Condé and Montmorency freed each other so they could negotiate the Peace of Amboise in March 1563. It was the first of the edicts of pacification that culminated in the Edict of Nantes. The freedom of worship granted to the Huguenots was more limited than the edict of January 1562: Calvinist worship would be allowed only in the suburb of one town in each administrative district and in the homes of Huguenot nobles. The edict required them to return all church property they had seized. Catherine and Chancellor L'Hôpital were probably the only ones satisfied with the peace, but it did end the organized fighting for a time, although minor encounters continued. Catherine's reconciliation of the two factions was complete enough that she could persuade many Huguenots to aid the royal army in retaking Le Harve from the English. The young king and his mother also went with the army. On their way to the coast, the royal party stopped at Rouen in August 1563. Its Parlement declared that Charles, who had just turned thirteen, had reached the age of majority because he was now in his fourteenth year, a new interpretation given to the edict of 1374.

Catherine felt that civil war and defiance of royal authority would be less likely if the people could see their king and be reminded of his power and majesty. Therefore, she took Charles on perhaps the longest royal progress ever made. Leaving Fontainebleau in March 1564, the court crossed Champagne to Lyon and made its way down the Rhône to Provence. While crossing Languedoc in the winter, Catherine negotiated with Philip II about a meeting with his wife Elisabeth, her daughter, and a marriage for the king with the Holy Roman Emperor's daughter. Philip, who hoped to persuade the French to cooperate in a campaign against Protestantism in the Low Countries, sent the duke of Alba to represent him. Neither side gained what they wanted from the meeting at Bayonne in May 1565. Certainly, there was no agreement to destroy the Huguenots as was claimed after the St. Bartholomew's massacre.[1]

The court resumed its progress north into Brittany and then east toward the Bourbonnais. Terrible weather forced it to stay at Moulins for the winter, where in February Charles promulgated the Ordinance of Moulins, which was largely concerned with the reform of justice and finance. The royal party finally reached Paris in May. The realm had been fairly quiet in the two years of the progress; there had been no major episodes of violence. However, rebellion had erupted in the Low Countries, and the situation there was a major complicating factor in French politics until 1648. Charles IX refused Philip's request to allow troops to cross France to Flanders, so Spanish forces under Alba took a route from Genoa through the Franche-Comté to Brussels, which became known as the Spanish Road. As they passed close to both Geneva and the French border, the distrustful French government strengthened its forces in Burgundy. The Huguenots saw both moves as a plot concocted at Bayonne against them and Geneva, and they returned to arms.

The king was at Meaux in September 1567 with only his usual array of guards, while Coligny and Condé secretly collected 1,500 men to seize the court. The plot was revealed at the last moment, and even worse for the scheme, 6,000 Swiss mercenaries had just arrived at Meaux, who protected the court as it dashed to Paris. This event touched off the Second War of Religion. Condé's forces, already prepared, had the early advantage and set up a blockade of Paris. That only frittered away the Condé's early edge, while the Catholics gathered their forces. In November 1567 a battle erupted near St-Denis, in which Montmorency, commanding the Catholic/royal army, was killed. Nonetheless, Condé was forced to withdraw from the vicinity of Paris. Negotiations led to a new edict of pacification in early 1568, which largely repeated the terms of the Peace of Amboise.

It was only a truce, as both sides remained armed. Events in the Low Countries, where Alba was repressing the revolt, raised Catholic hopes and Huguenot fears that the same could happen in France. Condé and Coligny, who were together in Burgundy, received word of a government plan to arrest them in August 1568. They successfully eluded the trap and retreated across France to La Rochelle, which by 1568 had emerged as the major Huguenot stronghold. The arrival of the Huguenot leaders and their forces foiled a government plan to seize the city. These developments led to the Third War of Religion. On the government's side it was far more openly a war of religion than the first two were. The cardinal of Lorraine had persuaded the clergy to provide the monarchy with funds, and he used it as leverage to force Chancellor L'Hôpital to retire. The Garde des sceaux, René de Birague, archbishop of Sens, took over his duties, and he was less committed to a policy of toleration, despite being a protégé of the queen mother. Two weeks after Birague was appointed, a new edict revoked the earlier edicts of pacification and expelled all Calvinist ministers. The upshot of these developments was that La Rochelle and the

Huguenot captains there received nearly total support from the Huguenots across France.

Preparing for new violence, Charles IX appointed his seventeen-year-old brother, Duke Henry of Anjou, lieutenant general of the realm in command of the royal army. The office of constable was left vacant after Montmorency's death. His oldest son, François, expected the post, and this snub was a major reason why he and his brother Henri de Damville, governor of Languedoc, grew cool toward the monarchy. Damville would soon ally with the Huguenots. Anjou, eager for glory, pushed the royal army into battle with Condé's forces in March 1569 at Jarnac near Angoulême. Condé, as usual for him, personally led his cavalry to the attack and was captured. As he was being led to Anjou, he was struck down by a royal captain whose motive remains obscure.[2] Coligny assumed command and successfully extracted the Huguenot forces from the battle. The royal army made no effort to pursue, so the admiral was free to regroup and receive German reinforcements.

With his army largely intact, Coligny the next spring made the most brilliant move of his career—marching his army from Gascony to Burgundy and then threatening Paris from the east. While his army was too small to lay siege to the city, its appearance was the last element Catherine de Medici needed to convince Charles to resume negotiations, which led to the Peace of St-Germain of July 1570. While repeating most of the elements of the previous edicts, it extended freedom of worship to all the towns the Huguenots held, which included most of those in the Midi. Calvinist burials were to be permitted but only at night. The edict granted four fortified places to the Huguenots for two years, and the king agreed to a general amnesty that returned all confiscated property on both sides. Not formally a part of the treaty but an integral part of it were two marriage proposals: The king would marry the Holy Roman Emperor's daughter, and the king's younger sister Marguerite was betrothed to Henry of Navarre. A year later, with the peace holding, Coligny was invited to the court as a member of the royal council, and for a second time the council acquitted him of any guilt in the murder of the duke of Guise, a verdict the duke's family would not accept. The admiral agreed to join the court because he felt he could convince Charles to aid the rebels in the Low Countries, who then were in dire straits. Coligny felt a foreign war would unite the realm against a common foe and draw the French away from battling each other.

In the summer of 1572, Huguenot volunteers were assembling to go to Flanders, and Coligny planned to lead them if the king did not. Meanwhile, preparations for the wedding of Marguerite of Valois and Henry of Navarre were proceeding. Jeanne d'Albret died in June 1572, removing a loud voice in objection to it. The wedding took place on August 18. Hundreds of Huguenot nobles had come to Paris, and their presence, both as nobles and Huguenots, in the ardently Catholic city raised tensions to a boiling point. On the morning of August 22, Coligny and his retinue were returning to his residence from the Louvre when three shots rang out. Two hit the admiral but only wounded him, and he was expected to live. Charles IX rushed to his bedside and swore that he would find the persons responsible.

One of the great controversies of French history involves the responsibility for the attack on Coligny. Traditionally, blame has been affixed to the queen mother, perhaps aided by her son Anjou, because she was convinced that the war with Spain the admiral was advocating would be a disaster for France and she was intensely jealous of his growing influence over her son. Several recent studies have argued against her direct culpability, but they do not make a better case against the other suspects: Anjou, the Guise, or the would-be assassin, who had a grudge against Coligny although he also had ties to the Guise, each acting alone or in any combination. It has also been proposed that the real responsibility for the massacre lay with the Catholic mob in Paris.[3] Most probably, the true culprit will never be identified.

The mood of the Huguenot nobles in Paris grew ugly, and the Parisian Catholics prepared for trouble. Whether or not Catherine was responsible for the attack on Coligny, it was apparently she who convinced Charles, who was not very stable, that Coligny and the Huguenot nobles were plotting a coup against him. Late in the evening of August 23, Charles met with the royal council and agreed to the summary execution of Coligny and his principal lieutenants. The captains of the Paris militia were called to the Louvre and told to expect trouble. The task of killing Coligny was given to Henri de Guise, first son of the duke killed in 1563, still eager for revenge. Before dawn the next morning, the feast of St. Bartholomew, Guise led a band of troops to Coligny's residence. The troops broke in, killed the admiral, and threw his body out to Guise in the street. Meanwhile, royal troops were hunting down the other prominent Huguenots marked for death.

Word spread with astounding speed through the streets of Paris that the king had ordered the killing of the Huguenots. The Paris mob swung into action with deadly zeal. Within a few hours of Coligny's death, the monarchy began to try to halt the killing, but it had little effect for three days. By the time the orgy of violence ended, at least 2,000, perhaps as many as 3,000, people, including women and children, had been killed. Many of the corpses were mutilated before being thrown into the Seine, the fate of most of the dead. There was also an orgy of looting of Huguenot homes and shops.

By the time the massacre had ended in Paris, it had spread to other towns, as the word that the Parisian Catholics were exterminating the heretics touched off new massacres in numerous cities. Royal letters written early on August 24 ordering provincial officers to take preventive measures against the Huguenots had an incendiary impact in many places. A second set of letters countermanding the first went out late the same day. Some royal officials chose to obey the first; others, the second. The result was a erratic pattern of killing in the provinces. The number of deaths was substantial in Toulouse, Rouen, and Lyon; while in Reims, Dijon, and Montpellier, there were none. Sporadic violence continued until October in the provinces, resulting in about 12,000 deaths.

At the very beginning of the Paris massacre, Henry of Navarre and his younger cousin Henry of Condé were taken before Charles IX and promised their lives if they recanted their heretical beliefs. It took several days of intense pressure before they agreed, and they were placed under tight watch to ensure they did not escape from the court. With Coligny dead and the two Bourbon princes neutralized, the Huguenots had lost their natural leaders and many of their captains, but enough had survived for a return to war. The Fifth War of Religion was largely a matter of the royal army besieging La Rochelle and several Huguenot strongholds in the Midi. Their stubborn resistance and his lack of money forced Charles to lift the sieges in July 1573.

By then the Huguenots of the Midi had gone a long way toward organizing Calvinist governments for the regions they controlled, a sort of "United Protestant Provinces of the Midi." It had essentially a republican type of government, with local assemblies making decisions. There was, however, a protector chosen from among the sympathetic grandees of the realm. For several years it was Henri de Montmorency-Damville, governor of Languedoc, despite his moderate Catholicism. Then in 1579 Henry of Navarre, who escaped from royal custody in 1576 and resumed his earlier faith, became the protector. There are intriguing similarities between the St. Bartholomew's massacre and the Spanish Fury of Antwerp of 1576 in that both might have led to independent Calvinist republics, but there was one key difference: Navarre's high place in the line of royal succession and the possibility that he might become king may have kept the French Calvinists from more actively pursuing their own separate state.

The odds that Henry of Navarre might gain the throne had improved when Charles IX died in May 1575 at age twenty-four without a son. Charles had been physically the strongest of Catherine's sons, but his health had deteriorated since August 1572. Guilt over the massacre may well have been a factor in his decline, as the Huguenots argued, but he had consumption (probably tuberculosis). Henry of Anjou, the third brother, was now king, and Navarre moved into second place in the line of succession behind François of

Alençon, the youngest brother. Henry III was not in France when Charles died; he had been elected king of Poland the previous year. The crown of that realm, which was elective, became vacant in 1572. Catherine had pushed Charles IX into providing a vast sum for bribing the electors (the Polish nobility). Henry arrived in Cracow in early February 1574, only to hear four months later that he was now king of France. The twenty-three-year-old king slipped out of Cracow the next day against the wishes of the Poles, who elected a new king the following year. Henry, who always called himself king of France and Poland, reached Paris via Italy in September. For the zealous Catholics, who turned out to be his most bitter foes, he brought to the throne the promise of being a Catholic champion and a reputation as a victorious commander. Both quickly proved to be inaccurate. In respect to the latter, he was the most sedentary king of the period, spending most of his time in Paris.

Henry III was intelligent and sophisticated, and he was more interested in the business of the monarchy than most other kings of the era. He planned to make numerous changes in the government, especially the tax system and the legal code. In respect to the former, he began the process of introducing the royal revenue officers, the *élus,* into the *pays d'état* where the provincial estates and their officers were responsible for the *tailles.* He succeeded in stripping the Norman estates of a role in setting the *tailles* in the province, but he was unable to achieve the same results in the other *pays d'état.* In an attempt to deal with his fiscal woes, Henry called a meeting of the Assembly of Notables in 1583. In preparation, he had his finance ministers prepare a lengthy analysis of royal rights and revenues across the realm, the first attempt to gain a thorough understanding of the revenue system.[4] Yet the assembly failed to achieve anything of note. Most of Henry's intended reforms failed to take hold, in large part because of the near anarchy of his reign but also because of his own personality, which made it difficult for him to follow through on his ideas. Did he have a flaw in his character, as most of his contemporaries, and historians ever since, have argued; or was he a victim of circumstances, as several historians have maintained? Certainly, the condition of the realm during his reign was atrocious. Whether he could have been a successful ruler if he had been more a man of action, as was Henry IV, who put into effect many of his reforms, is ultimately unanswerable. No other French king, not even Louis XI or Louis XVI, was as vilified as was Henry III. One of the taunts thrown at him was that his touch did not cure scrofula. The more vicious charges included homosexuality, incest with his sister Marguerite, and black magic.

By the time Henry III returned to France from Poland, the Huguenots, who already controlled the larger part of the Midi, had forged an alliance with a number of moderate Catholics, in particular the Montmorency clan and the duke of Alençon, who at twenty-one years of age was ready to assert himself. He entertained hopes of marrying Queen Elizabeth and becoming royal consort of England or being established as the prince of the Low Countries. Both required that he appear as a moderate Catholic friendly to the Huguenots, and he emerged as the leader of the Politiques, those French who were willing to accept religious toleration for the good of the state. They were far from being an organized party, but by 1570 the name Politique was being used for them. Chancellor L'Hôpital usually has been regarded as the first Politique. Intended originally as an insult for those Catholics who "wanted to join the religion to the state and not the state to the religion," the term came to identify the group who not only opposed the monarchy's religious policy since 1560 but also advocated a strong monarch in order to restore peace and stability in the realm. Despite their support for a powerful monarchy, the Politiques badly complicated matters for Henry III.

The worsening French economy, a product of both civil war and a string of poor harvests caused by cold, wet summers, exacerbated the government's fiscal distress. The monarchy was rapidly increasing its expenditures while losing control over the tax system in much of the realm, especially those regions controlled by the Huguenots. They sent the royal treasury only a small part of what they collected in taxes. In 1572 a Venetian ambassador reported that the Huguenots easily took in 200,000 *l* a year and could collect two or three times more, as they did in the next years.[5] By 1576 governors and officials elsewhere also were defrauding the monarchy on a large scale. The king's response to the decline in income was to raise taxes, which caused more hostility while making it easier for those in opposition to fill their coffers. In the Midi, the Huguenots and Politiques held local assemblies, which usually agreed to grant to their leaders the sums the king had set as taxes.

Efforts to determine what the royal revenue flow was during the religious wars are doomed to failure, because a large portion of the taxes, an increasing amount as the wars continued, never reached the treasury. By 1584 the official rate of taxation may have reached 15 million *l*, mostly in the form of *tailles*; perhaps half of it was being siphoned off. Numerous new taxes raised little additional money but upset those persons who were directly affected, as did a special tax of 1582 on woolen cloth. The *décimes* and other demands on clerical revenues raised tensions between the monarchy and the clergy without solving the fiscal crisis. Expanding venality was another expedient that raised the ire of the French populace. Rentes and forced loans were favorite means of dealing with the royal cash-flow problems, but they only increased the monarchy's long-term difficulties. The rentes on the Hôtel de ville of Paris reached 30 million *l* by 1584, and their interest totaled 3.75 million *l*, although the king regularly defaulted on the interest in order to promise the royal revenues raised in Paris to other lenders. Outright loans, largely from the Italian bankers at Lyon, remained the principal way the monarchy dealt with its most urgent expenses. Since there was good reason to fear the king might default on the loans, interest rates reached as high as 20 percent. Having poured enormous sums into the French monarchy, the bankers then had to continue to provide money to try to keep it solvent, despite a total debt that reached 101 million *l* in 1576. Given a situation in which expenses (22 million *l*) were estimated to have exceeded income (16 million *l*) by 6 million *l* in 1575, it was impossible to reduce the debt.[6]

The edicts of pacification created part of the problem by forgiving the Huguenots their seizures of royal taxes and revenues and usually agreeing to pay their troops and mercenaries. Both were major parts of a new edict Henry III issued in 1576. It became known as the Peace of Monsieur, for his younger brother, Alençon. The duke had fled the court the year before and put himself at the head of the Catholic malcontent nobles who were allied with the Huguenots. By then Henry of Navarre had begun to show the talent as military leader of the Huguenots that would make him one of the most respected captains of his generation. These two developments persuaded Henry III to negotiate peace. The edict granted the Religion Prétendu Reformé (RPR), as the Reformed Church was called for the first time in a legal document, liberty of conscience everywhere in France except Paris and wherever the court was. Again, a general amnesty and return of confiscated property was proclaimed. The edict created special courts in the Parlements with Catholic and Calvinist members to hear cases in which Huguenots were one party. They were declared eligible for royal officeholding. Eight fortified towns, mostly in the Midi, were given to the Huguenots as security places. Henry also agreed to call the Estates general.

The edict gave broad concessions to the Huguenot and Politique nobles. Alençon received the title of duke of Anjou and extensive additional lands as an appanage. Condé was named governor of Picardy and granted the Picard town of Péronne as a place to practice his religion freely. The ardent Catholic governor of Péronne, Jacques d'Humières, organized opposition to the decision. He enlarged on the idea of local Catholic leagues that had popped up and disappeared since 1561, calling on all the Catholic nobility to band together to defend Catholicism. This national Catholic League immediately gained a head of high standing—Henri de Guise, although he had little to do with organizing it.

The Catholic League was sufficiently well-organized across the realm to have a strong influence on the selection of deputies for the meeting of the Estates that Henry III called for December 1576 in Blois. The Huguenots complained that they were systematically excluded from the selection of deputies; and they boycotted the process, even in those areas they controlled. Not only was the number of Huguenot deputies very small, but the moderate Catholics were also poorly represented, leaving the Estates solidly in the control of the Leaguers.

When the 326 deputies assembled in December, the king himself, contrary to tradition, gave the opening address, since he was a fine speaker. He promised an extensive program for reform of justice and administration, if the Estates would agree to give him a large subsidy to pay his troops. It was directed at the Second and Third Estates, since the clergy had just agreed to aid the royal treasury. The nobility, however, declared that it violated their status to put a hand to sword and purse at the same time, while the Third Estate detailed the economic distress of the people and the heavy tax burden they were already bearing. It was proposed that a commission of 36 members chosen equally from the three estates be established, whose unanimous decisions on government reform would be binding on the king. Henry III, of course, objected, and squabbling between the Third Estate and the other two prevented the idea from being pushed with vigor. The very fact that it was proposed revealed the depths to which the monarchy had sunk, which was further demonstrated by the fact that this was the first meeting where the Estates refused to provide new revenues to the king when he asked for them.

The Catholic League pushed the Estates and the king into declaring that there was a fundamental law of Catholicity, by which the royal successor had to be Catholic, thereby excluding Henry of Navarre from the throne. In early March 1577, the Estates disbanded with no other significant results. Henry III had committed himself to a new war on the Huguenots, although the Estates failed to vote a subsidy for it, and he pursued it for six months with little enthusiasm. By late 1577 a new, somewhat less generous edict of pacification was in place. It did not detract enough from the Peace of Monsieur to force the Huguenots back to arms, while it satisfied the most urgent demands of the Leaguers. Henry moved to co-opt them by declaring he was in full agreement with their goals and proclaiming himself the head of the League. With the king as the chief, the Leaguers lost interest in it, and it declined rapidly. Whether it disbanded entirely by 1584 remains uncertain. The years from 1577 to 1584 were relatively quiet, certainly in comparison to the previous ones. A brief flare-up of violence in the Midi in 1579—counted as the Seventh War of Religion—resulted in the reaffirmation of the peace of 1577. Both royal finances and the economy had stabilized somewhat. It appeared that France might be on its way to a stable peace.

That it did not must be blamed in part on Henry III. He was busy making himself thoroughly hated by his often bizarre behavior and extravagance toward his *mignons*, the favored young noblemen of the court. After 1577 he had settled into Paris for good, and the Parisians were given an eyeful of the luxury and frivolities of the court in the midst of hard times. Henry was a devout Catholic, and he participated in the public devotions expected of a king with far more enthusiasm and devotion than did previous kings. He adopted for the royal chapel the liturgy proposed by the Council of Trent, something even Philip II had not done. On the other hand, he and his *mignons* would ride through the streets of Paris at night engaging in rough and raucous mischief, perhaps the same streets through which he had led a prayer procession that morning.[7] The contrast was jarring. Henry was excessively generous to the *mignons* with money, estates, titles, and royal offices. His fondness for his *mignons* and the Italian style in clothes, which the French regarded as highly effeminate, led to rumors that he was homosexual. Several modern historians have argued that he was not, although they agree he may well have been a transvestite. Whatever his sexual orientation was, what was important was that most of France believed he was homosexual. The fact that he was childless after ten years of marriage to Louise of Lorraine seemed to confirm it.

Henry III's lack of a son was what mattered the most in June 1584, when his unmarried younger brother died. The Salic Law, which governed the royal succession since 1328, dictated that in default of a direct father-to-son succession, the throne passed to the closest male relative who could trace his lineage in the male line (father to eldest son) to a kingly ancestor common to himself and the reigning king. In this case the successor was Henry of Navarre, whose Bourbon lineage went back to a sixth son of Louis IX. Although Navarre was twenty-two degrees of blood from Henry III and there were dozens of men who were more closely related to the king through females, the Salic Law made Navarre the royal successor.

Immediately reviving the Catholic League, the French Catholics served notice that they were not willing to accept a heretic on the throne. The League now consisted of two distinct elements—the Catholic nobles and the urban Catholics. They were tied together by their loyalty to Henri de Guise, who was the most popular man in France in 1584. The new League had two major items on its agenda—resisting Navarre by force and securing the succession of Navarre's uncle, Cardinal Charles of Bourbon. If, as the League proclaimed, there was a law of Catholicity that took precedence over the Salic Law, then the cardinal was the royal successor over his heretical nephew.

Philip II had a strong interest in the French succession, largely because of the impact on the Dutch Revolt. He had long been in contact with the Guise and other Catholic leaders. Once the League was reorganized, Philip sent envoys to carry on secret negotiations with the Guise. In late December 1584, at the Guise estate of Joinville, a secret agreement was signed, pledging Philip's support for the succession of the cardinal of Bourbon and a subsidy for the armed forces needed to make it good. The cardinal promised that once he was king he would cooperate with Philip in eliminating heresy from both France and the Netherlands. The next March the Catholic League made a public statement of its goals. Besides proclaiming its intention to place Bourbon on the throne if Henry III died without a son and restore Catholicism to its unique status in the realm, the League also pledged to implement the reforms called for by the Estates in 1576 and assemble the Estates every three years.

The adherence of a large portion of the Catholic nobility to the League allowed Guise to raise a substantial army, which he used in the spring of 1585 to seize control of much of eastern France. Catherine de Medici, who at age sixty-six was still active in politics, persuaded Henry III to negotiate with Guise, resulting in an agreement at Nemours in early July. The king agreed to pay the League's army, revoke all the edicts of pacification, and remove all Huguenots from royal offices. That created a legal barrier to Henry of Navarre's succession, which was quickly followed by papal excommunication of Navarre and Condé as relapsed heretics. The king agreed that Navarre could not succeed him under these circumstances but strongly urged him to become Catholic.

Navarre's response was a return to war, which is known as the War of the Three Henries. It was pursued in 1586 with little conviction, with the king trying to maneuver Guise and Navarre into destroying each other's forces while conserving his own. Then in February 1587, Queen Elizabeth approved the execution of Mary Stuart for plotting against her. Her execution convinced Philip that he had to conquer England, and he decided to send the Armada. He first needed to neutralize France until his fleet was victorious. His envoy in France was told to use the League to create diversions so that the French could not interfere.

In the spring of 1587 the pace quickened. A large force of German Protestants crossed the eastern frontier to join Navarre who was in the southwest. Henry III devised a risky strategy to deal with the situation: the duke of Guise was given a commission and some royal troops to join his Leaguers in attacking the Germans, while the royal favorite, the duke of Joyeuse, was sent with the bulk of the royal forces to battle Navarre. Henry hoped that Guise, with inadequate manpower, would be defeated while Joyeuse would drive the Germans out after Navarre's defeat, if they had not already left France. The king would then stand alone in France. Henry's plans backfired badly on him. In late 1587 Guise defeated the Germans at Auneau, near Chartres, while at Coutras Navarre crushed Joyeuse, who was killed in the battle. Joyeuse, who had some respect from his fellow nobles, was quickly replaced in the king's affections by the duke of Epernon, who had none. What offended the Leaguers the most about Epernon, beyond the gifts Henry lavished on him, was the fact that he had commanded a royal force that had moved between Guise and the Protestants after the battle of Auneau, preventing Guise from pursuing and perhaps destroying them.

The Leaguers were enraged at the king for his perfidy, while Guise's standing as the Catholic hero reached new heights. Nowhere was this more true than in Paris, the major stronghold of the League. The League was strong in a number of cities such as Toulouse and Nantes, with a loose organization tying them together and to the duke of Guise, but none matched Paris in its devotion to Guise and strength of the League. The Parisian Leaguers had organized in late 1584. Representatives were named to organize the 16 wards of the city; hence, the name "the Sixteen" (at least according to one account) for the more militant Parisian Leaguers. The group included most of the city's preachers, giving the League control over the principal means of spreading information and propaganda. From the beginning the Sixteen was as hostile to Henry III for his heavy taxes, bizarre behavior, and capriciousness as to the ostensible target of its efforts, Henry of Navarre. It planned at least twice in 1587 to stage riots that would allow it to take over the city, but a royal informer among its members leaked the plots to the king. Although only a few were arrested and lightly punished, the Leaguers' nerves were on edge, and they were eager for the duke of Guise to come to Paris, issuing an invitation to him in early 1588.

Henry III was equally on edge that Guise would appear in Paris, perhaps to depose him and take the throne himself as a descendant of Charlemagne, as many Leaguer pamphleteers were urging him. The king forbade the duke from entering Paris and ordered some 5,000 Swiss mercenaries into the vicinity of the city. Urged on by appeals from the Sixteen and the Spanish ambassador, since the Armada was about to set sail, Guise decided to go to Paris to justify himself to the king, so he claimed. When the duke entered Paris on May 9, the Leaguers were jubilant. Their emotion turned to rage when in the early morning of May 12 they found that the Swiss had entered the city and taken up positions. The Sixteen, using a plan created a year earlier and joined by a great number of the Parisians enraged at the presence of foreign troops in their city, barricaded the streets to prevent the movement of the troops. Under orders from Henry not to fire on the people and isolated in small squads surrounded by hostile mobs, the Swiss began to surrender en masse. In the evening Henry III, feeling that the Louvre was no longer safe, slipped out of Paris for Chartres.

This "Day of the Barricades," which is noteworthy as the first time barricades were used in Paris as an instrument of rebellion, made Henri de Guise "king of Paris," although it was largely the Parisian radicals who purged the city hall and put their own supporters into positions of power. Well before 1588 the Paris Sixteen had made contact with Leaguers in other cities; now it proposed a formal organization, a Sainte Union, against Henry III. About 300 cities and towns responded favorably, but whether a formal structure was ever instituted for the Sainte Union is not known.

Henry III carefully hid his rage and humiliation behind a facade of cooperating with the League. In July he accepted an Edict of Union the League had drawn up, and he declared that its terms, especially the law of Catholicity, were fundamental law of the realm. The king pledged his life to the eradication of heresy, agreed to implement the decrees of the Council of Trent in France, and gave a number of towns to the League as security places for six years. He repeated his promise to assemble the Estates general. A month later he named Guise lieutenant-general of the realm and recognized the cardinal of Bourbon as his nearest male relative. In return Henry was allowed to return to Paris.

In October 1588 the Estates met at Blois. The Catholic League completely dominated the First and Third Estates and had a majority in the Second. The Leaguers were well prepared for the meeting. The Parisian League had prepared a very lengthy cahier, which served for the entire Third Estate. Amid the requests for profound fiscal and administrative reforms and the total eradication of Calvinism in France, the crucial demand was that the king swear again the Edict of Union with the deputies. This act would have established the Estates as having a necessary role in the formulation of fundamental law, a dramatic enhancement of its powers. In a meeting with the leaders of the Third Estate, the king told them that some of his councilors were complaining that he was turning his monarchy into a semi-democratic state; "But, he said, I will do it."[8]

Henry III, however, was only buying time. He had made up his mind to eliminate those he regarded as the principal source of his troubles—the Guise. A week after the meeting with the deputies, he summoned the duke to meet with him at the château of Blois. Guise was warned that the king was not to be trusted, but he replied that Henry would not dare try anything. On the morning of December 23, 1588, as Guise waited to be admitted to the king's chambers, royal guards stabbed him to death. About 20 other leaders of the Leaguers were arrested, including the cardinals of Bourbon and Guise, the duke's brother. The latter was murdered in his prison cell the next day. The Estates remained in session for another three weeks, but the only piece of business was Henry's unsuccessful effort to get them to condemn the Guise for *lèse-majesté*, which would have justified his acts.

The Leaguers responded with rage to the events at Blois. Nowhere was it greater than in Paris, where a Guise sister, the duchess of Montpensier, led the chorus denouncing the tyrant Henri de Valois, as the Leaguers usually referred to the king after December 23. A Guise cousin became governor of Paris, and the 40-man general council of the Sainte Union named a third Guise brother, the duke of Mayenne, as lieutenant-general of the realm, "awaiting the assembling of the Estates." On January 7 the Faculty of Theology declared that the murders at Blois released the French people from their oath to the king.

Henry III's moment of exaltation at freeing himself from the Guise quickly disappeared. Catherine de Medici died in January 1589, removing his one confidante and the only person who might have been able to negotiate with the Leaguers, who now controlled well over half of France. By late April Henry had negotiated an alliance with the man who controlled much of the rest of the realm—Henry of Navarre. The king recognized Navarre as his successor, and they agreed to join forces in an attack on Paris. As the two approached Paris with 40,000 men, sermons and pamphlets proclaiming that killing the tyrant would be a holy deed stoked the hatred of the Parisians to a fever pitch.[9] Jacques Clément, a young Dominican lay brother, took them at their word and went to the royal camp near St-Cloud. On August 1 he gained entrance to the king by claiming to be bringing news from the royalists in Paris and fatally stabbed him.[10] Henry III lingered for a day, telling his loyalists to accept Navarre as king and begging him to convert to Catholicism. The Valois dynasty then came to an end.

On August 2, 1589, Henry of Navarre-Bourbon had become, according to Salic Law, the king of France. But whom did he rule? The Huguenots, of course, recognized him as king, but when two days later he issued a statement promising to maintain the Catholic Church in its entirety and to be instructed by a free, national council, some of the Huguenot nobles retired to their homes. Most, however, were back under his banner by the next spring. More serious a blow to Henry was the defection of a large number of Catholic royalists. Most took a position of neutrality and returned to Henry's service eventually, but a few did join the League. In the month after Henry III's death, the royal army shrunk from 40,000 men to 18,000.

With so drastic a reduction in his forces, Navarre had to abandon the attack on Paris. Overcoming his first thought of retreating to Gascony, he headed west into Normandy to make contact with the English. Caen and Dieppe were among the few cities that recognized him as king. Mayenne pursued him into Normandy and gave battle at Arques in late September 1589. Henry's foe outnumbered him by some three to one, but he had been able to entrench his men in a strong defensive position and withstood the Leaguer attack. Mayenne pulled back to Amiens. Henry, with 5,000 English and Scots troops as reinforcements, dashed on Paris. The city was caught by surprise, but the Parisian militia, aided by a large portion of the clergy with pikes and firearms, was able to hold the walls. Henry had to pull back to Normandy, where Mayenne again gave him battle at Ivry in March. Navarre personally led his cavalry into the Leaguer line and broke it. A hard pursuit of the defeated Leaguer army scattered it widely, and Paris again was vulnerable. But Henry delayed pushing toward Paris for two months, and when his forces did reach the walls at the end of May 1590, they settled into a blockade. As has often happened in a city under siege for a cause, the level of fanaticism among the Parisians rose to unimagined heights. They held out through the summer despite being reduced to eating cats and dogs. In late August a Spanish army from Flanders led by the Duke of Parma arrived, and Henry lifted the siege without a fight.

By September 1590 the military situation across France was in the same stalemate as the political. The Leaguer king "Charles X" had died earlier that year, and the League had no other candidate with a claim comparable to Henry's. But he had fallen in love with Gabrielle d'Estrées, and he undertook an ineffective siege of Chartres in order to be close to her. In July 1591 he issued the Edict of Mantes, in which he pledged again to maintain Catholicism while reenacting the broadest of the edicts of pacification granting freedom of worship to the Huguenots. It brought a number of Politique nobles back to his banner, and with increased forces he moved into Normandy in late 1591 to lay siege to Rouen. Parma pursued him into Normandy and drove him away from Rouen, but was wounded in the action. Leaving 1,500 Spanish troops in Paris, Parma returned to Flanders where he died six months later.

While Parma commanded the Leaguer forces, Mayenne was left to attend to the League's political agenda. Its main item was convoking the Estates to elect a Catholic king. The Leaguers had been seeking a meeting since their king died, but it was only in late 1592 that Mayenne, acting in his capacity of lieutenant-general of the realm, sent out letters calling for a meeting in Paris in January 1593. Henry declared that anyone who attended the Leaguer estates was guilty of lèse-majesté and used his forces to prevent many Leaguers from reaching Paris. Consequently, only 128 deputies comprised the Estates of Paris. Several of the cahiers were concerned with other matters, such as reducing both the *tailles* and the number of royal offices to what they had been under Louis XII, but the main matter at hand was the election of a Catholic monarch. Of the several possible choices, the favorite among the Leaguers was the young Charles de Guise. Philip II, however, had sent an ambassador with plenty of gold to promote the candidacy of his daughter Isabella, the granddaughter of Henry II. A small but vocal group of Leaguers, largely from Paris, loudly supported her election, especially if she were married to Guise. The issue of the Spanish candidacy badly split the Leaguers, and it prompted a group of moderate Leaguer magistrates in the Parlement, led by Guillaume Du Vair, to declare that the Salic Law was fundamental law.

Meanwhile, the moderate Leaguers had agreed to meet with Catholic supporters of Henry IV at Suresne in May 1593. It had become clear that the situation was thoroughly stalemated. In particular it seemed impossible for Henry to gain control of Paris. His financial situation was so desperate that it looked as if he would lose most of his mercenaries to the League, since he could not pay them. While the Leaguers probably coined the quip "Paris is worth a mass!" always attributed to Henry,[11] it summed up perfectly the situation of mid-1593: A Protestant king could never hope to rule France from Paris. On May 17 Henry's spokesman at Suresne, Archbishop Renauld de Beaune, announced Henry's intention to be received into the Catholic Church.[12] The Leaguers could only sputter that they hoped he was sincere, something many doubted for years to come.

In July Henry and a group of Politique prelates met at St-Denis, where he spent a day being instructed in the Catholic religion and drawing up an act of abjuration of his Calvinist beliefs. The next day, July 25, 1593, Henry attended mass in the abbey church. A great crowd outside greeted him with *Vive le Roi!* That religion was the League's primary motivation is made clear by the speed with which a rush of Leaguers came over to Henry's side. Many Leaguers were ready to abandon their factionalized party the moment Henry changed his religion. However, they did not come cheaply. Many of the same type of grants given to the Huguenot captains in the edicts of pacification were provided to the more important Leaguer captains and cities—forgiveness of the taxes they had appropriated and payment of their troops and debts. In addition the Leaguer chiefs received large monetary gifts and royal offices. Because they had much larger forces, the sums the Leaguers received were far greater than those for the Huguenots. In the case of the duke of Mayenne, for example, the king agreed to pay his debts of more than 1 million *l.* Although the amount of appropriated taxes he was forgiven is not known, the total sum involved in his capitulation was estimated in his own time at 2.46 million *l.* Mayenne's cousin, the duke of Lorraine, received over 2.7 million *l,* mostly in the form of a gift.

By 1596 Henry paid out about 20 million *l* to the Leaguer grands. Of course, if he had forced them to submit by war, the cost might have come to nearly the same, with the added price of permanent bitter feelings. The money granted as gifts was largely distributed over many years as pensions, and some of the Leaguer pensioners died before their full sums were paid out. In addition to the financial elements of the Leaguers' submissions, Henry IV gave the most prominent among them the right to exclude Calvinist worship from their lands, a concession that was made also to many Leaguer cities. Small wonder that when one of his servants said to Henry that his people had "rendered to Caesar what is Caesar's;" the king quipped: "Not rendered *(rendu)* but sold *(vendu)*."

Charles de Guise, who controlled Champagne, sold his loyalty to the king only in early 1595, which prevented Henry from using Reims when he decided to go ahead with his coronation in February 1594. The use of Chartres was one of a number of improvisations, such as reproducing several of the royal insignia, which were necessary for the ceremony that took place on February 26. Nonetheless, there were few who argued that it was not valid. Henry took the solemn coronation oath that included the promise to drive out of the realm all heretics denounced by the Church. Immediately after the ceremony, he touched for scrofula with many cures. This was seen as God's approval and brought many Catholics to his side.

These events had a powerful impact in Paris, which as of late March 1594 was still in the grips of the League, backed by a large Spanish force. Henry moved his army within a few miles of the city. The Leaguer governor of Paris, Charles de Cossé, secretly negotiated with the king to surrender the city to him. His payoff included more than 1.4 million *l* and the office of marshal. His confederates opened three gates to royal forces in the early hours of March 22. In four hours they had control of the city, and Henry felt secure enough to enter. He rode to Notre Dame where he devoutly attended mass. In the evening he and most of the Parisians cheered as the Spanish troops left, taking with them about 20 of the most radical Leaguers. The king extended an amnesty to most of the Parisian Leaguers, but three were executed for the murder of a president of the Parlement, and some 120 of the most ardent were expelled from France. Most did receive pardons eventually if they asked the king. There were widespread bonfires of the Leaguer pamphlets, and the records of the Leaguer-controlled offices were purged. Overall, Henry IV's reprisals against those who so vehemently had opposed him were singularly bloodless.

The king worked very hard at being a good Catholic. He devoutly attended the lengthy Holy Week services that soon followed his Parisian entry. By the end of April, the Sorbonne announced that it was satisfied he was a sincere Catholic and recognized him as king. Yet even the Sorbonne's approval was not good enough for some die-hard Leaguers. In late December 1594 Jean Chastel made an attempt on Henry's life, knocking out a tooth as he struck at him with a knife. At his trial Chastel declared that Henry was a tyrant because he had not received papal absolution, and according to his teachers, tyrannicide was justified. Chastel was executed. The king was already negotiating with the pope for absolution from the papal excommunication of 1585. In September 1595 Clement VIII absolved Henry in exchange for his pledge to reestablish Catholicism in Béarn and other places under Huguenot control and publish the Tridentine decrees in the realm. Henry may have intended to fulfill the first pledge, even if he never did; but he had no intentions of offending Gallican sensibilities by accepting Trent. Despite his failure to live up to the agreement, his relationship with Clement remained cordial, in large part because the pope wanted a Catholic French king as a counterweight to Philip II.

Papal absolution was not sufficient to convince a few unrepentant Leaguers. Plots against Henry's life continued to be uncovered at the rate of about one a year in the ten years after his conversion. Absolution, however, brought most of the remaining Leaguer nobles over to his side. In June 1595 Henry defeated a Leaguer/Spanish force near Dijon, which gave him control of Burgundy and brought about the submission of Mayenne. After that, the civil war became a war with Spain, in which some Catholic nobles sided with the foreigners. By the end of 1596 the only significant holdout was the duke of Mercouer, the Leaguer governor of Brittany. Picardy was the main theater of the war, where the Spanish seized Calais in April 1596. Henry sought aid from Queen Elizabeth, but she demanded Calais as payment. In early 1597 a Spanish force surprised Amiens, where Henry had been collecting supplies for an attack on Flanders. He had to retake the city if he wished to control Picardy. He assembled a force of some 30,000 men and put Amiens under siege. The Spanish commander was killed in September, and the garrison surrendered three weeks later. As often was the case in this era, such a quick turnabout in fortune was seen as revealing God's will for peace. In late 1597 Chancellor Pompone de Bellièvre was on his way to begin negotiations.

Meanwhile, Henry IV reassembled his army over the winter months and in early 1598 led it toward Brittany. Mercoeur quickly agreed to submit to the king. The financial elements of his submission came to about 4.3 million *l.* Arriving at Nantes in April, Henry signed the famous edict of toleration known as the Edict of Nantes.[13] It consisted of four parts. The major section was made of up of 92 published articles, which provided for a general amnesty and freedom of worship for the entire French population, Catholic and Reformed. Catholic services were to be allowed in those places where they were being barred. It was the articles on freedom of worship for the Huguenots for which the edict is famous. The Calvinist nobles were free to hold their services in their residences: the highest-ranking ones, whether or not they were present, the lower ranking, only if they were present in person. The Huguenots also received the right to worship in those places that they held in 1597 and, in addition, one town in every *bailliage*. They, however, were not allowed to hold their services in those Leaguer cities where Henry had promised to bar Protestant services when these cities submitted to him. As for Paris, Calvinist worship was prohibited in the city and for 12 miles around it. The Huguenots were granted special courts in which their cases were to be heard by judges who were equally divided between Calvinist and Catholic. The Calvinists were not to be denied entrance into royal offices, schools, and universities because of their religion. The 55 secret articles, so called because they were not published immediately, largely dealt with specific towns and persons to which special privileges or restriction applied.

The Edict of Nantes also included two royal brevets. One provided royal pay of 135,000 *l* a year for the Calvinist ministers, since the Huguenots were still obliged to pay the tithes. The second was the most controversial part of the edict. It allowed the Huguenots to maintain garrisons in those towns where they had them as of August 1597. The king paid their garrisons and named their captains, who had to be Huguenots. There were 49 places in all that served as the Huguenot surety places, mostly in the southwest. There was little in the edict that was not in earlier edicts of pacification. Henry pulled all of their elements together in a largely consistent way and expanded their applications. Did the edict permit the Huguenots to create "a state within the state," as has often been said? In one key way it did. No other group had the right to garrison fortified places for any reason other than royal service. The strongest argument against this point is that the privilege of having the surety places was to last for only eight years. While the kings regularly reaffirmed it until 1629, they always had the right to rescind the privilege. The religious toleration clauses, on the other hand, were in perpetuity. Perpetuity in France lasted 85 years.

The edict did not take effect until the Parlement of Paris registered it. Presumably Henry IV expected resistance, but surely not as much as he received. After two *lettres de jussion* failed to achieve results, he called the parlementaires to the Louvre to hear him in person. He clearly wanted to avoid a *lit de justice* at this point. His address to them was a masterpiece of bravado, cajolery, and pleading. For example, in dismissing the possibility of a new league, he exclaimed: "I have jumped over high walls, I will do the same to barricades, which are not so high." He made a strong statement about his power as king: "I am king now and speak as king. I want to be obeyed."[14] His oration to the Parlement was one of the strongest statements of a sixteenth-century king's perception of his own authority. Yet it took another such address before the magistrates registered the edict in late February 1599. Six of the provincial Parlements followed within the next year, but the Parlement of Rouen did not register it until 1609, despite heavy pressure from Henry.

Among French Catholics the edict stirred up a furor. In Paris the Parlement had to forbid street processions in late 1598 because they were occasions for denouncing the king . Henry could afford to be stubborn about the edict because the international situation had changed dramatically in the months after he issued it. Chancellor de Bellièvre led negotiations with the Spanish at Vervins on the Flemish border. The Peace of Vervins was accepted on May 2, 1598. It returned the status quo of 1559 on the northern frontier of France, both sides restoring places taken since then. France had the better of it, getting back Calais and several other towns, while Spain's right to Cambrai was affirmed. Philip II died in late September 1598, shortly after he had signed the treaty, removing a dedicated antagonist of France from the scene. His successor, Philip III, was neither as strong-willed nor as committed a defender of Catholicism. The death of the old king meant that the die-hard Leaguers, who might have rebelled against the Edict of Nantes, could not count on Spanish aid. This helped to defuse the situation in France.

One element of the Peace of Vervins led to further complications concerning the marquisate of Saluzzo on the border between Savoy and France. The duke of Savoy had occupied it in the midst of the anarchy in France of 1588. Vervins called for papal arbitration of the French claim to it, but the pope quickly conceded failure and withdrew. The duke came to Paris himself to negotiate with Henry IV and made broad concessions. When by August 1599 he had failed to follow through on his pledge, Henry declared war. The war involved assaulting several mountain top fortresses, in which the excellent French artillery played the major role. By January the duke accepted a treaty that gave France the territories of Bresse, Bugey, and Gex between the Saone River and Geneva. This acquisition soothed the Calvinists since it put the French in a good position to aid Geneva should the Spanish ever attack it and to occupy the Franche-Comté, as they would in 1678.

For the next ten years, France was at peace with itself and its neighbors. Henry IV and his advisers could turn their full attention to restoring the realm, especially royal finances, which were in a truly dismal state in 1594. They had already made good progress in that regard by 1600. The king had a good head for figures, but much of the credit for restoring the monarchy's solvency belonged to Maximilien de Béthune, who received the title of duke of Sully in 1606, the name by which he always is called. As a twelve-year-old boy, he had barely escaped the St. Bartholomew's Day massacre in Paris. Soon after that he joined Henry's entourage and became a respected captain. In 1593 he became involved in financial administration, which soon became his special domain. In 1600 he was named *surintendent des finances,* which was the most important of the five offices that he held. Had Henry IV been a less active king, Sully might well be regarded as the original first minister. Sully remained a Huguenot after Henry's conversion, but that hardly affected their relationship. Indeed, after 1600 much of the king's entourage was Calvinist, much to the great annoyance of many Catholics. Sully's memoirs reveal that the two of them engaged in easy bantering, which produced several of Henry's best-known bon mots.

In 1596 Henry IV hoped to call a meeting of the Estates but decided instead to have an Assembly of Notables. The 95 notables present recommended that the king levy a special sales tax of 5 percent on everything sold in the realm, except for wheat, thereby avoiding bread riots. It was estimated that this *pancarte* would raise up to 5 million *l*, but in its best year it produced only 1.56 million *l*. Opposition from nearly everyone in the realm convinced Henry to abolish it in 1602, but it had helped to restore solvency to the royal budget. He and Sully came up with a myriad of other expediencies to raise money, but the key to pulling the monarchy up from bankruptcy was simply to insure that the system of taxation worked efficiently. This was Sully's great achievement.

In 1600 the fiscal divisions of the realm consisted of the 15 *généralités*, which were divided into 153 *élections*, and the five provinces of the *pays d'états*—Brittany, Burgundy, Dauphiné, Languedoc, and Provence. Sully personally investigated the accounts of the *receveurs-généraux* and *trésoriers*, usually traveling to their cities. Those who failed to cooperate or whose accounts were inaccurate were often punished by having their salaries withheld; the worst were dismissed. By 1600 the tax system had been restored to full efficiency. The median sum in the ten years after 1600 collected as the *taille* was 10.8 *l* a year; from the *gabelles*, 1.6 million *l*; from the *aides*, 3.2 million *l*; and from the domaine, 1 million *l*. The *taille* was largely stable, although Henry routinely add *crues* of some 4 million *l* a year. The other taxes were rising rapidly by 1610. With the addition of the money from venality, including the new system of selling offices called the *paulette*, the *décime* from the church, and other sources, the median annual revenues came to about 26 million *l* a year.

With royal expenses running close to that, including pensions to great nobles of more than 2 million *l* a year and subsidies to the Netherlands and Geneva, it was impossible to have the sort of budget surpluses needed to reduce substantially the massive debt that may have reached 297 million *l*, as reported to the notables in 1596. That sum included loans totaling 147 million *l* and 150 million *l* in lands and revenues of the royal demesne that had been alienated. Sully negotiated ruthlessly with the creditors. He forced them to accept a sharply reduced rate of interest—for example, the interest on the *rentes* was dropped to 6.25 percent from 8.66. In many cases he reduced the sums owed by half and more. The king owed the Swiss cantons and captains 36 million *l*; Sully paid off 19.6 million *l* at most, and the rest was written off. In 1608 all of the debts from Henry III were repudiated, and some others were declared to have been fabricated and were disowned. Nonetheless, at Henry's death 130 million *l* in debts remained, mostly in the form of alienated demesne revenues. But perhaps as much as 15 million *l* had been collected in the royal treasury for a war chest, although that quickly was spent in the troubled times of Marie de Medici's regency.

Marie de Medici was the queen mother in 1610 through a fortuitous set of circumstances. Although Henry had married Marguerite of Valois in 1572, they had spent very little time together and had not seen each other since 1582. They had no children. Both had taken numerous lovers, but Henry was especially smitten by Gabrielle d'Estrées, who bore him two sons. If she had not died in 1599, he almost certainly would have married her. Thus, her death was a break for him, although he genuinely mourned her, because Pope Clement VIII would not have granted him an annulment of his marriage in order to wed Gabrielle. Part of the negotiations with the papacy for the annulment involved a discussion of the right choice for his new wife. When Clement granted the annulment on the grounds of coercion and consanguinity, it was already understood that Henry would marry the niece of the duke of Tuscany. Marie brought with her a dowry of 1.8 million *l,* of which 750,000 went back to her uncle to help pay Henry's debts to him, which totaled 3 million *l.* In October 1600 they were married by proxy. The next month she met her husband at Lyon, and ten months later the Dauphin Louis was born.

With a dauphin in the royal nursery, peace across the realm except for a few peasants' riots, and the war with Spain over, Henry IV devoted his attention after 1600 to restoring royal authority. He and his advisers did it so well that many historians regard the next ten years as the real foundations of royal absolutism in France. Henry made a number of statements that indicate a strong sense of royal power, but in fact they were little different from those of Francis I and Henry II. His contribution to absolutism was restoring the efficiency of the government so that it was again responsive to the king's will. He was little more inclined to absolutism than his predecessors, but after the 40-year intermission in the process of strengthening the monarchy, he returned to the task, which then continued after 1600 with only short pauses. Certainly, the atmosphere then was far more conducive to strengthening the monarchy than it had been 50 years earlier.

The actual changes Henry IV effected in the government were subtle enhancements of royal authority, which taken as a whole produced a stronger monarchy. Among them were placing royal tax officers, the *élus,* in the provinces of Guyenne and Dauphiné, although his efforts to put them in the other *pays d'état* failed. His use of *chambres de justice* to ferret out corruption among the revenue officers was a limited success, but it established an important precedent for future kings. Henry never called the Estates general, and he was effective in reducing the power of several of the provincial estates, particularly in Guyenne.[15]

Historians have sometimes pointed to Henry IV's handling of the great nobles as evidence that he was an absolute monarch, but there was precedent for that in the reigns of Louis XI and Francis I. The treason of the Constable Bourbon in Francis's reign was similar to the major case of noble revolt under Henry, involving Duc Charles de Biron. Spain was deeply involved in the conspiracy, although many involved were Huguenots. The Peace of Vervins did not end the hostility between the French and the Habsburgs. Such matters as a tariff war and French aid to the Spanish Muslims kept the relationship chilly. In early 1609 the duke of Jülich-Cleves died. The location of his lands on the eastern border of both the Dutch Republic and the Spanish Netherlands gave them major strategic importance. He left only distant relatives, Catholic and Protestant, with claims to his duchy. When it became clear that the Holy Roman emperor supported the Catholic claimant, the Lutheran princes made contact with Henry. As of late 1609 he could not decide whether to go to war over the issue.

Suddenly Henry's never-ending pursuit of beautiful women became a factor in deciding war or peace. He had become deeply smitten with an exquisitely beautiful fifteen-year-old, Charlotte de Montmorency, and arranged for her marriage to his cousin, Henri II de Condé, who was not expected to stand in the way as Henry seduced his bride. But Condé had fallen deeply in love and whisked her away to Brussels to escape Henry. Henry demanded that the Spanish authorities return the couple. When they refused, he agreed to support the Lutherans militarily in the Jülich-Cleves dispute. By May 1610 France was abuzz in anticipation of a war with the Habsburgs. The ardent Catholics, who had always suspected the sincerity of Henry's conversion, were convinced that the king was planning to wage war on Catholic rulers in league with the Huguenots. One of them, François Ravaillac, stabbed Henry to death as the king rode in his coach through Paris. Although he had been the object of at least 20 assassination plots since 1593, his guard was very small on that fateful May 14, 1610. Ravaillac was immediately seized. Extensively interrogated and tortured before he was executed, he insisted that he had acted alone, because the king was planning to wage war on the pope. The powerful suspicion that the Jesuits and the Spanish were behind Ravaillac has never been proven.

At age eight Louis XIII was now king of France. Of course, he needed a regent, his mother, Marie de Medici. She had been crowned queen only the day before the assassination so she could serve as regent while Henry led his army against the Habsburgs. The Parlement of Paris, in what appears to have been an attempt to enhance its authority, issued an *arrêt* the same afternoon as Henry was killed proclaiming Marie regent. She and her advisers, believing that the Parlement's act was an infringement on royal power, quickly arranged for a *lit de justice* to take place the next day. The boy king appeared in person in the Parlement and proclaimed his mother as regent. Having the new king appear in public in his formal capacity as king so quickly after his predecessor's death served to emphasize the perception that the successor gained the authority of kingship at the moment of death and not at his coronation. It was a concept that had been developing since before 1484, but it had never been so clearly expressed. The event also affirmed the emerging idea that it was the royal blood in the new king that gave him the right to rule, not the coronation. One tradition remained in place in respect to the coronation, however; Louis touched 868 people for scrofula the day after he was crowned.

Both the nature of Henry's death and his removal from the scene raised tensions between Catholics and Huguenots. Louis was being raised a Catholic by a pious mother; naturally, the Huguenots would be suspicious of their intentions. The quick reaffirmation of the Edict of Nantes did not remove those doubts entirely. In one respect the queen mother was in a weaker position than her cousin Catherine had been fifty years earlier: She had been in France only ten years compared with Catherine's 26. Marie was spared the serious troubles of the previous era largely because few wanted to resume the religious wars. Perhaps her own limited talent as a politician was also a factor, since her policies were cautious and uncomplicated, and she avoided the reputation for deviousness that plagued Catherine.

Marie defused the impending war with the Habsburgs over Jülich-Cleves by negotiating with Spain, resulting in a treaty in 1612. The disputed lands were split between the Catholic and the Protestant claimants, and the treaty also included a double marriage contract between Philip III's daughter Anna and son Philip with Louis XIII and his sister Elisabeth. The marriages took place in 1615. The peace with Spain and the Spanish marriage for the king were unpopular with many French nobles, who had expected an opportunity to fight in a foreign war. It added to the worst problem of Marie's regency—noble unrest. She hoped to buy their loyalty by opening up the royal treasury to them, quickly dissipating the surplus that Sully had built up. His complaints led to his dismissal in 1611. The leader of the malcontents was Henri of Condé, who had returned from exile expecting to have a major role in government. Even a huge pension failed to satisfy him. Although he was a Catholic, he worked well with the Huguenots. In early 1614 the malcontents sent a letter to the young king demanding that he replace his current evil advisers, especially the queen mother's favorite, the Italian Concini, and call a meeting of the Estates general. Marie opposed holding a meeting before her son had reached the age of majority on his fourteenth birthday, so in the summer of 1614 she took Louis into Brittany and the southwest, with the added purpose of influencing the election of the deputies.

Shortly after returning to Paris, Louis went to the Parlement in October to have his majority pronounced, and later that month 477 deputies assembled in Paris. The election process largely followed that of 1484, but unlike that meeting, this one proved to be highly contentious. The First and Third Estates engaged in bitter disputes over the Jesuits and the issue of whether the papacy could depose a French king. The Second and the Third heatedly debated tax policy, but they cooperated in opposing the clergy's demand that the decrees of the Council of Trent be published in France. The meeting of 1614 is remembered for giving Bishop Armand de Richelieu the opportunity to demonstrate to the court, already half-convinced, his talents as an orator and politician. It is far better known as the last meeting of the Estates for 174 years.

15

The Church: Tempered and Strengthened

Despite the failure of the Colloquy of Poissy and the Conference of St-German, the French monarchy and hierarchy remained confident that they could reform the Gallican Church without handing over the task to either Rome or Geneva. The French had little influence over either center of the two competing faiths. In regard to the papacy, one clear result of the troubles that hit France upon the death of Henry II was the loss of French influence in Rome. When Paul IV died a month later, French involvement in the conclave that elected Pius IV was minimal. The popes for the next 35 years were largely beholden to Philip II for their elections, and while not slaves to his will, they tended to see things his way. The clearest example of this occurred in the conclave of 1572 in which none of only five French cardinals participated in the election of Gregory XIII, who reigned until 1585. He actively supported the Catholic League and excommunicated Henry of Navarre despite the objections of the French government. His successor, Sixtus V, was elected with greater French participation, and his policy, while hardly hostile to Spain, reflected greater consideration of French interests, most obviously in his refusal to issue a summary excommunication of Henry III after the execution of the cardinal of Guise. The situation reached its worst point with the elections of Gregory XIV and Innocent IX in quick succession in 1591 without any French input whatsoever. Their ardent support of Spanish and Leaguer interests would have made Navarre's conversion impossible had both not died after reigns of only a few months. To be sure, Clement VIII's election had little French involvement, but he realized the danger to the papacy of being little more than Philip's chaplain and looked to France as a counterweight. Thus, he was accommodating to Henry IV, giving him absolution without clear evidence of his sincerity and granting him an annulment in 1600. His policy sharply revealed the value of having a friend of France on St. Peter's throne.

An earlier papal decision that rankled the French government was the reconvocation of the Council of Trent. Catherine de Medici expected it would reaffirm the decisions of the earlier sessions on such matters as justification and the Eucharist, which the Protestants vehemently opposed. Catherine and the cardinal of Lorraine declared that French bishops would attend a new council if Pope Pius IV would call one and not reconvene Trent. Vague promises from the French could not counter the pressure from Philip II, and the pope announced the reconvening of Trent in January 1562. Having just proclaimed the first edict of pacification the day before Trent reopened, the queen mother felt obliged to humor the Catholics and the pope on the issue of French representation. She sent six bishops, but they were very slow in getting underway, so when the council reconvened, only two Italians who held French sees were present. Catherine and the cardinal of Lorraine soon decided that a large French presence would be useful after all to look after Gallican interests, and at the end of March 1562, she told the pope she had ordered 24 bishops to attend. Early in April three French ambassadors left for Trent with explicit instructions: demand a new council at a place other than Trent; reform the Church in head (i.e. the papacy) and members; protect Gallican liberties; and work as hard as possible for a compromise with the Lutherans. Compromise with the Calvinists was seen as out of reach. Lorraine himself arrived at Trent in November 1562 with 13 prelates. When the last French arrivals wandered in, there was a total of 26 bishops and another 26 abbots and theologians. In alliance with the Imperial delegation, the French hoped to hold the balance of power between the Italians and the Spanish. They did win some concessions, but in general the decisions that the council reached were hostile to the Gallican point of view, especially in respect to the power of the papacy.

It was intended that Trent's decrees would be implemented through their publication by the Catholic rulers, as Philip II did in 1564 with several key reservations. A month after the pope had promulgated the Tridentine decrees, Catherine assembled the royal council at Fontainebleau in February 1564 to decide whether to publish them in France. Several staunchly Gallican jurists, in particular Charles Du Moulin, ardently protested that they violated Gallican liberties, and the royal council accepted their argument.[1] Nearly every papal communication to France henceforth included a request for the publication of the Tridentine decrees, but it did not happen during the ancien régime. Nonetheless, Trent soon began to have an impact on the French Church. Several of the bishops who attended began to implement some of the decrees in their dioceses; the cardinal of Lorraine, for example, abandoned politics after his return from Trent and worked diligently to reform his see of Reims. As the Catholic lands around France, especially those Philip II ruled, began to implement Tridentine reform, it created something of a moral imperative for the French Church to do the same. Archbishop Charles Borromeo of Milan, where the French still had many contacts, was the first truly Tridentine prelate; his example, writings, and several of his disciples, who became bishops in France, all had an effect on the French Church.

One serious abuse Trent condemned was pluralism. By accepting its decrees the papacy committed itself to eliminate the practice, which it could do unilaterally by refusing the bulls of office to would-be pluralists. Thus, the practice quickly disappeared from the French Church, which in turn reduced the problem of absenteeism. The kings issued several decrees against that abuse, urging the prelates to take up residence, but their success was limited and short term. As of 1559 absenteeism was truly chronic: 65 percent of the bishops had not set foot in their sees in the previous year. The outbreak of violence across France offset the newfound zeal of some prelates, keeping absenteeism at about that level until the late 1580s, when anarchy pushed it to 80 percent. Other Tridentine mandates slowly had an impact on such matters as preaching, holding annual diocesan synods and visitations, and building seminaries for the education of Catholic clergy. After 1600 there was widespread implementation of Tridentine reform in practice, even if it was never established in law.[2]

New religious orders were a significant factor in reforming the Catholic Church. The best known was the Society of Jesus. Although it was founded in Paris when Ignatius Loyola was a student there in the 1530s, French members were few in its first 20 years, and for decades to come most French regarded the society as an agency of the Spanish monarchy. Nonetheless, French prelates in Rome came to know the early Jesuits and were highly impressed. In 1550 the bishop of Clermont, Guillaume Du Prat, who had met a Jesuit at Trent, invited them to staff a college at Paris he intended to found for the students of his diocese. Keeping it going became a major problem when the Spanish Jesuits were forced to leave Paris in 1551 at the resumption of war, leaving only a small handful of French members there.

Despite the fact that the only Jesuits in Paris for the next several years were French, the Parlement and Bishop Du Bellay, strongly Gallican, fiercely opposed establishing the society in France on the inconsistent grounds that it was both too pro-papal and pro-Spanish. The Jesuits, however, had gained a powerful patron in the cardinal of Lorraine, who had met Loyola in Rome in 1550. He persuaded Henry II to grant letters of naturalization to the order, permitting it to own property in France. Continued opposition from the Parisian Gallicans persuaded the Jesuits to focus their efforts in Auvergne, where Bishop Du Prat invited them to found a college at Billom in 1558. It and other Jesuit colleges soon to be erected were seen as the conservatives' answer to the humanist colleges with their strong streak of Evangélisme. In 1565 the supporters and opponents of the order engaged in a bitter debate before the Parlement of Paris. The Gallicans threw their all into the fight, but the Parlement finally agreed to allow the Jesuits into the realm, under severe restrictions. By then the society had two provinces in France, with a third added in 1582. The Jesuits reached 316 men in 1575, a small majority of whom were natives. Even before then, their influence had became noticeable; such noted Jesuits as Ponce Cogordan, Juan Maldonado, and Emond Auger (even if he was not Henry III's confessor) had a strong impact in France and established the society's reputation as "the cutting edge of the Counter-Reformation."

While the Jesuits were struggling to get themselves established in France, another new order, the Capuchins, had a far easier time gaining acceptance. They were a branch of the Franciscans, which was founded early in the sixteenth century in a desire to return to a rigorous interpretation of St. Francis's rule. They adopted a four-cornered hood from which their name came. The Capuchins ministered to the urban poor, as Francis had instructed his followers to do, and earned a reputation for being good preachers. They first came to France in 1570, and soon had 13 houses in such places as Rouen, Lyon, and Paris. Their reputation was so high that when in 1599 Henri de Joyeuse, the governor of Languedoc, joined them, Henry IV quipped: "Peace is here to stay since our captains are turning into Capuchins."[3]

The Minimes were another new order active in France. Already a century old when this Italian order began to appear in France about 1540 with houses at Bordeaux and Paris, the Minimes were a mendicant order with an especially austere life-style. Their reputation for preaching won them numerous commissions as preachers of Lenten sermons, when the congregations were always the largest and most receptive. The Ursulines were another Italian order to gain a place in the French Church without resistance, probably because they were Italian and not Spanish. A female religious order, one of several new ones to appear, the Ursulines made a sharp break with the traditional cloistered orders of nuns, being active in the world largely as teachers of girls. Their first French house was established at Aix in 1600, and the order rapidly became the largest order for women in the realm, despite the fact that the papacy forced the Ursulines to change their rule, returning them to a more traditional style for nuns.

The new orders, which included several lesser-known ones, played a significant role in keeping France Catholic. While the Jesuits and Ursulines worked mostly with the elite, the other new orders labored effectively with the lower classes. Their zeal and austere lives contrasted sharply with the image presented by the traditional orders and the secular clergy. Even as Calvinism spread and religious war raged, the established clergy was very slow to reform itself. The zealous Catholic priest from Champagne, Claude Haton, denounced the life-style of the Catholic clergy as bitterly as any Protestant: "Beginning with the cardinals and archbishops down to the simplest curés . . . they make their residences where they can take their pleasures."[4] The attitude of the French people toward much of the hierarchy can be summed up in the story told about Bishop Philippe de Lenoncourt of Auxerre: After his death in 1570 his heart was placed in the chapel of one of his abbeys, and dogs broke in and ate it. The local people said its fate was the judgment of God on his sins.

While much of the hierarchy remained attached to a scandalous life-style, many prelates were attracted to Protestantism. As of 1561 the reputation of the French episcopate for orthodox Catholicism had dropped so low that the papal secretary wrote to the papal legate in France not to push the French prelates too hard on going to Trent because their doctrine was "little sure." A number of humanist bishops, largely Francis I's appointments, were accused of heresy or openly apostatized. A good example of the former was Charles de Marillac, archbishop of Vienne and a talented royal diplomat. His Erasmian address to the Assembly of Notables of 1560 brought down the wrath of the more conservative prelates, although it may well have enhanced his place at the court until his death two years later.

At least 12 bishops openly became Protestant, often marrying after their change of religion. The most notorious was Cardinal de Châtillon, but he was not one of the eight bishops whom the Holy Office in Rome accused of heresy. Eventually seven of them were judged guilty and deprived of their offices, although the guilt of three of them is not clear. They protested that the verdicts were an infringement of the Gallican liberties, and the Parlement of Paris refused to register the papal bulls stripping them of their offices. The best known among them, Jean de Monluc, bishop of Valence, kept both his see and his suspect beliefs until his death in 1579. Several bishops quietly slipped out of France for Geneva and other Protestant places.

At the Estates of 1560 and 1561, some of the bitterest complaints were not directed at the hierarchy's life styles or its lack of orthodoxy, but at the number of Italians in it. For a long time there had been a few Italians in French benefices, especially in the Midi, but the number rose after French involvement in Italy began in 1494. One side effect of the Italian wars was the flight of numerous Italian exiles to France, where their service to the French crown gave them a claim on royal patronage. Under Francis I, the number of Italians began to rise rapidly; it accelerated under Henry II; and when Catherine de Medici became regent, she patronized a large number of her Italian friends and relatives. In 1560 Marillac denounced the large crowd of Italians in the French hierarchy, "who suck our blood like leeches." Such complaints probably were a factor in the decline in the number of Italians in the hierarchy under Charles IX and Henry III, while Henry IV's reign saw their numbers return to those of a century earlier.

Widespread anger at the Catholic clergy, nearly as strong in the Catholic laity as among the Huguenots, gave broad approval to the efforts to transfer much of the Church's wealth to the monarchy. By 1562 the *décime* had been established as an annual "gift" from the clergy, but the king still needed the clergy's permission to collect it, and the sums involved varied vastly from year to year. To overcome these problems, the monarchy took advantage of the clergy's terror at the radical proposals made at the Estates of 1560 to hammer out the Contract of Poissy with the Church. The clergy agreed to provide 1.6 million *l* annually for six years and then 1.3 million *l* for the next ten years. The monarchy agreed to allow the clerics to supervise the collection of the funds, thus allowing them to escape royal audit of their incomes, and accepted the fiction that the money was still a gift.

The sums granted in the Contract of Poissy hardly solved the royal fiscal crisis. In the midst of the first civil war in 1563, Catherine de Medici mandated a forced sale or alienation of church properties and revenue-producing rights worth 3.6 million *l*. If a churchman had enough cash on hand to meet his quota, he was not obliged to sell anything. Royal commissioners traversed the kingdom supervising the alienations and collected the funds, often forcing the clerics to sell more than necessary to meet their quotas. Sometimes they required the sale of the best piece of property attached to a benefice. The royal edict had not provided for the possibility of the clergy's buying back alienated properties, but the loud complaints from the clerics and the pope's position that he would accept the fait accompli if repurchase were permitted, led to a new edict allowing buying back at the original sale price. Many of those who had bought church property, as often Catholics as Huguenots, refused to sell it back, prompting extensive litigation.

In 1567, when the annual *décime* was scheduled to drop by 300,000 *l*, Charles IX asked the clergy to continue to pay the larger amount. When it refused, he imposed a second alienation of church property totaling 1.8 million *l*. This time the clergy received the right to supervise the sales, but not the authority to repurchase. Since cleric commissioners were more favorable to their fellows, this second alienation resulted in far less litigation. Many benefice-holders, however, declared that they were unable to pay as much as demanded because the Huguenots had taken over their lands, especially in the Midi. Another problem affecting the clergy's finances were the tithe strikes that were widespread in the Midi. The monarch did make concessions to those dioceses worst hit.

As the monarch's fiscal distress continued to mount, it resorted to further impositions on the clergy's wealth: extraordinary *décimes* on top of the Contract of Poissy, such as one for 1.4 million *l* in 1571; additional alienations of Church property in 1569, 1574, and 1576; and steeple taxes in 1568 and 1574. When the clergy held its general assembly in 1579, it was asked to agree to a new contract with the monarchy. The clerics objected that in the 16 years since Poissy they had contributed 64 million *l*, a third of royal revenues in the period. Nonetheless, they negotiated a new contract for six years at 1.3 million *l* a year. Henry III agreed to call another assembly of clergy if the royal debt had not been paid off by then. Of course, it was not, and the clergy met again to forge a new contract. Thus the tradition that general assemblies of the churchmen would meet on a regular basis was established and continued to 1789.[5] The clergy also controlled the machinery of collecting its "gift" to the king, including the right to name the *receiver-général* of the clergy. The office never became venal and remained out of royal control. For the clergy in the 1580s, however, having regular assemblies hardly compensated for the severe depredations on its revenues resulting from the civil wars, Huguenot seizures, and royal de-mands. Little wonder so much of the clergy enthusiastically supported the Catholic League.

As for the French Reformed Churches, after 1562, they too had serious problems. The death of Jean Calvin in 1564 removed a dynamic, powerful leader who had the respect and loyalty of his followers. Theodore Beza, his designated successor as chief theologian and spokesman, had high social stand-ing as a French noble and the ability to provide strong leadership, but he could not truly replace Calvin. Quickly a quarrel broke out in France, which badly taxed Beza's leadership. In preparation for the second national synod of the French Reformed Churches at Orléans in 1562, Jean Morély de Villiers, a Calvinist since about 1547, published a book calling for a reconsideration of the manner of governance in the church. He wanted the synod to adopt an ecclesiastical organization that can be termed "congregationalist": All the mem-bers of a congregation collectively made decisions for it. Calvin had placed authority over the church in the pastors and elders, a structure called "presby-terian." Morély's proposal reflected at least partly the situation of the French Reformed Churches, where the lack of pastors had given the laity a major role in founding churches and governing them. By 1562 the pastors in Geneva were eager to bring the French into conformity with practice there. They did not welcome Morély's book.

Accordingly, the national synod of 1562, presided over by Antoine de La Roche Chandieu, a friend of Calvin and Beza, condemned Morély's book and ordered him to recant. The Geneva consistory ordered it burned. Morély recanted several times over the next two years, but they were never complete enough for his detractors. By 1565 he had gained a number of supporters, including Cardinal de Châtillon. His rather brief support of Morély persuaded him to hold firm against the Genevans. By the time the cardinal had withdrawn, he had another prominent advocate, Peter Ramus, whose efforts in behalf of congregationalism were more effective than those of Morély himself.

This issue was still the center of attention when the sixth national synod met at La Rochelle in 1571. The number of important persons who attended made it one of the major assemblies for French Calvinism. Beza, Jeanne d'Albret and her son, and Admiral Coligny were the most prominent attendees. The Confession of Faith accepted by the synod settled the dispute in favor of Presbyterianism, while the deaths the next year of Ramus and many other Parisian supporters of Morély on St. Bartholomew's Day made any further effort impossible. Morély apparently died in England some years later. The defeat of congregationalism was disconcerting to a number of French Calvinists. While it is difficult to believe that many of them were so disheartened that they embraced the rigid hierarchy of Catholicism, there is no question that the Morély affair had a negative affect on French Calvinism.

The impact of that affair on the Huguenots pales in comparison to that of the St. Bartholomew's Massacres. Without a doubt the high watermark of the Reformed Churches, in respect to momentum if not total number, was 1562. Much of its appeal, however, arose from curiosity, the appeal of something new, and the distinct possibility that the monarchy might join up. Over the next few years, the effect of those factors declined, leaving those who were committed to Calvin's religious principles as members of the Reformed Churches. The evidence is inconclusive on the question of whether their numbers were stable in the several years before 1572 or were declining at a slow pace. In particular Calvinism's appeal to artisans had much declined by then.

St. Bartholomew's Day was a traumatic shock to the Huguenots. While there had been religiously motivated killings by both sides since the late 1550s, the number of deaths in any one incident was always small. Protestant violence was directed first against religious objects, such as statues, that offended them, secondly against the Catholic clergy. The Catholics from the beginning were more likely to go after the persons of the other faith. The popular violence, however, had decreased over the previous ten years, while state-sponsored executions had all but disappeared. The sudden explosion of violence in August 1572 took the Huguenots by surprise, not only in the number of those killed but also the high rank of so many. Persons of quality had been relatively immune to the earlier violence.

If one accepts a figure of 1.5 million Huguenots prior to the massacres, then about 1 percent were killed, but a large portion of the Huguenot leadership was wiped out. In fear for their lives thousands of Huguenots rushed to be readmitted to the Catholic Church. Of course, perhaps a majority returned to the Reformed faith once it was safe, as did the two Bourbon princes, but many remained Catholic. Flight abroad, largely to Geneva and England, was another option taken by Huguenots, and while many exiles eventually returned home, not all did. The impact was considerably less in the Midi, where only Toulouse saw serious violence. A number of Huguenots fled to the south and west, especially to La Rochelle, and strengthened their presence there.

For those Huguenots who permanently embraced Catholicism, and even for those who remained Protestant or returned to it once the crisis had passed, the massacres raised the troubling question of whether God was in fact on the side of the Reformed. The deaths of Henry II and Francis II, for example, were used as proof that God favored the religion the two kings had been persecuting. Now the blood of the martyrs did not appear as the seed of the church but as drowning it. On several levels the massacre had a deeply negative impact on French Protestantism, placing it on the defensive. Not even the emergence in 1584 of Henry of Navarre as successor to the throne could restore its optimism.

French Catholics, for the most part, expressed little guilt over St. Bartholomew's Day, although fear of Huguenot revenge was an important factor in their support of the Catholic League. The massacre was only one manifestation, albeit the most important one, of a new militancy among the Catholics that was largely absent ten years earlier. Another aspect was a new zeal for the public display of their faith. Never completely absent earlier, it took on its most obvious form in the "white processions," which reached their peak in 1583 and 1584. So called because their often barefooted participants wore only the white shift of repentance, their purpose was in begging God's mercy on His people. They were an old medieval tradition, occurring when there were crises such as famine or plague, but rarely had they reached the level of participation they did in this era. An account of one procession across northern Champagne to the cathedral of Reims in late 1583 gave the number of persons involved as precisely 72,409. A powerful motivation within them was the desire to cleanse the land of the pollution of heresy, but perhaps equally important was the belief that the world was about to end, as predicted from the great comet of 1577 and the great conjunction of planets in 1583. The processions were largely the spontaneous creation of the Catholic poor and the village curés.[6]

Catholic zeal and dread were at a high level when the duke of Alençon died in 1584 and the Catholic League was regenerated to oppose Henry of Navarre's succession. The laity and lower clergy was far more supportive of the League than was the hierarchy. Among the bishops, 36 percent supported Navarre's right to the throne; the position of another 12 percent cannot be determined; and only about half were Leaguers of one stripe or another. When Navarre announced his intention to abjure his Protestant beliefs in May 1593, a large number of Catholic prelates were prepared to accept his sincerity without question. Eleven bishops led by the archbishop of Bourges, Renauld de Beaune, and other church leaders attended Henry at St-Denis in July when he formally returned to Catholicism. Much of the League, especially the lower clergy, was adamant that his conversion was a fraud, intended to trick the Catholics into accepting him as king. The quip attributed to Henry: "Paris is worth a mass!" may have originated with the Leaguers, but it summed up completely the situation in which he found himself. Henry hoped to overcome Catholic skepticism by a show of pious attention to the public rituals of Catholicism. He succeeded well enough to gain the loyalty of most Leaguers by 1595, although some, such as the Leaguer polemicist Jean Boucher, always regarded the conversion as a sham.

The last possibility that Protestantism might become the established religion of the realm disappeared, although it can be argued that it had been impossible since 1562. Henry's conversion prompted a significant number of defections from Calvinism by nobles and courtiers, who also thought ambition was worth a mass. Becoming Catholic, however, was not necessary to hold a place in Henry's court. The Duc de Sully was only one of a number of prominent officials who were openly Protestant. Even Henry's almoner was a Calvinist.

For the unrepentant Leaguers the presence of so many Protestants at the court was proof that Henry IV's conversion had been insincere. Many more Catholics felt that way when he promulgated the Edict of Nantes in 1598. The strong opposition to granting freedom of worship boded ill for the long-term permanence of the Edict, but it hardly bothered Henry and did little to affect its implementation. The Edict made the some 1 million Huguenots, not counting the 100,000 people of Béarn, which was still officially Reformed, heavily dependent on the monarchy to defend the rights it had granted. A strong monarchy, at least one committed to maintaining the Edict, was far more likely to protect freedom of worship than a weak one, easily buffeted by the waves of Catholic hostility. Numerous Huguenots became committed royal absolutists, believing that if they demonstrated their loyalty to the crown, it would protect them. Nonetheless there was an inherent tension arising out of the fact that the king was the head of religion in France. How could he be head of both? Louis XIV would eventually resolve that contradiction to the detriment of the Reformed.

Having become head of the Gallican Church by his conversion, Henry IV had broad authority over it, including the right of appointment. Even before his conversion he had attempted to exercise royal rights under the Concordat of Bologna, but the papacy refused to accept his nominees, which remained true until he received papal absolution in 1595. By then a third of the French sees were vacant. Henry thus had an excellent opportunity to remake the French episcopate, but he was slow to take full advantage of it. His early bishops were chosen from the Politique clergy, but after 1600 some Leaguers, at least those who had rallied to him early, appeared among his appointments. In 1605 he boasted about the quality of bishops he was appointing. Henry had reason to be pleased with the bishops he seated after 1600. They were better educated and better trained, more mature, and more zealous in performing their duties, even if the old abuses did not entirely disappear.[7] Most French bishops began to implement parts of the Tridentine decrees. The quality of the lower clergy improved as seminaries opened, episcopal visitations made, synods held, and discipline imposed. The monarchy, however, pushed by the Gallicans and the Huguenots, continued to refuse to publish Trent formally in the realm.

Gallicanism had won the day with Henry IV's conversion and coronation, but the Catholic League had revealed that there were more ultra-montane (pro-papal) French Catholics than was thought possible at mid-century. They looked to the Society of Jesus for inspiration and education for their sons. The Society's expulsion from the part of the realm under the Parlement of Paris after Jean Chastel's attack on Henry in 1594 was a result of the fact that he had studied in their college in Paris, but it also came about because of their image as too supportive of the papacy and the Habsburgs.[8] The Parlement of Paris, its strong Gallicanism still intact, was more responsible for the decision than was the king. When he received papal absolution, he felt he needed to make a gesture to the pope—the return of the Jesuits. The Parlement resisted it for several years and registered the edict in 1603 only after heavy pressure from Henry. One of the edict's clauses required that the society provide a preacher at the court, apparently as a hostage of sorts for its good behavior. He frequently wound up as the royal confessor, a post that the very capable Pierre Coton gained in 1608. The Jesuits impressed Henry IV, and he granted them a number of favors. Most importantly he gave them both permission and money to erect the famed Collège de La Flèche, an act he balanced by granting the Huguenots the same for their college at Die.

In the course of the sixteenth century, there was only one French saint canonized by the Catholic Church—Jeanne of France who died in 1505. It is one measure of the transformation of French Catholicism after 1600 that the number of saints increased dramatically, including four of the most loved French Catholics of any time—François de Sales, Vincent de Paul, Jeanne de Chantal, and Louise de Marillac. The last three were associated with education, and the greater emphasis on providing a Christian education to French children was a key feature of the Catholic Reformation. Schools run by religious orders competed strongly with municipal schools, which also increased dramatically in number. If anything, the Huguenots emphasized education even more.

The Tridentine clergy, created in the seminaries the council ordered bishops to found, was better prepared to preach, teach, and correctly perform the liturgy as mandated by Trent, but was also less likely to come from the same place and social milieu as its parishioners, as was true previously. It was now more willing to criticize the practices and behavior of the laity and insisted on the more rigorous code of morality that marked the Catholic Reformation. Although results were slow in coming, the consequence was a society in which the behavior of the common people was much more carefully regulated, to eliminate what Catholic authorities, joining with the Protestants, now regarded as superstition and paganism. The more vigorous the priests were in combatting these evils, previously condoned, the further removed from their parishioners they became. Yet it was precisely such priests whom the Church would regard as saintly. The close ties between a curé and his people became largely a thing of the past.[9]

One goal of much of the effort in reforming and revitalizing the Catholic Church was the conversion of the Huguenots. In that respect it had limited success. Once the wave of mostly noble conversions after Henry IV's abjuration had subsided, the Huguenot population remained stable for the next two decades, at a little above 1 million people worshipping in some 900 temples. The ease and, indeed, royal encouragement with which Huguenots converted to Catholicism, the disabilities that hampered them in fact albeit not in law, and the fact that they had to pay the tithe to the Catholic clergy while supporting their own churches, all meant that they had to be fully committed to their faith. The lukewarm were quickly gone. As before 1561, the Protestants comprised those who could not expect any advantage from their faith but a spiritual reward. More clearly than before, they were concentrated in the Protestant crescent of the Midi—from Grenoble through Languedoc to Béarn and Navarre and then up the Atlantic coast to La Rochelle. The Calvinist schools were largely in the south—Die, Nîmes, and Montpellier—but the intellectual center was the college at Saumur, near Angers. As the nobility declined in presence in the

Reformed Churches, the ministers and especially the theologians at Saumur emerged as the leadership cadre. The proper understanding of predestination and maintaining consistorial discipline were the major issues that held their attention.

One of the disabilities imposed on the Huguenots was the refusal to accept them as delegates for the First Estate at the Estates general. For all of the change that had taken place since 1561, the cahiers that the First Estates prepared in 1614 were remarkably similar to those from the earlier meetings. The call to correct the many abuses in the church could have been taken from cahiers prepared for previous Estates. It was, however, the Council of Trent that provided the blueprint on how to reform Catholicism. The First Estate made a strong appeal for publishing its decrees in France, except for those that threatened Gallican liberties, but the effort failed in the face of the powerful opposition of the Third Estate and the monarchy. The monarchy's efforts to extract money from the clergy were denounced. The clergy objected to the Edict of Nantes and even asked for the banning of the Religion Prétendue Réformée. The traditional ideal of *une foi, une loi, un roi* had not disappeared from France in 1614, nor would it for the duration of the ancien régime.

16

The Nobility:
A Return to Arms

Much of the nobility welcomed the outbreak of the wars of religion in 1562 as an opportunity to bear arms, but the wars proved to be costly to the Second Estate in many ways. The nobles had to bear most of the cost of fighting. Those on the Huguenot side had the heaviest burden from 1562 to 1589, while the monarchy helped support the Catholics until many of them joined the Catholic League. Even many royalists, however, found that serving a bankrupt king was a losing proposition. Properties were ravished or destroyed, and incomes drastically reduced. Heavy casualties caused a number of families to die out. Far less serious but probably as disconcerting to the nobles was a change in the style of war away from the traditional knight.

The last point was the first to become apparent. It was largely a product of the nature of the forces the Huguenots assembled. Their captains could call on large numbers of French nobles for their forces, but they were volunteers. As such they were usually reluctant to travel far from their homes, or if they did go far afield at the urging of the Protestant leadership, they were quick to dash home at any rumor of trouble. The inability of the prince of Condé, the Admiral Coligny, and Henry of Navarre to keep substantial forces together for long was a significant factor in the failure of the Huguenots to win the civil wars militarily, despite usually having greater élan and higher morale than the Catholic/royal forces. Huguenot captains recognized this from the beginning of the civil wars and sought to compensate by recruiting German *reitres,* who were mostly Protestant.

There were some 2,400 of these pistol-carrying horsemen in Condé's army at the Battle of Dreux (1562), the first major battle of the civil wars. Accounts of the battle mark the first mention of a new tactic the *reitres* used. Forming up in lines as many as 15 ranks deep and carrying their pistols in their right hands, they rode toward the enemy line; but instead of carrying the charge into the enemy ranks, they wheeled their horses to the left, fired their pistols, and retreated to the rear of their company. The second and subsequent lines did the same, until the first line, with pistols reloaded, was again in front to perform the same maneuver. The swirling movement of the *reitres* supposedly looked like a snail's shell, thus the word *caracole* (Italian for snail) for the tactic. Given the short range of the pistol, its gross inaccuracy when fired off a moving horse, and its lack of penetrating power against plate armor, the caracole could be effective only when executed by a large number of horsemen against an enemy line that was stationary or nearly so and weak in firepower, such as a line of pikemen. The tactic also had some success against heavily armored lancers, even when they were charging, because they moved so slowly. The reitres could stop lancers by hitting the lancers' horses and using their speed to get out of the way if that failed. The caracole was successful enough at Dreux, where the Catholic/royal *gens d'armes* still formed up in the single line, *en haye,* to persuade many nobles to adopt the pistol.

There were several reasons why the pistol rapidly replaced the lance among the French nobles after Dreux. One was that the heavy armor and horses the lancers needed were extremely expensive; only the wealthiest nobles could afford them. The pistol, although not cheap enough for the infantry to use, was affordable for the petty nobility, and horses *reitres* used were lighter. The lower levels of the nobility could again claim a place on the battlefield, which for the previous half-century had been tenuous. Using a pistol from horseback, while not easy, required far less practice than did using the lance. Probably most important, the pistol allowed the nobles to keep the place that God had ordained for them in battle—on horseback. The *reitres'* far cheaper style of fighting, however, also made it possible for commoners to take it up. By 1598 they made up perhaps as much as 20 percent of the French pistolers. The end of violence led to a reduction in that number, but enough were still serving as pistolers in 1614 to provoke complaints from the nobles at the Estates general. The effectiveness of the *reitres* in several battles after Dreux was clear enough by 1569 to Marshal Gaspard de Tavennes, the de facto commander of the Catholic/royal forces after the duke of Guise's death, to persuade him to recruit *reitres* for his cavalry. He did not favor the caracole but preferred that his pistolers charged into the enemy with swords after firing their pistols. He continued to use lancers as well, but required them to form up in squadrons several ranks deep instead of *en haye*. He further insisted that his cavalry march together in formation on the way to the battle so that they would become used to holding their places in the formation on the battlefield.

Although these developments marked the transition from the medieval knight to modern cavalry and from the groups of mounted warriors fighting as individuals to tactical bodies of cavalry, the style of command during the religious wars remained largely traditional. Condé and Henry of Navarre on the Huguenot side and Montmorency on the Catholic believed strongly that battles were won by the commander leading his cavalry in a charge against the enemy line in the decisive attack. The more modern idea of command with the commander at the rear of his forces directing all of his forces did not appeal to them, although it was the mark of two of the most successful commanders of the era, Guise and the duke of Parma. Parma, who faced Navarre in several battles in 1590 to 1592, commented about him: "I expected to see a general; this is only an officer of light cavalry."[1] Both Condé and Montmorency were killed in battle, while Navarre barely escaped death on several occasions. For Montmorency his adherence to the traditional style came from a lifetime of war; for Condé and more so Navarre, it was more a product of the type of forces they had. They led volunteers, who served as much because of the force of commander's personality as for the cause he represented.

That became even more true when Navarre took command of the royal army in August 1589. Many of its men were Catholic nobles who remained with him because they admired him, not his cause. His style of recruiting was to ask important nobles to "assemble as many of your friends and come."[2] He was successful with his style, winning most of the battles he fought without being seriously wounded. The cavalry that Henry led so effectively into battle consisted mostly of armored swordsmen. Lancers were still prominent in the Catholic forces. He disdained the caracole, requiring his men, five or six ranks deep, to charge into the enemy using their swords, while using mounted musketmen, *arquebusiers à cheval,* to provide firepower in support of his *gens d'armes.* He regarded the use of the sword as natural to the French nobles. Once he had taken effective control of France, he introduced his system to the entire army. Henri de Montmorency, whom Henry appointed constable in 1593 after a 25-year vacancy in the office, reduced the size of the lance companies to 30 lances consisting of only the lancers themselves; the support troops of former times disappeared. By 1614 the only lance company whose existence is certain was the royal guard with its two hundred *gens d'armes,* although the term *compagnies d'ordonnance* continued to be used for cavalry units.

Another reason why Henry's record in battle was better once he gained the title of king was that he then had command of the Swiss companies under contract to the monarchy. A serious flaw in the Huguenot forces was their lack of pikemen, which made their infantry of mostly harquebusiers vulnerable to charges by both heavy infantry and cavalry. The presence of the Swiss in the armies of their foes was a major reason for many of the Huguenot defeats, beginning with Dreux. By 1562 French infantrymen were more likely to appear in battle than 50 years earlier but mostly as harquebusiers; French pikemen were still rare.

During the civil wars, there was considerable movement among the nobles from one party to the other. It was more often from the Huguenot side to the Catholic from 1562 until 1589, after which a steady stream of Catholic nobles joined Henry IV. Antoine of Bourbon's change of allegiance was the most noteworthy example, but more typical were the sieur de Ludé in Guyenne, Jacques de Crussol in Languedoc, and François des Adrets in Dauphiné. Their behavior was notorious regardless of which side they were currently serving. Henry IV's conversion to Catholicism began a rush of religious changes, most notably by Henri II de Condé, son of Henry's old comrade-in-arms who had died in 1588, allegedly poisoned by his wife. The Huguenot party retained the loyalty of a small coterie of well-placed nobles to provide leadership. The highest ranking was the king's own sister, Charlotte of Bourbon, who stubbornly resisted heavy pressure from him to convert. Her presence at the court with her Calvinist ministers was a major scandal to many Catholics, but her influence was limited. Sully remained Protestant as did the dukes of Bouillon and Biron. Philippe Duplessis-Mornay, governor of Saumur under the Edict of Nantes, served as the elder spokesman for the Huguenots after Theodore Beza died in 1605. When Marie de Medici allowed them to hold a national synod at Saumur in 1611 as a way of showing the new government's commitment to the edict, a major topic was the need to replace Sully as the principal Huguenot representative at the court. Duc de Rohan, his son-in-law, emerged as the choice for that responsibility. He would later lead the Huguenots in the final outbreak of religious violence in 1625. The synod at Saumur also revealed the decline in noble presence among the Calvinists. Noble leadership would become less important after 1614 than it had been in the civil wars.

A major consequence of the religious wars was the extinction of many noble families. When French nobles battled French nobles in the wars, often brother against brother, casualties were high. According to *Le Secret des finances* of 1581, 775 Huguenot nobles and 880 Catholics were killed between 1560 and 1580.[3] The list of nobles killed in some cases included the last male member of the families. More often war deaths left noble lines so short-handed that a premature death or two ended them. A good example was the House of Cleves, which controlled the duchy of Nevers. Duke François II was killed in battle in 1562 and his only son died two years later. A daughter married Louis Gonzagua, and Charles IX allowed her to pass the duchy to her husband. In 1589 a Burgundian noble remarked on how many noble estates had changed hands in the previous 60 years, although extinction was only one of the ways it could happen.

It is a mistake, however, to think that the nobility as a whole as badly devastated by war casualties. The nobles were surprisingly resilient in keeping their overall number stable. Writing in 1591, Chancellor L'Hôpital's son Michel estimated that there were between 20,000 and 30,000 noblemen in France. If one were to accept the lower figure as more plausible, then it would match a similar calculation for 1547. Army rolls and other sources suggest that about one in five nobles was serving as a fighting man. The absence of so large a portion of the nobility from the military rolls led to a proposal at the Estates of 1589 that those who did not answer the summons for the *ban* be stripped of noble status. By 1614, however, the idea that much of the nobility would never provide military service was widely accepted. For many nobles the civil wars proved to be profitable. In some cases high offices opened up for them which they otherwise would not have received. For many others extortion, confiscations, and plunder more than made up for the frequent lack of pay for military service. Some of the provincial warlords such as Lesdiguières in Dauphiné, Monluc in Gascony, and Ludé in Guyenne did well without being called to account for their ill-gotten gains after the violence ended. A good portion of the lesser nobility probably profited in much the same fashion.

Certainly the economic problems of the period before 1598, which at times were true subsistence crises that threatened the lives of the poor, had an impact on the nobility, but for the most part the nobles were in a good position to weather the periods of dearth. They had first call on the yield of their peasants' labor, and only in the worst years were no crops harvested. Nonetheless, the many years of major reduction in yield between 1562 and 1598 emptied the noble coffers at times when prices were climbing and noble expenses were accelerating. The years in which the nobles found themselves profiting from war and those in which they were hurt by the widespread problems in French agriculture and commerce did not necessarily coincide. Many a nobleman felt himself on his way to ruin at the moment when he was given an opportunity to express his opinion on the state of affairs in the realm.

Complaints of the nobility about being ruined by the wars and royal policy were extensive and bitter. As was usually true for the sixteenth century, the best place to look for their complaints is in the cahiers prepared for the Estates general. The nobles, who included two Huguenot deputies (a third was elected but did not attend), produced a lengthy set of grievances for the meeting of 1576. The nobles enforced their demand that only old nobility be allowed to stand for election; the *anoblis* had to serve in the third, giving that estate more of an aristocratic cast than might have been expected. In their cahiers, the nobles included a call for religious unity but did not demand that the king resume the war to enforce it.[4] The central theme was the disorder into which the realm and the nobility had fallen because of the civil wars. Venality and the surge in false nobles were the principal targets of noble blasts. The nobility petitioned the king to stop creating new offices and reduce the number to what it had been under Louis XII. Another complaint, which also centered around the nobles losing their rightful place at the top of the government, was about the large number of Italians in the royal council and the fiscal administration. Catherine de Medici was generous to her fellow Italians, including many of her relatives. Chancellor Birague, from an Italian family living in Paris, was the target of particular complaint. The nobles also decried the dramatic reduction in the pensions and other gifts the monarchy traditionally gave them and the heavy expenses they bore while fighting for the king without compensation.

The strong Leaguer sentiment in the Second Estate at Blois has usually been contrasted with the more Politique attitude of the Third, led by Jean Bodin. But the Leaguers did not dominate the nobility, as shown by the failure of the League to get a resolution through the Second Estate demanding a new war to eradicate heresy. Nonetheless, the Catholic League of 1576 was a noble creation, motivated both by loyalty to the ancient faith and resentment toward the privileges given to numerous Huguenot nobles by the Peace of Monsieur. Ties with the urban Leaguers, which appeared after 1584, had not yet been forged. The Leaguer nobles swore an oath of union that pledged them to full, prompt obedience to the head of the League, whose name was not revealed at the time the oath was circulating. In 1576 the traditional bonds between king and his nobles were under great strain. Those bonds only became weaker in the following years as Henry III found a multitude of ways to upset the nobles, such as being rude or putting too much pressure on them to break with their longtime patrons in the religious parties.[5] In particular they were offended by his largesse to his *mignons,* few of whom were great nobles.

By the time the Estates met again in 1588, the usual goodwill a king could count on from his nobles was all but gone. Both Henry III and the Leaguer leadership worked hard at gaining the election of sympathetic deputies. The overall success of the League was revealed by the flight of all but 32 of the 102 noble deputies from Blois after the murders of the Guise brothers. It was also obvious in the cahiers from the Second Estate, which demanded that the king swear to the Edict of Union a second time and use force to eliminate the

Huguenots. The few passages that did not deal with those demands repeated the concerns of 1576. In the three-cornered struggle between the three Henrys, the League had the support of the most nobles, and upon Henry III's death, a large portion of the Catholic royalists abandoned the royalist camp, to take up a position of neutrality.

In late 1589 the League had at least the lukewarm support of a majority of the nobles. Relations between them and the more radical urban Leaguers, however, were cold at best. Guise's enormous popularity in both elements of the League had been the cement of the party. His death meant that fissures widened rapidly. When numerous nobles joined Henry IV even before his conversion, and many more after it, the radicals, especially the Paris Sixteen, began to write extremely hostile attacks against the nobility. The concept of a nobility of virtue, by no means new to the Leaguers, was taken up by the radicals: Only those who were virtuous, which meant fighting for the League's cause, had a right to noble standing. In the *Dialogue d'entre le maheustre et le manant* (*Dialogue between the Courtier and the Commoner,* [1593]), this concept was expressed the most clearly, especially when the Leaguer lamented that the nobles in the royalist camp follow heresy and those in the League follow money.

Complaints about the behavior of nobles and soldiers were legion in the civil wars, although it was only their volume that made the situation any different from any other time in early modern France. The nobles had their own list of grievances. Recently historians have challenged the nobles' assumption that they were worse off than they had been previously, but often perception is as important as reality. For example, the actual tax burden on the nobility had changed little, but there was strong opinion it had increased drastically. Nonetheless, there were some real problems in the finances of the great nobles detectable in their accounts, although the ability of modern historians to make informed comments about the circumstances of the petty nobility is more limited. The drastic reduction in royal pensions left most of the great nobles without that major source of income and largesse for their clienteles. The grands had to draw on their own resources to keep their clients in service.[6] Much of the resentment toward Henry III's *mignons* resulted from the fact that they were getting the sums other nobles had been receiving. Since the *mignons* were mostly from the lower nobility, they had not yet built up clienteles for distributing the money further.

Another problem for the nobles was the drastic rise in the size of dowries for their daughters, well beyond the rate of inflation. Probably the major cause was competition from the haute-bourgeoisie and *anoblis,* who had the liquid assets to pledge huge dowries in order to marry their daughters into the old nobility. The civil wars also caused many nobles to fall into the hands of their foes, requiring large ransoms. The most important reason, however, for the serious fiscal woes of many grands was raising armies to fight in the civil wars. In many cases they did it for the king, who did not repay them for their outlays in his behalf. Others spent most of their wealth in behalf of their religious parties. The Guise and the duke of Nevers were good examples of grands who nearly became bankrupt serving both the king and their religious cause. When Henry IV assumed Charles de Guise's debts of 900,000 *l* as part of his settlement for submitting to the king, a large portion of that money was owed to Guise by the monarchy.

By 1594 a substantial part of the nobility had good reason to believe that their world was crashing down around them. The speed with which most of them recovered from their problems as Henry IV restored peace and stability indicates that their difficulties were not created by a permanent pattern of decline, but by temporary dislocations. The new king was far more in tune with the attitudes of the nobles than was his predecessor. He had spent most of his life up to 1598 as a commander living in close proximity with his nobles and leading them personally into the fray. He loved to hunt, which he continued to do until his death, and his reputation as a lover, the *vert galent* (green gallant, the precise meaning of which is obscure) endeared him to all Frenchmen. Henry increased the royal pensions, but except for those Leaguer grands who received vast sums for submitting to him, the pensions were distributed to large numbers of nobles in small amounts.

Yet Henry IV faced some noble unrest. Sully created difficulties for the king with his program of demanding proof of noble status from those of dubious status who were claiming exemption from the *taille*. He imposed the tax on those who could not come up with such proof. Certainly it hit those whose claims were fraudulent, but a number of true nobles were caught up as well, at the least forcing some to prove their noble status. Many Huguenot captains who had served Henry prior to 1594 resented their loss of influence after his conversion, which was a factor in the most serious noble uprising of his reign led by the duke of Biron, a former Huguenot. The most serious difficulty Henry IV had with the French nobility involved the issue of dueling. The disappearance of judicial combat removed that method of resolving feuds between nobles, and the near elimination of the tournament removed that way for young nobles to prove their manhood and prowess. The fighting of the civil wars, and the opportunities that anarchy provided for settling feuds by murder and thuggery, disappeared after 1594, and dueling rapidly took their place in a society that was used to settling disputes by violence.

The word *duel* itself first began to appear in France after 1570. In 1578 three of Henry III's *mignons* fought a duel with three of the duke of Guise's retainers over an insult at a dinner. Only one of the duelists, a Guisard, survived. The king soon after issued an edict that attempted to control dueling, but he also erected a monument to his dead favorites. It was after 1594 that dueling became a significant problem because of the numerous deaths it caused. By then the procedure, as it would last unchanged for centuries, had been established. The gentleman whose honor was impugned would issue a challenge or cartel, which early on was usually written but later was presented orally. The move to oral cartels was one step in greatly shortening the time between the insult and the duel, but more important in speeding up the process was the fact that the duelists no longer sought the permission of the king. The man challenged would accept the cartel and gain the right to choose weapons. By 1600 duels were fought almost always on foot, without armor, and with a one-handed thrusting sword (rapier) rather than the heavy broad swords of the lancers, which were really hacking weapons. The rapier ensured a quicker death with far less chance of serious disfigurement. Carrying a rapier everywhere became a true mark of noble status. Pistols were a distant second as weapons of choice for duels. Duels were much more likely to be fought to the death than previously. Other innovations of Henry IV's era include the use of seconds, who often fought as well, and the fighting of duels in near privacy as opposed to the huge crowds of spectators for the judicial combats. The latter became more standard as kings began to crack down on the practice.

The monarchy began to object to dueling once it began to appreciate how many of its fighting men were killed and how duels were a continuation of the nobles' right of private war. When in 1602 Henry IV issued an edict condemning dueling as *lèse-majesté*, for which the penalty was death, he reflected the belief that dueling violated the monarch's right to decide how men should die violently. He included the requirement that feuding nobles seek the mediation of major royal officers. The president of the Parlement of Toulouse reported that in the first six months after the edict had been broadcast through his province, it had saved the lives of more than 300 noblemen.[7] Even if he exaggerated badly, the figure gives some sense of how many nobles must have died in duels and continued to die, since the edict was barely enforced. After all, most of those who were expected to enforce it had the same sense of honor as the duelists. In 1609 Henry repeated it almost verbatim, as later kings did through the century. Dueling became one of the marks of nobility after 1600 at a time when military service was becoming less and less important as a badge of noble status.

Despite the edicts outlawing duels, the monarchy's attitude was ambivalent. The king still believed himself to be the first peer among the nobles, not distinct from them, and was sympathetic to their ethos. Also it was argued that dueling released the aggression of the nobles, who might otherwise allow it to spill over into rebellion, although that argument was less than persuasive because noble revolts still occurred after 1600. The worst case involved a boon champion of Henry IV from long before 1594, Duc Charles de Biron, who converted to Catholicism shortly after the king and soon was named a marshal and governor of Burgundy. As one of the negotiators of the Peace of Vervins, he made contact with Spanish agents. The lure of Spanish gold and the promise of lands in Lorraine led him to organize a conspiracy to assassinate Henry. One of Biron's retainers informed on him, and Henry summoned him to the court to confess. Unaware of how completely implicated he was, he refused. He was quickly put on trial before the Parlement of Paris, where the peers of the realm were to serve as his judges; that old feudal principle had not yet disappeared. The peers, however, refused to judge him, and it was the last time that they would be asked to exercise that function. The counselors quickly found him guilty, and he was executed in July 1602.

A number of prominent nobles such as the Constable Montmorency and the duke of Epernon, Henry III's *mignon,* were on the fringes of Biron's conspiracy, as was one of Henry IV's former mistresses, Henriette d'Entragues, who had a promise from the king to marry her. Most important among them was the Huguenot Henri de Bouillon. He was implicated enough to flee to his stronghold at Sedan in Lorraine. There he actively worked against Henry, seeking to unite both French and German Protestants with some Catholic nobles who had been involved with Biron. When unrest broke out in several provinces in the southwest in 1605, Henry's response was to march to Sedan, an Imperial city, in early 1606 with a powerful force. When he arrived at its walls, Bouillon quickly submitted and was taken back to Paris in disgrace. He survived Henry's wrath, but five nobles involved in the unrest in the southwest were executed, and more fled to Spain. Henry's prompt and forceful response saved him from more serious trouble, but it did not end the tradition of noble rebellion. The period of Marie de Medici's regency saw further unrest on the part of nobles led by the prince of Condé.

The search for ways to domesticate the nobility was not successful until Louis XIV's reign, but one new approach that appeared in Henry IV's era was the creation of academies for young noblemen. Antoine de Pluvinel founded the first one in Paris in 1594 with royal support. Two more soon appeared at Toulouse and Aix. The concept originally came from Italy where schools for training young nobles to ride and use their swords existed at least 30 years earlier. Both skills were made major parts of the French academies, but other subjects— courtesy, politeness, languages, mathematics, and such military skills as map reading and fortification design—were part of the curriculum for the two years the young nobles were expected to attend. Being a cultured gentleman became a mark of nobility, although such a gentleman was still expected to take offense at any insult and challenge his insulter to a duel. The monarchy aided these academies with money and moral support in the view that they would put reins on the traditional independence of the French nobility.

It was with a sense that their traditional life-style was being threatened with significant change that the nobles at the Estates of 1614 drew up their cahiers. They objected to the presence of so many non-nobles in the royal administration and demanded that the proportion of nobles in royal office be vastly increased. Complaints about venality and the number of new nobles it was creating, or to be more accurate, the presence of so many non-nobles in the judiciary, were even more pronounced. The nobility demanded that nobles from old families were to be given preference in all royal and ecclesiastical appointments, and no grant of noble status given in the previous 30 years be valid unless granted for military service. The Second Estate's efforts to eliminate the *paulette* were finessed when the Third proposed that the resulting loss of revenue to the monarchy be compensated by the elimination of noble pensions. Nobles complained about the heavy taxes that they were paying, especially the *gabelles,* contrary to custom. As a historian who studied the Estates of 1614 has said, "Anything of recent origin that harmed the nobles was an abuse, but any privilege, exemption, or right that the nobles had held for thirty years was to be incontestable."[8] A sense of dissatisfaction with the direction that the realm and the monarchy were going in respect to noble privilege permeated the cahiers. It is easy see why noble unrest continued for another 15 years.

17

The People: Depression, Devastation, and Recovery

The situation in France deteriorated badly after 1562 for most common people. The religious wars devastated numerous villages and cities and killed many noncombatants; hyperinflation created severe disruption of the economy; and climatic conditions turned for the worse. Although the natural agricultural productivity of France saved it from falling completely into ruin and allowed it to recover rapidly once peace was restored and the economic fluctuations leveled off, it is readily understandable why numerous French people joined the parties of the religious wars, mostly the Catholic League. When the parties failed to satisfy popular resentments, the lower classes, in particular peasants, became involved in local revolts known collectively as the Croquants. Peace came later to the countryside than to the towns.

Other than local disruptions caused by the movement of armies and sieges of fortified towns, which affected the region around Paris most severely, the major problem for the ordinary people was an adverse change in climate. In the seven decades before 1560 in southern France, there were only one or two winters per decade described as cold to severe, while the number of mild winters was about the same. In the period from 1560 to 1610, there was an average of nearly five cold to severe winters per decade, while no winter after 1568 can be rated as mild.[1] While popular perception of what is a cold winter may be skewed by a long period of warm winters preceding a cold one, these categorizations depend on such events as olive trees being killed by cold or rivers freezing over. The vast expansion of the Alpine glaciers indicates that the weather was not only becoming colder year-round but that the amount of precipitation was increasing as well. This combination was ruinous to grain production, especially wheat. The results were year after year of scarcity and hyperinflation in the price of bread, the mainstay of everyone's diet.

War also had a hand in creating scarcity: Troops plundered granaries, trampled crops, disrupted transportation networks, and laid siege to towns, which placed extraordinary pressure on the grain supply in most of the years between 1562 and 1598. Frequently the major impact of an army's passage was stealing or killing a village's animals. Rebuilding animal herds took much longer than growing a new crop, and the result was a decline in the amount of both meat and manure for the fields, which hurt crop yields. The impact of the civil wars becomes obvious when the situation in France is compared with that in Alsace, which was at peace; the climatic changes were nearly the same, but grain prices did not exhibit the wild fluctuations found in France.

In the last five years of Henry III's reign the average price of a *setier* of wheat in the Parisian market was 12.5 *l*, compared to 3.9 *l* for the last five years of his father's. In much of France, 1586 saw the most serious crop failure, but in Paris, the hardest year (except for the siege year of 1590 and its aftermath) was 1587, when the prices of wheat, rye, barley, and oats, the four major grains, were all at least four times their 1559 price and wheat's rising five and a half times. Other inflationary rates for the same time period included 1.5 times the price for olive oil and eggs and three times for wine and meat. Soaring prices for bread affected the urban poor the most. Not only did bread take up a major part of their incomes; but they also had no way to store up grain for hard times, as the urban elite could, nor any opportunity to grow substitute foodstuffs, as peasants could in a limited way. Rural day-laborers, however, were no better off in those respects. At least in the towns, public alms helped the "deserving poor," the towns' own residents, while town fathers diligently worked to keep newcomers out. Private stocks of grain sustained the bourgeoisie in the towns for a while, unless the poor pillaged the granaries in a bread riot; but prolonged bad times, the norm for this era, pressed them as well. Hard on the heels of grain shortage and malnutrition came epidemics, which the movement of armies across France also helped to spread. The incidence of the plague rose substantially. In Languedoc one of the worst outbreaks of plague since 1348 followed the terrible summer of 1586 with its nearly complete crop failure.

An occasional year of scarcity jolted the poor hard but had little effect on the bourgeoisie. A prolonged period, however, hit everyone. For merchants and artisans, nearly as serious a problem as the grain shortage was the fact that high grain prices soaked up money that would have been used for other commodities, causing a serious downturn in commerce. Thus, one long-term result of the subsistence crises of this era was its deflationary impact on commodities other than foodstuffs. In the decade after 1562 there was considerable inflation in goods other than food, but by 1575, it began to level off. For example, there was a nearly 50 percent increase in the price of candles from 1562 to 1575; it then rose by only 7 percent in the next 15 years. The inflation in all manufactured products for the latter period was only slightly higher, although the anarchy of the five years after 1589 pushed prices up sharply until Henry IV returned the realm to stability. Wages for the lower classes did not rise as rapidly as inflation in prices. Unskilled laborers' earnings lagged behind inflation until 1589, when wages dropped. The effect of declining income, combined with an extraordinary rise in prices over the next five years, resulted in a drastic reduction in buying power.[2]

The concept of inflation was something that was completely foreign to the people of the era. The explanation for any price increase was to blame the merchants for price gouging, which they did often enough, but they were not responsible for the long-term price rise. In 1563 the monarchy ordered the Chambre des comptes to conduct an investigation of the problem, and one of its members, the Sieur de Malestroit, published his *Paradoxes* (1566) based on its work. He argued that inflation was really a monetary problem caused by changing the value of the money of account—the *livre*—and debasing the coinage, which involved reducing the bullion content of the coins and adding base metals such as copper or lead to them. Nearly every monarch in fiscal trouble resorted to debasing the coinage because it increased the face value of the bullion in the royal treasury, allowing the kings to mint more coins out of the same amount of precious metal. The coins continued to have the same face value as before but were reduced in real value; debasing the coins thus was another source of inflation since it required more coins to buy the same amount of goods. The monarchy used the debased coins to pay its obligations at a lower cost in bullion before those receiving the coins became aware that they were worth less than before. Thus, the kings were always one step ahead of the inflation that debasing the coinage created. Laborers, on the other hand, were hurt, since they were paid the same number of debased coins for their work over a long period, while merchants were quick to recognize the situation and raise their prices. Since the French kings had been debasing their coinage throughout the sixteenth century, Malestroit correctly identified one factor in the price rise of the era. It apparently was because of the conclusions of the Chambre des comptes and Malestroit that Henry III changed the monetary system. He raised the value of the *écu* to three *livres* from 2.25 and made it serve as the money of account as well, eliminating the *livre tournois* as the basic unit of money of account. The rapidly changing ratio of gold to silver in western Europe, largely caused by American silver brought in through Spain, was making it difficult to maintain the official rate between the *écu,* a gold coin, and the *livre,* based on silver. Henry's radical change in the monetary system was difficult to implement, because everyone, even the government, continued to express accounts in terms of *livres.* In 1602 Henry IV returned to the old system.

In 1568 Jean Bodin addressed the issue of inflation in *Response de Jean Bodin à M. de Malestroit.* He disagreed with Malestroit's analysis and argued that the huge increase in the money supply was largely responsible for rising prices, although he did note other factors, including debasement and population increase. He also noted the great numbers of French laborers who crossed the Pyrenees to work seasonally in Spain, where wages were substantially higher than at home. The money they brought or sent back to France was an important means of bringing American treasure into the realm and certainly was a factor in inflation. Bodin also cited the importance of trade with Spain in bringing bullion into France. He argued that it was something the monarchy should encourage. He also proposed that a heavy export tax be placed on the traditional major French exports: wheat, salt, and wine. The heavier prices, he maintained, would not reduce demand for them by their foreign buyers.

Seasonal or long-term migration to Spain was one strategy the poor, at least in the south of France, had for dealing with hard times. After 1562 joining the army as a foot soldier was a more common option than it was previously, although the Swiss pikemen and the German *landsknechtes* continued to be regarded as better soldiers than French infantrymen. Service in the army proved costly to many, as the *Secret des finances* stated that 12,237 ordinary soldiers were killed in religious violence from 1560 to 1580. On the other hand, commoner soldiers often rose in the military hierarchy. Of the 1,928 men admitted between 1560 and 1610 into the Order of St. Michael, an honor that was heavily dependent on military service, 13 percent were commoners.[3] One loud complaint from the Second Estate in 1576 was about the large number of commoners serving as officers in the royal army. It is difficult to get a sense of whether the Huguenot forces were any different in that regard. Apparently, few commoners who functioned as officers in the royal army were given the privileges of nobility.

Yet another strategy among the peasants for survival in hard times was rural industry. The trend toward doing more manufacturing in the countryside continued unabated between 1562 and 1614, although localized problems often caused drastic declines in productivity. Spinning wool and linen was the major industrial activity; large-scale production was centered in Picardy, where spun thread was made into cloth in cities such as Amiens and Abbeville. By the end of the sixteenth century, weaving cloth also was done in the rural villages, and urban centers of production began to decline. Peasant women provided a larger portion of the labor in the textile industry but at wages well below their urban counterparts.

For most French peasants, life in the late sixteenth century was more than ever fraught with uncertainty. Heavy taxation, whether collected by royal agents or those of the Huguenot or Leaguer captains, hit the peasants directly. The peasantry bore the brunt of rapidly increasing taxes, a trend that continued after 1598. Real taxes rose from a base index of 100 in 1560 to 191 for 1619. A significant portion of peasants went permanently into debt to moneylenders, who were quick to foreclose and take their land. Land purchases by nobles and tax-exempt bourgeoisie were a major factor in raising taxes on the remaining landholding peasants, creating a vicious circle that resulted in a substantial transfer of land and wealth into the hands of the elite.[4] The trend toward larger landholdings accelerated toward the end of the century. Some of those displaced from their holdings found work in their former fields as day-laborers, but others were forced to join the large number of footloose, propertyless peasants roaming the French countryside. The economic problems of the time pinched that class of people the hardest. The hardening attitude toward vagabonds and beggars and the closing off of the traditional escape valve for such people—migration to the cities—combined to make life truly miserable for the largest part of the peasantry.

One of the most serious problems in the late-sixteenth-century country-side was the increase in witch-hunting, which was largely a phenomenon of the villages and small towns, not the cities. Judges responsible for it were from the mid-levels of society, and most of the victims were from the lower classes, but most lower-class people were quick to cooperate with the judges and denounce others as witches. The extensive use of torture in witch trials intensified the witch craze by producing long lists of alleged accomplices, but there were other powerful elements at work as well. One was the bitter religious strife, in which each side denounced the other as doing the work of the devil. It created a strong feeling that evil was abroad. The powerful sense of eschatology was involved as well, for one of the marks of the Antichrist of the last days was his sending forth demons to prepare for his coming. Judges were far more willing to prosecute charges of witchcraft than they had been previously, because they were much more certain of the presence of evil. The deep economic crisis of the period also was a factor: Marginal members of society, of whom there were now a great many more, were far more likely to be accused. The typical victim of the witch-hunt was a old woman who was a poor, widowed beggar. Probably without family and lacking protectors, the poor widow had to resort to begging, but that had its risks in an era when few had enough for survival themselves. Should any harm come to the family in the days after they refused alms to a beggar, perhaps with curses from her, the family would blame the beggar and accuse her of being a witch. The judges would then take over and ensure that she was found guilty and probably executed, but not before she named her accomplices. Lower-class men in some number also fell victim to the witch-hunt, and when a full-blown panic hit a region, young women and even "respectable" persons did as well. At that point, however, the inquisitors came to their senses, and the panic died out, only to erupt in another region.

There is no good estimate of how many victims of the witch craze there were in France to 1614. Besides those executed (at least a thousand), there were also those who died or were maimed in torture and those whose lives were ruined by accusations of witchcraft. The burden of the witch craze hit the rural population particularly hard, in part because the peasants were quicker to accuse their neighbors of witchcraft. It was another factor that made the years from 1562 to 1598 truly miserable for most of the French peasantry.

Problems in the cities were not quite as severe, despite the suffering of the urban lower classes. The French urban population continued to rise. According to one calculation, the number of French cities with at least 10,000 inhabitants increased from 34 in 1550 to 43 in 1600.[5] Several cities suffered losses in population, however. Perhaps the worst affected was Abbeville in Picardy. It had been a major center of the cloth trade, dealing with the markets of Flanders. It was badly hurt by the movement of much of the cloth industry to the countryside. Abbeville also suffered from two severe outbreaks of the plague in the 1590s. It soon slipped from being one of the major cities of northwestern France to a provincial backwater. Toulouse did not actually suffer a decline in size, but its economy and privileged classes took a hard hit when the bottom collapsed out of the woad trade. In 1560, because of bad harvests and problems in the French financial markets, a large number of the woad magnates in Toulouse went bankrupt. Fighting during the religious wars in the vicinity of the city prevented the woad industry from recovering from the crisis of 1560. By 1594 indigo from the Americas was making serious inroads in the woad market; it was both cheaper and regarded as a better dye. Lyon was another city that suffered economic decline after 1562 that was structural rather than episodic. The monarchy's fiscal crisis of 1557 hurt the Lyonnaise bankers, and the end of extensive French involvement in Italy harmed the city's ability to recover. More seriously the general shift in the commerce of western Europe away from Italy was a long-term problem that by 1614 cost Lyon dearly. The city probably lost population between 1560 and 1614.

Although during the civil wars nearly every French city suffered at least one crisis, and many several, some cities emerged from the strife with their economies enhanced. They were mostly the cities with several royal institutions and substantial numbers of officers. The dramatic rise in the number of royal officers resulted in a significant redistribution of wealth from the countryside to the cities. The salaries of the royal officers kept up with inflation far better than did workers' wages. From 1550 to 1575 they appear to have kept pace with inflation, and by 1600 they had risen well above it.[6] Montpellier, Dijon, and Paris were among the cities that came out of the civil wars in a much better position. Paris in particular profited immensely from both the great buildup in the bureaucracy and royal spending in the city under Henry III and Henry IV. Paris truly became a "center of consumption," drawing in enormous quantities of every commodity and a vast number of migrants.[7] The urban elite, again especially in Paris, also profited from the unquenchable royal demand for loans at higher and higher interest rates. The wealthy bourgeoisie invested huge sums in *rentes* and other forms of royal borrowing, although the fear, very strong after 1584, that the monarchy would default on them was a factor in much of the broad bourgeois support for the League, even from many who ought to have been ardent royalists.

Most of the notable episodes of popular violence during the religious wars took place in the cities. Peasant violence was common enough, but it was on a small scale until major rural uprisings occurred at the end of the wars. The peasants more often directed their rage against the local warlord or his troops than against persons of the other religion. They did, however, join with urban dwellers in some violent outbreaks, most notably at Romans in Dauphiné in 1579-80, although the elite in Romans were more responsible for the violence there.[8] Within the cities serious violence erupted in 1560-62. Some of it involved Huguenot efforts to take control of such places as Rouen, Toulouse, Lyon, and Dijon and a long list of towns in the Midi. More common but not as bloody was Huguenot violence directed against Catholic images and clerics. Calvinist iconoclasts destroyed statues, relics, and church decorations, but their most frequent target was the host of the Eucharist, especially when it was used in the sacred processions that were so much a part of Catholic devotion in this era, most notably on the feast of Corpus Christi. Catholics regarded desecration of the host as the clearest manifestation of the satanic nature of the new religion. For Calvinists the Catholic sacred objects were idols for whose worship God was punishing His people with hard times. Another term the Calvinists often used in context of the religious violence was *pollution:* The use of religious objects and the presence of priests and monks, whom the Protestants usually denounced as sexual libertines, were polluting society and causing its ills. Violence to cleanse society and prepare for Christ's second coming was a necessary task for the elect. While the Huguenots were quick to kill clerics, they did not intentionally target the Catholic laity, and the deaths of lay Catholics in such violence were usually regarded as unfortunate.[9]

Equally convinced that the presence of the heretics was proof of the coming of the Antichrist as foretold by astrology and other portends, Catholics also felt that they were preparing the way for the end of the world. For them the sense of pollution was even stronger since the Protestant presence was new in contrast with the long tradition of Catholic practice. One could reasonably ask why God had not punished His people earlier if Catholic practice was idolatry, while it was much easier to blame problems on the new presence in society. Lacking tangible Protestant objects to destroy except for the French Bibles, Catholics targeted persons of the new faith, whose bodies were often seen as being as pestilent as their minds.[10] While the incidence of violence by both sides was quite similar in the first decade of the religious strife, the number of Huguenots killed was much higher.

The participants in urban religious violence were generally not from the lowest levels of society. Had the day-laborers and vagabonds been extensively involved, it would have terrified the city fathers, who would have intervened to put them back in their place, whereas the authorities frequently condoned the violence that did occur. The perpetrators were mostly artisans and others of higher social status. Both perpetrators and victims so often came from the same social level that class and social antagonisms could not have played a major role in sparking the violence. While it is not clear that religion was the major motive for nobles and peasants who participated in the violence of the era, for urban dwellers it seems to have been the principal one. This conclusion is supported by the frequent presence in the mobs of the clergy from both sides, more often the Catholic. Their participation helped to reinforce the sense that what the mobs were doing was right and sanctioned by God.

For Catholics, miracles often served to emphasize divine sanction. The best example came during St. Bartholomew's Day, when a hawthorn tree in a Parisian cemetery suddenly began to bloom during the massacre. The sudden bursting forth of the new star later in 1572 was taken as proof by the Catholics of divine sanction, while the Protestants saw it as a sign of impending divine judgment on the perpetrators of the crime. The Catholics also frequently claimed royal sanction, when royal officials joined in the violence or stood by without attempting to stop it. It was again the massacre in Paris that most clearly shows this, when royal soldiers and the city militia participated in the killings.

St. Bartholomew's Day is, of course, the most notorious episode of popular violence of the religious wars. Except for the role played by the king and nobles and the huge number of casualties, it was similar to most other episodes of Catholic violence against the Protestants. A number of them occurred in Paris in the decade preceding the massacre.[11] In one key respect, however, it was atypical: The Huguenots, despite the presence of a great number of their nobles, did not make any real effort to resist, as they usually did in other episodes of violence directed against them, albeit often ineffectively. It is all the more remarkable since in the hours after the bungled assassination attempt on Admiral Coligny, the Huguenot nobles seemed to be preparing for violence. The lack of resistance is yet another mystery of the event. Perhaps the shock of royal involvement completely paralyzed the Huguenots.

St. Bartholomew's Day and its aftermath in the provinces had a deep, negative impact on the Huguenot population, but it hardly marked the end of popular violence. After an interlude of 12 years in which there was little violence, the reemergence in 1584 of the Catholic League with its strong urban component produced the most prolonged period of popular unrest between 1484 and 1614. A powerful reason for the broad support that the League enjoyed across urban France was the emergence of a new style of religious confraternities that mostly favored the League. The dominant confraternity of earlier years was the guild brotherhood, which provided opportunities for social, business, and religious activities for the artisans. There always had been another type of confraternity intended for the religious edification of its members drawn from a wider range of society, but it had been less popular and visible. When Francis I banned artisan confraternities in 1539 because of the unrest of the previous decade, these religious brotherhoods took center stage. They increased dramatically in size after 1562, broadened the range of their recruitment, and emerged as the centers of opposition to Protestantism in many cities, although their role as harbingers of Catholic Reformation spirituality for the urban classes must not be overlooked.[12] They provided political leadership for the ardent Catholics in many cities, especially since urban elites also joined them, and gathered arms in expectation of armed conflict with the Protestants and, later, the royalists and Politiques. Although they often had conflicts with the noble leaders of the League, they served as a ready-made constituency for the League as it began to organize across the realm in 1584.[13]

The best-known group in the League was the Paris Sixteen. Few other topics of sixteenth-century France have been the subject of as much recent scholarship.[14] Some 225 Parisians have been identified as being part of the Sixteen at some point between 1584 and 1594.[15] Their social positions were quite diverse—they were master artisans, merchants, lawyers, lower-level officers in the royal courts, clerics. Besides their ardent Catholicism what they had in common was a desire to defend the city of Paris from royal encroachment, particularly as perpetrated by the Parlement. Both motives were found widely in the cities of France, which allowed the League to gain control of many. While both the social makeup of the Leaguer groups and the details of their takeover of such towns as Angers, Rouen, Reims, Toulouse, and Nantes varied some-what, the nature of the movement remained the same.[16] Yet the presence of the same elements in other cities failed to secure them for the League. Tours, Rennes, Bordeaux and Châlons-sur-Marne were Catholic-controlled places that remained loyal to the king. In Rennes and Bordeaux, the Parlements remained staunchly royalist and kept control of the cities. In the case of Tours, extensive financial ties to the monarchy kept it loyal, while in Châlons, the passions of the city's Catholics never were aroused enough to reject the king.[17]

Apart from the Paris Sixteen, which has fascinated historians with its radical political thought, quasi-democratic structure, and support of regicide, the most interesting example of the urban League was in Marseille. The city never reconciled itself to being annexed to France a century before, and the Leaguers made effective use of the memory of its medieval status as an indepen-dent city-state to rally the people against Henry III. In April 1588 a coup ousted the royalist city government, killing several of its members, and established the League in control. Three years later, Charles de Casaulx, from a prominent merchant family, seized power and held it for five years. Although he can be called a tyrant because he seized power illegally, he was immensely popular in the city. He carried on diplomatic relations with the papacy, Savoy, and Spain. The "republic" of Marseille refused to submit to Henry IV even after he gained control of the rest of Provence, which for the most part had been Leaguer-controlled. Royal forces advanced on Marseille in late 1595. Casaulx called on Philip II for help, who dispatched troops and a small fleet to the city. The direct Spanish involvement upset several of Casaulx's allies, who arranged to have him assassinated and the city gates opened to the royal forces in February 1596. The Breton seaport of St-Malo had a similar experience as a Leaguer urban republic for several years. Its leaders were able to negotiate a satisfactory settlement with Henry IV, which included amnesty for murdering the royal governor in 1590. While Marseille and St-Malo were two clear examples of the desire on the part of much of the urban elite to protect the traditional faith and return their towns to the greater freedom of previous centuries, those motives were prevalent in towns across France.[18] The concessions Henry IV made to the Leaguer towns to return them to obedience to the crown suggest that he understood the motives behind their rebellion. His tax policy toward the towns was reasonable, and his edicts rarely created dissent among the urban elite.

While the towns quickly returned to normalcy, the countryside continued to experience unrest well into Henry's reign. The term for one group of peasant rebels in Guyenne, the Tard-Avisés (the Slow-to-catch-on), referred to their taking arms while the towns of their province were submitting to the king. A more general term for these peasant rebels was Croquant, which came to mean any poor peasant who was not properly submissive to social superiors. The Croquant movement extended from Brittany across the south to Dauphiné, but its heart was in Guyenne, where the term was first used for a large peasant revolt that began in 1594. The previous decade saw considerable peasant violence in northern provinces such as Normandy, but it was harshly crushed, and the north was quiet while the Croquants were under arms in the Midi.

These uprisings, which were a large series of local events rather than a widespread organized movement, had many features in common. The major motivation was the heavy burden of royal taxation. Henry IV asserted his authority in the southwest earlier than elsewhere, and his desperate need for money meant that the people of that region bore much of the financial burden of the last years of the religious wars. Some of the efficiency in fiscal matters that would mark his later reign was present in the southwest early on, so the ability of many peasants elsewhere to escape taxation because of the anarchy of the era was curtailed. The peasants were well aware of the settlements Henry was negotiating with the towns in the region and the broad concessions he was granting, especially in respect to taxes. They assumed that the sums being conceded to the towns would be extracted from them. There was, therefore, an element of anti-royalist anger in the uprisings of 1594 in Guyenne.

More immediate a cause was the widespread rapacious behavior of the local warlords and their troops. Hostility to the nobility was not paramount in the peasant movements, but they revealed anger that many of the local nobles were not behaving as good seigneurs ought to. Instead of protecting their tenants against harm, they were contributing to their ruin. The peasants, who in the course of the religious wars became used to being called on to help the nobles defend their region against forces from the opposite side, began to assemble and take arms for their own cause. In late 1593 vast assemblies of armed peasants, one of which may have reached 40,000 men, began to meet in northern Guyenne and neighboring provinces. They sent delegates to the king to ask for tax relief, but they also organized for violence. In early 1594 armies of peasants, armed with harquebuses and pikes and led by men who had extensive military experience, took control of the countryside, spreading out from their original bases in Turenne and Périgord. In particular they aimed at seizing the strongholds of the warlords who were ravishing their regions. Violence, however, was limited until the royal governors assembled their forces in mid-1594. Unable to hold together in the face of the *gens d'armes* and professional troops of the governors, the peasant forces quickly broke up when attacked and suffered heavy casualties. By late 1595 the violence ended with defeat for the Croquants, who fled to their homes, hid their weapons, and returned to the fields.

The Croquant assemblies, which called themselves the Third Estate of the people, had greater success in achieving their political goals than their military goals. The petitions their delegates carried to the king urgently requested his aid in removing the terror of the marauding bands of troops, who were robbing the poor people of their subsistence, torturing them, imprisoning them for ransom, and ruining their families. They also condemned the war profiteers in the cities and the financial officers who were demanding far more from the peasants than the official tax rate. The Croquants asked for the right to elect syndics who would represent their interests in the name of the king, and see to it that rural people received justice. Already in 1594 the royal council, having heard the Croquant delegates, agreed not to collect the taxes that were in arrears from the peasants and acknowledged that what they paid to the local warlords would be regarded as payments of royal taxes. Henry IV confirmed the concessions in 1596 and granted amnesty to the Croquants.

The attempt in 1597 to impose the *pancarte* led to riots by the urban poor in a number of towns, which helped to convince the king to abandon the tax, but the countryside was quiet. Once peace returned to the entire realm in 1598, the peasantry flourished for the next two decades. French agriculture adjusted to the climatic downturn, and the weather was somewhat better in the two decades after 1595. Maize was successfully introduced into the southwest shortly before 1600, although it was slow to spread out of that region. Those who grew it usually kept it for their own use and sold the other grains.[19] With improving conditions, Henry IV, who once cracked that if he had more time, he would become a Croquant himself, became immensely popular among the peasants. One reason was his famous remark, which he apparently first made to the duke of Savoy during his visit to Paris in 1599, that he would see that "there is not a peasant without a chicken in the stewpot."[20] Word spread rapidly across the realm, and Henry became known as *le roi poule au pot*.

Economic and commercial development was something that was on the mind of Henry IV and Sully, and their efforts in that respect also helped to make them popular with the bourgeoisie. Sully's appointment as *grand voyer* in 1599, a new office, to oversee the roads and other aspects of the transport system, gave him the authority to put into effect his ideas on improving transportation of goods and communications. One reason for the hard work that the king and his minister put into the task was the need to improve communications between the court and the provinces if the monarchy was to enhance its control over the realm.[21] The *grand voyer* was one of several new offices, which included the *grand maître des mines et minières*, designed to give Henry and Sully the sort of control over economic affairs they felt they needed to bring prosperity to France.[22]

As *grand voyer* Sully had the authority to appoint a lieutenant in every generality and command the treasurers to provide money for local projects. Sully's accounts indicate that many of the funds he controlled were used for bridges; the destruction of so many of them in the civil wars was a major hindrance to commerce.[23] Henry's reign was also the first time a real effort was made to dig canals, although many of them were proposed long before. The major canal begun under Henry was the Briare Canal, which joined the Loire with a tributary of the Seine, but it was not completed until 1642. It and several shorter canals initiated by Sully had a direct economic impact, because land transportation cost three to five times more than by water.

The mercantilist impulse in the two French leaders was more clearly revealed by their direct intervention in the economy. Henry created a Conseil de commerce to promote new economic ventures. Its first head was Barthelemy de Laffemas, who, even more than Sully, was a protectionist. The textiles industry was one place where protectionism was in effect. Heavy tariffs were imposed on foreign cloth, especially silk, to benefit native production. The success of the plan was obvious in regard to silk, whose production expanded vastly, in particular around Tours. The carrying trade, where French merchants were finding increasingly strong competition from the Dutch, was another area where royal intervention occurred. In 1604, in imitation of the Dutch, Henry chartered an East Indies Company, which was granted an exemption from customs duties, a pledge of royal support against attack by a foreign power, and protection against derogation for any nobles involved in the company. In 1608 he gave a charter to a national bank, but it, like the East Indies Company, succumbed to Dutch competition after 1614.

Henry IV had more success in another area of competition with the Dutch and other foreign powers—colonization. It was an area in which he, rather than Sully, was the driving force, although his minister was active in working to improve harbors, especially on the Atlantic coast. Official French interest in overseas exploration was nonexistent prior to 1515, but private maritime enterprises appeared well before then. Most of the French maritime and colonial efforts made before 1614 were privately funded. By 1500 Normans and Bretons were fishing the Grand Banks off Newfoundland, and by then French pirates were raiding Iberian shipping. French corsairs were the major problem for Spain and Portugal until 1560. In 1504 a Norman ship, headed for India, was blown off course to Brazil and returned home the next year with exotic plants and several natives, beginning a long-term French interest in Brazil. Serious royal involvement in overseas expeditions began in 1522, when Francis I commissioned an Italian pilot, Giovanni da Verrazzano, to explore new lands and provided one of the four ships in his expedition. Verrazzano sailed in 1524 with the goal of finding a direct passageway through the New World to China. He explored the North American coast from Cape Fear in North Carolina to Cape Breton in Canada.

Strong protests from Spain and Portugal about French violations of Pope Alexander VI's bull dividing the unknown world between them led to Francis's famous quip questioning where in Adam's will was the world so divided. He gave his answer by sending Jacques Cartier, a Norman navigator, to find the passage to China that Verrazzano had not, and claim the land for France. Cartier reached Newfoundland in the spring of 1534 and explored the Gulf of St. Lawrence and the mouth of the St. Lawrence River. A year later he returned to sail upriver as far as Montreal. Although he failed to find the passage to the East nor any quantity of gold or silver, he was dispatched again in 1541 to found a colony in Canada. The sieur de Roberval, appointed royal governor for the colony, sailed the next year with 200 colonists. The colony, on the St. Lawrence above Québec, quickly floundered, in part because the French efforts to exploit the natives turned them against the colonists. In late 1543 some one hundred survivors returned to France.

The next attempt at colonization occurred under Henry II in Brazil. Nicolas de Villegaignon, the vice-admiral of Brittany, received three royal ships and funds to lead an expedition to Brazil in 1555. Its goals were to develop trade in the valuable plants of the region and challenge Iberian control of South America. He chose a site near Rio de Janeiro for the colony. There was a large contingent of Protestants among the colonists, but it may have reflected the fact that many were drawn from prison. A second fleet sailed the next year with 300 settlers, who had a higher proportion of Calvinists and included two ministers from Geneva, as the first colonists asked Calvin for them. Whether the king saw the colony as a place to settle French Protestants is impossible to say, but he seems to have been aware of the large number of them among the colonists. In Brazil, however, religious dissension broke out, which compounded the usual problems of the first years of any colony. In 1559 Villegaignon returned to France for more funds and reinforcements, but Henry II's death prevented him from acquiring royal support. In 1560 the Portuguese destroyed the colony.

The next French colony was planned as a Protestant refuge in the New World. Admiral Coligny, who had a role in the Brazil colony, was the main force behind it, but Catherine de Medici was solidly in favor of the project as a way to solve the religious crisis in France. In the next century the monarchy refused to allow the Huguenots to settle overseas on the grounds that they would aid France's enemies, but that did not hold in 1562, since the principal enemy was Spain, and the Huguenots would have ardently defended the colony against it. Coligny intended to plant a colony along the southeast coast of North America as a base to challenge Spain's control of the Caribbean and seize its treasure ships. Jean Ribault led the first attempt to found such a colony, which was located on the coast of South Carolina. It failed within a year because of inadequate provisions. Ribault returned to France seeking more settlers and funds, but the outbreak of civil war forced him to turn to England, where he received considerable help. In 1564, while Ribault was still in England, his lieutenant commanded a fleet that landed some 200 men near St. Augustine, Florida. The usual problems of a new colony and the relentless search for gold taxed its leadership, but the colony, called Fort Caroline, survived until Ribault arrived the next year with eight ships and another 600 people, mostly men. They had not finished offloading when a Spanish fleet arrived and demanded that they leave. The French refused, and the Spanish attacked Fort Caroline. Some of the French got away by sea, but most were massacred at the site or after they were tracked down in the surrounding region.

The destruction of Fort Caroline ended any organized French overseas efforts for three decades, but a great number of French fishermen, whalers, and fur traders spent their summers in the region around Newfoundland. The monarchy again became involved in colonization in 1597 when Henry IV gave the Marquis de La Roche a monopoly on fur trading and the title of lieutenant-general of New France. The king did not provide any financial support to La Roche, however; he was determined to strengthen the French presence in the New World at no cost to his treasury. La Roche and other private entrepreneurs who received royal commissions to found colonies in New France were expected to use their own funds. Among the concessions the king granted the colony-builders was an exemption from the rule that required the derogation of nobles engaged in commerce. Nonetheless, they had a difficult time finding enough French settlers for their colonies, a problem already obvious to Villegaignon and one that would plague the French in Canada until 1763. They filled out their contingents of colonists by turning to prisoners.

The attempts of La Roche and several others to colonize Canada failed, and Henry turned to a former Huguenot captain, Pierre Du Monts, who was given a commission to found the New France Company in 1604 with a monopoly in the fur trade. Du Monts's efforts may have not gone anywhere had he not gotten Samuel de Champlain involved in his company. Champlain had a keen sense of how to describe the new lands in a way that caught the attention of many in France without distorting the difficulty of life in Canada.

More importantly, he had the ability to deal firmly but fairly with both the native peoples and the colonists, and he possessed the resourcefulness to keep his colony going where others might have failed. In 1608 he founded Québec. In the same year Henry IV funded the voyage of two Jesuits to Canada, beginning the long tradition of French missions among the Indians. Although the profits of the New France Company were meager for some time, Champlain had great success in working with the natives. He established the pattern of French rule in Canada—cordial relations with most of the tribes and the mutual defense of both peoples' interests. This allowed the French to build a successful colony in New France with only a small number of settlers, compensating for the lack of interest on the part of the French people to leave their homes. As of 1614 French colonization was creating wealth for a small but increasing number of merchants and sea captains in seaports such as La Rochelle, Rouen, Dieppe, and Le Harve, but it had virtually no impact on France as a whole.

The lack of interest in colonies on the part of the French people was obvious at the Estates of 1614, where the only mention of them involved requests that all French merchants be free to trade in them and money be provided for missionaries. What concerned the Third Estate the most, beyond its attack on papal authority to depose a French king, were taxes, the *paulette,* the number of royal offices, and the problems of commerce. The Third's cahiers reflected the fact that far more than earlier meetings, it consisted of nobles of the robe and royal officeholders. About half had a noble title of some sort, while only ten deputies represented the peasants—nine syndics and one simple peasant. The urban poor, artisans, and merchants were hardly better represented. It can be argued that the failure of the Estates and its disappearance from France for the next 175 years were results of the failure of the Estates to represent more than at best 10 percent of the French people. That, however, would ignore the solid program of reform the Estates, led by the Third, did propose. They included abolition of venality and a drastic reduction in the number of offices; a lower *taille,* to be used exclusively for the military; the implementation of a tax on the clergy and nobles for use on roads, canals, and bridges; and the removal of internal tolls. These were all good ideas whose implementation would have done much to build a more prosperous and better governed France. The monarchy, intent on strengthening its power yet loathe to upset the privileged corporations that had a stake in the established system, ignored the Estates. Shortly, there were few in France who saw any reason why another unproductive meeting ought to be held.

18

Justice:
Bulwark of Absolutism

The era of the French Wars of Religion was one of profound instability in the patterns of French life, and this included the judicial system. Contemporaries often stated that a major cause of the troubles was the maladministration of justice. Everyone in France agreed on that. Even the king and the chancellor professed their belief in the proposition before the assembly of notables at Moulins in early 1566. In their addresses to the assembly, both Charles IX and Michel de L'Hôpital declared that the royal grand tour of the realm, which was drawing to a close, had been undertaken in order that the king might hear the complaints of the people and see at firsthand the judicial system at work. They stated that the ills the king witnessed convinced him of the need for a great ordinance mandating a thoroughgoing reform of justice.

The result was the Ordinance of Moulins, consisting of 86 articles. There is no question that the inspiration for it, as was true of the ordinance of 1561, was L'Hôpital. His dislike of venality in the judicial system clearly shows through. He wanted the rule strictly enforced that prevented the heirs of officeholders who died within 40 days of a letter of resignation in favor from taking the office. Nearly 1,500 offices were to be abolished, but incumbents would keep their offices until their deaths. This did not satisfy the parlementaires completely, but the real bone of contention between chancellor and Parlement had nothing to do with venality: It was the mandate that the Parlement could not refuse to register royal edicts once it was clear that the edicts were the king's will. This revealed the chancellor's sense of royal power: When it was known what the king's will was, his subjects were obliged to carry it out. Therefore, royal officials were required to enforce royal edicts once they were published, regardless of whether the Parlement registered them. Ironically, the court never registered the articles in question.

The Ordinance of Moulins, responding to the request of the Estates, also required the magistrates to resume a practice known as *grands jours* that took parlementaires into disorderly regions to enforce the king's laws. The practice remained strong under Francis I, in whose reign 12 were held; the most notable one was at Moulins in 1534, emphasizing the return of Constable Bourbon's appanage to royal control. L'Hôpital believed the use of annual *grands jours* would help restore order where it had disappeared. The Parlement ignored the order, and it is not certain whether there were any *grands jours* through 1614, although they did reappear under Louis XIV in the *grands jours* of Auvergne.

The edict of 1566 contained numerous clauses designed to reduce the jurisdiction of traditional local authorities and enhance that of the king. The authority of the seignorial and municipal courts was substantially reduced, while governors, technically royal officers but autonomous ones, lost the power to give pardons and levy taxes. Nobles who defied royal orders or officials were to have their castles razed. Feudal relationships had been based on the premise that there was mutual obligation between lord and vassal and loyalty was reciprocal: A vassal could withdraw his loyalty from a lord who injured him. In 1566 the monarchy repudiated the concept of conditional loyalty; loyalty owed to the king was absolute.

In regard to the law itself, the Ordinance of Moulins established the priority of written testimony over oral in cases involving 100 *l* or more. L'Hôpital reiterated most of the procedural changes mandated in the Ordinance of Villers-Cotterêts, with small changes where experience revealed the need for clarification. Some 40 years later, the noted French historian Jacques-Auguste de Thou proclaimed that the edict of 1566 "is now everywhere received and justice is administered according to its rules in almost all the sovereign courts and the other lower jurisdictions of the realm."[1] He exaggerated the extent of compliance to the edict, probably because his father, a president of the Parlement of Paris, was involved in drawing it up, but it is accurate to say that L'Hôpital's revision of Villers-Cotterêts became the law code for ancien-régime France.

In 1566 the chancellor called for the completion of the task of redacting the *coutumes,* which had slackened off in the previous three decades. The great jurist Charles Du Moulin just finished a work on the *coutumes,* which was published the next year. In it he called for the use of Roman law as the means of standardizing French customary law across the realm. He gave special attention to the *coutumes* of Paris, which were partially edited. Du Moulin's comments served as a basis for legal opinion until 1789. When the Parisian *coutumes* were finally published in toto in 1580, they became the major code of law for northern France and were adopted in the French colonies.

L'Hôpital, Du Moulin, and other legal scholars regarded the multiplicity of law codes in France as a major obstacle to the proper administration of justice and the enhancement of royal authority. Their goal was to put together a single code of law by synthesizing the major *coutumes*, guided by the principles of Roman law. Despite the influence of supporters of such a process, there was far too much inertia from tradition and too much resistance from those who benefited from keeping the established system in place. The redaction of the *coutumes* accelerated only slightly after 1566, and standardization was not achieved before 1789.

Another area in which codification was seen as highly desirable involved the royal edicts. The Estates of Orléans and Blois both included a request for such a code. Henry III gave the task to a president of the Parlement of Paris, Barnabé Brisson. In May 1587 he published a massive code of royal law called the Code Henri. It was done in some haste, but Brisson did make modifications in the edicts in order to be more consistent with Roman law. Probably because Henry was overwhelmed by trouble, the code was not put in force; but it went through five editions by 1622 and influenced the Code Louis of Louis XIV.[2]

As a legal humanist, Chancellor L'Hôpital was convinced that Roman law had much to offer the French in reforming their law codes, especially for private law. Another of their number, François Hotman, who became the most effective Huguenot polemicist, reached a different conclusion: Since the history of the Gauls and Franks and the nature of their monarchies were far different from those of the Romans, Roman law had little bearing on French law. His scheme for reforming French law, which he acknowledged was badly needed, involved going back to the foundations of the French nation, not drawing extensively on the Roman experience. Hotman argued this point in his *Anti-Tribonian* (Tribonian was a Roman legalist), which he dedicated to L'Hôpital and published in 1567. In the book he praised the Ordinance of 1539 for mandating the use of French in the courts. He repeated much of his case for the importance of French history and customs in understanding French law and government in his *Francogallia* of 1573, one of the major French works on politics.

The proper understanding of French history became important after 1559 because of the debate over fundamental law of the realm. The term *fundamental law* was not used until Theodore Beza apparently coined it for *Du Droit des magistrats sur leurs sujets (On the Rights of Magistrats over their subjects,*

1573);[3] but the concept that there were certain laws in effect since the first Frankish kings was long-standing. The laws were seen as immutable, and even the king was subject to them. No one doubted their existence; the debate was over what they were. The rapid successions of the two young kings, Francis II and Charles IX, raised the issue of whether there were fundamental laws establishing the age of majority for a minor king and choosing a regent for him. These points were settled in favor of the king's thirteenth birthday and the queen mother. The next controversy over fundamental law erupted over the issue of the inalienability of the royal demesne. Francis I used the argument that there was such a law to prevent the concession of Burgundy to Charles V in 1527. By 1566 the issue involved the king's demesne revenues and royal offices. L'Hôpital wanted to establish as fundamental law the proposition that the king had no right to alienate permanently any revenue source or office. Therefore, the chancellor argued, not only did the king have a perpetual right of repurchase, but all alienated demesne revenues reverted to the king after a certain period of time. Had this become law, it would have boosted royal revenues, but the chancellor also proposed it as part of his attack on venality. He wanted to define royal offices as part of the royal demesne and have them revert to the king at some point without a refund of their sale price. The parlementaires sharply opposed him on these points and prevented his views from being established as fundamental law.

Hardly a year after the Ordinance of Moulin appeared, the monarchy backed away from the clauses on venality. The clause enforcing the 40-day rule in resignations was lifted, although the fee for allowing such resignations was increased. A new chamber of *enquêtes* was erected in the Parlement of Paris in 1568. The reduction in the number of *généralités* was soon reversed, but those who had held those offices were obliged to pay a fee to return. L'Hôpital was frustrated not only in his efforts to reduce venality but also by the enforcement of several anti-Protestant decrees he opposed. Late in 1568, he was persuaded to give up the seals of office. Like the rest of the government, there was instability in the office of chancellor in the next years. None of the three men who exercised the functions of chancellor, two of whom under the title of *garde des sceaux,* over the following two decades had any interest in legal reform.

The failures of both meetings of the Estates general of 1560-61 and L'Hôpital to effect significant legal reform meant that the issue would be a concern again at the Estates of Blois in 1576. Whether the religious situation dominated the discussions or people were beginning to accept the procedures established in 1539, there was considerably less comment on the judicial system in the cahiers of the three estates. The Third Estate again asked that the accused have the right to learn the names of accusers at the beginning of the process.

The Ordinance of Blois, which was drawn up after the meeting, took note of the request by emphasizing that judges and royal prosecutors were obliged to find out the truth while interrogating the witnesses, thereby serving the defense as well as the prosecution. The ordinance also required judges to ask witnesses to reveal ties to plaintiffs and defendants at the beginning of interrogations. The edict also required *grands jours* every year in the provinces most distant from the Parlements.

The Ordinance of Blois contained articles on marriage, responding to the Third Estate's request for a stronger ban on clandestine marriages. Priests were forbidden to perform marriage ceremonies for persons from outside their parishes in the expectation that this would reduce the opportunities for secret marriages. The Catholic Church sanctioned marriages with only the consent of the couple, but the Council of Trent changed the nature of the sacrament of marriage by requiring the presence of a priest and two witnesses. The French delegates were responsible for that decree, but it did not require parental consent for a couple who had reached the age of majority. The French government took matters in its own hands in the Ordinance of Blois, which not only reaffirmed the 1556 ban on clandestine marriages but also declared that those responsible for such a marriage, usually but not always the would-be husband, were guilty of rape. In that era the term had not only its modern sense of *rapt de violence* but also referred to *rapt de séduction,* in which someone, again usually the male, would abduct or seduce an unwilling prospective spouse, thereby threatening her with dishonor if she did not wed him. The death penalty was mandated for a convicted rapist, which dramatically raised the stakes in respect to clandestine marriages. It also meant that the civil courts had greatly enhanced authority over matrimony. For several decades after 1579, there were numerous executions for *rapt de séduction,* especially when a case involved a daughter of a well-placed family who married a male of lower status against her parents' will. When the case involved a son who married below the family's station, the decision was to dissolve the marriage, leaving the woman dishonored and often with children deemed illegitimate.[4]

After 1562 witch trials became a major part of the case load of French judges. They were found in larger numbers on the fringes on the kingdom, especially along the frontier with the Holy Roman Empire, where the witch craze was more virulent than in France. France never had any episodes of the sort found in Germany and Lorraine where more than a thousand witches were executed, although one report placed the number executed at 300 in Toulouse in 1577. The half of France under the jurisdiction of the Parlement of Paris had far fewer executions for witchcraft than most of western Europe.[5] Of the 1,123 cases the Parlement heard on appeal, it reduced the death sentence imposed by local courts in 359 cases and let it stand in 115. It is not that the Paris magistrates were any more skeptical about witchcraft than their provincial counterparts, but they were sticklers for proper judicial procedure, which the lower court judges violated consistently in cases of witchcraft. It is noteworthy that the Leaguer Parlement confirmed a far higher proportion of death sentences. During the years from 1581 to 1590, appeals to Paris surged, as was to be expected considering that period's strong sense of the presence of the Antichrist, and remained at a high level for the next two decades.

It was, however, the legal issues surrounding the presence of Protestantism in the realm that held center stage before 1600. Prior to the meeting of the Estates, Henry III issued a new edict of pacification in May 1576, called the Edict of Beaulieu but better known as the Peace of Monsieur. By extending toleration to the Huguenots, the edict dealt with a legal problem, and it included several elements more specifically dealing with the judiciary. It repeated the lifting of the ban on Protestants entering schools, universities, and royal offices found in the Edict of St-Germain of 1570. However, it went well beyond the 1570 edict's clause that allowed Huguenots to object to four judges in any case before the Parlements by creating what become known as *chambres mi-parties*. Each Parlement would have a chamber in which the judges were half Catholic and half Protestant to hear civil and criminal cases involving Huguenots as one party. Only the Parlement of Languedoc made even a halfhearted effort to organize one, and the fierce opposition of the Catholic magistrates forced the *chambre mi-partie* to meet outside of Toulouse, eventually settling in Castres, where it met sporadically until 1598.[6]

The issues of the last religious war, specifically the agenda of the Catholic League, thoroughly dominated the next meeting of the Estates in 1588, again at Blois. Legal procedure was of little concern compared to the issue of whether there was a fundamental law of Catholicity, although there were recommendations on how to speed up criminal proceedings. The death of the duke of Anjou in 1584 passed first place in the line of succession to Henry of Navarre, if the usual interpretation of the Salic Law were followed. After Navarre's escape from the royal court in 1576, he returned to the Reformed faith and became the head of the Huguenot party. The Catholic League tried several tactics to deny him the right of succession. Armed force was one; defining fundamental law to eliminate Navarre from the line of succession was another. Some Leaguers simply denied that the Salic Law was a fundamental law on the grounds that it had been fraudulently perpetrated at the time of the disputed successions of the sons and nephew of Philip IV before the Hundred Years War. The key feature of the Salic Law was its requirement that the throne passed only to males through the male line. Accordingly, a vast number of male relatives of Henry

III whose blood ties to him came through women were ineligible for the throne. If the Salic Law was not fundamental law, then the Guises, as great grandsons of Louis XII through Renée of France, had a solid claim to the crown. Another tactic was to declare that the Salic Law required the succession of the male relative closest in blood to the reigning king through the male line of the royal family. According to this argument, the Cardinal of Bourbon, as the younger brother of Antoine of Bourbon and Navarre's uncle and therefore one degree closer to Henry III (although both were in fact remote—20 and 21 degrees respectively), was the royal successor.

The Leaguers were on more solid ground when they proclaimed that there was a fundamental law of Catholicity, dictating that the French king had to be Catholic, which took precedence over the Salic Law. They based this law not only on French history and tradition, especially the baptism of Clovis in 496, but also on the coronation oath, in which the new king swore to conserve the Catholic Church and keep it free of heretics. While there were Leaguers who argued all three points without regard for the resulting inconsistency, most of them preferred to proclaim that the law of Catholicity was the first fundamental law, taking precedence over the Salic Law. Since the religion of the royal successor had never before been in dispute, the Huguenot and Politique authors who rejected the Leaguer claim had an advantage in proclaiming that there was no evidence in French history for a law of Catholicity. They strongly defended the Salic Law as the first of the fundamental laws; whoever it designated as the royal successor was the next king regardless of his religion, even if he were Muslim, as several argued.

The Leaguers, who made the argument for a law of Catholicity since 1576, thought they won their case at the Estates of 1588. Earlier that year Henry III signed the Edict of Union drawn up by the League, which declared that fundamental law barred a heretical prince or favorer of heresy from the throne regardless of whatever rights in blood he might have. The Leaguer deputies at Blois constrained Henry to swear the edict again in conjunction with the Estates. Clearly they intended to gain for the Estates a role in deciding what fundamental law was. This point of view seemingly won a major victory when the king declared that he "would enact no fundamental law except with the agreement of the Estates," a phrasing that indicated the king believed he had the power to define fundamental law. Less than a month later, the duke of Guise and his brother were killed at Henry III's command, and the Cardinal of Bourbon was in prison. The cowed deputies of the Estates made little protest at the king's declaration that the Guises were guilty of *lèse-majesté* and his renunciation of the Edict of Union with its implication for fundamental law.

The League responded to the deaths of the Guises with open rebellion across the realm. The prospect of rebelling against one's king was terrifying for all but the most ardent Leaguers, but no one faced a more excruciating dilemma in early 1589 than did the parlementaires. Would they support the League in revolt and act contrary to the monarchy, or would they join with Henry III and Henry of Navarre and oppose what seemed to be the interests of their faith? The difficulty of this choice is made clear in the divisions in the Parlements; 45 percent of the magistrates manifested support for the League by serving in Leaguer-controlled Parlements. The League seized control of six cities where Parlements were located—Aix,[7] Dijon, Grenoble, Paris, Rouen, and Toulouse. The royalists kept control of two—Bordeaux and Rennes. The argument that many parlementaires remained in the Leaguer Parlements simply out of inertia is countered by Henry III's explicit order that all magistrates flee to royalist cities where rival Parlements were being established; for example, at Tours for Paris, and Caen for Rouen. The Leaguers set up their own court for the royalist Parlement of Brittany, while the court at Bordeaux was so completely royalist that no attempt was made to establish a Leaguer rival.

Most parlementaires who stayed in Paris found that their fellow Leaguers regarded them as suspect, despite often being fully committed to the Leaguer agenda. This suspicion culminated in 1592, when the radical Leagues executed Barnabé Brisson, a president of the Parlement, and two other magistrates, all moderate Leaguers. Any magistrate who remained in Paris after that had to be dedicated to the League, but that group of parlementaires performed a far greater service to the monarchy than did those who fled to Tours. When in early 1593 the League convoked the Estates general to Paris in order to elect a Catholic king (the Cardinal of Bourbon died in 1590), proposals were presented to the deputies to elect, among several others, Philip II's daughter Isabella, granddaughter of Henry II, on the grounds that the Salic Law was bogus. Before the Leaguer Estates could act, President Jean Lemaistre introduced a resolution in Parlement calling on the Estates not to interfere with the fundamental law of the realm. Of the several addresses in favor of the resolution, the most noteworthy was that of the prominent conseiller, Guillaume Du Vair. He supported Henry of Navarre's right to the throne if he converted to Catholicism. Now he powerfully defended the Salic Law as the first fundamental law. The Parlement quickly accepted Lemaistre's resolution requesting that a Catholic French prince be accepted as king. A week later France had such a king when Henry of Navarre abjured his Protestant beliefs at St-Denis.

In large part this debate over fundamental law in the decade after 1584 settled it for the ancien régime. With the victory of Henry IV there was no longer any question about the Salic Law and its several elements. Some historians propose that there was no law of Catholicity in the next two centuries, but Henry's conversion established that law as surely as his coronation demonstrated the status of the Salic Law as fundamental law.

Henry IV found himself in 1594 a Catholic king who had to deal with a powerful Protestant minority in his realm. His solution was the same as his predecessors'—an edict of pacification. The Edict of Nantes was, like its precursors, a legal document. The right to public worship it conceded to the Calvinists was a legal privilege the king granted out of his absolute power. The edict defined three types of places in which this right applied: places where Protestant services were regularly conducted in 1597, the estates of nobles who held rights of justice, and two sites in every *bailliage* and *sénéchausée* in the realm. Royal commissioners were to select the latter. When a number of Leaguer cities submitted to Henry, they wrung the concession from him that Protestant worship would not be allowed within their walls. Protestant services were held in the suburbs of several cities, including Paris and Rouen. The edict removed all of the legal disabilities imposed on the Huguenots by earlier royal edicts, such as the prohibition on holding royal offices, attending universities, and purchasing property. Henry granted a full pardon to anyone who had fallen afoul of royal justice in respect to religion since 1559.

The king realized that there would be innumerable matters over which legal disputes would erupt between Huguenots and Catholics. On some of these issues, such as marriages, wills, and burials, the two religions would have differing practices. The king knew that the Huguenots would not trust Catholic judges to be impartial in such cases. Accordingly, he established four special courts in the Parlements of Paris, Grenoble, Toulouse, and Bordeaux to hear cases involving Protestants. The predominance of Huguenots in the Midi is made clear in that three of these courts were placed there. The court at Paris originally consisted of a president and 16 conseillers, six of whom had to be Protestants. The strong objections to the edict from the Parlement of Paris and the Catholics in general forced him to reduce the number of Protestant judges in it to one. This Chambre de l'Edit, as it was known, served the area under the jurisdiction of the Parlement of Paris and had temporary responsibility for Normandy and Brittany, until courts could be erected in their Parlements. None ever were. Huguenots in Burgundy had the option of taking their cases to Paris or Grenoble. The three courts in the Midi were assigned two presidents and 12 magistrates, evenly divided between Catholic and Protestants. The members of these *chambres mi-parties* had membership in the Parlements with all of the privileges accorded to their magistrates. The Parlement at Toulouse objected so strongly to the creation of the *chambre mi-partie* for Languedoc that it was placed at Castres. Although it was officially part of the Toulouse court after 1598, it remained in Castres.[8]

Any civil or criminal case involving a Huguenot as one party could be taken to these courts, either as the court of first instance or appeal. Their decisions were without appeal, except in theory to the king, but there seems to have been few cases appealed to him. This suggests that the system must have worked well enough to alleviate the Protestants' worst fears about getting justice under a government still formally Catholic. Other evidence supports this, especially the fact that the courts quickly became busy once they began to function. That, however, took three or four years because of the Catholic opposition. Huguenot complaints about the Parisian court, with its minute Protestant presence, were the loudest. The existence of a legal process, often long drawn out, reduced substantially the possibility of violence in disputes between Catholics and Huguenots and helped to secure the peace established by the Edict of Nantes.[9] The offices in the courts of the edict immediately became venal. As the only judicial offices effectively open to Huguenots, their prices rose far more rapidly than for the seats in the Parlements to which they were attached.

The prices of all the venal offices increased substantially once peace was established, even before Henry IV published the major edict on venality in 1604. The *paulette* was a product of the king's need for money, but it also reflected the increasing hereditary nature of royal office. The one remaining obstacle to venal offices being truly hereditary was the 40-day rule in respect to resignations in favor: An officeholder had to have resigned his office at least 40 days before his death in order for his designated successor to take it over. The 40-day period began at the point when the tax for such resignations was paid. By the time an officeholder who was seriously ill arranged to pay the tax, he may have been on his deathbed. The office then reverted to the king, who was free to sell it to whomever he pleased, often to the designated heir, but at the full price. Families frequently resorted to hiding the deaths of incumbents, often by salting the bodies to preserve them until the 40-day rule was fulfilled. In the case of a president of the Parlement of Paris, his death was concealed for 52 days.

A royal financier named Charles Paulet proposed a solution that satisfied both the king's need for money and the problems of the 40-day rule: the incumbent would pay an annual fee of $1/60$ of the tax for resigning an office in order to guarantee that the resignation, regardless of when it was made, would be effective. The king still collected the resignation tax, so the new annual fee was a new sum for his treasury. In the first several years after 1604, it came to 1 million *l.* Paulet held the office responsible for collecting the fee for a year, hence *paulette*. Nothing now prevented a diligent officeholder from passing on his office to his heir, although the king had the right to repurchase any or all offices. The hereditary principle was now universal in the royal offices, except for the military, where rank and merit still had a role in commissions. One result of the *paulette* was that the price for offices rose dramatically for those few that still came on the market, even as the return from salaries and *épices* remained stagnant. Although such situations as the lack of an heir or conviction for treason caused offices to revert back to the king and put them back on the market, the main reason was the sale of the office by the incumbent. The wealthy haute-bourgeois families traded in offices like any other commodity, and although women could not exercise an office, they could hold the right to sell or assign one to a male. As prices went up, so did both the resignation tax and the *paulette*. By 1614 the sum of the latter reached 1.6 million *l.*

From two points of view the *paulette* was a brilliant success. The monarchy gained a significant sum of money, and the officeholder class was highly grateful to the king for the new arrangement that so benefited their families. It tied those families even tighter to the crown. But there was a negative side, which Chancellor Pomponne de Bellièvre laid out when he objected to the *paulette* when it was discussed in the royal council. He asserted that the king would lose control of the royal bureaucracy and magistracy, which would be permanently in the hands of wealthy *robin* families. Also, he objected, the king could no longer reward loyal service with an office; at least it would become rare. The aristocracy also complained that the *paulette* reduced their influence in the government by pricing offices beyond the reach of most nobles, while the grands who still could afford offices were not interested in purchasing them. The grands, however, had their own objection: the *paulette* worked to the detriment of the system of noble clientage. In the past, the great nobles succeeded in pressing the king to name their clients to offices. The nobles' complaint touched on a point that was not necessarily bad for the monarchy; if the kings realized it, it may explain, along with the sums being collected, why they resisted abolishing the *paulette,* despite frequent demands that it be done. Pomponne, for his part, continued to object until Henry asked him to give up the seals of his office in 1605.

Loud complaints about the *paulette* were heard from the First and Second Estates at the Estates of Paris in 1614. The nobles and their allies in the clergy were eager to regain what they regarded as properly belonging to the nobility— royal office. They assigned a specific percentage to the different categories of offices that the nobles would receive: all of the positions of provost-marshal and superintendent of the forests and waters, $1/3$ of the seats in the Parlements, and $1/3$ of all other offices. They specifically attributed the dramatic decline in officeholders from the *noblesse d'epée* to the *paulette,* which, they argued, priced them out of the market. The Third Estate, with its large representation of parlementaires, made a brilliant counter suggestion. Its deputies proposed that the monarchy abolish the *paulette,* making the king give up 1.6 million *l,* and reduce the *taille* by 4 million *l;* the king would recoup these loses by eliminating 5.6 million *l* in pensions to the nobility. The nobles erupted in rage over that proposal, and after three months of bickering, the Estates closed with a vague promise from Louis XIII to end the *paulette* in 1617. That year came and went with no change in the system of venality.

Squabbling over the *paulette* was one reason why the institution of the Estates was discredited at the 1614 meeting. In regard to justice the meeting was unproductive. The secret legal procedure of 1539 had been in place for 75 years, and everyone, especially the judges and *avocats,* was used to it. In their cahiers, all three estates repeated an old call that only one judge, aided by his clerk, handled the interrogation of the accused and witnesses. Another repeat request was that the authority of the provost marshals be restricted to soldiers and military matters. The cahiers of the nobility called for the elimination of the presidial courts as an infringement on the authority of the seignorial courts and requested the erection of a special chamber in the Parlements for the cases of the nobility. The tiers requested the use of *grands jours* as a means of enforcing royal justice in the provinces. It also suggested that the king travel in person to give justice, as Louis IX did.

The monarchy's response to the cahiers was delayed until 1629, when it published an ordinance on justice called the Code Michaud. Its impact was limited, and it did little to change the system established by Villers-Cotterêts and revised by Moulins. In respect to the law and those who were involved in its application, the Ordinance of Villers-Cotterêts and the *paulette* largely settled matters. Although the men of the long robe benefited from both, especially the latter, the monarchy profited far more. Although there was no uniform code of law for the realm, royal justice triumphed over seignorial and ecclesiastical courts. Justice devolved entirely from the king; there was no separate judicial authority. Grateful for their enhanced authority and the *paulette,* the magistrates worked diligently to implement the royal will. They were not always a docile instrument of royal authority, as the early phases of the Fronde would reveal, but they were predisposed to decide issues in the favor of royal authority. By 1614 royal power had firm allies in the law and the magistracy.

19

Culture and Thought:
On to Classicism

The violence of the Wars of Religion had a profound impact on the intellectual and cultural activities of the last decades of the sixteenth century. While it did not end the French Renaissance, it sorely disrupted the work of the humanists and artists just as their achievements peaked under Henry II. Yet the era was not a cultural desert; some notable work persisted throughout. Catherine de Medici was imbued with her ancestors' ideal that governments and powerful persons should patronize artists and humanists, and she provided considerable support for culture. Had times been better, she might have gone down in history as one of the great patrons of the arts. Furthermore, the religious violence helped to inspire one of the great French intellectuals, Michel de Montaigne, and produced a major body of political thought.

It was in art that the impact of the religious wars appears to have been the deepest. Only two painters, Antoine Caron and Jean Cousin the Younger, merit special attention for the years before 1598. Caron worked at Fontainebleau under Primaticcio, and his work reveals the elements of mannerism—its elongated human figures and love of ceremony and festivals. He became Catherine de Medici's favorite artist and painted several allegorical pieces on the court and its members. His two paintings depicting astrologers at work touched on her favorite subject. (See illustration XII). Perhaps his best-known work is the *Massacres under the Triumvirs* (1566). As a Catholic who later did several paintings supportive of the League, it is improbable that he was attacking

XII. Astronomers observing an Eclipse. By Antoine Caron, c. 1580, Private Collection. Giraudon/Art Resource, New York.

Catholic leaders, but neither is it clear he was praising them.[1] Jean Cousin, son of a painter with the same name, was highly regarded in his time, but not enough of his work has survived to permit a thorough scholarly evaluation. Influenced by Rosso, Cousin also seems to be anticipating the Baroque in his best-known piece, *Last Judgment,* with its crowding of human figures and frenetic activity.

In sculpture, Germain Pilon dominated the era. His funerary pieces for Henry II, his first major work, won him the admiration of the queen mother, who gave him many more commissions. Pilon did funerary statues in both marble and bronze for the Birague, a wealthy Italian mercantile family from which came a royal chancellor of the 1570s. There are hints of the baroque in the emotionalism and flowing drapery of these and other pieces from his late career, which ended in 1596. Pilon's statues, especially those on Henry II's tomb, had a powerful influence on French sculptors for the rest of the century, but only Barthelémy Prieur produced enough work of high quality to warrant mention, especially his monument for the heart of Constable Montmorency.

The reigns of Charles IX and Henry III saw more building than might have been expected, given the state of the French economy and royal finances and the political anarchy. Having ordered the destruction of the old Tournelles because it was the place where her husband died, Catherine de Medici began to build the Tuileries close to the Louvre, with Philibert de L'Orme as its architect until his death in 1570. Before then he designed the Hôtel de la Reine in Paris for her, with its famous tower for astrologers. Jean Bullant completed both projects for Catherine, and received numerous other commissions from her and prominent courtiers. The most notable was the gallery on the bridge at Chenonceaux, done in the classical style. His later work moved away from the rules of classical architecture and showed signs of the inventiveness that marks mannerism. The best-known architect of the period was Jacques Du Cerceau the Elder, the founder of a dynasty of noted architects. He completed only a small number of structures, but sketched many existing buildings and drew up designs for many more. They appeared mostly in his *Les plus excellents Bastiments de France (The Most Excellent Buildings of France* [1576, 1579]), which was dedicated to the queen mother. Many of his plans for new buildings provide the best examples of mannerist architecture in France, since they were highly fanciful and on a scale too large to be achieved; but he also included some practical designs for town houses, being the first architect to address that theme. His designs influenced the rebuilding Paris that occurred during Henry IV's reign. In literature the Pléiade still dominated the writing of poetry; the last member died in 1605. As a group they were pleased with the queen mother's generosity, but it was Pierre Ronsard who benefited the most, becoming poet laureate. Much of his poetry after 1562 flattered the courtiers, but it is not as well regarded as earlier poems written in some anger when he felt that he was not getting the recognition he deserved from Henry II. After he retired from the court at about 1580, Ronsard wrote mostly religious poetry, solidly Catholic in doctrine, and polemical pieces hostile to the Huguenots.

Many of the poems of the Pléiade were set to music. Orlando di Lasso, a native of the Low Countries despite his name, put several of Ronsard's poems to music, of which the best known is *Bonjour mon coeur*. He used rich harmony and counterpoint for these poetic pieces, which mark him as one of the early masters of polyphony. The member of the Pléiade most involved in combining music and poetry was Jean-Antoine de Baif, who founded the Academie de poèsie et musique in 1570 to set French poetry to music following the rules of the ancients. Charles IX issued a royal patent that set out the academy's statutes, and he declared himself to be its patron. Among the musicians who wrote the music and played at Baif's house for the king and members of the court were the Huguenot Claude Le Jeune and the Catholic Jacques Maudit, who rescued Le Jeune and his works during the siege of Paris in 1590. Baif's academy existed for only a short time, but it did much to establish the rules for setting poetry to music, which had wide influence in the next century.

Better known than Baif's academy was one that Henry III established in 1576. It is unclear whether this Palace Academy was a continuation of the earlier one or a new foundation. It placed greater emphasis on rhetoric and philosophy, but its sessions always ended with a musical selection, usually a piece by Maudit. The Palace Academy had largely the same membership as Baif's, but it included two noblewomen who took an active part in the discussions on moral and natural philosophy. The latter topic has been the focus of modern interest in the Palace Academy, because heliocentrism was debated. Jacques Davy Du Perron, a Huguenot savant who later converted to Catholicism and became a cardinal, reportedly annoyed the king when, after arguing in favor of heliocentrism, he told him that he could argue equally well to the contrary. According to some historians, the academy had its last formal meeting in late 1579,[2] although it is also possible that the notorious Italian savant Giordano Bruno lectured before the king in 1581 under the auspices of the academy. He was in Paris from 1581 to 1583, until he went to London as Henry's representative.

Pontus de Tyard, a prominent member of the Pléiade and both academies, was known for using the dialogue, a literary form he introduced to France. In 1551 he translated into French an Italian dialogue from the previous century, and the next year he published his own, the *Solitaire premier*. By presenting differing opinions of the participants and allowing the author to serve as the moderator with the final word, the dialogue genre permitted the discussion of dangerous ideas that, if presented in a different context, would have exposed the author to censorship. Thus, in his *L'univers* (1557) Tyard had one of his speakers discuss heliocentrism in a positive manner, while a second one argued against it; Tyard himself mediated the dispute with a moderate skepticism toward the certainty of human knowledge. The dialogue was also a device to discuss love (as used by Louis Le Caron and Etienne Pasquier) and religion. It provided the ideal format for the Politiques to argue for a moderate approach to religion and politics, allowing them to stand between vehement defenders of Catholicism and Calvinism.

Ronsard's replacement as court poet under Henry III was Philippe Desportes, a cleric who received a number of abbies for his poetry, which often flattered the king. Given the hostile press Henry received from almost everyone else, his desire to reward Desportes is understandable. Desportes spent some time in Italy before 1567, and much of his poetry is either a direct translation of Italian pieces or imitations of them. The feature for which he is best known is his coining of French words from Latin, Greek and Italian. He also is noted for his extravagant similes and complicated analogies, which contain a hint of the baroque. Much of his poetry was set to music. Desportes also translated the Psalms into French to provide a Catholic alternative to those of Marot, which were so completely identified with the Calvinists. He had a wide public in England, which is somewhat surprising since he joined the Catholic League after Henry III's assassination. He demonstrated his political facility by becoming court poet for Henry IV, a post he held to his death in 1606.

Religion provided the inspiration for a large number of literary works written after 1562. A Dominican nun, Anne de Marquets, wrote sonnets that emphasized Catholic beliefs, while her counterpart, Georgette de Montenoy from Rouen, dedicated a book of poetry in 1566 to Jeanne d'Albret. The Huguenot works are regarded more highly, because they included such masterpieces as Agrippa d'Aubigné's *Les Tragiques*. Wounded while fighting in Navarre's army, d'Aubigné began to write the work while he was recuperating. It was largely finished by 1589 but not published until 1616. *Les Tragiques* is a history of Christianity in poetic form, with special emphasis on the St. Bartholomew's massacre, which d'Aubigné blamed squarely on the queen mother and the cardinal of Lorraine. His hostility toward Catherine was especially vigorous, and he had much to do with creating her image as the evil Italian woman. The same point of view reappeared in his better-known *Histoire universelle*.

In the late sixteenth century, Guillaume Saluste du Bartas, whose noble title came from an estate that a bishop sold during an alienation of Church property, had the highest reputation among the Protestant poets. His masterpiece is a set of two poems of more than 20,000 lines, which are known collectively as *Les Semaines* (*The Weeks* [1578, 1584]). The work was intended to be much longer, since du Bartas, another of Navarre's comrade-in-arms, planned to write on all seven days of creation, but only finished the first four days. It is an epic with God the Creator as its hero. The device of writing on the days of the creation gave the author the opportunity to engage an enormous number of topics. Heliocentrism was one of them, and du Bartas gave Copernicus a favorable mention. Less blatantly partisan than d'Aubigné's poetry, *Les Semaines* still had a Calvinist core. Du Bartas highly admired the Pléiade and took to heart Joachim Du Bellay's prescription to write long epics in French. His work was immensely popular, going through 25 editions by 1610 and numerous translations, including the famous English edition of 1592 by Joshua Sylvester.

The French theater developed rapidly after Jodelle's *Cléopatre* was performed in 1553. He continued to be productive to his death in 1573, but he lost royal patronage and died in poverty. Henry III's tastes ran toward the theater, and he patronized a large number of playwrights, including Jean de La Taille. La Taille published the two plays of his brother Jacques as well as his own long repertoire. He wrote a treatise, *L'art de la tragédie,* which laid out the rules that a playwright had to follow to seize hold of the audience's emotions. The most notable playwright whom Henry patronized was Robert Garnier. He wrote love poetry as well as a broad range of plays, which Ronsard, his friend, praised extravagantly. He had a law degree from Toulouse and served in the judicial system of his native Maine until Henry III appointed him to the Grand Conseil in 1586. Most of his plays were tragedies, in which he followed the conventions of the ancients, especially Seneca. His *Les Juifves* (1583) was probably the first religious drama from a French Catholic, and he was the first French writer of a tragicomedy, *Bradamante* (1582), about a female warrior who promises to marry the first man who can defeat her in single combat. Garnier eliminated the chorus from this work, and his characterizations are the strongest in sixteenth-century French drama. Another important innovation in the play was that his characters address their soliloquies to a person on the stage, not to the audience. The Calvinists contributed a large number of religious dramas to French literature, beginning with Theodore Beza's *Abraham sacrifiant* (1552), which was probably the best. It dramatizes the Calvinist view that sinners, even Satan, must praise God. For Beza, Satan was a tragic figure, not a buffoon as he was portrayed in earlier farces.

The late sixteenth century is best known in French literature as the era of Michel de Montaigne, regarded today as one of the great virtuosos in writing French. He was born in 1533 near Bordeaux. His father's family were wealthy merchants who purchased the estate of Montaigne, while his mother's family included converted Iberian Jews who settled in France. His father, a committed humanist, gave his son a tutor, who did not speak French or Gascon, to teach him Latin from early childhood. Thus Montaigne became exceptionally fluent in classical Latin. He gained a seat in the Parlement of Bordeaux at the age of twenty-four, but resigned 13 years later to take up residence at Montaigne. He was deeply pained by the religious strife he saw about him and the inability of the law and its servants to end the violence and injustice. He first tried Stoicism, staying in his tower at Montaigne with his books and remaining aloof from the world's problems. Stoicism, however, was not compatible with his nature, and by 1575, he moved toward skepticism—questioning the ability of human reason to reach the truth. It led him to two positions that were not inherently contradictory but seemed so in the context of his era. One was that since the human mind was incapable on its own of knowing the truth, it was best to rely on the collective wisdom of vast numbers of people over centuries of time. This led him to remain a Catholic, albeit not a zealous one. The other was a strong belief in religious toleration. It is, he commented, putting a high price on one's own beliefs to burn someone else for them, since no one can be certain of the truth of those beliefs.

Montaigne expressed his ideas in short pieces he called *essais*—from the word to try out or test. In his *Essais* he tried out ideas and presented them to others for response. He published his first two books in 1580, and the public response was enormous. Although his writing was interrupted by two terms as mayor of Bordeaux from 1581 to 1585 and then by diplomatic missions for Henry of Navarre, he published a third book in 1588. Montaigne died in 1592 while attending mass. His adopted daughter, Marie de Gournay, did most of the work of putting his scraps of writing, marginal notes, and the published *Essais* into a coherent edition in 1595. Few literary works have had the profound long-term impact as Montaigne's essays, which still serve as exemplars of good French style. Their author stands as a prime example of the "Renaissance man": at home in a enormous range of topics but especially in classical literature, eager to achieve the golden mean in every respect, including religion, and fiercely individualistic. The *Essais* are modern in their psychological understanding of human nature and sense of the relativism of experience, which, Montaigne argued, determines an individual's behavior, not some sort of ultimate truth.

In the first decades after the publication of the *Essais*, their skeptical philosophy had the greatest impact. Pierre Charron, a canon in the cathedral at Bordeaux and friend of Montaigne, made skepticism a key part of the French Counter-Reformation. In *Les Trois Verités (The Three Truths* [1594]) he argued that Protestantism necessarily sowed confusion because of its insistence on the ability of the individual to read and understand the Bible. The inability of the human mind to be certain of the truth meant that the 16 centuries of the collective experience and tradition of Catholicism had to be relied upon, and not the ever-erring minds of Protestant leaders. In 1601 Charron published a second skeptical text, *La Sagesse (Wisdom),* which again made the case that only the Church's understanding of divine revelation points to the truth, but added that there is a natural code of ethics that can be discerned from the study of human societies. Christian morality is superior to this natural code because it is based on divine revelation, but Charron was one of the first in Christian Europe to postulate a code of ethics separate from religion. This use of skepticism became a mainstay of Catholic controversialists after 1594. The Jesuits, in particular François Veron, were skilled in making use of it to confound the Huguenots. Their college at La Flèche was the stronghold of skepticism for the next several decades, when René Descartes was educated there. He left the college a complete skeptic, against which he later would react.

Montaigne's skeptical toleration was not much in evidence in the era of the French religious wars, certainly not in most of the extensive political literature written then. Periods of civil strife tend to be highly productive for political theory, when attention is paid to the questions of public authority and political rights. When stable government breaks down, these questions receive an urgent reexamination. Most of the political works of the era were mediocre at best, but several became classics of political thought. The Huguenots, perhaps because they were "people of the Book," were quick to recognize the potential of the printing press as a means of spreading their political propaganda. Already in 1560 a noteworthy work appeared—François Hotman's *Le Tigre de France,* written in response to the Tumult of Amboise. He was from a German family that settled in Paris after 1470. His father was a magistrate in the Parlement, and most of his many siblings remained Catholic. Like many other Reformers, he was a legal humanist. He fled into exile in 1548 and was in Strasbourg when the Tumult occurred. The "mad tiger" of his work was the cardinal of Lorraine, who, along with his brothers, were deemed the evil advisers to the young king responsible for the troubles in France. The participants in the Tumult were only seeking to free the king from those who illegally seized power and return France to its ancient constitution. The latter point was a consistent theme in Hotman's writings. Jean Du Tillet, another parlementaire, was the principal respondent to Hotman. He added little to the debate beyond asserting that the king was at the age of majority and the Guise government was legal.

The political works of the next 12 years added little to the discussion, except that the queen mother was as often the target of the Huguenot attacks as the Guise. St. Bartholomew's Day drastically changed the nature of the Huguenot works. After this they were directed against the king instead of using the fiction of the evil advisers. The right of the people to resist an evil ruler who harmed the true religion was openly expressed. Many of the authors, however, sought revenge, more on the queen mother than her son, as she was widely blamed for the massacre. Even the best of the Huguenot works expressed a desire for revenge, but they subordinated it to significant discussions of political theory. The anonymous *Reveille-matin des Français (Alarm bell of the French)* was published in 1573 in both Latin and French. It may have been collaborative work of several authors, as was true of many anonymous works of the religious wars. It presented more fully—if not more precisely—a thesis that had already appeared in some pre-1572 Huguenot writing. The people conferred power on the king but did not give over the whole of sovereign authority; some remained in the hands of the lesser magistrates who had the duty to resist an evil ruler. Their identity, however, was left vague. The *Reveille-matin* proposed that this authority was granted in the ancient constitution of France, which had been subverted by the recent kings. When a king injures his people as cruelly as Charles IX had, who was alleged to have fired on the Huguenots himself and was responsible for the death of 10,000 of his loyal subjects in Paris alone, he can and must be deposed.

The *Tocsain contre les massaceurs et auteurs des confusions en France (Alarm against the massacrers and authors of confusions in France* [1577]) denied that Charles shot at the Protestants and placed the number of the massacred at 2,000, but it bitterly attacked the queen mother as a student of "that atheist Machiavelli." That same theme, argued at greater length but less vehemently, is the subject of Innocent Gentillet's *Anti-Machiavel* (1576). He, like many other Huguenot authors, blamed the influence of Machiavelli for the troubles in France, especially the illegal and immoral behavior of the monarchy. They contrasted the Italian's pernicious ideas about government with the pure and virtuous ancient constitution of the French realm and denounced the powerful influence of both Machiavelli and the many prominent Italians in France.[3] One often repeated story from the era was that Henry III carried *The Prince* in his pocket and carefully consulted it when he wanted to pull off something underhanded or wicked.

The three major Huguenot works on political thought are not known for such stories but for the depth of their views. The authors of these and numerous other polemics were often referred to as "monarchomachs" (king eaters) for their bitter attacks on the French monarchs.[4] Hotman's *Francogallia* was written before August 1572, but in his preface and several places in the text, he made clear the work's relevance to the massacre.[5] Hotman, who was in Geneva when it was published, contrasted the virtue of the governmental system of the founders of the French state with the corruption in the French monarchy of his time, which drew on the corrupt tyranny of Rome and Italy. The twin founders of France, the Franks and the Gauls, loved liberty, which led both to resist the tyranny of Rome. The Gauls were unsuccessful, but the Franks successfully freed the Gauls from Roman tyranny. If anyone happened to miss the analogy to religion, Hotman made it obvious: the French needed to free themselves from the new tyranny of the Italians both in government and the church, with the help of the Germans in regard to the latter. Much of the work discusses the ancient constitution of the Franco-Gauls, who had an elective monarchy with a public council possessing authority to depose a tyrannical king. Hotman identified that council with the Estates general.

More obviously a *livre de circonstances* was the *Du Droit des Magistrats sur les sujets,* in which the question of who had the power to depose a wicked king was addressed more immediately. Published anonymously in both French and Latin, its author was Theodore Beza. He proposed that the people created the monarchy and granted authority to it, which was limited, not absolute. The Estates and the lesser magistrates had authority from God to resist and even rebel against an evil ruler who was transgressing those limits. Beza argued that the ancient French constitution empowered the Estates and the lesser magistrates with control of the king, but Louis XI in particular had succeeded in eliminating their authority. Good government and respect for true religion would return to France when the ancient constitution was restored. More radical yet probably the most influential of the Huguenot political works, was the *Vindiciae contra Tyrannos (Defense against Tyrants),* which was published under a pseudonym in 1579. It may have been a collaborative work, but there is little doubt that Philippe Duplessis de Mornay was a major contributor, if not the sole author.[6] He was a nobleman with a good education, who fought with Henry of Navarre and by 1576 was a major adviser to him. After 1594 he emerged as the elder statesman for the Huguenots. The *Vindiciae* consists of four questions and their answers. Are subjects bound to obey a prince if their orders contradict the law of God? The answer, of course, is no. Who may resist such a prince? The people as a whole, the officers of the people, but also a private person who has received a special call from God to save the people from a tyrant. The author then turns from religion to ask whether a prince who devastates the commonwealth can be resisted. His answer demonstrates that the people created the French monarchy and the officers of the kingdom, and the Estates general elect the king. There is a covenant between king and people in which the king pledges to rule justly. If he violates that pledge by bad law or overtaxation, the people or their officers can resist and depose him. The final question establishes that neighboring princes are obliged to aid the subjects of a prince who is a tyrant. There is in the *Vindiciae* a sense that France was a federation of communities, in which communities such as La Rochelle or Montauban were sovereign in their own right and contracted with the king to rule them. One of the most common accusations hurled at the Huguenots was that they intended to "cantonnize" France in imitation of the Swiss Confederation; the *Vindiciae* provides some justification for the charge.

Catholic political theory until 1576 remained little more than a defense of the status quo and the king's right to full obedience in all matters, including religion. The Peace of Monsieur provoked a drastic change in the minds of the Catholics who joined the League, because they now doubted the monarchy's commitment to eradicate heresy. The League's manifesto pledged its adherents to oppose anyone who was not in full accord with its goal. Henry III was intended, even if the manifesto proclaimed the League's loyalty to the monarchy. At about the same time the first works advocating the fundamental law of Catholicity appeared, which would be a mainstay of Catholic thought until 1594. Leaguer political thought began to develop as a distinct body of literature in 1584, concentrating on the issue of the royal succession. The most notable Leaguer author writing prior to the executions at Blois was Louis d'Orléans, whose several works, especially the *Advertissement des Catholiques anglois aux Catholiques françois* (1586), were intended to prove that the presence of a second religion in the realm was a deadly threat to the state. The death of the Guise at the hands of Henry III was a dramatic turning point in Leaguer political theory. A floodtide of hatred was directed at Henri de Valois, for the Leaguers no longer acknowledged him as king.[7] Pamphlets and sermons proclaiming the right of the good Catholics to depose him as king thundered across France. Some of them advocated tyrannicide as the only solution to the evil that infected the kingdom. Jacques Clément took them at their word and killed the last of the Valois.

The Leaguer propagandists are noteworthy for that fact alone, but several Leaguer works are important in their own right. The first of them was Jean Boucher's *De Justa Henrici Tertii Abdicatione a Francorum rege* (*The Just Deposition of Henry III as King of the French* [1589]). Curé of a parish in Paris, Boucher became so influential in the Catholic League as a preacher and author of polemical works that he was called the "the one-eyed king" of Paris. Borrowing extensively from the Huguenot works, Boucher asserted that both the church and the people have a right and an obligation to depose Henry III as a tyrant. The people's right is based on common law, in which it is clear that the people are superior to the monarchy, which they created, and they elect each new king. Thus, they can depose a king who is harming their interests. The pope, as the supreme authority in religion, also has the power to depose a king and order the election of a new dynasty. Boucher added a new conclusion after Henry III's assassination, praising Jacques Clément as the new David killing Goliath, and proclaimed that the Estates must meet quickly to elect a Catholic king.

Another major Leaguer work from shortly after Henry III's death, was the *De Justa Reipublicae Christianae Authoritate* (*The Just Authority of the Christian Republic* [1590]). Published under the pseudonym of "G. Guilielmus Rossaeus," contemporary sources and internal evidence suggest several possible authors, both English Catholics in exile in France and French Leaguers. Given that the first part of the work is an extensive discussion of political theory in which the author reveals broad knowledge of English history and historians, and the second is a far-ranging demonstration of the "perversity" of Protestant doctrine, in which the author refers to "the Burgundian blood that is within me," the book probably was a collaborative work by an English exile and a French theologian. Among the key points in the work is the argument that the monarchy was elective and the people, acting through their officers, can depose an evil king and even kill him if that is the only way to remove him from the throne. One of the ways in which a legitimate king can become a tyrant is through taxing the people without the consent of the Estates. There is a binding contract between king and people in which the people promise to obey the king only if he rules justly in a Christian manner. Since Henry of Navarre as a heretic could never do that, he cannot be allowed to take the throne, and a Catholic prince must be elected king.

A third major Leaguer political work was the most radical piece to appear during the religious wars. The *Dialogue d'entre le manant et le maheustre* appeared anonymously in late 1593, after Henry's conversion. Its author probably was Louis de Cromé, a Parisian magistrate of the Grand Conseil, who was involved in the murder of Barnabé Brisson.[8] Its identity as a Leaguer work was hidden for centuries because Henry IV commissioned a royalist version of it and ordered the destruction of all the original copies. In the nineteenth century a copy of the first version reappeared, revealing that it was originally a work from the radical Paris Sixteen. Like several other works, it was a product of the months after Henry's conversion, when many Leaguers were convinced the act was fraudulent. Its author was a firm believer in the elective nature of the French monarchy, but extended a role in the election to all French Catholics. Its most radical element, however, was its fierce attack on the nobles, including the Leaguers, for betraying the cause of the faith. They and the royal officers were parasites who lived off the sweat and blood of the poor people, who alone upheld the true cause of the League. The *manant's* (commoner's) attack on Leaguer leaders, especially the duke of Mayenne, was so strong and bitter that the royalist who rewrote it only changed a few lines to turn it into a piece of royalist propaganda.

Among the several prominent Politique authors who may have done the redaction of the *Dialogue,* the most probable was Pierre Pithou, a Parisian parlementaire and humanist. Early in the religious wars, there was little difference between works by ardent Catholics and Politiques. Both wanted a strong monarchy, although they disagreed over how it was to be maintained: the Catholics argued that the eradication of heresy was necessary; the Politiques, that religious toleration was the only solution. Politique literature diverged drastically from the Leaguer in 1576, when it became clear that the zealous Catholics were prepared to oppose the monarchy if it was not active enough in rooting out heretics. The most active Politique writer was Pierre de Belloy, who held an office in the Parlement of Toulouse. In several books from after 1584 that responded mostly to the works of Louis d'Orléans, he argued for the inviolability of the Salic Law, maintaining that nothing, not even being a Muslim, could keep the successor designated in that law off the throne. He was still active in 1598, when he supported the Edict of Nantes.

The major Politique piece appeared after Henry IV's conversion. The *Satyre Menippée*, which refers to the ancient author Menippus of Gadara, was a collection of satirical pieces by several authors, organized by Pierre Le Roy. A first draft appeared in late 1593, and an expanded edition came out in 1594. It made effective use of satire to attack the die-hard Leaguers. Much of it is a parody of the Leaguer Estates that petered out several months earlier. Although the entire range of Leaguer adherents was subjected to biting satire, its most effective aspect, which touched an exposed nerve for most French Catholics, was the attack on Leaguer ties to Spain.[9]

Jean Bodin, the most highly regarded political writer of sixteenth-century France, should be regarded as a Politique, although he did join the League, probably out of prudence, when it was the height of its power. He was born in Angers, joined a Carmalite monastery for several years, and then took a law degree at Toulouse, where he taught until about 1560. There is reason to suspect that he was in Geneva for a short time after 1550. He was knowledgeable in Calvinist theology, but his later writings did not have the hint of sympathy for it that can be sensed in his early ones. He knew Hebrew and Judaic thought well and revealed an enthusiasm for Judaism in some of his works, to the point that some historians have suggested he had an Iberian Jewish mother. Bodin was involved in politics as a deputy for the Third Estate in 1576 and a member of the entourage of the duke of Anjou until Anjou's death in 1584. At the Estates of Blois he was active in successfully opposing both the League's demand for a war on the Huguenots and the king's request for approval of the alienation of royal property. His attitude toward the Estates general was succinctly expressed in his statement that the sovereignty of the monarch was in no way reduced by their presence: "On the contrary, his majesty is much greater and more illustrious seeing his people acknowledge him as their sovereign."[10] Royal power is the theme of Bodin's major work, *Six livres de la République (The Six Books of the Republic)*. First published in 1576 in French, it went through six new editions in the next seven years, a Latin edition in 1586 that was reprinted in 1588 and 1591, and translations into most major European languages. Filled with lengthy digressions, few works on political thought are as confusing, but that was fairly typical of the Politique authors, who performed a careful balancing act between the warring factions. It also was common to second-generation legal humanists, who looked to both Roman law and French custom for their concepts.

The *Republic* was a product of its time, intended to answer the question of how the king should deal with the anarchy in France. Its solution was to place all sovereign power in the monarch. Contemporary Huguenot authors were advocating a mixed constitution in which sovereignty was shared between the king and the people through such institutions as the Estates. Bodin believed that such a division of power was currently found in France, but it was contrary to the principles of good government and was partly responsible for the disorders across the realm. He defined sovereignty as the exercise of the absolute power invested in the state. It is indivisible. The sovereign depends on no one, makes and enforces law for everyone, and has the power to command his subjects and take a reasonable part of their property as taxes. However, he is subject himself to divine and natural law; to disobey either is to be guilty of treason against God. Bodin's sovereign had to be a moral prince, not Machiavelli's amoral one. Furthermore, the king must obey the fundamental laws of the realm, such as the Salic Law, which are part of the very nature of the French *respublica*.

Shortly before Bodin wrote his book, Protestant theorists began to use the word *state* as a synonym for *republic*. Bodin did not use state in that sense, but as of 1614 it was more common than republic. The two words had differing connotations: republic implied a sense that the people had a stake in "the public thing;" state, that there was a permanent entity apart from the people centered in the king. It is difficult to imagine Louis XIV saying "La république, c'est moi!" (Of course, "L'Etat, c'est moi!" may be apocryphal.)

Bodin began the *Republic* with a powerful statement on the king's indivisible sovereignty, but by its conclusion kingly authority, especially his right to make new law, a key aspect for Bodin, was in fact hedged considerably.[11] Nonetheless, through his discussion of royal power Bodin hoped to justify a potent monarchy that could reestablish law and order without depending on traditional religious sanctions for political authority. When religion itself was openly subject to divisive interpretations, its ability to provide a solid basis for the well-ordered state was destroyed. In fact, religion was responsible for the disorders threatening to ruin France. The king had to have the power to prevent religious zealots from disrupting the state and force them to obey the law, but the source of that power could not be religious, since that would simply add to the divisions, not prevent them. The foundation of the political system had to be based on something other than traditional Christian doctrine. Only then would the king have the power to force religious sects to give up their quarrels and live in peace. The king was to serve as the guarantor of justice, which for Bodin the Politique included the right to practice one's religion in peace. There is reason to believe that he extended this right to Jews and Muslims as well as

Protestants. In a dialogue published long after he died in 1598, the *Colloquium Heptaplomeres,* two of the seven speakers, a Jew and a follower of natural religion, sharply criticized both sides of the split in Christianity and suggested that true religion may well be found outside of the Christian faith. It is ironic, therefore, that Bodin became a member of the Catholic League in 1589. Perhaps because he felt that tradition required the king to be Catholic, he supported the right of the cardinal of Bourbon to the throne before his nephew Navarre. While Navarre was next in line, he had to convert before he could wear the crown, which Bodin in 1591 accurately predicted would occur within two years.[12]

While Bodin's political thought was a product of the worst years of the religious wars, Charles Loyseau's came out of the period of the restoration of order and royal authority. He was a member of a family that was rising rapidly in the French social order. His grandfather was a rural *laboureur;* his father, a lawyer who settled in Paris. Loyseau became a royal bureaucrat and ended his career as the president of the lawyers' council in Paris. His grandson completed the family's rise by becoming a magistrate in the Parlement of Paris. Perhaps because his family was rising through the levels of the French social hierarchy, he was intensely interested in its composition. His many works, mostly written between 1600 and 1610, have titles such as *Traité des seigneuries, Traité des Ordres et simples dignités, Traité des Offices.* Loyseau saw France as a society arranged by God into a clearly defined set of orders and ranks. Within each of the three orders of clerics, nobles, and commoners, there was an enormous range of ranks, meaning a group of persons who share the same social, legal, and political standing. Although historians need to be careful not to take everything Loyseau wrote about the social structure of his time as fully accurate, his works provide a most useful insider's description. Loyseau also had much to say about the monarch who had sovereignty—the exercise of power without a superior. Like Bodin, Loyseau saw sovereignty as delineated by the laws of God and nature and the fundamental laws of the realm, but more clearly than Bodin, he found the absolute power of the king was also limited by property rights, which included the rights of the seigneur on his estates. The king's major powers were specifically defined: to make law, create officials, decide on peace or war, be the final appeal in justice, and mint coins. In regard to taxation the king could tax only with the consent of those taxed, since it involved taking private property. Consent came through the Estates general, although Loyseau was vague about its powers and functions. Befitting to the period in which he wrote, he had little interest in the Estates. Both Bodin and Loyseau used the phrase "absolute sovereignty" and, therefore, have been seen as advocates of the absolute monarchy of the ancien régime, but in fact they carefully hedged its power. Their sovereign's authority was vast, but he was not the Leviathan.

Loyseau's political thought has a sense of order that was absent in works from before 1594. It reflected the success of Henry IV in restoring peace and stability to France. While one legacy of the anarchy of the previous decades was the enormous royal debt, the monarchy could return after 1594 to large building projects of the sort little seen since 1559. Most of Henry IV's building was done in Paris; enhancing the appearance of his capital was important to him. Paris was far more the center of French culture after 1600 than it was a century earlier when Lyon was a close rival. Henry's most durable project in Paris was the Pont neuf. Henry III conceived of building a bridge across the Seine at the tip of the Ile de Cité, but it was left to Henry IV to see the project to completion. A comparison between the original plans for the bridge with what was built for Henry IV reveals his sense of simplicity and order, characteristics of French classicism, in contrast with the ornateness and grandiosity of Henry III's mannerist design. In 1614 Marie de Medici placed the famous equestrian statue of Henry IV at the point of the island where the bridge cut across it. Henry also finished Catherine de Medici's new palace, the Tuileries, and her scheme of replacing the old Tournelles, which she ordered torn down, with a square of fine houses. The plan for the Place Royal, today's Place des Vosges, was his. Except for two large royal houses, the square was surrounded with uniformly designed houses of moderate cost for bourgeois Parisians, not grand hôtels for the great nobility. This was a new idea in town planning—a plaza of private houses for comfortable living, not great public and church buildings as found in Italy. The square was used as a place for public celebrations, such as for the wedding of Louis XIII in 1612. Henry planned several similar places in Paris, but none were as successful as the Place Royal.

Most of Henry's architects were Huguenots; among the most prominent was Solomon de Brosse. His best-known projects reveal a return to classicism from the mannerism of the previous generation of architects. This is clear in his design for the Luxembourg Palace begun in 1615 for Marie de Medici. Since these royal projects were completed after 1600, their decoration constituted a major part of the painting and sculpture done in France for the next two decades. The artists were heavily influenced by the art they saw at Fontaine-bleau, and they constituted what is known as the Second School of Fontaine-bleau, led by Toussaint Dubreuil. Their works were the last gasp of mannerism in France. After 1610 Fontainebleau and the Loire châteaux were bypassed for Paris, but aspiring artists continued to make pilgrimages to see the splendid works there.

The major poet of Henry IV's reign revealed the same shift away from the style of the previous half-century. François de Malherbe, a son of a Protestant lawyer of Caen, who converted to Catholicism before 1585, received the position of court poet in 1605. The Pléiade had influenced heavily his early work, but he later abandoned their style. He sharply criticized Ronsard and Desportes—whom he replaced as court poet and for whom he had a strong antipathy—for extravagance in their poetry. Malherbe, already about fifty when he began his reform of French poetry, demanded discipline and order in writing poetry. He objected to the creation of new French words from classical languages and recommended that his disciples go down to the docks, listen to the workers there, and return their words to respectability by using them in literary works. He established strict rules for rhyme and required a mathematical balance in his verses. In short he, along with his large group of disciples that included the playwright Racan, established French classicism in literature.

Malherbe's sense of mathematical exactitude in verse writing may well have come from his contacts with the large group of natural philosophers and mathematicians he met while he was in Aix for ten years before his arrival at court. Guillaume Du Vair, the first president of the Parlement of Aix, was their major patron, although he contributed little directly to their achievements except a strong interest in Stoicism, which had a different outlook on cosmology than that of the dominant Aristotelianism. Stoics contended that there was only one element, either air or fire, extending from earth to the stars.[13] Skepticism also played a role in creating interest in the new astronomical ideas proposed by Nicolaus Copernicus. Montaigne argued that the only conclusion to be drawn from the Polish astronomer's skill in championing heliocentrism was that one should be unconcerned over which of the two systems of cosmology was true. The human mind was incapable of reaching certain knowledge on such matters; therefore, discussion of them was not dangerous to the faith but was simply hypothesizing. Such a position hardly seems productive of scientific advances, but it did have a positive aspect. It allowed French savants to discuss Copernicanism in the midst of the religious wars, when ardent Leaguers like Jean Boucher declared that heliocentrism was another Satan-induced error of the times. The skeptical position continued to serve French Catholic thinkers after 1616 when Rome condemned heliocentrism.[14]

One of those for whom the skeptical approach proved useful was Pierre Gassendi, a members of the Provencal School of astronomy. Its founder was a Fleming, Godefroy Wendelin, who arrived in Provence in 1599 in order to take advantage of the favorable conditions for viewing. He was an accomplished observational astronomer at a time when France was decidedly lacking in such expertise. He taught Gassendi, Joseph Gaultier, and Nicolas Fabri de Peiresc, all noted names in French astronomy, the techniques of observation. Peiresc, a member of the Parlement of Aix, spent time with Galileo earlier, so he was probably the first in France to hear about Galileo's discoveries with the telescope. Peiresc wrote to him asking for a telescope and a copy of *Starry Messenger*. With both in hand, he and Gaultier became the first Frenchmen to view Jupiter's moons in November 1610. By 1614 there was a large group of astronomers making astronomical observations in Provence.

French contributions in mathematics were more noteworthy in the context of the history of the discipline, largely through the work of François Viète. A lawyer and parlementaire who was an adviser to Henry IV, he used his mathematical skills to break the cipher the Spanish were using for their diplomatic correspondence. His *In artem analyticem isagoge* (*Introduction to the Analytical Art* [1591]) was the first work to use letters for both known and unknown numbers in algebra. In his system consonants denoted known numbers, and vowels, unknown ones. He defined the rules for transferring terms from one side of an equation to the other and dividing both sides by a common denominator. In later works to his death in 1603, he was especially concerned with using algebraic equations to solve geometric problems. Viète was the founder of a major school of French mathematicians in the seventeenth century who included Fermat, Pascal, and Descartes. The certainty of mathematics proved to be an effective corrective to the skepticism prevalent in France in the early 1600s. It became the language of the mechanical physics rapidly being developed, and together they were largely responsible for French rationalism.

20

Epilogue

Looking at France from the vantage point of 1614, what happened in the 130 years since 1484? One major development was a vast strengthening of the sense of being French among the common people and the spread of the French language into most corners of the realm, although many would still have answered a query about their *pays* (country) with their town or province. This stronger identity of being *bon françois* was associated with the king, not the Estates general. The brief moment in the late fifteenth century when it was possible that being French might have been identified with the Estates had flitted away, along with any chance that the Estates might have bridled the king and created a limited monarchy, although no one in 1614 would have predicted that it would not be called again for 175 years.

By 1614 the feudal suzerain had become the royal sovereign, and part of this process involved raising the arbitrary authority of the king over the consultative element. In lockstep with that development was the new emphasis on blood right to the throne. Although the elements that went into the greater importance of blood right had been developing for many years, Henry IV's succession was the key one. His right to succeed was based on the fact that he had in his veins the royal blood of Louis IX, despite Henry's remote relationship to the last Valois, Henry III. St. Louis became the model king whose sanctity justified the French monarchy in perpetuity. Now the new king had authority at the moment of his predecessor's death: "The King is dead! Long live the King!" The significance of the *sacre* conferring the right to rule on the new king had largely disappeared, although the ceremony itself became more elaborate. Louis XII, who was cited in the era of the religious wars as the model king for his tax policy and consultation, nearly disappeared after 1594 from the popular mind.[1] Perhaps even more significant in the rise of absolute monarchy was the change in the royal bureaucracy, which was both much larger, reaching perhaps 25,000 members,[2] and tied more tightly to the king than it was a century earlier.

The French monarchy came out of the extremely turbulent times of the religious wars so greatly strengthened that the succession of an eight-year-old boy in 1610 caused only minor ripples in the realm. The monarchy was not free of domestic troubles until the adult years of Louis XIV, but after 1614 it did not face such major crises as the captivity of Francis I, the religious wars, or the assassination of Henry IV. The untroubled succession of Louis XV in 1715 at five years of age demonstrated the continued enhancement of royal authority in the century after 1614.

Between 1484 and 1614, the Catholic Church withstood the most serious challenge to its place in French society prior to the French Revolution. The Catholics had to tolerate, however reluctantly, the presence of some one million Huguenots in the realm, but they never truly accepted the concept of toleration and were able to achieve their goal of a return to *une foi* in 1683. The king gained vastly greater authority over the Church, but the Catholic clergy, with a few exceptions, preferred to see him exercise that authority instead of the pope. It cost the clergy the annual payment of the *décime,* but that had its compensation in the form of the national assemblies of the clergy every three years. These provided the clergy with some opportunity to influence royal policy, even if the monarchy skillfully manipulated the meetings. In several respects, especially its judicial power, the clergy saw its authority eroded since 1484, but the reform of the worst abuses, even if the decrees of the Council of Trent were never accepted in toto, strengthened the hold of Catholicism on the French people, which was unchallenged until 1789.

French Counter-Reformation Catholicism, in place by 1614, was quite different from the religion of 1484. The most significant changes echoed Calvinism, although it can be argued that both faiths reflected a broad reforming spirit within Christendom, which affected them both. One development was the more rigorous morality demanded of clergy and laity; both Catholics and Calvinists were expected to be saints. A second, which may have helped to bring about the first, was the concept that salvation was really a matter for the individual soul. The sense that salvation was a communal affair—found in the confraternity, the parish, the monastery—disappeared almost entirely in Calvinism, and it became far less important in Catholicism. Individuals were to be obedient subjects of God, as they were to be the king's. In both church and state, the commune was much less important in the seventeenth century than it had been in the fifteenth.

The nobility too had lost much of its autonomy and power to the monarchy, but it certainly had not conceded its place as the most prestigious status. By 1614 nobles no longer were regarded as the exclusive military caste, and perhaps a majority of them never went to war. With the *paulette* reducing the number of new nobles appearing, the strong antagonism of the nobles of the sword toward the *anoblis* declined considerably, although it never completely disappeared, and intermarriage between the two groups became common. The *recherche* became a tool by which the monarchy could remove pretenders to noble status from the roll of the noblesse, which did much to satisfy the old nobility that those who claimed noble privileges were worthy of them.

For the common people, the broad prosperity that touched nearly all of them in the decades after 1484 had largely disappeared, especially for the large portion of them who were day-laborers. Heavy taxes also burdened the commoners. The *taille* was most exasperating to the wealthy peasants, who hid their prosperity in order to avoid paying more taxes. While the artisans and their guilds largely stagnated, the merchants were doing well, especially those who took advantage of changing trade patterns, centered on the Atlantic coast. The cities lost much of their autonomy to the monarchy, but it was the group of medieval urban republics that lost the most. The Huguenot towns, in particular La Rochelle, held out the longest in that regard, until after 1614.

Although the Parlement of Paris was chastised in 1610 when it presumed to take for itself a larger role in the affairs of state than was traditional, that event by no means reversed the gains the legal profession had made since 1484. Lawyers and legal bureaucrats clearly benefited from the changes in government and law. That in turn aided the rise in royal power because most in the legal profession were advocates of enhanced royal authority and even absolutism. French law was codified in the years since 1484 and remained little changed to 1789. Despite Bodin's assertion that the sovereign had the power to make new law, the king was still viewed as the provider of justice who saw that the good law of the past was justly applied. The concept of the king as sovereign lawmaker took nearly another century to become established. The monarchy, however, took effective control of the judicial system throughout the realm; it gave the king real power of the sort about which theorists of absolutism could only speculate.

French culture and intellectual activities reflected the turbulence of the century before 1614, most especially in mannerism and skepticism. The appearance of French classicism indicated the return to a more stable society, which also was reflected in the rejection of skepticism. The certainty of royal absolutism also contributed to the demise of both mannerism and skepticism and the corresponding rise of classicism. It is the nature of architecture, art, and literature to leave a more permanent record of a period's achievements than any other area of human behavior. In a way that is not true for Francis I, Catherine de Medici, or a Croquant, today François Rabelais, Louise Labé, and Philibert de L'Orme can still speak to us of the glory of sixteenth-century France.

In the 130 years after 1484, France made the transition from the Middle Ages to the ancien régime for most aspects of French society. Certainly, ancien-régime France was far from a static society, but the rate of change was far less over 175 years to 1789 than it had been during the "Long Sixteenth Century." The society and government that would be destroyed by the French Revolution was already mostly in place in 1614.

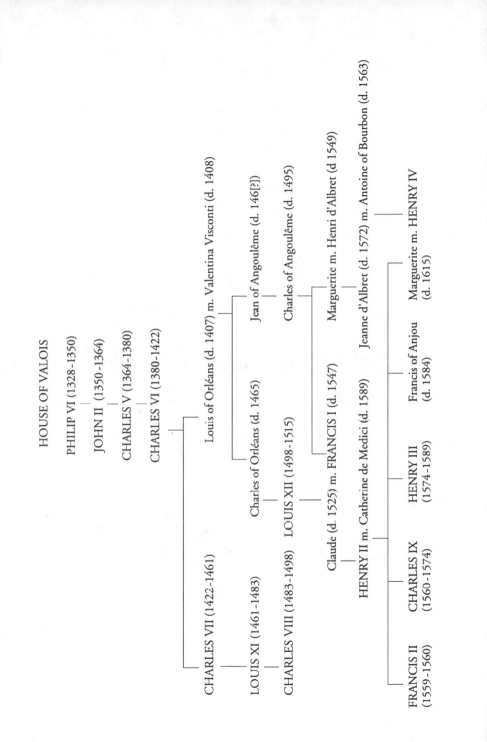

HOUSE OF VALOIS

PHILIP VI (1328–1350)

JOHN II (1350–1364)

CHARLES V (1364–1380)

CHARLES VI (1380–1422)

CHARLES VII (1422–1461)

Louis of Orléans (d. 1407) m. Valentina Visconti (d. 1408)

Jean of Angoulême (d. 146[?])

Charles of Orléans (d. 1465)

Charles of Angoulême (d. 1495)

LOUIS XI (1461–1483)

LOUIS XII (1498–1515)

Marguerite m. Henri d'Albret (d 1549)

CHARLES VIII (1483–1498)

Claude (d. 1525) m. FRANCIS I (d. 1547)

Jeanne d'Albret (d. 1572) m. Antoine of Bourbon (d. 1563)

HENRY II m. Catherine de Medici (d. 1589)

Francis of Anjou (d. 1584)

Marguerite m. HENRY IV (d. 1615)

HENRY III (1574–1589)

CHARLES IX (1560–1574)

FRANCIS II (1559–1560)

HOUSE OF BOURBON

LOUIS IX (d. 1270)

|

Robert of Clermont (Sixth son, d. 1317) m. Béatrix de Bourbon

|

Louis I of Bourbon (d. 1341)

Pierre I of Bourbon (d. 1356)   Jacques of Bourbon-La Marche (d. 1377)

|

Louis II of Bourbon (d. 1410)   Jean of Bourbon-La Marche (d. 1393)

|

Jean I of Bourbon (d. 1434)   Louis of Bourbon-Vendôme (d. 1446)

Charles I of Bourbon (d. 1456)	Louis of Montpensier (d. 1486)	Jean of Bourbon-Vendôme (d. 1477)
Pierre of Beaujeu (d. 1504)	Gilbert of Montpensier	Francis of Bourbon-Vendôme (d. 1495)
Suzanne of Bourbon m. Charles of Bourbon (d. 1523) (d. 1527)		Charles of Bourbon-Vendôme (d. 1537)

Antoine of Bourbon m. Jeanne (d. 1572)   Louis of Condé   Charles, Cardinal
(d. 1563)   (Queen of Navarre)   (d. 1569)   of Bourbon (d. 1590)

|

HENRY IV (d. 1610) m. (1) Marguerite of France (d. 1615)

m. (2) Marie de Medici (d. 1642)

|

LOUIS XIII (d. 1643)

HOUSE OF MONTMORENCY

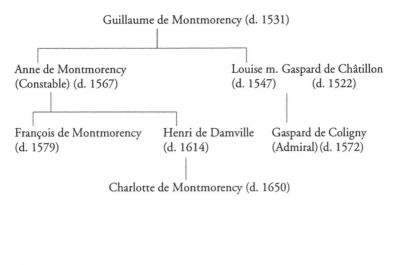

Guillaume de Montmorency (d. 1531)

Anne de Montmorency (Constable) (d. 1567)

Louise m. Gaspard de Châtillon (d. 1547) (d. 1522)

François de Montmorency (d. 1579)

Henri de Damville (d. 1614)

Gaspard de Coligny (Admiral) (d. 1572)

Charlotte de Montmorency (d. 1650)

HOUSE OF GUISE

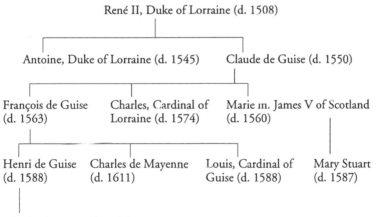

René II, Duke of Lorraine (d. 1508)

Antoine, Duke of Lorraine (d. 1545)

Claude de Guise (d. 1550)

François de Guise (d. 1563)

Charles, Cardinal of Lorraine (d. 1574)

Marie m. James V of Scotland (d. 1560)

Henri de Guise (d. 1588)

Charles de Mayenne (d. 1611)

Louis, Cardinal of Guise (d. 1588)

Mary Stuart (d. 1587)

Charles de Guise (d. 1640)

Glossary of Terms

Aides The earliest tax collected by the French monarchy. It was a form of sales tax and was so called because it was originally imposed as part of the subjects' obligation to give aid to the king for war or a crusade.

Anobli New noble, generally used for a family that had been ennobled since 1400. The term is more appropriate for the sixteenth century than *noblesse de robe*, since many new nobles had received their noble status for reason other than service in royal office.

Appel comme d'abus The right to appeal a verdict from a church court to a royal court on the grounds that the church court had exceeded its authority.

Bailli, bailliage The terms used in northern France for the major local royal officers and their some hundred districts into which France was divided. In the Midi the terms *sénéshal, sénéchausse* were used.

Ban and *Arrière-ban* The king's right to summon his vassals and subvassals for military service, the feudal levy.

Benefice A church office with an income irrevocably attached to it.

Bonnes villes The king's "fair cities," a term used for the towns and cities that were exempted from the major tax, the *taille.*

Cahiers Petitions drawn up by the three estates to present to the king at meetings of the Estates general, detailing perceived problems in the governance of the realm and their recommended solutions. They were produced both at the local level as the local estates chose their deputies to the Estates general and at the meetings of the Estates.

Cas royaux Legal cases that pertained to the person of the king, his family, and his edicts.

Chambres mi-parties Judicial units created by the Edict of Nantes (1598) to hear cases involving French Protestants. Their membership was half Catholic and half Protestant.

Communautés des habitants Self-governing peasant villages that controlled most aspects of peasant life and were responsible for tax collection.

Compagnies d'ordonnance Royal companies of heavy cavalrymen created by royal decree in 1445. Also known as lance companies.

Décime   The royal tenth, in theory a gift of a tenth of its annual income that the French clergy gave to the king. By 1614 it clearly was a tax, but it was also well less than a tenth of clerical revenues.

Demesne   Lands and revenues that pertained to the king as feudal lord. The revenues that came to him from the *demanse* (as it was called at the time) were referred to until the middle of the sixteenth century as his "ordinary revenues," while taxes were known as "extraordinary revenues."

Dîme   The tithe, a first portion of all agricultural production owed to the Catholic clergy. It rarely was as high as a tenth but was more commonly a fifteenth.

Elu, Election   The royal officer responsible for the collection of the *taille* and his district. Originally, he was elected by the local taxpayers, hence the name. The system of *élection* extended to about two-thirds of the realm, which was know as the *pays d'élection*.

Epargne   More properly, the tresor de l'Epargne. It was created in 1523 to collect most royal revenues in treasure chests in the Louvre; its treasurer and his subordinates soon became responsible for most of the royal revenue collection and expenditure.

Evangélisme   Term used for the early French movement seeking church reform. The Evangéliques were largely convinced that meaningful church reform could take place without breaking with the Catholic Church.

Franc-fief   A fee paid to the king in lieu of military service by commoners who acquired noble estates.

Gabelles   A tax on salt. The tax varied enormously across the realm, thus encouraging salt smuggling.

Gallicanism   Theory that the French Catholic Church was free of papal control in regard to its finances and the appointment of its prelates while accepting the pope's authority in matters of doctrine and discipline.

Gens d'armes   "Men at arms." Term in common use after 1450 for heavy armored cavalrymen (knights).

Gens de finances   Royal financial officials, more specifically used for those in place before the Epargne was created in 1523.

Grands Jours   Special courts using magistrates from the Parlements held sporadically in provinces distant from the Parlements to enforce royal justice.

Généralités des finances   The four divisions of France, excluding the *pays d'états*, for the collection of the king's "extraordinary revenues" (taxes). In 1542 they were subdivided into sixteen *recettes-générales*.

Hôtel du roi   The royal court, including the members of the king's household and the royal guards.

Lance   The basic unit in the French cavalry, referring to the fact that it was centered around the armored heavy lancer with several support troops; hence, "lance company" as a synonym for *compagnie d'ordonnance.*

Lettre de jussion   A royal command given to one of several courts and royal officials who had sovereign authority to refuse to register a royal edict, which ordered them to effect the registration. When in the case of the Parlement, such a letter failed to have the desired results, the king would appear in person in a *lit de justice.*

Lit de justice   The king's appearance in the Parlement to order the magistrates to register a controversial edict or to promulgate a decree of major importance.

Midi   The region of France south of a line roughly from Bordeaux to Lyon. In the sixteenth century, it was still largely distinct from northern France in culture, language, and law.

Mortmain   "Dead hand," referring to the fact that once property had passed into the control of the Church, it almost never again changed hands.

Noblesse d'épée   Nobility of the sword, the traditional nobility whose ancestors had won noble status by military service to the king in the Middle Ages. Essentially synonymous with *Noblesse de race.*

Noblesse de robe, robins   Nobles whose status was conferred by service as a royal official or magistrate, especially in the Parlement. Often used as synonym for *anobli, robin* was somewhat less inclusive, since some *anoblis* had gained their status through other means.

Officialité, Official   The bishop's court and its principal officer, to hear cases such as heresy that fell under clerical jurisdiction.

Paulette   Term used for the edict of 1604 allowing those who purchased royal offices to pass them on to their heirs without restrictions in return for an annual payment to the king of $1/60$ th of the price of the offices.

Pays d'élu   Those provinces, already under royal control by 1439, in which the king imposed the *taille* without consultation. For the most part they did not have provincial estates

Pays d'état   Those provinces, largely those on the frontiers which came under royal control after 1439, in which the king negotiated with the provincial estates over the amount of taxes collected.

Progress   A royal tour of the provinces, intended to boost loyalty to the king through his presence among his people.

Reitres   Pistol-carrying horsemen, originally Germans, who began to appear in the French army in the 1550s and largely replaced armored lancers as the French cavalry.

Recettes-générales   The seventeen fiscal divisions of France created in 1542 whose *Receveurs-généraux* collected nearly all of the royal revenues, ending the distinction between "ordinary" and "extraordinary" revenues.

Recherches   Scrutiny of a family's right to its claim of noble status. The monarchy used them primarily to determine whether those claiming an exemption from paying the *taille* as a privilege of noble status had a legal right to do so.

Rentes   A form of royal loan taking in which the king rented out a source of income such as a toll for a sum of money. The sum served as the principal while the revenue served as interest. This avoided the Church's prohibition on usury. The most important *rentes* were those managed for the king by the city of Paris.

Resignation in favor   A device by which a holder of a royal office or a church benefice could designate his successor in the process of resigning the position.

Roturier   A commoner, anyone who did not belong to the clergy or the nobility.

Sénéchal, sénéchaussé   See *Bailli.*

Setier   A measure of volume used for grain.   In the Parisian system of measurements, it contained 156 liters.

Sovereign court   One of several royal courts that had the right of registering royal edicts affecting their areas of jurisdiction. Appeals from them were taken directly to the royal council.

Taille   The largest royal tax. Originally imposed to pay the *gens d'armes* in times of war, it became permanent under Charles VIII. In most of France it was collected from persons deemed as commoners—*taille personelle;* in the Midi it was based on property that conferred commoner status—*taille réelle.*

Venality   The selling of royal offices. By 1614 all royal offices had become venal except those of military command. The *Paulette* of 1604 ensured that those holding venal offices could pass them to their heirs.

Abbreviations Used in the Notes

AHR—*American Historical Review*

Annales—*Annales Economies, Sociétés, Civilisations*

BSHPF—*Bulletin de la Société de l'histoire du Protestantisme français*

BHR—*Bibliothèque d'humanisme et renaissance*

FHS—*French Historical Studies*

Proceedings, WSFH—*Proceedings of the Western Society for French History*

RHEF—*Revue d'histoire de l'Eglise français*

SCJ—*The Sixteenth Century Journal*

Notes

Chapter 1

1. B. Doumerc, "La lente agonie des ports du Midi: Narbonne, Montpellier et Marseille confrontes l'evolution des circuits d'échange (fin XV—début XVI siècles)," *Annales du Midi,* 106, (1994):317-31.
2. M. Brun, *Recherches historiques sur l'introduction du français dans les provinces du Midi* (Paris: 1923).

Chapter 2

1. Quoted in B. Quillet, *Louis XII* (Paris: 1986), 180.
2. J. Freeman, "Louise of Savoy: A Case of Maternal Opportunism," SCJ, 3 (1972): 77-98.
3. J. Bosher, "'Chambres de Justice' in the French Monarchy," in *French Government and Society 1500-1850,* J. Bosher, ed. (London: 1973), 19-40.
4. V. Bourilly, ed. *Mémoires de Martin et Guillaume Du Bellay,* 4 vols. (Paris: 1908-19), vol. I, 332-57.
5. R. Knecht, "Francis I and the *lit de justice:* A 'legend' defended," *French History,* 7 (1993): 53-83.

Chapter 3

1. B. Chevalier, *Les Bonnes Villes de France du XIVe au XVIe Siècle* (Paris: 1982), 242; J. Farr, *Hands of Honor: Artisans and Their World in Dijon, 1550-1650* (Ithaca, N.Y.: 1988), 246.

2. J. Bergin, "Between estate and profession: The Catholic parish clergy of early modern western Europe," in *Social Orders and Social Classes in Europe since 1500*, M. Bush, ed. (London: 1992), 66-85.

3. P. Gagnol, "Les décimes et les dons gratuits," RHEF, 10 (1922): 465-81.

4. R. Darricau, "La réforme des réguliers en France de la fin du XVe siècle à la fin des guerres de religion," RHEF, 65 (1979): 5-12.

5. B. Palustre, "L'Abbesse Anne d'Orléans et la réforme de l'ordre de Fontevrault," *Revue des questions historiques*, 66 (1899): 210-17.

6. H. Heller, "Marguerite of Navarre and the Reformers of Meaux," BHR, 33 (1971): 271-310.

7. H. Heller, "The Briçonnet case reconsidered," *Journal of Medieval and Renaissance Studies*, II (1972): 223-58.

8. J. Vidal, "Une crise épiscopale à Pamiers 1467-1524," RHEF, 14 (1928): 305-64.

9. R. Knecht, "The Concordat of 1516: A Reassessment," in *Government in Reformation Europe 1520-1560*, H. Cohn, ed. (London: 1971), 91-112.

10. M. Edelstein, "The Social Origins of the Episcopacy in the Reign of Francis I," FHS, 8 (1974): 377-92.

11. F. Baumgartner, "Louis XII's Gallican Crisis, 1510-1514," in *Politics, Ideology and the Law in Early Modern Europe*, A. Bakos, ed., (Rochester, N.Y.: 1994), 56-72.

12. L. Sandret, "Le Concile de Pise," *Revue des questions historiques*, 34 (1883): 425-56.

13. A. Giustinian, *Dispacci*, ed. by P. Villari, 3 vols. (Florence: 1876), II: 175.

14. M. Piton, "L'idéal épiscopal selon les prédicateurs français de la fin du XVe siècle," RHEF, 108 (1911): 77-118, 393-423.

Chapter 4

1. P. Contamine, *Guerre, Etat et Société à la fin du Moyen Age: Etude sur les armées des rois de France 1337-1494* (Paris: 1972), 315-17.

2. Claude de Seyssel, *The Monarchy of France*, trans. by J. H. Hexter (New Haven, CT.: 1981), 58-59.

3. R. Kalas, "The Noble Widow's Place in the Patriarchal Household: The Life and Career of Jeanne de Gontaut," SCJ, 24 (1994): 519-39.

4. J. Woods, *The Nobility of the Election of Bayeux, 1463-1666* (Princeton, N.J.: 1980), 24.

5. Ibid., 22.

6. W. Weary, "Royal Policy and Patronage in Renaissance France: The Monarchy and the House of La Trémoille," Ph.D. diss., Yale University, 1972, 76.

7. P. Contamine, *Histoire militaire de la France* (Paris: 1992), vol. I, 249.

8. Contamine, *Guerre, Etat et Société*, 660-63.

9. B. Monluc, *Commentaires*, ed. by P. Courteault (Paris: 1964), 34-35.

10. A. Spont, "La Marine française sous le règne de Charles VIII," *Revue des questions historiques*, 55 (1894): 387-454.

11. A. Spont, "Les galères royales de la Mediterranée 1496-1575," *Revue des questions historiques*, 58 (1897): 238-74.

12. A. Santosuosso, "Italian and French Art of War: The Battle of Fornovo (1495)," *International History Review*, 16 (1994): 221-50.

13. A. Spont, "Marignan et l'organisation militaire sous François Ier," *Revue des questions historiques*, 60 (1899): 59-77.

Chapter 5

1. M. Baulant, "Les prix des grains de 1431 à 1789," *Annales*, 23 (1968): 520-40; D. Richet, "Croissance et blocages en France du XVe au XVIIIe siècles," *Annales*, 23 (1968): 759-87; G. Blois, "Le prix du froment à Rouen au XVe siècle," *Annales*, 23 (1968): 1262-82.

2. F. Brumont, "La commercialisation du pastel toulousain (1350-1600)," *Annales du Midi*, 106 (1994): 25-40.

3. E. Leroy Ladurie, *Carnival in Romans*, trans. by M. Feeney (New York: 1979), 2-9.

4. Archives départementales des Hautes-Alpes, Fonds G, ms. 1207.

5. B. Diefendorf, "Widowhood and Remarriage in Sixteenth-Century Paris," *Journal of Family History*, 7 (1982): 379-95.

6. C. Loats, "Gender and Work in Paris: The Evidence of Employment Contracts, 1540-1560," Proceedings, WSFH, 20 (1993): 25-37.

7. N. Davis, "Women in the Crafts in Sixteenth-Century Lyon," in B. Hanawalt, ed., *Women and Work in Preindustrial Europe* (Bloomington, IN.: 1986), 167-97.

8. A. Voisin, "Notes sur la vie urbaine au XVe siècle. Dijon La Nuit," *Annales de Bourgogne*, IX (1937): 265-79.

9. R. Muchembled, *Popular Culture and Elite Culture in France 1400-1750*, trans. by L. Cochrane (Baton Rouge, LA.: 1985), 119.

Chapter 6

1. D. Parker, "Sovereignty, Absolutism, and the Function of the Law in Seventeenth-Century France," *Past and Present,* 122 (1989): 36-74.
2. Quoted in F. Baumgartner, *Louis XII* (New York: 1994), 250.
3. Royal letter of March 1498, quoted by J. Dawson, "The Codification of the French Customs," *Michigan Law Review,* 38 (1940): 774. See also J. Filhol, "The Codification of Customary Law in the 15th and 16th Centuries," in *Government in Reformation Europe, 1520-60,* H. Cohn, ed. (London: 1971), 265-83.
4. J. Dewald, *Pont St-Pierre 1398-1789* (Berkeley, CA: 1987), 216-24.
5. C. Stocker, "Public and Private Enterprise in the Administration of a Renaissance Monarchy: The First Sales of Office in the Parlement of Paris (1512-1524)," SCJ, 9 (1978): 4-30.
6. R. Giesey, "Rules of Inheritance and Strategies of Mobility in Prerevolutionary France," AHR, 82 (1977): 271-89.
7. The nature of the *lit de justice* is the subject of a dispute between S. Hanley, in her *The "Lit de Justice" of the Kings of France* (Princeton, N.J.: 1983); and R. Knecht, "Francis I and the *lit de justice*. A 'legend' defended," *French History,* 7 (1993): 53-83. Hanley would restrict the use of the term to a small number of occasions when the king was present in Parlement for major constitutional disputes.

Chapter 7

1. The Venetian Ambassador Contarini, in *Relazioni degli ambasciatori veneti,* E. Alberi, ed. (Florence: 1860), IV, 15.
2. H. Bernard-Maître, "Les 'Théologastres' de l'Université de Paris au temps d'Erasme et de Rabelais (1496-1536)," BHR, 27 (1965): 248-64.
3. P. Jodogne, "Les Rhétoriqueurs et l'humanisme," in *Humanism in France at the End of the Middle Ages and in the Early Renaissance,* A. Levi, ed. (New York: 1970), 150-75.
4. E. Rummel, "*Et cum theologeo bella poeta gerit.* The Conflict between Humanists and Scholastics Revisited," SCJ, 23 (1992): 713-26.
5. G. Di Stefano, "L'Hellénisme en France à l'orée de la Renaissance," in Levi, *Humanism in France,* op. cit.

6. M-M. de La Garanderie, "Guillaume Budé, A Philosopher of Culture," SCJ, 19 (1988): 379-88.

7. J. Beard, "Letters from the Elysian Fields: A Group of Poems for Louis XII," BHR, 31 (1969): 27-38.

8. Y. Labande, *Charles VIII, le vouloir et la destinée,* (Paris: 1986), 495.

9. E. Thomas, "Les logis royaux d'Amboise," *Revue de l'Art,* 100 (1993): 44-57.

10. M. Melot, "Politique et architecture: Essai sur Blois et Le Blésois sous Louis XII," *Gazette des beaux-arts,* 70 (1967); 317-28.

11. R. Scheller, "Gallia Cisalpina: Louis XII and Italy 1499-1508," *Simiolus,* 15 (1985): 5-63.

12. J. Perouse de Montclos, "Nouvelles observations sur Chambord," *Revue de l'Art,* 102 (1993): 43-53; J. Guillaume, "Léonard de Vinci, Dominique de Cortone et l'escalier du modele en Bois de Chambord," *Gazette des Beaux-arts,* 1 (1968): 93-108.

13. B. Meyer, "Louis XII, Leonardo and the *Burlington House Cartoon,*" *The Art Bulletin,* 51 (1975): 371-76.

14. A. de Montaiglon, "La famille des Juste en Italie et en France," *Gazette des Beaux-Arts* (1875): 385ff; (1876): 552ff.

15. P. Chaillon, "Les musiciens de Nord à la cour de Louis XII," in *La Renaissance dans les provinces de Nord,* F. Lesure, ed. (Paris: 1956), 63-69; J-M. Vaccaro, "L'Apogée de la Musique Flamande à la Cour de France à la fin du XVe siècle," in *La France de la Fin du XVe siècle,* 253-64.

Chapter 8

1. R. Doucet, "La Mort de François I," *Revue historique,* 83 (1913): 309-16.

2. H. Furgoet, "L'attitude de Henri II le landemain de la journée de Saint-Quentin," *Revue des Questions historiques,* 32 (1882): 464-93.

3. D. Potter, "The Duc de Guise and the Fall of Calais, 1557-1558," *The English Historical Review,* 388 (1983): 483-96.

4. L. Romier, "La mort de Henri II," *Revue historique,* 108 (1911): 225-50; 109 (1912): 27-55.

5. M. Antoine, "Genèse de l'institution des intendants," *Journal des savants,* (1982): 283-318.

6. P. Gagnol, "Les décimes et les dons gratuits," RHEF, 2 (1911): 465-79.

7. R. Doucet, "Le Grand Parti de Lyon au XVIe siècle," *Revue historique,* 171 (1933): 471-513; 172, 1-41.

8. N. Sutherland, "Calvinism and the Conspiracy of Amboise," *History*, 47 (1962): 111-38.

Chapter 9

1. M. Mann, *Erasme et les débuts de la Réforme française* (Paris: 1934), 23.
2. L. Febvre, *Au coeur religieux du XVIe Siècle* (Paris: 1968), 66.
3. D. Nicholls, "The Nature of Popular Heresy in France, 1520-1542," *The Historical Journal,* 26 (1983): 261-75; Nicholls, "France," in *The Early Reformation in Europe,* A. Pettegree, ed. (Cambridge: 1992), 120-41.
4. G. Griffiths, "Louise of Savoy and Reform of the Church," SCJ, X (1977): 29-36.
5. N. Davis, "Strikes and Salvation at Lyon," *Society and Culture in Early Modern France* (Stanford, CA.: 1975), 1-16.
6. G. Brasart-de Groër, "Le Collège, agent d'infiltration de la Réforme," in *Aspects de la propagande religieuse,* G. Berthoud, ed. (Geneva: 1957), 172-98.
7. A. Moliner, "De la religion des oeuvres à la Réformation dans les Cévennes (1450-1600)," RHEF, 72 (1986): 245-63.
8. J. Rott, "Documents strasbourgeois concernant Calvin. Un manuscrit autographe: la harangue du recteur Nicolas Cop," in *Regards contemporain sur Jean Calvin* (Paris: 1960), 28-43.
9. N. Weiss, "Episode de la Réforme à Paris—L'assemblée de la rue Saint-Jacques," BSHPF, 65 (1916): 195-235.
10. A. Delmas, "Le procès et la mort de Jacques Spifame," BHR, 5 (1944): 105-37.
11. L. Johnson, "The Politics of Conversion: John Calvin and the Bishop of Troyes," SCJ, 25 (1994): 809-22.
12. H. Baird, *History of the Rise of the Huguenots of France,* 2 vols., reprint (New York: 1970), vol. I, 52.
13. F. Baumgartner, "Henry II and the Conclave of 1549," SCJ, 16 (1985): 301-14.
14. M. Venard, "Une réforme gallicane? Le projet de concile national de 1551," RHEF, 76 (1981): 201-21.
15. D. Kelly, "The *Fides Historicae* of Charles Du Moulin and the Gallican View of Historical Tradition," *Traditio,* 22 (1966): 347-403.
16. M. Lelièvre, "Le procès et le supplice d'Anne du Bourg," BSHPF, 37 (1888): 281-95, 337-55, 506-29.
17. P. de Felice, "Le Synode national de 1559," BSHPF , 105 (1959): 1-8.
18. L. Romier, "Les Protestants français à la veille des guerres civiles," *Revue historique,* 124 (1913): 1-51; 225-86.
19. P. Benedict, *Rouen during the Wars of Religion* (Cambridge: 1981), 53.

Chapter 10

1. M. Greengrass, "Property and Politics in Sixteenth Century France: The Landed Property of Constable Anne de Montmorency," *French History*, 2 (1987): 371-88.

2. J. Major, "Noble Income, Inflation, and the Wars of Religion,"AHR, 86 (1981): 21-48.

3. J.Wood, *The Nobility of the Election of Bayeux, 1463-1666* (Princeton, N.J.: 1980), 82-83.

4. François de Rabutin, *Commentaires des Guerres en la Gaule-Belgique*, 2 vols. (Paris: 1923), vol. I, 303.

5. F. Baumgartner, "The Demise of the Medieval Knight in France," in J. Friedman, ed., *Regnum, Religio et Ratio* (Kirksville, MO.: 1987), 9-18.

6. N. Roelker, "The Role of Noblewomen in the French Reformation," *Archive for Reformation History*, 63 (1972): 168-95.

7. R. Kingdon, *Geneva and the Coming of the Wars of Religion in France: 1555-1563* (Geneva: 1956).

Chapter 11

1. E. LeRoy Ladurie, *The Peasants of Languedoc*, trans. by J. Day (Urbana , IL.: 1974), 53.

2. J. Powis, "Guyenne, 1548: The Crown, the Province, and Social Order," *European Studies Review*, 12 (1982): 1-15.

3. N. Davis, "Poor Relief, Humanism and Heresy," in *Society and Culture in Early Modern France* (London: 1975), 17-64.

4. H. Hauser, "Une grève d'imprimeurs parisiens au XVIe siècle 1539-1542," *Revue internationale de sociologie*, 3 (1895): 597-616.

5. M. Morineau, "Lyon l'italienne, Lyon la magnifique," *Annales*, 29 (1974): 1537-50.

6. F. Irvine, "From renaissance city to ancien régime capital: Montpellier, C. 1500-C.1600," in *Cities and Social Change in Early Modern France*, P. Benedict, ed. (London: 1989), 105-33; J. Farr, "Consumers, commerce, and the craftsmen of Dijon, 1450-1750" in ibid., 134-73.

7. M. Lamet, "French Protestants in a Position of Strength: The Early Years of the Reformation In Caen, 1558-1568," SCJ, 9 (1978): 35-56; R. Mentzer, "Heresy Suspects in Languedoc prior to 1560: Observations on their Social

and Occupational Status," *Bibliothèque d'Humanisme et Renaissance,* 39 (1977): 561-68; N. Nicholls, "Social Change and Early Protestantism in France: Normandy, 1520-1562," *European Studies Review,* 10 (1980): 279-80.

Chapter 12

1. E. Meynail, "Etudes sur l'histoire financière du XVIe siècle," *Nouvelle Revue historique de Droit français et étranger,* 44 (1921), 143-77; 45 (1921), 23-65.
2. P. Bondois, "Les chancelleries présidials au XVIe siècle," *Revue du Seizième Siècle,* I (1913): 521-28.
3. A. Soman, "La Justice criminelle aux XVIe-XVIIe siècles: Le Parlement de Paris et les sièges subalternes," in *Philologie et histoire jusqu'a 1610,* (Brest: 1982), 31-44.
4. S. Hanley, "Engendering the State: Family Formation and State Building in Early Modern France," FHS, 16 (1989): 4-27; B. Gottlieb, "The Meaning of Clandestine Marriage," in *Family and Sexuality in French History,* R. Wheaton and T. Hareven, eds. (Philadelphia: 1980), 49-83.
5. D. Nicholls, et al., "The European Witchcraze Revisited," *History Today,* 30 (November 1980): 23-34.
6. Quoted by M. Gilmore, *The Argument from Roman Law in Political Thought 1200-1600* (New York: 1967), 5.
7. M. Smith, "Early French Advocates of Religious Freedom," SCJ, 25 (1994): 27-51; M. Turchetti, "Concorde ou tolerance? Les Moyenneurs à la veille des guerres de religion," *Revue de théologie et de philosophie,* 118 (1986): 255-67.
8. S. Kim, "'Dieu nous garde de la messe du chancelier': The Religious Beliefs and Political Opinion of Michel de L'Hôpital," SCJ, 24 (1993): 596-620.
9. Quoted in A. Esmein, *A History of Continental Criminal Procedure with Special Reference to France,* trans. J. Simpson (Boston: 1913), 168.
10. S. Neely, "Michel de L'Hospital and the Traité de la Réformation de la Justice: A Case of Misattribution," FHS, 14 (1986): 339-68.

Chapter 13

1. F. Marias, "De Madrid à Paris: François Ier et la Casa de Campo," *Revue de l'Art,* 91 (1991): 26-35.
2. L. Caron, "The Use of Color by Rosso Fiorentino," SCJ, 10 (1988): 355-78.

3. D. Panofsky and E. Panofsky, "The Iconography of the Galerie François Ier at Fontainebleau," *Gazette des beaux-arts,* 52 (1958): 113-90.

4. M. Chatenet, "Le logis de François Ier au Louvre," *Revue de l'Art,* 97 (1992): 72-75.

5. A. Smart, *The Renaissance and Mannerism outside Italy* (London: 1972), 185.

6. D. Baker, "Louise Labé's Conditional Imperatives: Subversion and Transcendence of the Petrarchian Tradition," SCJ, 21 (1991): 523-41.

7. J. Lapp, "Pontus de Tyard and Science," *The Romanic Review,* 38 (1947): 16-23.

Chapter 14

1. A. de La Ferrière, "L'Entrevue de Bayonne," *Revue des questions historiques,* 34 (1883): 457-522.

2. D. d'Aussy, "L'assassin du prince de Condé à Jarnac (1569)," *Revue des questions historiques,* 49 (1898): 573.

3. A good example of the first viewpoint is J. Neale, *The Age of Catherine de Medici* (London: 1943); the second, N. Sutherland, *The Massacre of St. Bartholomew and the European Conflict, 1559-1572* (New York: 1973); the third, J. Bourgeon, "Pour une histoire, enfin, de la Saint-Barthélémy," *Revue historique,* 282 (1989): 83-142.

4. A. Karch, "L'assemblée des notables de St-Germain-en-Laye," *Bibliothèque de l'Ecole des chartes,* 30 (1956): 115-62.

5. M. Wolfe, *The Fiscal System of Reniassance France* (New Haven, CT.: 1972), 146.

6. J. Major, "The Assembly at Paris in the Summer of 1575," *Monarchy, Estates and Aristocracy,* (London: 1988), V, 710.

7. J. Boucher, "Henri III mondain ou dévout?" *Cahiers d'histoire,* 15 (1970): 113-26.

8. G. Picot, *Histoire des Etats généraux de 1355 à 1614,* 4 vols., reprint (Geneva: 1959), vol. III, 372.

9. A. Gérard, "La révolte et le siège de Paris, 1589," *Mémoires de la société de l'histoire de Paris,* 33 (1906): 64-150.

10. P. Chevallier, "Nouvelles Lumières sur le fait de Jacques Clément assassin de Henri III," *Annuaire-Bulletin de la Société de l'Histoire de France,* 122 (1985-86): 39-66.

11. M. Wolfe, "The Conversion of Henri IV and the Origins of Bourbon Absolutism," *Historical Reflections/Reflexions Historiques,* 14 (1987): 287-309.

12. F. Baumgartner, "Renaud de Beaune, Politique Prelate," SCJ, 9 (1978): 99-114.

13. The most accessible text of the Edict of Nantes in English is in R. Mousnier, *The Assassination of Henry IV* (New York: 1973), 316-63.
14. P. L'Estoile, *Mémoires-Journaux,* 12 vols. (Paris: 1875-96), vol. VIII, 157.
15. J. Major, "Henri IV and Guyenne: A Study concerning the Origins of Absolutism," FHS, 4 (1966): 363-83.

Chapter 15

1. T. Crimando, "Two French Views of the Council of Trent," SCJ, 19 (1988): 169-85.
2. A. Degert, "Les premiers seminaires français," RHEF, 2 (1911): 24-38; 129-44.
3. Quoted in M. Greengrass, *France in the Age of Henry IV* (London: 1984), 178.
4. C. Haton, *Mémoires 1553-1582,* F. Bourguelot, ed., 2 vols. (Paris: 1857), vol. I, 89.
5. M. Peronnet, "Naissance d'une institution: Les assemblées du clergé," in *Pouvoir et instituions en Europe au XVIe siècle,* A. Stegmann, ed. (Paris: 1987), 249-62.
6. D. Crouzet, "Recherches sur les processions blanches 1593-1584," *Histoire, Economie et Société,* 1 (1982): 511-64.
7. J. Bergin,"Crown and Episcopate in the Age of Henry IV and Louis XIII," Proceedings, WSFH, 20 (1993): 63-74.
8. M. De Waele, "Pour la sauvegarde du roi de du royaume. L'expulsion des Jésuites de France à la fin des guerres de religion," *Canadian Journal of History,* 29 (1994): 267-88; C. Sutto, "Henri IV et les Jésuites," *Renaissance and Reformation,* 17 (1993): 17-24.
9. A. Barnes, "The Social Transformation of the French Parish Clergy, 1500-1800," in *Culture and Identity in Early Modern Europe (1500-1800),* B. Diefendorf, ed. (Ann Arbor, MI.: 1993), 139-58.

Chapter 16

1. Quoted in R. Love, "'All the King's Horsemen': The equestrian Army of Henri IV, 1585-1598," SCJ, 22 (1991): 511-33.
2. D. Buisseret, *Henry IV* (London: 1984), 66.
3. J. Wood, "The Impact of the Wars of Religion: A View of France in 1581," SCJ, 15 (1984): 131-67.

4. M. Holt, "Attitudes of the French Nobility at the Estates-General of 1576," SCJ, 18 (1987): 489-504.

5. N. Le Roux, "The Catholic Nobility and Political Choice During the League, 1585-1594: The Case of Claude de Châtre," *French History*, 8 (1994): 34-50.

6. S. Kettering, "Clientage during the Wars of Religion," SCJ, 20 (1990): 221-39.

7. M. Greengrass, *France in the Age of Henri IV: The Struggle for Stability* (New York: 1984), 183.

8. J. M. Hayden, *France and the Estates General of 1614* (Cambridge: 1974), 187.

Chapter 17

1. E. Leroy Ladurie, *Times of Feast, Times of Famine: A History of Climate since the Year 1000* (New York: 1988), 234.

2. M. Baulant, "Prix et salaires à Paris au XVIe siècle Sources et résultats," *Annales*, 31 (1976): 954-95; P. Raveau, "La crise des prix au XVIe siècle," *Revue historique*, 162 (1929): 1-44, 268-93; R. Gascon, *Grand Commerce et la vie urbaine au XVIe siècle*, 2 vols. (Paris: 1972), vol. II, 543; 932-33.

3. P. Contamine, *Histoire militaire de France*, 2 vols. (Paris: 1992), vol. I, 328-29.

4. P. Hoffman, "Taxes and Agrarian Life in Early Modern France: Land Sales, 1550-1730," *Journal of Economic History*, 46 (1986): 37-55.

5. J. de Vries, *European Urbanization 1500-1800* (Cambridge, MA: 1984), 29.

6. F. Irvine, "From Renaissance City to Ancien Régime Capital: Montpellier, c.1500-c.1600," in *Cities and Social Change in Early Modern France*, P. Benedict, ed. (London: 1989), 113-14.

7. M. Morineau, "Problèmes de l'économie française au temps de Henri III," in *Henri III et son temps*, R. Sauzet, ed. (Paris: 1992), 293-312.

8. L. Van Doren, "Revolt and Reaction in the City of Romans, Dauphiné (1579-80)," SCJ, 5 (1974): 71-100.

9. N. Davis, "The Rites of Violence," *Society and Culture*, 152-87.

10. A. Benoit, "La Peste soit des Huguenots Étude d'une logique d'exercration au XVIe siècle," *Histoire, Economie, Société*, 11 (1992): 553-70.

11. B. Diefendorf, "Prologue to a Massacre: Popular Unrest in Paris, 1557-1572," AHR, 90 (1985): 1067-91.

12. A. Barnes, "Religious Anxiety and Devotional Change in Sixteenth Century French Penitential Confraternities," SCJ, 19 (1988): 389-405; J. Bossy, "Leagues and Associations in 16th-Century French Catholicism," *Studies in Church History*, 23 (1986): 171-89.

13. R. Harding, "The Mobilization of Confraternities against the Reformation in France," SCJ, 9 (1980): 85-107.

14. Despite the valuable works by R. Descimon, E. Barnavi, and D. Richet (see bibliography), the basic work on the Paris Sixteen remains J. Salmon, "The Paris Sixteen, 1584-1594: The Social Analysis of a Revolutionary Movement," *Journal of Modern History*, 44 (1972); 540-76.

15. R. Descimon, *Qui étaient les Seize? Mythe et réalités de la Ligue parisienne (1585-1594)* (Paris: 1983).

16. R. Harding, "Revolution and Reform in the Holy League: Angers, Rennes, Nantes," *The Journal of Modern History*, 53 (1981); 379-416; M. Greengrass, "The Sainte Union in the Provinces: The Case of Toulouse," SCJ, 14 (1983): 469-96.

17. D. Nicholls, "Protestants, Catholics and Magistrates in Tours,1562-1572: The Making of a Catholic City during the Religious Wars," *French History*, 8 (1994): 14-33; M. Konnert, "Provincial Governors and Their Regimes during the French Wars of Religion: The Duc de Guise and the City Council of Châlons-sur-Marne," SCJ, 25 (1994): 823-40.

18. P. Ascoli, "French Provincial Cities and the Catholic League," *Occasional Papers of The American Society for Reformation Research* (St. Louis: 1977), 15-40.

19. P. Hohenberg, "Maize in French Agriculture," *Journal of Economic History*, 6 (1977): 79-80.

20. Quoted in Greengrass, *France in the Age of Henry IV* (London: 1984), 160. Like most of Henry's bon mots, it first appeared in a source written well after 1610.

21. R. Trullinger, "The *Grand Voyer* as an Instrument of Royal Centralization in Brittany under Henry IV," Proceedings, WSFH, 3 (1975): 26-34.

22. B. Barbiche, "Une révolution administrative: la charge de grand voyer de France," in *Pouvoir et Institutions en Europe au XVIe siècle*, A. Stegmann, ed. (Paris: 1987), 283-96.

23. D. Buisseret, "The Communications of France during the Reconstruction of Henri IV," *Economic History Review*, 2nd Series, 18 (1965): 267-77.

Chapter 18

1. Quoted in P. van Dyke, *Catherine de Médicis* (New York: 1922), 337.

2. M. Reulos, "L'Action legislative de Henri III;" in *Henri III et son temps*, R. Sauzet, ed. (Paris: 1992), 177-82.

3. M. Thompson, "The History of Fundamental Law in Political Thought from the French Wars of Religion to the American Revolution," AHR, 91 (1986): 1103-128.

4. M. Cummings, "Elopement, Family, and the Courts: The Crime of *Rapt* in Early Modern Europe," Proceedings, WSFH, 4 (1976): 118-24.

5. A. Soman, "The Parlement of Paris and the Great Witch-Hunt (1565-1640)," SCJ, 9 (1978): 31-44.

6. R. Mentzer, "The Formation of the chambre de l'édit of Languedoc," Proceedings, WSFH, 8 (1981): 47-56.

7. S. Kettering, "Political Parties at Aix-en Provence in 1589," *European History Quarterly*, 24 (1994): 181-211.

8. R. Mentzer, "Bipartisan Justice and the Pacification of Late Sixteenth-Century Languedoc," in *Regnum, Religio et Ratio,* J. Friedman, ed. (St. Louis: 1986), 125-32.

9. D. Margolf, "The Edict of Nantes' Amnesty: Appeals to the *Chambre de l'Edit,* 1600-1610," Proceedings, WSFH, 16 (1989): 49-55.

Chapter 19

1. J. Ehrmann, "Massacre and Persecution Pictures in Sixteenth-Century France," *Journal of the Warburg and Courtauld Institutes,* 8 (1945): 195-99.

2. R. Sealy, "The Palace Academy of Henry III," BHR, 40 (1978): 61-83.

3. D. Kelly, "Murd'rous Machiavel in France," *Political Science Quarterly,* 85 (1970): 545-49.

4. R. Giesey, "The French Monarchomach Triumvirs: Hotman, Beza, and Mornay," BHR, 32 (1970): 41-56.

5. R. Giesey, "When and Why Hotman Wrote the *Francogallia,*" BHR, 29 (1967): 581-611.

6. G. Jagger, "On the Authorship of the *Vindiciae contra tyrannos,*" *Durham University Journal* (1968): 73-80.

7. D. Bell, "Unmasking a King: The Political Uses of Popular Literature Under the French Catholic League, 1588-89," SCJ, 20 (1989): 371-79.

8. P. Ascoli, "A Radical Pamphlet of the Late Sixteenth Century France: *Le Dialogue d'entre le Maheustre et le Manant,*" SCJ, 5 (1974): 3-22.

9. J. Salmon, "French Satire in the Late Sixteenth Century," SCJ, 6 (1975): 57-88.

10. Quoted in J. Major, "The Renaissance Monarchy: A Contribution to the Periodization of History," in *The Monarchy, the Estates and the Aristocracy in Renaissance France* (London: 1988), 122.

11. D. Parker, "Law, Society, and the State in the Thought of Jean Bodin," *History of Political Thought,* 2 (1981): 253-85.

12. J. Moreau-Reibel, "Bodin et la Ligue," *Humanisme et Renaissance,* 2 (1935): 422-40; P. Rose, "The Politique and the Prophet: Bodin and the Catholic League 1589-1594," *The Historical Journal,* 21 (1978): 783-808.

13. P. Barker, "Stoic Contributions in the Early Modern Science," in *Atoms, "pneuma," and Tranquillity: Epircurean and Stoic Themes in European History,* M. Osler, ed. (Cambridge: 1991), 135-54.

14. F. Baumgartner, "Scepticism and French Interest in Copernicanism to 1630," *Journal for the History of Astronomy,* 17 (1986): 77-88.

Chapter 20

1. F. Baumgartner, "Le Roi de Bonté: The Image of Louis XII during the French Wars of Religion," in *Politics, Religion and Diplomacy in Early Modern Europe,* M. Thorp and A. Slavin, eds. (Kirksville, MO.: 1994), 113-26.

2. J. Nagle, "L'Officier 'moyen' dans l'espace français de 1568 à 1665," *L'Etat moderne: Genèse* (Paris: 1990), 185-97.

Bibliography

The following bibliography is a list of studies of sixteenth-century France that served as major sources for this book. Works cited in the notes are not repeated here.

P. Ardouin, *Maurice Scève, Pernette du Guillet, Louise Labé: l'amour à Lyon au temps de la Renaissance* (Paris: 1981).

E. Armstrong, *Before Copyright: the French Book-Privilege System, 1498-1526* (Cambridge: 1990).

E. Armstrong, *The French Wars of Religion: Their Political Aspects* (Oxford: 1904).

L. Batiffol, *The Century of the Renaissance,* reprint (New York: 1967).

J-P. Babelon, *Châteaux de France au siècle de la Renaissance* (Paris: 1989).

————, *Nouvelle histoire de Paris: Paris au XVIe siècle* (Paris: 1986).

E. Barnavi, *Le parti de Dieu. Etude sociale et politique des chefs de la Ligue parisienne: 1585-1594* (Louvain: 1980).

E. Barnavi and R. Descimon, *La Sainte Ligue Le Juge et La Potence* (Paris: 1985).

M. Baulant and J. Meuvret, *Prix des céréales extraits de la mercuriale de Paris, 1520-1698* (Paris: 1960).

F. Baumgartner, *Change and Continuity in the French Episcopate: The Bishops and the Wars of Religion: 1547-1610* (Durham, N.C.: 1986).

————, *Henry II King of France 1547-1559* (Durham, N.C.: 1988).

————, *Radical Reactionaries: The Political Thought of the French Catholic League* (Geneva: 1976).

Y. Bellenger, *La Pléiade: la poésie en France autour de Ronsard* (Paris: 1988).

P. Benedict, *Rouen during the Wars of Religion* (Cambridge: 1981).

S. Bequin, *L'Ecole de Fontainebleau* (Paris: 1960).

G. Berthoud, *Antoine Marcourt* (Geneva: 1973).

C. Beaune, *The Birth of an Ideology: Myths and Symbols of Nation in Late-Medieval France,* trans. by S. Huston (Berkeley, CA.: 1991).

F. Billacois, *The Duel Its Rise and Fall in Early Modern France,* trans. by T. Selous (New Haven, CT.: 1990).

D. Bitton, *The French Nobility in Crisis: 1560-1640* (Stanford, CA.: 1969).

P. Blet, *Le clergé de France et la monarchie* (Rome: 1959).

J-R. Bloch, *L'annoblissement en France au temps de François Ier* (Paris: 1934).

M. Bloch, *French Rural History,* trans. by J. Sondheimer (Berkeley, CA.: 1966).

A. Blunt, *Art and Architecture in France: 1500-1700* (Middlesex: 1981).

———, *Philibert de L'Orme* (London: 1958).

G. Bois, *The Crisis of Feudalism* (Cambridge: 1984).

M. Boulet, "Les élections épiscopales en France au lendemain de Concordat de Bologna," *Mélanges d'archéologie et d'histoire d'école française de Rome,* LVII (1940): 190-234.

E. Bourassin, *Charles IX* (Paris: 1986).

J. Boutier, et al., *Un tour de France royal: le voyage de Charles IX (1564-1566)* (Paris: 1984).

W. Bouwsma, *John Calvin: A Sixteenth Century Portrait* (Oxford: 1989).

F. Braudel, *The Identity of France,* trans. by S. Reynolds, 2 vols. (London: 1989).

———, *The Mediterranean and the Mediterranean World in the Age of Philip II,* trans. by S. Reynolds, 2 vols. (New York: 1973).

J. Bridge, *A History of France from the Death of Louis XI to 1515,* 5 vols. (Oxford: 1921-36).

H. Brown, *Music in the Renaissance* (Englewood Cliffs, N.J.: 1976).

L. Bryant, *The King and the City in the Parisian Royal Entry Ceremony* (Geneva: 1986).

D. Buisseret, *Sully and the Growth of Centralized Government in France* (London: 1968).

K. Cameron, *Louise Labé Renaissance Poet and Feminist* (Munich: 1990).

———, ed., *Montaigne and His Age* (Exeter: 1981).

V. Carrière, et al., *Introduction aux études d'histoire ecclésiastique locale,* 3 vols. (Paris: 1936).

H. Chambard, *Histoire de la Pléiade,* 4 vols. (Paris: 1961).

P. Champion, *Henri III Roi shakespearien* (Paris: 1978).

H. Chardon, *Robert Garnier: sa Vie, ses Poésies Inédites* (Paris: 1905).

M. Chassaigne, "Un manuel de procedure criminelle au XVIe siècle," *Revue des études historiques,* 79 (1913): 202-37, 294-317.

P. Chaunu and R. Gascon, *Histoire économique et sociale de France,* 3 vols. (Paris: 1977).

B. Chevalier, ed., *La France de la fin du XVe siècle: renouveau et apogée* (Paris: 1985).

———, *Tours, Ville royale, (1356-1520)* (Louvain: 1975).

J. Clamageran, *Histoire de l'impôt en France,* 3 vols. (Paris: 1867-76).

A. Clergeac, *La curie et les bénéficiers consistoriaux* (Paris: 1911).

I. Cloulas, *Catherine de Médicis* (Paris: 1979).

————, *Henri II* (Paris: 1985).

————, *La vie quotidienne dans les châteaux de la Loire au temps de la Renaissance* (Paris: 1983).

J. Collins, *Classes, estates, and order in early modern Brittany* (Cambridge: 1994).

J-M. Constant, *Les Guises* (Paris: 1984).

————, *Nobles et paysans en Beauce aux XVIème et XVIIème siècles* (Lille: 1981.)

————, *La vie quotidienne de la noblesse française aux XVIe-XVIIe siècles* (Paris: 1985).

L. Crété, *Coligny* (Paris: 1985).

J. de Croze, *Les Guise, les Valois et Philippe II*, 2 vols. (Paris: 1866).

S. Cuttler, *The Law of Treason and Treason Trials in Later Medieval France* (Cambridge: 1981).

N. Davis, *The Return of Martin Guerre* (Cambridge, MA.: 1983).

J. Dawson, *A History of Lay Judges* (Cambridge, MA.: 1960).

————, *The Oracles of The Law*, reprint (Westport, CT.: 1978).

F. Decrue, *Anne de Montmorency, connétable et pair de France sous les rois Henri II, François II, et Charles IX* (Paris: 1889).

P. Desan, ed., *Humanism in Crisis: The Decline of the French Renaissance* (Ann Arbor, MI.: 1991).

R. Descimon, *Qui étaient les Seize? Mythe et réalités de la Ligue parisienne: 1585-1594* (Paris: 1983).

C. Devic, et al., *Histoire générale de Languedoc*, 15 vols. (Toulouse: 1872-92).

Dictionnaire de Biographie française, 17 vols. to date. (Paris: 1933- ————).

B. Diefendorf, *Beneath the Cross: Catholics and Huguenots in Sixteenth-Century Paris* (Oxford: 1991).

————, *Paris City Councilors in the Sixteenth Century: The Politics of Patrimony* (Princeton, N.J.: 1983).

L. Dimier, *French Painting in the 16th Century* (New York: 1911).

————, *Histoire de la peinture de portrait en France au 16e siècle*, 2 vols. (Paris: 1924-46).

————, *Le Primitice* (Paris: 1900).

C. Dolan, *Entre Tours et Clochers* (Sherbrooke, Québec: 1981).

R. Doucet, *L'etat des finances de 1523* (Paris: 1923).

————, *Les Institutions de la France au XVIe siècle*, 2 vols. (Paris: 1948).

G. Duby, ed., *Histoire de la France urbaine*, vol. III, ed. by E. Leroy Ladurie (Paris: 1981) .

J. Dupâquier, et al. *Histoire de la population française*, 3 vols. (Paris: 1988).

S. Eurich, *The Economics of Power: The Private Finances of the House of Foix-Navarre-Albret during the Wars of Religion* (Kirksville, MO.: 1994).

H. Evenett, *The Cardinal of Lorraine and the Council of Trent* (Cambridge: 1930).

J. Farge, *Orthodoxy and Reform in Early Reformation France: The Faculty of Theology of Paris: 1500-1543* (Leiden: 1985).

S. Farmer, *Communities of Saint Martin: Legend and Ritual in Medieval Tours* (Ithaca, N.Y.: 1991).

J. Farr, *Authority and Sexuality in Early Modern Burgundy (1559-1730)* (New York: 1994).

———, *Hands of Honor: Artisans and their World in Dijon: 1550-1650* (Ithaca, N.Y.: 1991).

L. Febvre, *Life in Renaissance France,* trans. by M. Rothstein. (Cambridge, MA.: 1977).

J-L. Flandrin, *Les Amours paysannes (XVIe-XIXe siècles)* (Paris: 1975).

M. Fleury, *Le château de Louvre* (Paris: 1990).

J. Franklin, *Jean Bodin and the 16th-Century Revolution in the Methodology of Law and History* (New York; 1963).

N. Fustel de Coulanges, "La Justice en France sous la monarchie absolue," *Revue des deux mondes,* 95 (1871): 570-611.

A. Galpern, *The Religions of the People in Sixteenth-Century Champagne* (Cambridge, MA.: 1976).

J. Garrisson-Estèbe, *Protestants du Midi (1559-1598)* (Toulouse: 1980).

J. Garrisson, *Guerre civile et compromis 1559-1598* (Paris: 1991).

———, *Royaume, Renaissance et Réforme 1483-1559* (Paris: 1991).

F. Gebelin, *Les châteaux de la Renaissance* (Paris: 1927).

B. Geremek, *Les marginaux parisiens aux XIVe et XV siècles,* trans. by D. Beauvais (Paris: 1976).

R. Giesey, *The Royal Funeral Ceremony in Renaissance France* (Geneva: 1960).

G. Gigon, *La révolte de la Gabelle en Guyenne* (Paris: 1906).

M. Greengrass, *The French Reformation* (Oxford: 1987).

B. Guenée, *Tribunaux et Gens de Justice dans le bailliage de Senlis à la fin du moyen âge* (Paris: 1963).

M. Gueudrie, *Histoire de l'ordre des Ursulines en France* (Paris: 1963).

W. Gundersheimer, ed., *French Humanism 1470-1600* (New York: 1970).

S. Hanley, *The "Lit de Justice" of the Kings of France* (Princeton, N.J.: 1983).

R. Harding, *Anatomy of a Power Elite* (New Haven, CT.: 1978).

H. Hauser, *Etudes sur la réforme française* (Paris: 1909).

———, *Les sources de l'histoire de France au XVIe siècle,* 4 vols. (Paris: 1906-15).

H. Heller, *Blood and Iron: Civil Wars in Sixteenth-Century France* (Montreal: 1991).

———, *The Conquest of Poverty: The Calvinist Revolt in Sixteenth-Century France* (Leiden: 1986).

P. Hoffman, *Church and Community in the Diocese of Lyon, 1500-1789* (New Haven, CT.: 1984).

G. Huppert, *Public Schools in Renaissance France* (Urbana, IL.: 1984).

J. Hurry, *The Woad Plant and Its Dye* (Clifton, N.J.: 1973).

P. Imbart de La Tour, *Les Origines de la Réforme*, 4 vols. (Paris: 1905-35).

R. Jackson, *Vive Le Roi! A History of the French Coronation from Charles V to Charles X* (Chapel Hill, N.C.: 1984).

J. Jacquart, *Le Crise rurale en Ile-de-France, 1550-1620* (Paris: 1974).

————, *François Ier* (Paris: 1981).

L. Jensen, *Diplomacy and Dogmatism: Bernardino de Mendoza and the French Catholic League* (Cambridge:MA.: 1964).

A. Jouanna, *Le Devoir et révolte: La Noblesse française et la gestation de l'état moderne* (Paris: 1989).

————, *L'idée de race en France au xvie siècle et au début du xviie siècle (1498-1614)*, 3 vols. (Paris:1976).

C. Julien, *Les voyages de decouverte et les premiers établissements* (Paris: 1948).

R. Kingdon, *Geneva and the Consolidation of the Reformation in France* (Madison, WI.: 1956).

R. Knecht, *French Renaissance Monarchy: Francis I and Henry II* (London: 1984).

————, *The French Wars of Religion 1559-1598* (London: 1989).

————, *Renaissance Warrior and Patron: The Reign of Francis I* (Cambridge: 1994).

S. Kettering, "Patronage and Kingship in Early Modern France," *French Historical Studies*, 16 (1989): 408-35.

A. Krailsheimer, *Rabelais and the Franciscans* (Oxford: 1963).

M. Kuntz, *Guillaume Postel: Prophet of the Restitution of All Things: His Life and Thought* (The Hague: 1981).

O. de La Brosse et al., *Latran V et Trente* (Paris: 1975).

C. de La Roncière, *Histoire de la Marine française*, 4 vols. (Paris: 1899-1906).

J. Langbein, *Prosecuting Crime in the Renaissance England, Germany, France* (Cambridge, MA.: 1974).

J. Lavaud, *Un poète de cour du temps des derniers Valois: Philippe Desportes (1546-1606)* (Paris: 1936).

E. Lavisse, ed. *Histoire de France*. Vol. V., *Les Guerres d'Italie,* by H. Lemonnier; vol. VI, *La réforme et le ligue, l'Edit de Nantes (1559-1598),* by J. Mariejol (Paris: 1903-11).

M. Lazard, *Rabelais: L'Humaniste* (Paris: 1993).

A. Lebigre, *La Justice du Roi: La Vie judiciaire dans l'ancienne France* (Paris: 1988).

————, *La Révolution des Curés 1588-1594* (Paris: 1980).

A. Lemaire, *Les lois fondamentales de la Monarchie française,* reprint (Geneva: 1975).

N. Lemaitre, *Le Rouergue flamboyant: le clergé et les fideles du diocèse de Rodez: 1417-1563* (Paris: 1988).

C. Lenient, *La Satire en France; ou, la litterature militante au XVIe siècle* (Paris: 1866).

E. Leroy Ladurie, *The French Peasantry: 1450-1660,* trans. by A. Sheridan (Urbana, IL.: 1974).

————, *The French Royal State 1460-1610,* trans. by J. Vale (Oxford: 1994).

P. Lewis, *Later Medieval France* (London: 1968).

F. Lot, *Recherches sur les effectifs des armées françaises des guerres d'Italie aux guerres de religion 1494-1562* (Paris: 1962).

I. McFarlane, *A Literary History of France: Renaissance France: 1470-1589* (London: 1974).

A. McGrath, *A Life of John Calvin* (Oxford: 1990).

D. McNeil, *Guillaume Budé and Humanism in the Reign of Francis I* (Geneva: 1975).

J. Major, *The Assembly of Notables of 1596* (Philadelphia: 1974).

————, *From Renaissance Monarchy to Absolute Monarchy* (Baltimore, MD.: 1994).

————, *Representative Government in Early Modern France* (New Haven, CT.: 1980).

————, *Representative Institutions in Renaissance France, 1421-1559* (Madison., WI.: 1960).

R. Mandrou, *Introduction to Modern France: 1500-1614,* trans. by R. Hallmark. (New York: 1976).

A. Martin, *Henry III and The Jesuit Politicians,* (Geneva: 1973).

V. Martin, *Les origines du Gallicanisme,* 2 vols. (Paris: 1939).

E. Maugis, *Histoire du Parlement de Paris à l'avenement des rois Valois à la mort de Henri I,.* 3 vols. (Paris: 1913-16).

R. Maulde La Clavière, *Les origines de la Révolution française au commencement du XVIe siècle* (Paris: 1889).

R. Mentzer, *Blood & Belief: Family Survival and Confessional Identity among the Provincial Huguenot Nobility* (West Lafayette, IN.: 1994).

————, *Heresy Proceedings in Languedoc: 1500-1560* (Philadelphia: 1984).

C. Michaud, *L'Eglise et l'argent sous l'ancien régime. Les receveurs généraux du clergé de France aux XVIe et XVII siècles* (Paris: 1991).

F. Mignet, *La rivalité de François Ier et de Charles-Quint,* 2 vols. (Paris: 1875).

S. Minta, *Love Poetry in sixteenth-century France* (Manchester: 1977).

R. Mousnier, *Le Conseil du roi Louis XII à la Révolution* (Paris: 1970).

———, *La vénalité des offices sous Henri IV et Louis XIII* (Paris: 1971).

K. Neuschel, *Word of Honor: Interpreting Noble Culture in Sixteenth-Century France* (Ithaca, NY: 1989).

D. Nugent, *Ecumenism in the Age of the Reformation: The Colloquy of Poissy* (Cambridge, MA: 1974)

C. O'Malley, *Andreas Vesalius of Brussels 1514-1564* (Berkeley, CA: 1964).

C. Oman, *A History of the Art of War in the XVIth Century* (New York: 1937).

A. Parent, *Les métiers du livre à Paris au 16e siècle (1530-60)* (Geneva: 1974).

L. von Pastor, *The History of the Popes from the Close of the Middle Ages,* 36 vols. (St. Louis: 1952).

M. Peronnet, *Les évêques de l'ancien France,* 2 vols. (Paris: 1978).

R. Pillorget, *Les Mouvements insurrectionnels de Provence entre 1596 et 1715* (Paris: 1972).

R. Popkin, *The History of Scepticism from Erasmus to Spinoza* (Los Angeles, CA.: 1979).

E. Quentin-Bauchert, *La bibliothèque de Fontainebleau: 1515-89* (Paris: 1891).

M-F. Quignard, *Vie de Monsieur de Malherbe* (Paris: 1991).

A. Renaudet, *Preréforme et humanisme à Paris pendant les premières guerres d'Italie* (Paris: 1953).

D. Richet, "Aspects socio-culturels des conflits religieux à Paris dans la seconde moitié du XVIe siècle," *Annales* (1977), 764-89.

P. Roederer, *Histoire de Louis XII* (Paris: 1825).

L. Romier, *Le royaume de Catherine de Médicis,* 2 vols. (Paris: 1922).

P. Rose, *Bodin and the Great God of Nature* (Geneva: 1980)

J. Rott, *Jean Morély et l'utopie d'une démocratie ecclésiastique (1524-ca.1594)* (Geneva: 1993).

J. Salmon, *Society in Crisis: France in the Sixteenth Century* (Cambridge: 1975).

E. Schalk, *From Valor to Pedigree: Ideas of Nobility in France in the Sixteenth and Seventeenth Centuries* (Princeton, N.J.: 1986).

B. Schnapper, *Les rentes au XVIe siècle* (Paris: 1957).

R. Schneider, *Public Life in Toulouse: 1463-1789: From Municipal Republic to Cosmopolitan City* (Ithaca, N.Y.: 1989).

R. Schoeck, *Erasmus of Europe* (Savage, MD.: 1990.)

M. Screech, *Marot évangélique* (Geneva: 1967).

———, *Rabelais* (London: 1979).

———, *Rabelais and the Challenge of the Gospel* (Baden-Baden: 1992).

W. Sewell, *Work and Revolution in France: The Language of Labor from the Old Regime to 1848* (Cambridge: 1980).

J. Shennan, *The Parlement of Paris* (London: 1968).

Q. Skinner, *The Foundations of Modern Political Thought,* 2 vols. (Cambridge: 1978).

A. Spont, *La taille en Languedoc de 1450 à 1515* (Toulouse: 1890).

F. Spooner, *The International Economy and Monetary Movements in France, 1493-1725* (Cambridge: 1972).

P. Sueur, *Histoire du droit public français, XVe-XVIIIe siècles,* 2 vols. (Paris: 1989).

N. Sutherland, *French Secretaries of State in the Age of Catherine de Medici,* (Westport, CT.: 1975).

————, *The Huguenot Struggle for Recognition* (New Haven, CT: 1982).

F. Taylor, *The Art of War in Italy, 1494-1529* (Cambridge: 1921).

L. Taylor, *Soldiers of Christ: Preaching in Late Medieval and Renaissance France* (Oxford: 1992).

C. Terrasse, *Germain Pilon* (Paris: 1930).

J. Thomas, *Le Concordat de 1516, ses origines, son histoire au XVIe siècle,* 3 vols. (Paris: 1910).

J. Thompson, *The Wars of Religion in France: 1559-1576* (New York: nd).

D. Thomson, *Renaissance Paris Architecture and Growth 1475-1600* (Berkeley, CA.: 1984).

A. Tilley, *The Dawn of the French Renaissance,* reprint (New York: 1968).

M. Trudel, *The Beginnings of New France: 1524-1663* (Toronto: 1973).

P. de Vaissière, *Charles de Marillac: ambassadeur et homme politique* (Paris: 1896).

P. Van Dyke, *Catherine de Médicis,* 2 vols. (New York: 1922).

M. Vigne, *La Banque à Lyons du XVe au XVIIIe siècles* (Paris: 1903).

J. Viguier, *Les contracts et la consolidation des décimes à la fin du XVIe siècle* (Paris: 1906).

M. Weisner, *Women and Gender in Early Modern Europe* (Cambridge: 1993).

N. Weiss, *La Chambre ardente,* reprint (Geneva: 1970).

M. Weisser, *Crime and Punishment in Early Modern Europe* (Brighton: 1982).

W. Wiley, *The Gentleman of Renaissance France,* reprint (Westport, CT.: 1971).

C. Winn, *The Dialogue in Early Modern France, 1547-1630: Art and Argument* (Washington, D.C.: 1993).

R. Wolf, et al., *Renaissance and Mannerist Art* (New York: 1968).

M. Yardeni, *La conscience nationale en France pendant les guerres de religion (1559-1598)* (Louvain: 1971).

F. Yates, *The French Academies of the Sixteenth Century* (London: 1947).

Index